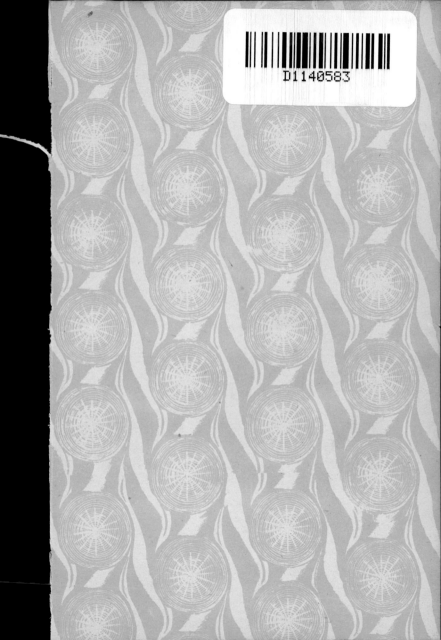

Everyman, I will go with thee, and be thy guide,
In thy most need to go by thy side.

# EVERYMAN'S LIBRARY
## EDITED BY ERNEST RHYS

## ESSAYS & BELLES-LETTRES

# THE BOOK OF THE COURTIER
BY BALDASSARE CASTIGLIONE · TRANS-
LATED BY SIR THOMAS HOBY · INTRO-
DUCTION BY W. H. D. ROUSE, D.LITT.
AND CRITICAL NOTES BY PROFESSOR
DRAYTON HENDERSON

BALDASSARE CASTIGLIONE, born at Casanatico in 1478. In the service of the Duke of Milan from 1496 to 1500. In 1506 went·to England on a diplomatic mission for the Duke of Urbino. Visited Spain, 1524, became naturalized there, and was given the bishopric of Avila. Died at Toledo in 1529.

# THE BOOK OF THE COURTIER

## BALDASSARE CASTIGLIONE

LONDON: J. M. DENT & SONS LTD.
NEW YORK: E. P. DUTTON & CO. INC.

# INTRODUCTION

"MANNERS makyth man," says William of Wykeham's motto; and our forefathers were well aware how precious good manners are in life. A modest and gracious bearing, with deference for those set above and consideration for the rights and feelings of all, adds so much to the happiness of men at so small a cost, and so commends the person to others' affections, that the wonder is how anyone can be rude. Yet nature has not taught us this in the cradle, and to acquire it there must be careful and long training. To help in this, by setting forth the standard of polite society for those who may not have the entry to such, many writers have compiled books of good manners, both in this country and in others. A number of the most simple from the fifteenth and sixteenth centuries have been gathered into a volume of the Early English Text Society, called the *Babees Book* (F. J. Furnivall, 1878). "O yongë Babees," says the author of the title-piece,

> whom blood royall
> With grace, feature, and high ability
> Hath enormyd, on you is that I call
> To know this book: for it were great pity
> Syn that in you is set sovreyne beauty.
> But if virtue and nurture were with all:
> To you therefore I speak in speciall . . .
>
> When ye enter into your lordis place,
> Say first, God speed, and all that be before
> You in this stead, salute with humble face:
> Start not rudely; come in an easy pace;
> Hold up your head, and kneel but on one knee
> To your sovereyn or lord, whether he be.

They are to kneel on one knee to their lord, on both knees to God. So he continues directing them as to demeanour and posture, how they are to answer, how to serve at table, how to accept an act of favour from their lord. Hugh Rhodes, in his *Book of Nurture*, describes the manner of serving a Knight, Squire, or Gentleman; how to order your master's chamber at night to bed-ward; how to behave at table; and what

else makes a school of manners for man or for child. He
says:

> I am full blind in poet's art,
>   thereof I can no skill;
> Take the best, and leave the worst,
>   of truth I mean no ill.

He begins with the opening day, when you get up:

> Brush them and sponge thy clothës too
>   that thou that day shalt wear,
> In comely sort cast up your bed,
>   lose you none of your gear.
> Make clean your shoes, and comb your head
>   and your clothes button or lace,
> And see at no time you forget
>   to wash your hands and face.

In this artless style, Master Rhodes gives his instructions
to gentle and simple. No one then thought it beneath him to
do menial service to his elders and betters; it was rather an
honour so to serve those who were honourable. Sir Thomas
More was brought up in Cardinal Morton's household; and
Morton said of young More, "Whosoever shall live to see it,
this child here waiting at the table will prove a marvellous
man."

It was indeed a part of the child's education to be brought
up in the house of some nobleman or great gentleman, and
many of them had their schoolmaster without to help in the
bookish part. The training was often strict, but that has its
advantages. Lady Jane Grey says:

One of the greatest benefits that God ever gave me, is that He
sent me so sharp and severe parents, and so gentle a schoolmaster.
For when I am in the presence either of father or mother, whether
I speak, keep silence, sit, stand or go, eat, drink, be merry or sad,
be sewing, playing, dancing, or doing anything else, I must do it
. . . ever so perfectly as God made the world, or else I am so
sharply taunted, so cruelly threatened, yet presently sometimes with
pinches, nips, and bobs, and other ways which I will not name
. . . so without measure misordered, that I think myself in hell
till time comes that I must go to Mr. Elmer, who teaches me so
gently, so pleasantly, with such fair allurements to learning, that
I think all the time nothing whiles I am with him.

But the breeding in courtesy was not confined to children;
with all the elaborate ritual of manners and precedence, which
was practised at Court and in the great houses, the utmost
care was applied to the conduct of young men and women.
The more finished treatises on this subject are not English in

origin; it is Italy, the seat of the most ancient civilisation of Europe, which has continued in its old place, where the chief works on this subject have appeared. Of these, three were translated into English, and became the standard works on the subject. They did not introduce a new practice into England, for the practice of good manners was here before; but they in a manner fixed it, and served as a convenient court of appeal. In fact they deserved their success; for they were books full of a beautiful courtesy of the heart, marked by a winning grace as well as intellectual power.

Chief of these is *The Courtier*, by Baldassare Castiglione, translated by Sir Thomas Hoby, and published by him in 1561. In 1588 it was again published, with texts in French and Italian on the same page. It is so witty and entertaining, that it is surprising that except for the edition of 1900 in the Tudor Translations, with an Introduction by Sir Walter Raleigh, it has not been reprinted in modern times. This is the matter of our present reprint, and no more need be said of it, except a few words as to the author and how he made his book.

Castiglione was born in 1478 of a good family. His manhood was spent in the field or at Court; and the happiest days of his life were passed with Guidobaldo Duke of Urbino (1504-8), whom he served in many diplomatic missions, one of which brought him to England. His book in reality describes the Court of Urbino, and the persons in it, to the life. He wrote his first draft in 1508, but it was not published until 1528; later it was translated into Spanish, French and English. The author's later life need not detain us. In 1516 the Pope seized Urbino, and his last years were spent as Papal Nuncio to Spain, where he died in 1529.

Sir Thomas Hoby, his English translator, was born in 1530 and died in 1566. He spent two years at St. John's College, Cambridge, and then travelled abroad, remaining some years in Italy. His life was passed in the public service, and he died as ambassador to France.

The second of the three great Books of Courtesy appeared in English as *Galateo of Manners and Behaviour*, by Giovanni della Casa, Archbishop of Benevento, and was published in 1576, as translated by Robert Peterson, of Lincoln's Inn, Gentleman. It was translated later, as a Treatise on Politeness, by the Rev. Richard Graves, M.A. This book deals more with the middle classes than with the more exalted personages of Baldassare's work. It is a charming book, and won a well-deserved popularity. It was reprinted, with an Introduction by J. E. Springarn, in 1914 (Grant Richards).

The third of these works is *La Civile Conversazione* of Stefano Guazzo, was published in 1574, and the English translation of Books I.–III. by George Pettie in 1581, the Fourth Book being added in 1586 by Bartholomew Young. This has been reprinted, with an Introduction by Sir Edward Sullivan, in the second series of Tudor Translations (Constable, 1925). Like the last, this is addressed rather to persons of the middle classes.

The present reprint has been checked by the edition of 1588.

The influence of Hoby's *Courtier* upon writers of the Elizabethan age was great. It has been well surveyed by Sir Walter Raleigh, in his Introduction; and although there is no direct evidence that Shakespeare used it, there are many passages in which they treat of the same ideas.[1]

# BIBLIOGRAPHY

Libro del Cortegiano (Venice, 1528), reprinted 1531, 1533, 1537. Over forty editions subsequently appeared in Italy during 16th century: banned by the Spanish Inquisition, 1576, and placed on the Index in 1590 by Pope Sixtus V. Only the expurgated edition of Antonio Ciccarelli was allowed to appear in 1584, reprinted 1601, 1606. Volpi in 1733 reprinted the original Aldine version of 1528 (reprinted 1766 with Life by Abate Serassi). First critical edition from author's MSS. in the Laurentian Library edited by Professor V. Cian (Florence, 1894, reprinted 1908, 1910); The Book of the Courtyer done into English by T. Hoby (1561, reprinted 1577, 1588, 1603, and in 1900 in the Tudor Translations series with an introduction by Walter Raleigh; Il Courtegiano or the Courtier: written by B. C., and a new version of the same into English: Together with several of his celebrated pieces, as well Latin as Italian, both in prose and verse. To which is prefix'd the life of the author, by A. P. Castiglione. (Italian and English. London, 1727.) In this version were printed several letters and poems thirty years before they appeared in Serassi's edition; The Courtier or the Countrie Gentleman and Gentlewoman, translated by Robert Samber (1724, reprinted 1729); The Book of the Courtier, translated and annotated by L. E. Opdycke (1901, reprinted 1902). P. A. Serassi: Delle Lettere del Conte B. Castiglione, con annotazioni storiche illustrate (Padua, 2 vols., 1769–1771); A. Vernazza di Freney: Lettere inedite di B. Castiglione (Turin, 1811); F. Coutin: Lettere diplomatiche di Castiglione (Padua, 1875); R. Renier: Notizia di lettere inedite di B. Castiglione (Turin, 1889); B. Feliciangeli: Alcune lettere inedite

---

[1] See Note by Prof. Drayton Henderson, p. xiii.

di B. Castiglione (Bologna, 1892); G. Bufardeci: Su la vita letteriara del Conte B. Castiglione (Ragusa, 1900); Carmina quinque illustrium postarum (Venice, 1548, 1558, 1576; Florence, 1549, 1552, 1740, 1753); Stanza pastorali, ed. by G. A. Corso (Venice, 1553); Poesie volgari e latine, ed. P. A. Serassi (Rome, 1760); B. Marliam: Vita del Conte B. Castiglione (Padua, 1733); G. Ferri: De Vita et scriptis B. Castiglionis (Mantua, 1780); G. Benini: Elogio del Castiglione (Vicenza, 1781); A. Tobbler: Castiglione und sein "Hofmann" (Berne, 1864); E. Narducci: Vita inedita (Rome, 1877); E. Bottari: B. di C. e il mo libro del Cortigiano (Pisa, 1877); C. Martinati: Notizie storico—biografiche intorno al Conte Baldassare Castiglione con documenti inediti (Florence, 1890); P. Toldo: Le Courtisan dans la littérature française et ses rapports avec l'œuvre du Castiglione (Brunswick, 1900); Philarète Charles: Du Roman et de ses sources dans l'Europe moderne: Observateurs des mœurs en Italie et en Espagne (Revue des Deux-Mondes, 15 mai, 1842); M. A. Scott: The Book of the Courtyer, Modern Language Association of America, vol. xvi. No. 4 (Baltimore, 1901); and Elizabethan Translations from the Italian (Boston, 1916); Christopher Hare: Courts and Camps of the Italian Renaissance (1908); Julia Cartwright (Mrs. Ady): B. Castiglione, the perfect courtier, his life, and letters (2 vols. 1908: bibliography and unpublished documents in Appendix); Sir Walter Raleigh: Some Authors (Sir Thomas Hoby, pp. 41-121) (London, 1923).

# A NOTE ON CASTIGLIONE AND ENGLISH LITERATURE

ENGLISH Literature owes a debt to Castiglione, and to his circle, which it is juster to overpay than set aside with the caution that the amount is hard to reckon. In all likelihood Spenser's Hymns of *Heavenly Love* and *Heavenly Beauty* are derived from Bembo's oration in this *Book of the Courtier*. Shakespeare's Sonnets show something of the same influence. It has been said, and plausibly, that Lady Emilia Pia and Lord Gaspar Pallavicino may have suggested—it can be said unhesitatingly that they suggest—Beatrice and Benedick of *Much Ado About Nothing*. Julia Cartwright (Mrs. Ady), Castiglione's most recent biographer, draws a parallel between his *Elegy of Alcon*, in memory of his friend Falcone, and Milton's *Lycidas*. It is plain that the form of the latter was suggested by the Italian poem, however much Bion or Virgil may also have given it:

For we lived together from our tendrest years and shared the heat of the day and the cold of the winter night and reared our flocks by our common labour.

Again, it is a possibility that another of Castiglione's friends, Raphael, may have prompted *Paradise Lost*. The first-composed lines of that poem are, as everyone knows, those in adoration of the sun, which appear in the Fourth Book. They were written not more than three years after Milton's return from Italy. Spoken by Satan, they are now framed after he has left the sphere of the *primum mobile* and has voyaged down through the intervening spaces to Earth and Mount Niphates.

Raphael's picture (in the Stanza of Heliodorus of the Vatican) is of a gigantic celestial angel or archangel, kneeling on the outer crystalline curve of the *primum mobile*, the right hand raised in surprise, the head bent in adoration, as he looks down through the starred spaces upon the brightness of Earth's sun.[1]

[1] It is on the corner arch or corbel between "The Freeing of St. Peter from Prison" and "The Eviction of Heliodorus from the Temple." In the adjoining stanza is "The School of Philosophy," whose design Castiglione is said to have influenced, and in which that perfect courtier (as Pythagoras) stands looking towards Raphael himself.

But we can approach our obligation closer than through these conjectures. We may even venture to say, if a trifle hyperbolically, that without Castiglione we should not have Hamlet. The ideal of the courtier, soldier, scholar, developed first in Italy, and perfected in the narrative of *Il Cortigiano*, was Castiglione's gift to the world, and Hamlet (even admitting that his chief end is not soldiership[1]) is the high exemplar of it in our literature:

> The courtier's, soldier's, scholar's, eye, tongue, sword.
>
> (III. i. 159).

According to Bradley, the Hamlet of the play's commencement is almost paralysed by shock arising from his mother's hasty and dishonourable second marriage. From what was he paralysed?—From the ideal of courtiership; and especially from that phase of it which regarded women as the inspiration and mainstay of courtliness. He believed that Beauty and Goodness were one. In shock and in recovery this true Hamlet is discernible, not least in Ophelia's triple praise. He was "the Courtier," he was *the* Prince. The terms are almost interchangeable. Indeed, Lord Julian suggests that "the Courtier" they have fashioned is greater than a prince. Being courtier-prince, or prince of courtesy, Hamlet, in addition to the endowments of physical strength, courage, and comeliness, and to the acquirement of skill in fence and the like (which are natural fulfilments of Belleforest's perfect prince of the North), adds certain characteristics which are peculiarly of Castiglione's School. He is a scholar—of Wittenberg University —much given to the classics.

He knows how to use puns and jests, is a master of the retort courteous and the retort discourteous, and can twist words into whatever ironies he will. Not least is his address among those "merry sayinges . . . that arise when a man at a nipping talk of his fellow taketh the very same words in the self same sense and returneth them back again, pricking him with his own weapon." Hoisting him, as it were, with his own petard. But of any one of his jests, almost, it might be said: "See this taunt: how pleasant, witty, and grave it is, and worthy in very deed for the noble courage of an Alexander."

He is a passionate friend. He could have been this, no doubt,

[1] Great is the difference between Hamlet and the courtier of an Italian city-state in this respect. But the balance of *Il Cortigiano* is so decidedly moral and intellectual, that, in comparison, Hamlet's lack of soldiership is unimportant.

without any other instruction than that of life, or of the Bible, or of that somewhat Anglicised pattern of gentility which develops through Ascham's *Scholemaster*, Elyot's *Governor*, Lyly's *Euphues*, Sidney's *Arcadia*, and Spenser's *Faerie Queen*. But combined as this passion is with certain other characteristics, such as the last-named, it is reasonably attributable to Castiglione's influence. "That high degree of friendship," says Sir Frederick, ". . . ministereth unto us all the goodness contained in our life. . . . I would have our courtier, therefore, to find him out an especial and hearty friend, if it were possible, of that sort we have spoken of."

He is the "sweet prince" (V. iii. 270) through most of his life. But he is capable of violence, of that dramatic sort which Castiglione advises. "He therefore that we seek for, where the enemies are, shall show himself most fierce, bitter, and evermore with the first. In every place beside, lowly, sober, and circumspect, fleeing above all things bragging and unshameful praising himself."

He dresses his part. "Customary suits of solemn black" are not mourning garments only. They are what Castiglione recommends for the Courtier's ordinary wear. For war, let him adopt colours over steel. For peace, "methinks a black colour hath a better grace in garments than any other."

He is a musician. At least he fingers a pipe as though accustomed to its stops and ventages. This also is fitting.

More than musician, he is potentially painter. He plays with cloud shapes as no other of Shakespeare's heroes does, except Antony. He regards the external world with that appreciation of line, form, mass, chiaroscuro, without which, Castiglione says, man cannot be great. "And in very deed who so esteemeth not this art [of painting] is, to my seeming, far wide from all reason." The succeeding passages in praise of the beauty of earth should be compared with Hamlet's "this most excellent canopy, the air"; and Hamlet's celebration of the masterpiece, man, with such passages from *The Courtier* as that beginning "Think now of the shape of man"; or as the following:

"In conclusion, this comely and holy beauty is a wondrous setting out of everything. And it may be said that Good and beautiful be after a sort one selfe thing, especially in the bodies of men: of the beauty whereof the nighest cause (I suppose) is the beauty of the soul."

These then are the elements of Hamlet's character. Perhaps he also, in meditation upon Beauty, knew the ecstasy of the

soul which "fleeth to couple herself with the nature of Angels
. . . [and] hath no more neede of the discourse of reason, for
being changed into an Angell she understandeth all things that
may be understood. . . ."

We can infer it through the inverse he shows, now that his
mother has done what "a beast that wants discourse of reason"
would not have done: now that he has lost that delight in man,
"in acting how like an angel, in apprehension how like a god!"
which once was his.

Fallen from his old belief, he abuses women. Beauty is a bawd.
"I have heard of your paintings too." Jeremiah had also heard.
But, even for this, Castiglione suggests himself as the most
immediate literary source; because of his combination of disgust
at artifice and trickery, with other qualities, of appreciation,
all of them in the courtier, and all of them in Hamlet also.

Hamlet's manner of speech, the range of his vocabulary,
his freedom and dignity of utterance, are what we should
expect (if we were wise enough) from the suggestions in *The
Courtier*. All his doings are, besides, marked by that "certain
Recklessness" or nonchalance which is Castiglione's hall-mark
of gentility.

But it is not only Shakespeare's Hamlet that seems to follow
Castiglione. Shakespeare himself does so. More surely than
anywhere else he paints (rather than poetizes) a background of
the natural world. It is a night piece—the battlements of
Elsinore, the sea deep below, the town inland under the glow
of the impetuous forges, the westering stars. And then:

> . . . look, the morn, in russet mantle clad,
> Walks o'er the dew of yon high eastward hill.[1]

In doing so, he cannot have forgotten (for none can forget
who reads it) that passage, at the end of *The Courtier*, in which
human conversation and dreams in a palace are set off by the
fair morning like unto the colour of roses, already risen over the
high top, eastward, of Mount Catri.

**W. B. DRAYTON HENDERSON.**

[1] *Hamlet*, I. i. (quarto version).

# BOOK OF THE COURTIER

## CHIEF PERSONS OF THE DIALOGUES

LADY ELIZABETH GONZAGA ("my Lady Dutchesse"), wife of Guidobaldo di Montefeltro, Duke of Urbino. Aged 46.

LADY EMILIA PIA,[1] friend and companion of the duchess, and
widow of the duke's half-brother. Aged about 30.

THE LORD GENERALL (Francesco Maria Della Rovere), nephew and
heir adoptive of Duke Guidobaldo, whom he succeeded the
year following these dialogues. Aged 17.

COUNT LEWIS (LUDOVICO) OF CANOSSA,[2] a kinsman of the author,
afterwards made Bishop of Bayeux. Aged 31.

SIR FREDERICK (FEDERICO) FREGOSO, half-nephew of the duke.
Aged 27. He and his brother were exiles from Genoa. They
were, both, soldiers and poets. Federico became Archbishop
of Salerno.

LORD JULIAN (GIULIANO) DE MEDICIS ("my Lord Magnifico"),
son of Lorenzo the Magnificent. He was one of Castiglione's
dearest friends. Sharing the exile of his family from Florence
(1494–1512), he was residing at the Court of Urbino. Aged 29.
Subsequently he became Duke of Nemours, and, dying in 1516,
was immortalised by Michael Angelo, at the instance of Pope
Leo X., in the Chapel of San Lorenzo. "Night" and "Day"
are at his feet.

M. BERNARD BIBIENA (Bernardo Dovizi da Bibbiena), an adherent
of the Medici, afterwards made a cardinal. Aged 27.

LORD OCTAVIAN FREGOSO, elder brother of "Sir Frederick," afterwards Doge of Genoa.

M. PETER (PIETRO) BEMBO, a Venetian humanist, afterwards made
a cardinal. Aged 37. He lived for six years at Urbino, studiously
following his fortunes.[3]

LORD CESAR GONZAGA, a kinsman of the duchess, and cousin as
well as close friend of the author. Aged about 32.

[1] It is possible that Castiglione's picture of her, and of the amusing
misogynist, L. Gaspar Pallavicino, with whom she is constantly sparring
(cf. p. 324, "I recken him a wavering starter"), suggested Beatrice and
Benedick for Shakespeare's *Much Ado*. See *The Book of the Courtyer* by
Mary Augusta Scott, Ph.D., *Mod. Lang. Ass. of America Pubs.*, vol. xvi.,
1901, No. 4.
[2] Some twenty years later, the bishop paid a visit to Urbino. Only the
Lady Emilia was left of all the old circle; and she was living, sick and
alone, in a corner of the great palace. He read to her from the book of
*The Courtier*, alive with her youth. As he read she seemed to revive, then
suddenly died. See Julia Cartwright, *Baldassare Castiglione*, vol. ii. 381.
[3] Cold and calculating as is Bembo, he delivers the rapt eulogy of
Platonic Love in Book IV., which is probably one of the sources of the
Platonism of Shakespeare's Sonnets. See G. Wyndham, *The Poems of
Shakespeare*.

"UNICO ARETINO" ("the unique Aretine"), BERNARDO ACCOLTI, a courtier-poet and popular extemporiser.

LORD GASPAR PALLAVICIN. Aged 21. (He plays Benedick to the Lady Emilia's Beatrice.)


TIME: MARCH 1507

URBINO at this time had come into a decade of happiness. The duchy had been overrun by the Borgia power—Pope Alexander VI. and Cesare Borgia in 1503–6—and Duke Guidobaldo and his family exiled. It was soon to be appropriated by the Medici, under Leo X., in 1516, when the young Duke Francesco was driven out; and this time there was no return. But the present happiness was large. It was the gift of Pope Julius II., and of that fortune which took off both the Borgias in 1603, and also Alexander's immediate successor Pope Pius III.—after a reign of twenty-six days. Julius II. favoured Urbino; his nephew was heir adoptive to its reigning duke. Returning to Rome after reducing Bologna, in March 1506, he paid a three days' visit to the little city; "and there were some," as Castiglione says, "who, attracted by the charm of the company, remained for many days at Urbino after the Pope and his court had left, during which time not only were the usual festivities and amusements held, but . . . fresh games and diversions were held every evening."

This was the occasion of the dialogues of *The Courtier*.

Whether or not the theme of *The Courtier* was actually discussed after the manner reported, at that time, or ever, it was most natural to the interests and fashion of the Court of Urbino.

Furthermore, most of the persons introduced were actually present at the court during that memorable week. Castiglione himself was there; though he introduces a polite fiction by which he was away and therefore unable to take part.

# CONTENTS

CONTENTS

# THOMAS SACKEVYLL IN COMMENDATION OF THE WORKE

## TO THE READER

*These royall kinges, that reare up to the skye*
*Their pallace tops, and deck thē all with gold :*
*With rare and curious workes they feede the eye :*
*And shew what riches here great Princes hold.*
*A rarer worke and richer far in worth,*
*Castilios hand presenteth here to thee.*
*No proude, ne golden Court doth he set forth,*
*But what in Court a Courtier ought to be.*
*The prince he raiseth huge and mightie walles,*
*Castilio frames a wight of noble fame :*
*The king with gorgeous Tissue clads his halles,*
*The Count with golden vertue deckes the same,*
*Whose passing skill, lo Hobbies pen displaies*
*To Britaine folke, a worke of worthy praise.*

## TO THE RIGHT HONORABLE THE LORD HENRY HASTINGS,

### Sonne and Heire Apparant to the Noble Earle of Huntington

THEMISTOCLES the noble Athenian in his banishment entertained most honorably with king of Persia, willed upon a time to tell his cause by a spokesman, compared it to a peece of Tapistrie, that being spread abroad, discloseth the beautie of the workmanship, but foulded together, hydeth it, and therefore demaunded respite to learne the Persian tongue to tell his owne cause: Right so (Honorable Lord) this Courtier hath long strayed about this Realme, and the fruite of him either little, or unperfectly received to the common benefite: for either men skilful in this tongue have delighted in him for their owne private commoditie, or else he hath eftsones spoken in peecemeale by an interpreter to such as desired to know his mind, and to practise

1

his principles: the which how unperfect a thing it is, Themistocles and experience teach. But now, though late in deede, yet for all that at length, beside the principall languages, in the which he hath a long time haunted all the Courtes of Christendom, he is become an Englishman (which many a long time have wished, but fewe attempted, and none atchived) and willing to dwell in the Court of England, and in plight to tell his owne cause. In whose commendation I shall not neede to use any long processe of wordes, for he can so well speake for himselfe, and answere to the opinion that men have a long time conceyved of him, that whatsoever I should write therein, were but labour in wast, and rather a diminishing, than a setting forth of his worthines, and a great deale better it were to passe it over with silence, then to use briefenesse. Onely for the litle acquaintance I have with him, and for the generall profit is in him, my desire is, hee should now at his first arrivall, a new man in his kind of trade, be well entertained and much honored. And for somuch as none, but onely a young Gentleman, and trayned up all his life time in Court, and of worthy qualities, is meete to receive and entertaine so worthie a Courtier, that like may felowship and get estimation with his like, I do dedicate him unto your good Lordship, that through your meanes, and under your patronage he may be common to a great meany. And this doe I not, for that I suppose you stand in neede of any of his instructions, but partly because you may see him confirme with reason the Courtly fashions, comely exercises, and noble vertues, that unawares have from time to time crept into you and alreadie with practise and learning taken custome in you: And partly to get him the more authoritie and credit through so honorable a Patrone. For no doubt, if you be seene willingly to embrace him, other young and Courtly gentlemen will not shun his companie: And so both he shall get him the reputation now here in England which he hath had a good while since beyond the sea, in Italy, Spaine and Fraunce, and I shall thinke my small travaile well imployed and sufficiently recompensed. The honour and entertainement that your noble Auncestours shewed Castilio the maker, when he was in this Realme to be installed knight of the Order, for the Duke his Maister, was not so much as presently both he, and this his handy worke shall receive of you. Generally ought this to be in estimation with all degrees of men: For to Princes and great men, it is a rule, to rule them selves that rule others, and one of the bookes that a noble philosopher exhorted a certaine king to provide him, and diligently to search, for in them he should find written such matters, that friendes durst not utter unto kings. To men growen in yeares, a pathway to the beholding and musing of the mind, and to whatsoever else is meete for that age: To young Gentlemen, an encouraging to garnish their minds with morall vertues, and their bodies with comely exercises, and both the one and the other with honest qualities to attaine unto their noble end. To Ladies and Gentlewomen, a mirrour to decke and trimme themselves with vertuous conditions, comely behaviours and honest entertainment toward all men: And to thē all in generall, a storehouse of most necessarie implements for the conversation, use, and trayning up of mans life with Courtly demeaners. Were it not that the ancientnes of time, the degree of a Consul, and the eloquence of Latin stile in these our dayes beare a great stroke, I know not whither in the invention and disposition of the matter, as Castilio hath folowed Cicero, and applyed to his purpose sundrie examples and pithie sentences out of him, so he may in feat conveyance and like trade of wryting, be compared to him: But wel I wot, for renowme among the Italians, he is not inferiour to him. Cicero an excellent Oratour, in three bookes of an Oratour unto his brother, fashioneth such a one as never was, nor yet is like to be: Castilio an excellent Courtier, in three bookes of a Courtier unto his deare friend, fashioneth such a one as is hard to find, and perhaps unpossible. Cicero bringeth in to dispute of an Oratour, Crassus, Scevola, Antonius, Cotta, Sulpitius, Catullus, and Cesar his brother, the noblest and chiefest Oratours in those daies. Castilio, to reason of a Courtier, the Lord Octavian Fregoso, Sir Frideric his brother, the Lord Julian de Medecis, the Lord Cesar Gonzaga, the L. Frances comaria Della Rovere, Count Lewis of Canossa, the Lord Gaspar Pallavisin, Bembo, Bibiena, and other most excellent Courtiers, and of the noblest families in these daies in Italie. Which all afterwarde became Princes, Cardinalles, Bishops and great Lordes, and some yet in life. Both Cicero and Castilio professe, they folow not any certaine appointed order of precepts or rules, as is used in the instruction of youth, but call to rehearsall, matters debated in their times too and fro in the disputation of most eloquent men and excellent wittes in every worthy qualitie, the one company in the olde time assembled in Tusculane, and the other of late yeares in the new Pallace of Urbin, where many most excellent wittes in this Realme have made no lesse of this booke, than the Great Alexander did of Homer. I cannot sufficiently wonder that they have not all this while from time to time done a common benefite to profit others as well as themselves: In this point (I knowe not by what destiny) Englishmen are much inferiour to most of all other Nations: For where they set their delight and bend themselves with an honest strife of matching others to turne into their mother tongue, not onely the wittie writings of other languages, but also of all the Philosophers, and all Sciences both Greeke and Latin, our mē weene it sufficient to have a perfect knowledge, to no other end, but to profit themselves, and (as it were) after much paynes in breaking up a gap bestow no lesse to close it up againe, that others may with like travaile followe after. And where our learned men for the most part holde opinion, to have the sciences in the mother tongue, hurteth memorie and hindreth learning, in my opinion, they do full ill cōsider from whence the Grecians first, and afterward the Latins set their knowledge. And without wading to any farther reasons that might be alleadged, if they will marke well the truth, they shall see at this day, where the Sciences are most turned into the vulgar tongue, there are best learned men, and comparing it with the contrarie, they shall also find the effects contrarie. In Italy (where the most translation of authors is) not onely for Philosophie, Logike, Humanitie and all liberall Sciences, both in Greeke and Latin (leaving a part Barbarus, Naugerius, Sannazarus, Bembus, Lazarus and the rest that of late dayes florished) Genua, Tomitanus, Robertellus, Manutius, Piccolhomineus, are presently very singular, and renowmed throughout all Christendome: but also for the same in the vulgar tongue with little or no sight at all in the Latin, Aretino, Gelli (a taylor in Florence) the Lord Victoria columna, the L. Dionora Sanseverina, the L. Beatrice Loffreda, Veronica Gambera, Virginea Salvi, and infinite other men and women are most famous throughout Italy, whose divine workes and excellent stile both in rime and prose give a sufficient testimonie, not onely of their profound knowledge and noble wit, but also that knowledge may be obtained in studying onely a mans owne native tongue. So that to be skilfull and exercised in authours translated, is no lesse to be called learning, then is the very same in the Latin or Greeke tongue. Therefore the translation of Latin or Greeke authours, doth not onely not hinder learning, but furthereth it, yea, it is learning itselfe, and a great stay to youth, and the noble ende to which they ought to apply their wittes, that with diligence and studie have attained a perfect understanding, to open a gap for others to follow their steps;

and a vertuous exercise for the unlatined to come by learning, and to fill their mind with the moral vertues, and their bodies with civill conditions: that they may both talke freely in all companie, live uprightly, though there were no lawes, and be in a readinesse against all kinde of worldly chaunces that happen, which is the profit that commeth of Philosophie. And he said well that was asked the question, How much the learned differed from the unlearned, "So much (quoth he) as the well broken and readie horses, from the unbroken." Wherefore I wot not how our learned men in this case can avoyde the saying of Isocrates, to one that among sundry learned discourses at Table spake never a word: "If thou be unlearned, thou doest wisely: but if thou be learned, unwisely." As who should say, learning is il bestowed where others be not profited by it. As I therefore have to my small skill bestowed some labour about this peece of worke, even so could I wish with all my heart, profound learned men in the Greeke and Latin should make the like proofe, and every man store the tongue according to his knowledge and delight above other men, in some piece of learn- ing, that wee alone of the world may not be still counted bar- barous in our tongue, as in time out of mind we have bene in our maners. And so shall we perchaunce in time become as famous in England, as the learned men of other nations have bene and presently are: And though the hardnesse of this present matter be such, and mine unskilfulnesse to undertake this enter- prise so great, that I might with good cause have dispayred to bring to an end it that many excellent wittes have attempted, yet could I not choose but yelde to the continuall requestes and often perswasions of many young gentlemen, which have (may chaunce) an opinion that to be in me, that is not in deede, and unto whom in any reasonable matter I were skilfull in, neither I could nor ought of duetie to want in fulfilling their desire. Notwithstanding a great while I forbare and lingered the time, to see if any of a more perfect understanding in the tongue, and better practised in the matter of the booke (of whom we want not a number in this realme) would take the matter in hand, to do his countrie so great a benefit: and this imagination prevailed in me a long space after my dutie done in translating the third booke (that entreateth of a Gentlewoman of the Court) perswaded thereunto, in that I was enformed, it was then in some forwardnes by an other, whose wit and stile was greatly to be allowed, but since prevented by death he could not finish it. But of late being instantly craved upon a fresh,

I whetted my stile and setled my selfe to take in hand the other three bookes (that entreat of the perfection of a Gentleman of the Court) to fulfill their petition in what I am able, having time and leisure thereto, the which I have done, though not in effect, yet in apparance, and that in a great deale shorter time, than the hardnesse of the matter required. And where it shall not perhaps throughly please, by reason my small understanding in the tongue, and lesse practise in the matters herein contained, is not of force to give it the brightnesse and full perfection in this our tongue that it hath in the Italian, it shall suffice yet that I have shewed my selfe obedient in the respect a man ought to have toward his betters: And no more can they avoyde the blame to charge me withal, than I to undertake it. Beside that, I have declared my good will and well meaning no lesse then if my cunning were greate, and could extend much farther. But peradventure the rudenesse of this shall be an encouraging of some other to give the onset upon other matters with a better ripenesse of stile and much more aptnesse, and so shall this yet profit both waies. But the estimation it must get by your Honour, is the principall cause that setteth it out, and maketh it worne with the handes of heedfull readers: For in case you cheerefully receive it, men wil reckon it good: If you allowe it, worthy to be practised: If you commend it, worthy to passe from hand to hand. Therfore among the other good opinions men generally hold of you, let it not be the least, that they may hold also no lesse of this that you allowe and commend. And so shall you shew undeserved kindnesse, I bound in duety, and al others in good wil, to imbrace and to welcome it out of Italy into England. And thus shal Castilio be estemed such a one as he is in deede, and waxe familiar with all men, that of late was knowne of very few, and so mangled with varietie of judgements, y$^t$ he was (in a maner) maymed, and lost a good peece of his estimation. But in case judgements now feint, or mine interpretation seeme not pithie, but rude, not proper, but colde, there is no more imperfection in this Courtier, then in Cirus himselfe, in the translation of Xenophon into the Italian or any other tongue, the one as necessarie and proper for a Gentleman of the Court, as the other for a king. And I shall desire my labour may so be taken well in worth, as I have endevoured my selfe to follow the very meaning and wordes of the Authour, without being misledde by fantasie, or leaving out anye parcell one or other, whereof I know not how some interpreters of this booke into other languages can excuse themselves, and the more they be conferred, the more it will perchaunce appeare. Wherefore receive you this, as a token of my good will, and so receive it, that the fruit, what ever it be, may be acknowledged at your hāds: and you passe the expectation of mē in this, as in all other things, which, no doubt, is very great of you: and I, to acknowledge this benefit, where my habilitie stretcheth to nothing else, shall at the least evermore wish unto your Lordship long life, that you may go forward, as you do, in these beginnings; which promise a luckie end, to the honour of your selfe, comfort of your friendes, and forwardnes of the common weale of your Countrie.

Your L. most bounden,

THOMAS HOBBY.

## A LETTER OF SYR J. CHEKE

### To his loving frind Mayster

#### THOMAS HOBY

FOR your opinion of my gud will unto you as you wriit, you can not be deceived: for submitting your doinges to mi judgement, I thanke you: for taking this pain of your translation, you worthilie deserv great thankes of all sortes. I have taken sum pain at your request cheflie in your preface, not in the reading of it for that was pleasaunt unto me boath for the roundnes of your saienges and welspeakinges of the saam, but in changing certein wordes which might verie well be let aloan, but that I am verie curious in mi freendes matters, not to determijn, but to debaat what is best. Wheurin, I seek not the besines haplie bi truth, but bi mijn own phansie, and shew of goodnes.

I am of this opinion that our own tung shold be written cleane and pure, unmixt and unmangeled with borowing of other tunges, wherin if we take not heed by tijm, ever borowing and never payeng, she shall be fain to keep her house as bankrupt. For then doth our tung naturallie and praisablie utter her meaning, when she bouroweth no counterfeitness of other tunges to attire her self withall, but useth plainlie her own, with such shift, as nature, craft, experiens and folowing of other excellent doth lead her unto, and if she want at ani tijm (as being unperfight she must) yet let her borow with suche bashfulnes, that it mai appeer, that if either the mould of our

own tung could serve us to fascion a woord of our own, or if
the old denisoned wordes could content and ease this neede,
we wold not boldly venture of unknowen wordes. This I say
not for reproof of you, who have scarslie and necessarily used
whear occasion serveth a strange word so, as it seemeth to grow
out of the matter and not to be sought for: but for mijn own
defens, who might be counted overstraight a deemer of thinges,
if I gave not thys accompt to you, mi freend and wijs, of mi
marring this your handiwork. But I am called awai, I prai
you pardon mi shortnes, the rest of mi saienges should be but
praise and exhortacion in this your doinges, which at moar
leisor I shold do better. From my house in Woodstreete the
16 of July, 1557.

Yours assured<br>JOAN CHEKE.

## EPISTLE OF THE AUTHOR

### Unto the Reverend and Honourable

#### Lorde Mychaell de Sylva

##### BISHOP OF VISEO

AFTER the Lorde Guidubaldo of Montefeltro Duke of Urbin [1]
was departed out of this life, certein other Gentilmen and I
that had bine servauntes to him, continued in servyce wyth
Duke Francescomaria Della Roveré hys heire and successor in
the state: and whyle the savour of the vertues of Duke Guidubaldo was fresh in my mynde, and the great delite I took in
those yeeres in the loving companie of so excellent Personages
as then were in the Court of Urbin: I was provoked by the
memorie therof to write these bookes of the *Courtier*.[2] The which
I accomplished in a fewe dayes, myndinge in time to amende
those faultes that spronge of the desire that I had speedilie to
paye this debt. But fortune now manie yeeres hath alwayes
kept me under in suche continuall travayles, that I coulde
never gete leyser to bringe it to the passe that my feeble judge-

[1] Guidubaldo of Montefeltro, Duke of Urbino (born 1472, died 1508),
in all respects but that of physique the ideal prince of the Renaissance.
Castiglione's praise is confirmed by other witnesses. Long an invalid (which
explains his absence from the conversations) and unsuccessful as a soldier,
his fame rests upon his character and intellectual accomplishments.
See p. 18. See also note on p. 231.

[2] Castiglione may have made his first sketch of the work in a few days
in 1508; but it was not until 1513–16 that he finally worked out the idea
—not until 1518 that he brought it to its present form.

ment might be throughlie satisfied withall. At such time therfore as I was in Spayne, being advertised out of Italy how the
Lady Vittoria Colonna[1] Marquesse of Pescara, unto whom in
foretime I had graunted a Copie of this booke, contrarie to
her promise, had made a great part of it to be copied out: it
greeved me somwhat whether I would or no, standinge in doubt
of the sundrie inconveniences that in the like cases may happen.
Yet had I a hope that the witt and wisdome of that Lady
(whose troth I have alwaies had in reverence, as a matter from
above) was sufficient to provide, not to be harmfull unto me
my beeinge obedient to her commaundement. At last I hard
an yncklinge that part of the booke was rief in Naples in many
mens handes: and as men are alwayes desirous of noveltie, it
was thought that they attempted to imprint it. Wherfore I,
amased at this mischaunce, determined wyth my self to over-
looke by and by that litle in the booke that time served me
therto, with entent to set it abrode, thinking it lesse hurtful
to have it somwhat corrected with mine owne hande, then
much mangled with an other mannes. Therfore to have this
my pourpose take effect, I tooke in hande to reade it over
afresh, and sodeinlie at the first blush by reason of the title, I
tooke no litle grief, which in proceadinges forward encreased
much more, rememberinge that the greater part of them that
are brought in to reason, are now dead. For beside those that
are mentioned in the Proheme of the last booke, M. Alphonsus
Ariosto him self is dead, unto whom the booke was dedicated,
a noble yonge Gentilman, discreete, full of good condicions,
and apt unto every thing meete for one livinge in court. Likewise Duke Julian de Medicis, whose goodnesse and noble
Courtesy deserved to have bene a longer time enjoyed of the
world. Also M. Bernard, Cardinall of S. Maria in Portico, who
for his livelie and pleasant promptness of witt, was most acceptable unto as manie as knew him, and dead he is. The Lord
Octavian Fregoso is also dead, a man in oure tymes verie rare,
of a most noble courage, of a pure lief, full of goodnesse, witt,
wisdome and Courtesie, and a verie frende unto honour and
vertue, and so worthy prayse, that his verie ennemies could
say none other of hym, then what sounded to his renoume:
and the mishappes he hath borne out with great steadinesse,

[1] Vittoria Colonna (born 1490, died 1547), a sister of Duke Guidobaldo.
She married the Marquess of Pescara in 1509. Both before and after her
husband's death (in 1525) she was an ardent humanist, and friend of
scholars. Perhaps her chief claim upon memory is that she comforted
Michael Angelo's last years, but, dying before he did, left him desolate.

were sufficient inoughe to geve evidence, that fortune, as she hath alwayes bene, so is she in these dayes also an enemie to vertue. There are dead in like maner manie other that are named in this boke, unto whom a man wold have thought that nature had promised a verie longe lief. But the thinge that should not be rehersed wythout teares is, that the Dutchesse[1] she is also dead. And if my minde be troubled with the losse of so manye frindes and good Lordes of myne, that have left me in this lief, as it were in a wildernes full of sorow, reason would it should with much more grief beare the heavinesse of the Dutchesse death, then of al the rest, bicause she was more woorth then all the rest, and I was much more bounde unto her then unto all the rest. Therfore for leesinge time to bestowe that of dutye I ought upon the memorye of so excellent a Ladye, and of the rest that are no more in lief, provoked also by the jeopardye of the booke, I have made him to be imprinted, and setforth in such sort, as the shortnes of time hath served me. And bicause you had no acqueintance, neither with the Dutches, nor with any of the rest that are dead, saving only with Duke Julian, and with the Cardinal of S. Maria in Portico, while they lived, therfore to the entent, in what I can do, you may have acqueintance with them after their death, I send unto you this booke, as a purtraict in peinctinge of the Court of Urbin: not of the handiwoorke of Raphael,[2] or Michael Angelo, but of an unknowen peincter, and that can do no more but draw the principall lines, without settingfurth the truth with beawtifull coulours, or makinge it appeere by the art of Prospective that it is not. And wher I have enforced my self to setfurth together with the communication the propreties and condicions of such as are named in it, I confesse I have not only not fully expressed, but not somuch as touched the vertues of the Dutchesse. Bicause not onlye my stile is unsufficient to express them, but also mine understanding to conceive them. And if in this behalf, or in

---

[1] "The Dutchesse": Elizabetta Gonzaga, second daughter of Marquess Federico Gonzaga of Mantua—from all accounts a woman of noble mind and appearance. She was Castiglione's faithful friend; and he, if this and other expressions of his grief for her death have weight, rather her lover than her courtier.

[2] Raphael was the son of Giovanni Santi, for many years court-painter at Urbino. The Dutchesse Elizabetta gave the boy his first commissions. Castiglione may have known him at this time. Later they became intimate friends, as is attested by Raphael's "School of Philosophy" in the Stanza of the Vatican—a picture whose design is said to have been influenced by Castiglione. In it both the painter and the courtier appear close together, Castiglione in the character of Zoroaster, looking toward his friend. Raphael painted yet another portrait of Castiglione, which is now in the Louvre.

anie other matter woorthy reprehension (as I know well there
want not manie in the booke) fault be found in me, I will not
speake against the truth. But bicause men somtime take such
delite in finding fault, that they find fault also in that deserveth
not reproof, unto some that blame me bicause I have not
folowed Boccaccio, nor bound my self to the maner of the
Tuscane speach used nowadayes, I will not let to say, for all
Boccaccio was of a fine witt, according to those times, and in
some part writt with great advisement and diligence: yet did
he write much better whan he lett him self be guided with witt
and his owne naturall inclination, without anie other maner
studie or regarde to polish his writinges, then whan with al
travaile and bent studye he enforced him self to be most fine
and eloquent. For his verie favourers affirme that in his own
matters he was far deceived in judgement, litle regarding such
thinges as have gotten him a name, and greatlye esteaminge
that is nothing woorth. Had I then folowed that trade of writing
which is blamed in him by such as praise him in the rest, I
could not have eschewed the verye same reprooffes that are
laied to Boccaccio himself as touching this. And I had deserved
somuch the more, for that his errour was then, in beleavyng
he did well, and mine should be nowe, in knowinge I do amisse.
Again if I had folowed that trade which is reckened of many
to be good, and was litle regarded of him, I should appeere in
folowing it to disagree from the judgement of him whom I
folowed: the which thing (in mine opinion) were an inconvenience. And beeside yf this respect had not moved me, I
could not folowe him in the matter, forsomuch as he never wrott
any thing in treatise like unto these bookes of the *Courtier*:
and in the tunge, I ought not in mine advise, bicause the force
or rule of speach doeth consist more in use, then in anye thinge
els: and it is alwayes a vice to use woordes that are not in
commune speach.[1] Therfore it was not meete I should have
used many that are in Boccaccio, which in his time were used,
and now are out of use emonge the Tuscanes them selves.
Neyther would I binde my self to the maner of the Tuscane
tunge in use nowe a dayes, because the practising emonge

[1] Castiglione's defence of his liberal use of words is part of that warfare
of the Ancients and the Moderns which was waged on so many wordy
battlefields throughout Europe. Our translator, Hoby, being of Sir John
Cheke's School of English pure and undefiled, though not too strict an
adherent, was therefore not the most ideal reproducer of the courtly
Italian. High Renaissance fashions are sometimes ill at ease in English
homespun. No less Hoby's translation is praised as "conscientious,
intelligent, and able."

sundrye Nations, hath alwayes bene of force to transport from
one to an other (in a maner) as merchaundise, so also new
woordes, which afterward remaine or decaye, according as
they are admitted by custome or refused. And this beside the
record of auntient writers, is to be evidently seene in Boccaccio,
in whom there are so manie woordes French, Spanish, and pro-
vincial, and some perhappes not well understood of the Tuscanes in these dayes, that whoso woulde pick them out, should
make the booke much the lesser. And bicause (in mine opinion)
the kinde of speach of the other noble Cities of Italy, where
there resorte men of wisdome, understandinge and eloquence,
which practise great matters of government of states, of letters,
armes, and diverse affayres, ought not altogether to be neglected for the woordes whiche in these places are used in commune speach: I suppose that they maye be used welinough,
writing such as have a grace and comlynesse in the pronun-
tiation, and communly counted good and of propre signification,
though they be not Tuscane, and have also their origion out
of Italy. Beeside this in Tuscane they use many woordes cleane
corrupte from the Latin, the which in Lumbardye and in the
other partes of Italy remaine wholl and without any chaunge
at al, and they are so universallye used of everye man, that of
the best sorte they are allowed for good, and of the commune
people understood with out difficulty. Therfore I thinke I have
committed no errour at all, yf in writing I have used any of
these, and rather taken the wholl and pure woord of mine owne
Countrey, then the corrupt and mangled of an other. Neyther
doeth that rule seeme good unto me, where many say the vulgar
tung, the lesse it is like unto the Latin, the more beawtiful it is:
and I can not perceive why more authoritie should consist in
one custome of speach, then in an other. For if Tuscane be
sufficient to authorise corrupt and mangled Latin woordes, and
to geve them so greate a grace, that mangled in such sort everye
man may use them for good (the which no man denieth) should
not Lumbardy or any other countrey have the authoritye to
allow the very Latin woordes that be pure, sounde, propre and
not broken in any part so, but they may be well borne: and
assuredly as it may be called a rash presumption to take in
hand to forge new wordes, or to set up the olde in spite of
custome: so is it no lesse, to take in hande against the force of
the same custome to bring to naught, and (as it were) to burye
alive such as have lasted nowe many yeeres, and have ben
defended from the malice of the time with the shield of use,

shute at one marke, where none of them hitteth the pinn, he that is nighest is out of doubt better then the rest. Some again say that my meaning was to facion my self, perswading my self that all suche qualities as I appoint to the Courtier are in me. Unto these men I will not cleane deny that I have attempted all that my mynde is the Courtier shoulde have knowleage in. And I thinke who so hath not the knowleage of the thinges intreated upon in this booke, how learned so ever he be, he can full il write them. But I am not of so sclender a judgment in knowing my self, that I wil take upon me to know what soever I can wish. The defence therfore of these accusations and peraventure of many mo, I leave for this once, to the judgement of the commune opinion: bicause for the most part the multytude, though they have no perfect knowleage, yet do they feele by the instinct of nature a certein savour of good and ill, and can geve none other reason for it: one tasteth and taketh delite, an other refuseth and is against his stomake.

Therfore if the booke shall generally please, I wil count him good, and think that he ought to live: but if he shall displease, I will count him naught, and beleave that the memorye of him shall soone perish. And if for all this mine accusers will not be satisfied with this commune judgemente, let them content them selves with the judgement of time, which at length discovereth the privie faultes of every thing: and bicause it is father to truth and a judge without passion, it accustometh evermore to pronounce true sentence of the life or death of writynges.

and have preserved their estimation and dignitye, wh[...]
the warres and turmoiles of Italy, alterations were bro[...]
up both of the tunge, buildinges, garmentes and maners. [...]
beeside the hardnesse of the matter, it seemeth to be (as it w[...]
a certein wickednesse. Therfore where I have not thought go[...]
in my writing to use the wordes of Boccaccio which are us[...]
no more in Tuscane, nor to binde my self to their law that thin[...]
it not lawful to use them that the Tuscanes use not nowadayes
me thynke I ought to be held excused. But I suppose both in
the matter of the booke and in the tunge, forsomuch as one
tung may help an other, I have folowed Authores asmuch
woorthie praise, as Boccaccio. And I beleave it ought not to be
imputed unto me for an errour, that I have chosen to make
my self rather knowen for a Lumbard, in speaking of Lumbard,
then for no Tuscan, in speaking of tomuch Tuscan. Bicause
I wil not do as Theophrastus did, which for speaking tomuch
the meere Athenian tunge, was of a simple olde woman knowen
not to be of Athens. But bycause in thys point there is sufficyent
talke in the first booke, I will make no more a do. And to avoid
al contention I confesse to my fault-finders, that I have no
knowleage in this their Tuscan tunge so hard and secrete: and
I say that I have written it in mine owne, and as I speak, and
unto such as speake as I speake: and so I trust I have offended
no man. For I beleave it is forbed no man that is, to wryte and
speake in his owne tunge, neyther is anye man bound to reade
or heare that contenteth hym not. Therfore if they will not
reade my *Courtier*, they shall offende me nothing at all. Other
say, bicause it is so hard a matter and (in a maner) unpossible
to finde out a man of such perfection, as I would have the
Courtier to be, it is but superfluous to write it: for it is a vaine
thing to teach that can not be learned. To these men I answere,
I am content, to err with Plato, Xenophon, and M. Tullius,
leaving apart the disputing of the intelligible world and of the
Ideas or imagined fourmes: in which number, as (according
to that opinion) the Idea or figure conceyved in imagination of
a perfect commune weale, and of a perfect king, and of a perfect
Oratour are conteined: so is it also of a perfect Courtier. To the
image wherof if my power could not draw nigh in stile, so much
the lesse peynes shall Courtiers have to drawe nigh in effect
to the ende and marke that I in writing have set beefore them.
And if with all this they can not compasse that perfection, such
as it is, which I have endevoured to expresse, he that cummeth
nighest shall be the most perfect: as emong many Archers that

# THE COURTIER

## FIRST BOOK

### THE FIRST BOOKE OF THE COURTIER OF COUNTE BALDESSER CASTILIO, UNTO MAISTER ALFONSUS ARIOSTO.

I HAVE a long time douted with my self (moste loving M. Alphonsus) whiche of the two were harder for me, either to denie you the thing that you have with such instance many times required of me, or to take it in hand: because on the one side mee thought it a verie hard matter to denie any thing, especially the request being honest, to the person whom I love dearely, and of whom I perceive my selfe dearly beloved. Againe, on the other side, to undertake an enterprise which I doe not know my selfe able to bring to an ende, I judged it uncomly for him that weyeth due reproofes so much as they ought to bee weyed.

At length, after much debating, I have determined to proove in this behalfe, what ayde that affection and great desire to please can bring unto my diligence, which in other things is woont to encrease the labour of men.

You then require me to write, (what is to my thinking) the trade and maner of courtiers,[1] which is most convenient for a gentleman that liveth in the Court of Princes, by the which he may have the knowledge how to serve them perfitely in every reasonable matter, and obtaine therby favour of them, and praise of other men.

Finally of what sort hee ought to bee that deserveth to be called so perfit a Courtier, that there be no want in him:

Wherefore I considering this kinde of request (say) that in case it shoulde not appeare to my selfe a greater blame, to have you esteeme me to be of small friendship, than all other men of

---

[1] "The trade and maner of courtiers." The excellent modern translation (1902) of Castiglione by L. E. Opdycke, which these notes use as a check on Hoby, renders this passage, "the form of courtiership most befitting a gentleman who lives at the court of princes"; and even so apologises for "courtiership" as a "sadly awkward rendering of the Italian *corteziania* which implies the perfect gentleman, complete as courtier, soldier, scholar." What then must be said of "trade and maner"?

little wisdom, I would have ridde my hands of this labour, for feare least I should be counted rash of al such as knowe, what a hard matter it is, among such diversitie of maners, that are used in the Courts of Christendome, to picke out the perfectest trade and way, and (as it were) the floure of this Courtiership. Bicause use maketh us many times to delite in, and to set little by the selfe same things: whereby sometime it proceedeth that maners, garments, customes, and fashions, which at somtime have ben in price, become not regarded, and contrariwise, the not regarded, become of price.

Therefore it is manifestly to be discerned, that use hath greater force than reason, to bring up new inventions among us, and to abolish the olde, of the which who so goeth about to judge the perfection, is oftentimes deceived.

For which consideration, perceiving this and many other lettes, in the matter propounded for me to write upon, I am constreined to make a peece of an excuse, and to open plainely that this error (if it may be termed an errour) is common to us both, that if any blame happen to me about it, it may be partned with you. For it ought to bee reckned a no lesse offence in you, to lay upon me a burthen that passeth my strength, than in me to take it upon me.

Let us therefore at length settle our selves to beginne that that is our purpose and drift, and (if be it possible) let us fashion such a Courtier, as the Prince that shall be worthie to have him in his service, although his state be but small, may notwith-standing be called a mighty Lord.

We wil not in these books follow any certaine order or rule of appointed preceptes, the which for the most part is woont to bee observed in teaching of any thing whatsoever it bee: But after the manner of men of olde time, renuing a gratefull memorie: we will repeate certaine reasonings that were debated in times past, betweene men very excellent for that purpose. And although I was not there present,[1] but at the time when

---

[1] "And although I was not there present." A graceful fiction, which permits Castiglione to keep himself off his own stage. The first of these dialogues is set on the evening after the departure of Julius II. from Urbino after a visit, on 7 March, 1507. Castiglione had been away, in England, where, as proxy, he had received the companionship of "the most noble order of the Garter" for his lord, Duke Guidobaldo, from Henry VII. But he had returned to Urbino on 5 March. It is of interest that, besides gifts of falcons, dogs, and horses, sent with him to the English king, Castiglione took a small panel picture of St. George, specially painted for the occasion by Raphael. Unless misfortune has overcome it, this is now in the Hermitage at Leningrad.

they were debated, it was my chaunce to be in Englande, yet soone after my returne, I heard them of a person that faithfully reported them unto me. And I will endevour my selfe, for so much as my memory will serve me, to call them particularly to remembrance, that you may see, what men worthy great commendation, and unto whose judgement a man may in every point give an undoubted credite, have judged and beleeved in this matter.

Neither shall we swarve from the purpose to arrive in good order at the ende, unto the which all our communication is directed, if we disclose the cause of the reasonings that hereafter follow.

As every man knoweth, the little Citie of Urbin is situated upon the side of the Appennine (in a manner) in the middes of Italy, towards the Goulfe of Venice. The which for all it is placed among hilles, and those not so pleasant as perhappes some other that we behold in many places, yet in this point the Element hath beene favourable unto it, that all about, the Countrey is verie plentifull and full of fruites: so that beside the holesomnes of ayre, it is verie aboundant and stored with all thinges necessarie for the life of man. But among the greatest felicities that man can reckon to have, I count this the chiefe, that now a long time it hath alwaies bene governed with very good princes, in the common calamities of the wars of Italie it remained also a season without any at all.

But without searching further of this, we may make a good proofe with the famous memorie of Duke Fridericke,[1] who in his daies was the light of Italy. Neither do wee want true and very large testimonies yet remaning of his wisedome, courtesie, justice, liberalitie, of his invincible courage and policy of warre. And of this doe his so manye victories make proofe, chiefly his conquering of places impugnable, so sodaine readines in setting forward to give battaile, his putting to flight sundrie times with a small number, very great and puissant armies, and never sustained losse in anye conflict. So that we may, not without cause, compare him to many famous men of olde tlme.

[1] "Duke Fridericke." Federico di Montefeltro (born 1422, died 1482), made Duke of Urbino, 1474, and also Captain-General of the Church. He was an able commander, and a loyal adherent to one after another of various causes he undertook for Pope, Emperor, King, League, or Prince. From these services came his revenue, amounting at the close of his life to about £330,000 in our values, annually. He spent his money freely for the benefit of his subjects, and the maintenance and enrichment of his cultured court. The library was the jewel of the court, as the court was of Italy. Its MSS. collection now forms part of the Vatican Library.

This man among his other deedes praise-worthie, in the hard and sharpe situation of Urbin buylt a Palace, to the opinion of many men, the fairest that was to bee found in all Italie, and so furnished it with all necessarie implementes belonging thereto, that it appeared not a Palace, but a Citie in forme of a Palace, and that not onelye with ordinarye matters, as Silver plate, hangings for Chambers of very rich cloth of Golde, of Silke and other like, but also for sightlines: and to decke it out withall, placed there a wondrous number of auncient Images, of Marble and Mettall, very excellent paintings and Instruments of Musicke of all sortes, and nothing would he have there but what was most rare and excellent.

To this with verie great charges hee gathered together a great number of most excellent and rare bookes, in Greeke, Latin, and Hebrue, the which all hee garnished with gold and silver, esteeming this to be the chiefest ornament of his great Palace.

This Duke then following the course of nature, when he was threescore and five yeares of age, as he had lived, so did he end his lyfe with glorie.[1] And left Duke after him a child of ten yeres having no more male, and without mother, who hight Guidubaldo.

This childe, as of the state, so did it appeare also that he was heire of all his fathers vertues: and sodainly with a mar-veilous towardnes, began to promise so much of himselfe, as a man would not have thought possible to bee hoped of a man mortall. So that the opinion of men was, that of all Duke Frede-rickes notable deedes, there was none greater than that he begat such a sonn. But fortune envying this so great vertue, with all her might gainstood this so glorious a beginning, in such wise that before Duke Guidubaldo was xx. yeares of age, he fell sicke of the goute, the which encreasing upon him with most bitter paines, in a short time so nummed him of all his members, that hee coulde neither stand on foote, nor move himselfe. And in this manner was one of the best favoured, and towardliest personages in the world, deformed and marred in his greene age.[2] And beside, not satisfied with this, fortune was so contrarie to him in al his purposes, that verye seldome he brought to passe any thing to his mind. And for all hee had in him most wise counsaile, and an invincible courage, yet it seemed that whatsoever he tooke in hand, both in feats of armes, and in

---

[1] Duke Federico was, in fact, sixty when he died.
[2] "In his greene age": cf. Opdycke, "in tender youth."

everye other thing small or great, it came alwaies to ill successe.[1]

And of this make proofe his manye and diverse calamities, which hee alwaies bare out with such stoutnesse of courage, that vertue never yeelded to fortune. But with a bold stomacke despising her stormes, lived with great dignitie and estimation among all men: in sicknesse, as one that was sounde, and in adversitie, as one that was most fortunate. So that for all hee was thus diseased in his bodie he served in time of warre with most honourable entertainement under the most famous kings of Naples, Alphonsus and Ferdinande the yonger. Afterward with Pope Alexander the sixt, with the Lordes of Venice and Florence.

And when Julius the second[2] was created Pope, hee was then made General Capitaine of the Church: at which time proceeding in his accustomed usage, hee set his delight above all thinges to have his house furnished with most noble and valiant Gentlemen, with whom hee lived verie familiarly, enjoying their conversation.

Wherein the pleasure which hee gave unto other men was no lesse, than that he received of other, because hee was verie well seene in both toongs,[3] and togither with a loving behaviour and pleasantnesse[4] hee had also accompanied the knowledge of infinite things. And beside this, the greatnesse of his courage so quickned him, that where hee was not in case with his person to practise the feates of Chivalrie, as he had done long before, yet did he take verie great delight to beholde them in other men, and with his wordes sometime correcting, and otherwhile praising every man according to his deserts, he declared evidently how great a judgement hee had in those matters.

And upon this at Tilt, at Tourney, in playing at all sorts of weapon, also in inventing devices in pastimes, in Musicke, finally in all exercises meete for noble Gentlemen, every man strived to shew himselfe such a one, as might deserve to bee judged worthie of so noble assembly.

Therefore were all the houres of the day divided into honourable and pleasant exercises, as well of the bodie, as of the minde.

---

[1] Duke Guidobaldo was rarely successful in war. In 1498, fighting under the banner of the Church, he was captured by the Orsini: his duchess had to sell her jewels to pay his ransom. See also note 1 on p. 8.

[2] Pope Julius II. acceded 1503.

[3] Latin and Greek.

[4] Cf. Opdycke, "affability and pleasantness" (in the sense of our modern "pleasantry").

But because the Duke used continually, by reason of his in-firmitie, soone after Supper to goe to his rest, everie man ordin-arily, at that houre drew where the Dutchesse was, the Ladie Elizabeth Gonzaga, where also continually was the Ladie Emilia Pia, who for that shee was indued with so lively a wit and judgement, as you know, seemed the maistresse and ringleader of all the company, and that everie man at her received under-standing and courage.

There was then to bee heard pleasant communications and merie conceites, and in everie mans countenance a man might perceive painted a loving jocundnesse. So that this house truely might wel be called the very Mansion place of mirth and joy. And I beleeve it was never so tasted in other place, what manner a thing the sweete conversation is that is occasioned of an amiable and loving company, as it was once there.

For leaving apart what honour it was to all us to serve such a Lorde, as hee whom I declared unto you right now, everye man conceived in his minde an high contentation[1] every time we came into the Dutchesse sight. And it appeared that this was a chaine that kept all linked together in love, in such wise that there was never agreement of wil or hartie love greater betweene brethren, than there was betweene us all.

The like was betweene the woman, with whom we had such free and honest conversation, that everye man might commune, sitte, dallye, and laugh with whom hee had lusted.

But such was the respect which we bore to the Dutchesse will, that the selfe same libertie was a very great bridle.[2] Neither was there any that thought it not the greatest pleasure he could have in the world, to please her, and the greatest griefe to offend her.

For this respect were there most honest conditions[3] coupled with wondrous great libertie, and devises of pastimes,[4] and laughing matters tempred in her sight, beside most witty jestes, with so comely and grave a Majestie, that the verye sober moode and greatnes that did knit together all the actes, woordes and gestures of the Dutchesse in jesting and laughing, made them all that had never seene her in their lyfe before, to count her a verie great Ladie.

And all that came in her presence, having this respect fixed in their breast, it seemed shee had made them to her becke.

---

[1] Cf. "a supreme contentment."

[2] "A very great bridle." But it must be remembered that freedom of expression was also very great.

[3] Cf. "most decorous manners."     [4] Cf. "games and laughter."

So that everie man enforced himselfe to followe this trade, taking (as it were) a rule and ensample of faire conditions at the presence of so great and so vertuous a Ladie. Whose most excellent qualities I entend not now to expresse, for it is neither my purpose, and againe they are well ynough knowne to the world, and much better than I am able either with tongue, or with pen to indite.

And such as would perhaps have lien hid a space, fortune, as shee that wondreth at so rare vertues, hath thought good with manye adversities and temptations of miseries to disclose them, to make triall thereby that in the tender breast of a woman, in companie with singular beautie, there can dwel wisedome, and stoutnes of courage and all other vertues that in grave men themselves are most seldome.

But leaving this apart, I say that the maner of the gentlemen in the house was immediately after supper to assemble together where the Dutchesse was. Where among other recreations, musicke and dauncing, which they used continually, sometime they propounded feate questions,[1] otherwhile they invented certayne wittye sportes and pastimes at the device sometime of one sometime of another, in the which under sundry coverts oftentimes the standers by opened subtilly their immaginations[2] unto whome they thought best.

At other times there arose other disputations of divers matters, or else jeastings with prompt inventions. Many times they fell into purposes,[3] (as we now a daies terme them) where in this kinde of talke and debating of matters, there was wonderous great pleasure on al sides: Because (as I have said) the house was replenished with most noble wittes. Among which (as you know) were most famous the Lord Octavian Fregoso, Sir Friderick his brother, the Lord Julian de Medicis, M. Peter Bembo, the Lord Cesar Gonzaga, Counte Lewis of Canossa, the Lord Gasper Pallavicin, the Lorde Lodovicus Pius, Maister Morello of Ortona, Peter of Naples, Maister Robert of Bari, and infinite of other most worthy knights and gentlemen.[4]

Beside these, there were many that for all ordinarilye they dwelled not there, yet spent they most of all their time there, as Maister Bernard Bibiena, Unico Aretino, John Christopher

---

[1] "Feate questions": cf. "neat questions."
[2] Cf. "disclosed their thoughts figuratively."
[3] Cf. "'devices' (*impresse*)": these were patterns painted or cut or moulded and worn on the person: the Duchess's "S," worn on her brow, is such a device.
[4] "Octavian Fregoso," etc. See "Chief Persons," pp. xvii, xviii.

Romano, Peter Mount, Therpander, Maister Nicolas Phrisio, so that thither ran continually Poets, Musitions, and all kind of men of skill, and the excellentest in every faculty that were in all Italy.

After Pope Julius the second had with his owne presence by the ayde of the Frenchmen brought Bolonia to the obedience of the Apostolique sea againe, in the yeare a thousande five hundred and sixe, in his returne toward Rome he took Urbin in his way, where hee was received as honorably as was possible,[1] and with as sumptuous and costly preparation, as could have bene in any other City of Italie whatsoever it be. So that beside the Pope, all the Cardinals and other Courtiers thought themselves thorowly satisfied.

And some there were that provoked with the sweetnes of this company, after that the Pope and the Court was departed, continued many daies together in Urbin. At which time they did not onely proceede in their accustomed trade[2] of disporting and ordinarye recreations, but also every man set to his helping hande to augment them somewhat, and especially in pastimes, which they had up almost every night.

And the order thereof was such, that as soone as they were assembled where the Dutchesse was, every man sat him downe at his will, or as it fell to his lot, in a circle together, and in sitting were devyded a man and a woman, as long as there was women, for alwaies lightly,[3] the number of men was far the greater.

Then were they governed as the dutchesse thought best, which many times gave this charge unto the Ladye Emilia.

So the day after the Pope was departed, the companye being gathered to the accustomed place, after much pleasant talke, the Dutchesse pleasure was that the Ladye Emilia shoulde begin these pastimes.

And she after a little refusing of that charge, said in this manner: Sith it is your pleasure [Madame] I shall be she that must give the onset in our pastimes this night, because I ought not of reason disobey you, I thinke meete to propound a pastime,[4] whereof I suppose shall ensue little blame, and lesse travaile.

And that shall be to have every man, as nigh as he can, propound a device not yet heard of, then shal we choose out such a one as shall be thought meete to be taken in hand in this company.

---

[1] "As honorably as was possible": cf. "with all possible honour."
[2] "Accustomed trade," etc.: cf. "ordinary pastimes and diversions."
[3] Cf. "nearly always."          [4] Cf. "to propose a game."

And after she had thus spoken, she turned her to the Lord Gaspar Pallavicin, willing him to propound his: who immediately made answere.

But first (Madame) you must begin to propound yours. Then said the Ladye Emilia:

I have already done. But your grace must commande him (Madame) to be obedient.

Then the dutchesse laughing, to the intent (quoth she) every man shall obey you, I make you my Deputie, and give unto you all mine authority.

It is surely a great matter, answered the Lord Gaspar, that it is alwaies lawful for women to have this priviledge, to be exempt and free from paines taking.[1]

And truely reason woulde we should in any wise know why.[2] But because I will not be he that shall give example to disobey, I shall leave this untill an other time, and will speake of that I am now charged withall, and thus I begin.

Mine opinion is, that our mindes, as in other thinges, so also in loving are diverse in judgement, and therefore it chaunceth often times, that the thing which is most acceptable unto one, is most abhorred of an other. Yet for all that they alwaies agree in that everye man counteth most deare the wight beloved. So that many times the overmuch affection in lovers doth deceive their judgment, that they weene the person whom they love, to be so garnished with al excellent vertues and without fault, that he hath no peere in the world.

But because the nature of man doth not admit such full perfections, and there is no man that hath not some default or want in him, it can not be said that such as these be, are not deceyved, and that the lover doth not become blind as touching the beloved.

I would therefore our pastimes should be this night to have everye man open what vertues he would principally the person he loved should be indued withall. And seeing it is so necessarily that we al have some sport, what vice he would also have in him: to see who can find out most praise-worthy and manly vertues, and most tollerable vices,[3] that should be least hurtfull both to him that loveth, and to the wight beloved.

After the L. Gaspar had thus spoken, the L. Emilia made a signe unto the Lady Constaunce Fregosa, because she was next

---

[1] Cf. "allowed this exemption from toil."
[2] "And truely reason," etc.: cf. "And it certainly would not be unreasonable to wish in some way to learn the reason why."
[3] Cf. "the most excusable faults."

in order, to follow: who was now about to speake when the Dutchesse solemnly saide.

Seeing the L. Emilia will not take the paines to finde out some pastime, reason willeth that the other Ladies should be partakers of the same privilege, and bee also free from this burden for this night, especially seeing there are so many men in place, for assure your selfe wee shall want no pastime.

So shall we doo, answered the L. Emilia, and putting the L. Constance to silence, turned her to the L. Cesar Gonzago that sat next her, commaunding him to speake, and thus began.

Who so will diligently consider all our dooing, hee shall finde alwaies in them sundry imperfections. And that happeneth, because nature doth vary, as well in this, as in all other things. Unto one she hath given the light of reason in one thing, and unto an other, in an other thing.

Therefore it commeth to passe, where one man knoweth that an other knoweth not, and is ignorant in the thing that the other hath understanding in, eche man doth easily perceive the errour of his fellow, and not his owne, and wee all thinke our selves to be verie wise, and paradventure in that point most, wherin we are most foolish.

So that we have seene by experience in this house many men which at the beginning were counted most wise, in processe of time were knowne to bee most foolish, which hath proceeded of no other thing but of our owne diligence.[1]

Like as it is said to be in Pulia,[2] of them that are bitten with a Tarrantula, about whom men occupy many instruments of musicke, and with sundry sounds go searching out, untill the humour that maketh this disease, by a certain concordance it hath with some of those soundes, feeling it, do sodenly moove, and so stirreth the pacient, that by that stirring he recovereth his health againe. In like maner wee, when wee have felt some privie operation[3] of folly, we provoke it so subtilly, and with such sundry persuasions, and so divers waies, that at length wee understand whether it tended.

Afterward the humour knowne, we so stir it, that alwaies it is brought to the perfection of open folly. And some is wexed foolish in verses, some in musicke, some in love, some in dauncing, some in making antiques,[4] some in riding, some in playing at

[1] Cf. "watchfulness."
[2] "In Pulia." In Apulia music was believed to cure the bite of the tarantula.          [3] Cf. "a hidden touch."
[4] "Making antiques": cf. "inventing mimes." The *moresco*, mime, or morris dance, was dance in the true sense, an expression of story and delicate sentiment by harmonious bodily movement.

fence, everie man according to the mine of his mettall: wherby hath ensued (as you know) marvellous great pastime.

I hold therfore for certaine, that in every one of us there is some seede of folly, the which beeing stirred may multiply (in a maner) infinite.

Therefore I would this night our pastime were to dispute upon this matter: and that everie man might say his mind, seeing I must be openly foolish, in what sort of folly I am foolish, and over what matter, judging it the issue for the sparkles of folly that are daily seene to proceede from mee. And let the like be said of all the rest, keeping the order of our devises.

And let every man doe his best to grounde his opinion upon some sure signe and argument, and so by this our pastime shall everie one of us get profite, in that we shall know our defaults, and then shall we the better take heede.

And in case the vaine of folly which wee shall discover, be so ranke that it shall appeare to us past remedie, we shall set thereto our helping hand, and according to the doctrine of Frier Marian, wee shall gaine a soule, which shall be no smal gain.

At this devise there was much laughing, and none could refraine from speaking.

One saide, I should bee found foolish in imagining.[1] An other, in viewing. An other said, he was already become foolish for love: and such like matters.

Then Frier Seraphin, after his manner, laughing. This (quoth he) should bee too tedious a matter. But if you will have a pretie pastime, let everie man tell his opinion, how it commeth that (in a maner) all women abhorre rattes, and love serpents, and you shall see that none wil hit upon it, but I, that know this misterie by a straunge meane. And now began hee to enter into his trifling tales, but the L. Emilia commanded him to silēce, and overskipping the Ladie that sat there, made a signe to Unico aretino that was next in order, and hee went without looking for anie more bidding.

I (quoth he) would gladly bee a judge of authoritie, that I might with all kinde of torment boult out the truth of offenders[2]: and that, to discover the deceits of an ungrate woman, who with the eyes of an angell, and heart of a Serpent, never agreeth her toong with her minde, and with a fained deceivable compassion, purposeth nothing els but to make Anatomie of hearts.

---

[1] Cf. "I should make a fool of myself over imagining."
[2] Cf. "search the heart of evil-doers."

Neither is there in all the sandie country of Libia to be found so venimous a serpent that is so desirous of mans bloud, as is this false creature. Which not onely for the sweetenesse of voice and pleasant sound of words, but also for her eyes, for her laughing, for her countenance, and for all her gestures is a most perfect Marmaide.[1]

Therefore seeing it is not lawfull for me, as I would, to use chaines, ropes, or fire, to understand a matter of trueth, my desire is to compasse the knowledge of it with a merry pastime, which is this: That everie man should expresse his fansie what the S. doth signifie that the Dutchesse carieth in her forehead.

For although this be also an artificiall covert, the better to beguile, perhaps there may bee an interpretation which she never thought upon. And who knoweth whether fortune, with pitie beholding ye torments of men, hath stirred her with his small token, to discover against her will the inwarde desire she hath to slea and bury alive in calamitie him that honoureth and serveth her.

The Dutchesse laughed, and Unico perceiving shee would have excused her selfe of this interpretation, no (quoth hee) speake you not, madam, for it is not your turne to speake now.

The L. Emilia then turned her and said: M. Unico there is none of us all here that giveth not place to you in everie thing, and especially in knowing the disposition of the Dutchesse. And as you by your divine wit know her better than all the rest, so doe you love her better than all the rest, which like birds of feeble sight, that cannot looke stedfastly into the circle of the Sun, cannot so well perceive the perfection of it.

Therefore all labour were in vaine in clearing of this doubt, saving your judgement alone.

This enterprise then is reserved onely to you, as unto him that alone can bring it to an end, and none other.

Unico, after he had pawsed a while, being still called upon to say his fansie, at length rehearsed a rime[2] upon the foresaid matter, expounding what signified the letter S., the which manie judged to be made at the first sight. But because it was more wittie and better knit than a man would have believed the shortnes of time required, it was thought he had prepared it before.

[1] Cf. "a very siren" (*verissima Sirena*). Hoby misses the point, which touches the "S" the Duchess wears on her brow.

[2] Unico's sonnet (?), of an incredible lack of poetic feeling and phrase, suggests that the "S" may signify a variety of experiences between his Suffering and his Salvation.

So after mens favourable voice given in the prayse of this rime, and after sufficient talke, the L. Octavian Fregoso, whose turne was then next, began in this sorte smyling.

My Lordes, if I shoulde say unto you that I never felt passion of love in my dayes, I am sure the Dutchesse and the L. Emilia, although they believe it not in deede, yet would they make semblance to believe it, and would say that it proceeded because I mistrusted I should never frame any woman to love me.

The which truely I have not hetherto proved with such instance, that of reason I should dispaire to obtaine it once. Neither have I forborne the doing of it, because I set so much by my selfe, and so litle by women, that I thinke none worthie to bestow my love and service upon. But rather amased at the continuall bewailing of some lovers,[1] that with their palenesse, sorrow, and silence, it appeareth they have evermore their owne discomfort painted in their eyes. And if they speake accompanying every worde with certaine treblefolde sighes, they reason of nothing else but of teares, of torments, of desperations, and of longing for death. So that whensoever any sparke of love hath begonne to kindle in my brest, I have by and by enforced my selfe with all diligence to quench it: not for any hatred that I have conceived against women (as these Ladies suppose) but for mine owne health.

On the other side, I have knowne some other cleane contrarie to these sorrowful, which do not onely advance and content them selves, with the chearefull lookes, loving wordes, and sweete countenances of their Ladies, but also sauce their sorrowes with sweetnes, so that they count debates, the angers, and the disdaines of them, most sweete.

Therefore these men seeme unto mee to bee much more than happie: for whereas they finde so much sweetnesse in the amorous disdaines, which some mē recken much more bitter than death, I believe in loving gestures they should feele that woonderfull blisse, which we seeke for in vaine in this world.

Therefore would I our pastime were this night, to have every man shew, where there must bee a disdaine against him in the person beloved, what the cause should be that should make the person conceive this disdeine. For if there be any here that have proved those sweet disdaines, I am sure they will desire for

---

[1] They were the stock in trade of the tribe of sonneteers, particularly: not least of Shakespeare, who could also use them to another advantage. Consider Mercutio mocking Romeo; or Rosalind, Orlando; or Don Pedro, Benedick.

courtesie one of these causes that make them so sweete. And perhaps I shall with a better will proceede somewhat farther in love, in hope that I shall also finde this sweetnesse, where as some finde bitternesse.

And so shall not these Ladies give me any more this slanderous report, that I am not in love.

This pastime was much praised, and therfore did every man settle himselfe to reason upon this matter. But ye L. Emilia holding her peace, M. Peter Bembo that sat next in order, spake in this maner:

My Lords, this pastime that the L. Octavian hath propounded, hath raised no smal doubt in my minde, where he hath reasoned of the disdaines of love, the which though they be sundry, yet unto me have they alwaies beene most bitter.

Neither do I believe, that I can learne any sauce that shall bee sufficient to sweeten them.

But peradventure they are the more and the lesse bitter, according to the cause whereof they arise. For I have in my daies (I remember) seene the woman whom I served, stirred against me, either upon a vaine suspition that shee conceived her selfe of my trustinesse, or els upon some other false opinion that had been put into her head by some mens report to my hinderance, so that I beleeved no griefe might be compared to mine.

And me thought that the greatest sorrow I felt, was to suffer without deserving, and to susteine this affliction, not for any offence of mine, but for the small love that was in her.

At other times I saw her disdainful for some oversight of mine, and knew that her anger proceeded of mine offence, and at that instant I judged the former vexation to be very light, in comparison to that which I felt then. And me thought to be in displeasure, and that for mine owne trespasse, with the person whom onely I coveted, and with such diligence sought to please, was the greatest torment of all other.

Therefore would I our pastime were to have everie man declare his opinion, where there must be a disdaine against him in the person beloved, of whom hee would the cause of this disdaine should have his beginning, whether of her, or of himselfe: to know which is greater griefe, either to displease the wight beloved, or to receive displeasure of the wight beloved.[1]

Every man looked what the L. Emilia woulde make answere to this, but without any word speaking to Bembo, she turned

---

[1] "Wight beloved": cf. "her who is loved."

her, and made a signe to sir Fridericke Frigoso to shew his devise. And hee incontinently beganne thus.

Madame, I woulde it were lawfull for me, as the maner is many times, to remit me to the judgement of an other,[1] for I for my part would with all my heart allow some of the pastimes that have been alreadie propounded by these Lords, because indeed mee thinke they would be worth the hearing. Yet least I should breake the order, this I say: who so would take in hand to praise our Court, leaving apart the deserts of the Dutchesse, which ghostly spirit[2] with hir influence is sufficient to draw from the earth up into heaven the simplest wits in the world, he might well doe it without suspition of flatterie. For peradventure in all Italy a man shall have much a do to find out so many Gentlemen and noble personages that are so worthie, and beside the principall profession of Chivalrie so excellent in sundrie things, as are presently here.

Therefore if in any place men may bee found that deserve y$^e$ name of good Courtiers, and can judge what belongeth to the perfection of Courtiership, by reason a man may believe them to be here.

To disgrace therfore many untowardly Asseheades, that through malapartnesse[3] thinke to purchase them the name of a good Courtier, I would have such a pastime for this night, that one of the company might bee picked out, who should take it in hand to shape in wordes a good Courtier, specifying all such conditions and particular qualities, as of necessitie must bee in him that deserveth this name.

And in such thinges as shall not appeare necessarie, that it may bee lawfull for everie man to reply against them, as the maner of Philosophers schooles is against him that keepeth disputations.

Sir Fredericke proceeded still forwarde in his talke, when the L. Emilia interrupting him, said: If it be my Ladie the Dutchesse pleasure, this shall be our pastime for this once. The dutchesse answered: I am well pleased.

Then (in maner) all the company began to say both to the Dutchesse and among themselves, that this was the trimmest pastime they could have.

And without looking for answere the one of the other, they

---

[1] Cf. "to assent to another's proposal."
[2] "Which ghostly spirit": cf. "which with her divine virtue."
[3] "Untowardly Asseheades," etc.: cf. "So, to repress the many fools who, by impudence and folly . . ." Sir Frederick is explicit and urbane. Hoby must both name and chastise the offence in a phrase.

craved upon the L. Emilia, to appoint who should first begin. Who turning toward the Dutchesse, said.

Command you, madame, whom shall please you to take this enterprise in hand, for I will not by choosing more one than another, declare my selfe to judge in this behalfe, whom I thinke to be better skilled than the rest, and so do wrong to some.

The Dutchesse answered: make you this choise your selfe, and take heede that in disobeying, you be not a president to the rest to bee disobedient.

Then the L. Emilia saide laughing unto Lewis Count of Canosse: therfore for leesing anye more time, you (Counte) shalbe he that shal take this enterprise upon him in forme and manner as sir Fredericke hath declared. Not for that wee know ye are so good a Courtier, that ye have at your fingers ends that belongs therto: but because in repeating everie thing arsiversie, as we hope ye wil, we shal have so much the more pastime, and everie one shall be able to answere you.

Where if an other more skilfull than you should take it in hand, there should bee nothing said against him for telling the truth, and so should we have but a cold pastime.

The Counte answered by and by: we need not feare (Madame) that wee shall want contrarying in words against him that telleth the truth, as long as you be here.

And after they had laughed a while at this answere, he proceeded on: but truely I would with all my heart be rid of this burthen, for it is too hard for mee. And I know that to be most true in me, which you have spoken in jeast: namely, that I have no understanding in that belongeth to a good Courtier. And this doe I not seeke to prove with any other triall: for seeing I do not y$^e$ deedes, a man may judge I understand it not, and I believe I am the lesse to bee blamed. For out of doubt, it is a worse matter not to do wel, than not to understand how to do it.[1] Yet seeing your pleasure is, that I shall take the charge upon me, I cannot, nor will refuse it, for withstanding your order and judgement, the which I know is much better than mine.

Then the L. Cesar Gonzaga. Because it is now (quoth hee) well forward in night, and we have here readie for us other sortes of pastimes, peradventure it shuld not be amisse to deferre this reasoning untill to morrow, and the Counte shall have leisure to thinke better upon that he hath to say: for in verie

---

[1] "For out of doubt," etc.: cf. "For sure it is worse not to wish to do well than not to know how."

deed, to entreat upon such a matter at the first sight, it is a hard thing.

Then answered the Counte: I will not do as he did, that stripped himselfe into his doublet, and leaped lesse ground than he did before in his Coate. And me thinke my lucke is good that it is late, because the shortnesse of time shall make me use fewe words, and the sodainesse of the matter shall so excuse me, that it shall be lawfull for me to speake without blame, whatsoever commeth first to minde.

Because I will not therfore carry this burthen of duetie any longer upon my shoulders, this I say: in everie thing it is so hard a matter to know the true perfection, that it is almost unpossible, and that by reason of the varietie of judgemēts.

Therfore many there are, that delight in a man of much talke, and him they call a pleasant fellow. Some wil delight more in modestie, some other will fancie a man that is active and alwaies dooing: other, one that sheweth a quietnesse and a respect in everie thing. And thus doth everie man praise or dispraise according to his fancie, alwaies covering a vice with the name of the next vertue to it, and a vertue with the name of the next vice: as in calling him that is sawcie, bold: him that is sober, dry: him that is seelie, good: him that is unhappie, wittie[1]: and likewise in the rest.

Yet doe I thinke that eche thing hath his perfection, although it be hid, and with reasonable discourses,[2] might be judged of him that hath knowledge in that matter.

And for as much as the truth (as I have said) is oftentimes hid, and I take not upon me to have this knowledge, I can not praise, but that kinde of Courtiers which I set most by, and allow that which seemeth unto me most nigh the truth, in my small judgement. The which you shall follow if ye thinke it good, or els sticke to your owne, if it shall varie from mine. Neither will I (for all that) stand stiffe, that mine is better than yours, for not onely one thing may seeme unto you, and an other to me.

But also unto my selfe it may appeare sometime one thing, sometime an other.

I wil have this our Courtier therefore to bee a gentleman borne and of a good house. For it is a great deale lesse dispraise for him that is not borne a gentleman to faile in the actes of

---

[1] Cf. "calling an impudent man frank, a modest man dull, an ignorant man good, a knave discreet."
[2] Cf. "through rational discussion."

vertue, then for a gentleman. If he swerve from the steps of his ancestors, hee staineth the name of his familie.

And doth not onely not get, but looseth that is alreadie gotten. For noblenesse of birth, is as it were a cleare lampe that sheweth forth and bringeth into light, workes both good and bad, and inflameth and provoketh unto vertue, as well with the feare of slaunder, as also with the hope of praise.

And whereas this brightnesse of noblenesse doth not discover the workes of the unnoble, they have a want of provocation and of feare of slaunder, and they reckon not them selves bound to wade any further than their ancestors did before them, whereas the noble of birth counte it a shame not to arrive at the least at the bounds of their predecessors set forth unto them.

Therefore it chanceth alwaies in a manner, both in armes and in all other vertuous acts, that the most famous men are Gentlemen. Because nature in every thing hath deepely sowed that privie seed, which giveth a certaine force and propertie of her beginning, unto whatsoever springeth of it, and maketh it like unto her selfe.

As we see by example, not onely in the race of horses and other beastes, but also in trees, whose slippes and graftes alwaies for the most part are like unto the stocke of the tree they came from: and if at any time they grow out of kinde,[1] the fault is in the husbandman. And the like is in men, if they be trained up in good nurture, most commonly they resemble them from whom they come, and often times passe them, but if they have not one that can well traine them up, they growe (as it were) wilde, and never come to their ripenesse.

Truth it is, whether it be through the favor of the Starres or of nature, some there are borne indued with such graces, that they seeme not to have beene borne, but rather fashioned with the verie hand of some God, and abound in all goodnes both of bodie and minde. As againe we see some so unapt and dull, that a man will not believe, but nature hath brought them into the world for a spite and mockerie.

And like as these with continuall diligence and good bringing up for the most part can bring small fruit: even so the other with litle attendance climbe to the full perfection of all excellencie.

And to give you an example, marke me the Lord Hyppolitus da Este[2] Cardinall of Ferrara, he hath had so happie a birth,

---

[1] Cf. "degenerate."

[2] Ippolito d'Este (born 1479, died 1520) was the third son of Duke Ercole I. of Ferrara; to the archbishopric of which city he came, by extremely

that his person, his countenance, his words, and all his gestures are so fashioned and compact with this grace, that among the most ancient prelates (for all he is but young) he doth represent so grave an authoritie,[1] that a man would weene he were more meete to teach, than needfull to learne.[2]

Likewise in companie with men and women of al degrees, in sporting, in laughing, and in jesting, he hath in him certaine sweetnes, and so comely demeanours, that who so speaketh with him, or yet beholdeth him, must needes beare him an affection for ever.

But returning to our purpose, I say, that betwene this excellent grace, and that fond foolishnes, there is yet a meane, and they that are not by nature so perfectly furnished, with studie and diligence may polish and correct a great part of the defaults of nature.

The Courtier therefore, beside noblenesse of birth, I will have him to bee fortunate in this behalfe, and by nature to have not onely a wit, and a comely shape of person and countenance, but also a certaine grace, and (as they say) a hewe,[3] that shall make him at the first sight acceptable and loving unto who so beholdeth him.

And let this bee an ornament to frame and accompany[4] all his acts, and to assure men in his looke, such a one to be worthie the companie and favour of everie great man.

Here without any longer tarrying the L. Gasper Pallavicin said: that our pastime may have the forme and maner agreed upon, and least it should appeare, that we litle esteeme the authoritie given us to contrary you, I say (in mine advise) that this noblenesse of birth is not so necessarie for the Courtier. And if I wist that any of you thought it a strange or a new matter,[5] I would alledge unto you sundry, who for all they were borne of most noble bloud, yet have they been heaped full of vices: and contrariwise, many unnoble that have made famous their posteritie.

And if it be true that you said before, that the privie force of the first seede is in everie thing, we should all bee in one

lucrative ways of ecclesiastical preferment, before he had reached the age of twenty-four. His chief claim on memory derives from his friendship for Leonardo da Vinci, and his patronage of Ariosto.

[1] Cf. "such weight of character."
[2] Cf. "he seems fitter to teach than to be taught."
[3] Cf. "and (as we say) air."
[4] "Frame and accompany": cf. "dispose and unite."
[5] Cf. "and if I thought I were saying what is new to any of us."

maner condition, for that we had all one selfe beginning, and one should not be more noble than an other.

But beside the diversities and degrees in us of high and low, I believe there be many other matters, wherein I judge fortune to bee the chiefe, because we see her beare a stroke in all worldly things, and (as it were) take a pastime to exalte manie times whom pleaseth her without any desert at al, and bury in the bottomles depth the most worthie to be exalted.

I confirme your saying as touching the happinesse of them that are borne abounding in all goodnesse both of minde and bodie: but this is seene as well in the unnoble, as in the noble of birth, for nature hath not these so subtile distinctions: yea (as I have said) we see many times in persons of most base degree, most hie gifts of nature.

Therefore seeing this noblenes is gotten neither with wit, force, nor art, but is rather a praise of our ancestors than our owne, me thinke it a strange opinion that the parents of our Courtier being unnoble, his good qualities should be defaced, and those other good conditions which you have named shuld not be sufficient to bring him to the top of all perfection: that is to say, wit, beautie of phisnomy, disposition of person,[1] and the grace which at the first sight shall make him most acceptable unto al men.

Then answered Counte Lewis, I denie not, but in men of base degree may raign the very same vertues that are in Gentlemen. But to avoide rehearsall of that wee have alreadie said, with many other reasons that might be alleaged in commendation of noblenes, the which is evermore honored of all men, because it standeth with reason, that good should spring of good: for so much as our intent is to fashion a Courtier without any maner default or lack in him, and heaped with all praise, me thinke it a necessary matter to make him a Gentleman, as well for many other respects, as also for the common opinion, which by and by doeth leane[2] to noblenes.

For where there are two in a noble mans house, which at the first have given no proofe of themselves with workes good or bad, as soone as it is knowne that the one is a Gentleman borne, and the other not, the unnoble shall be much lesse esteemed with everie man, than the Gentleman, and he must with much travell and long time imprint in mennes heades a good opinion of himselfe, which the other shall get in a moment, and onely

[1] Cf. "talent, beauty of feature, comeliness of person . . ."
[2] Cf. "is at once disposed in favour of."

for that he is a Gentleman: and how waightie these imprintings [1] are, everie man may easilie judge.

For to speak of our selves, we have seene men come to this house, which for al they were fooles and dulwitted, yet had they a report through al Italy of great Courtiers, and though at length they were discovered and knowne, yet many daies did they beguile us, and maintained in our mindes that opinion of themselves, which at the first they found there imprinted, although they wrought according to their small skill.

Wee have seene other at the first in verie small estimation, and afterward in the ende, have acquitted themselves marvellous well. And of these errors there are divers causes, and among other the obstinateness of Princes, which to prove maistries,[2] oftentimes bend themselves to favour him, that to their seeming, deserveth no favor at all.

And many times in deede they are deceived: but because they have alwaies many that counterfaite them,[3] a verie great report dependeth upon their favor, the which most commonly the Judges follow. And if they finde any thing that seemeth contrary to the common opinion, they are in doubt for deceiving them selves, and alwaies looke for some matter secretly, because it seemeth, that these generall opinions ought to bee founded upon a troth, and arise of reasonable causes.

And forasmuch as our mindes are verie apte to love and to hate: as in the sights of combates and games, and in all other kinde of contention, where the lookers on are affectionate without manifest cause unto one of the two parties, with a greedy desire to have him get the victorie, and the other the losse.

Also as touching the opinion of mens qualities, the good or ill report at the first brunt moveth our minde to one of these two passions.

Therefore it commeth to passe, that for the most part we judge with love, or els with hatred.

You see then of what importance this first imprinting is, and how he ought to endevour him selfe to get it good at first, if hee entend to be set by, and to purchase him the name of a good Courtier.

But to come to some particularitie, I judge the principall and true profession of a Courtier ought to bee in feates of armes, the which above all I will have him to practise lively, and to bee

---

[1] Cf. "impressions."
[2] Cf. "who in their wish to perform miracles . . ."
[3] Cf. "their many imitators."

knowne among other of his hardines, for his atchieving of enterprises, and for his fidelitie towarde him whom he serveth. And
hee shall purchase himselfe a name with these good conditions,
in doing the deedes in every time and place, for it is not for him
to fainte at any time in this behalfe without a wondrous reproch.

And even as in women honestie once stained doth never
returne againe to the former estate: so the fame of a gentleman
that carrieth weapon, if it once take a foyle in anye litle point
through dastardlinesse[1] or any other reproch, doth evermore
continue shamefull in the world and full of ignorance.[2]

Therefore the more excellent our Courtier shall be in this arte,
the more shall he be worthie praise: albeit I judge not necessarie
in him so perfect a knowledge of things and other qualities that
is requisite in a Captaine. But because this is overlarge a scope
of matters, we wil holde our selves contented, as wee have saide,
with the uprightnesse of a well meaning mind, and with an
invincible courage,[3] and that he alwaies shew himself such a one.

For many times men of courage are sooner knowne in small
matters than in great. Often times in dangers that stand them
upon, and where many eyes be, ye shal see some that for all
their hart is dead in their bodie, yet pricked with shame or
with the company, goe forwarde, as it were, blindfield and doe
their duetie. And God knoweth both in matters that litle touch
them, and also where they suppose that without missing they
may convey them selves from danger, how they are willing
inough to sleepe in a whole skinne.

But such as thinke them selves neither marked, seene, nor
knowne, and yet declare a stoute courage, and suffer not the
least thing in the world to passe that may burthen them, they
have that courage of spirite which we seeke to have in our
Courtier. Yet will wee not have him for all that so lustie to make
braverie in wordes, and to bragge that hee hath wedded his
harnes for a wife, and to threaten with such grimme lookes,
as wee have seene Berto[4] doe often times.

For unto such may well be said, that a worthie gentle woman
in a noble assemblie spake pleasantly unto one, that shall bee
namelesse for this time, whom she to shew him a good countenance, desired to daunce with her, and hee refusing it, and
to heare musicke, and many other entertainments offered him,

[1] Cf. "if once it be in the least tarnished with cowardice . . ."
[2] Cf. "ignominy."
[3] "The uprightnesse," etc.: cf. "perfect loyalty and unconquered
courage."
[4] "Berto": a buffoon of the papal court in the time of Julius II. and Leo X.

alwaies affirming such trifles not to be his profession, at last the gentlewoman demaunding him, what is then your profession? he answered with a frowning looke, to fight.

Then saide the Gentlewoman: seeing you are not now at the warre nor in place to fight, I would think it best for you to bee well besmered and set up in an armory with other implements of warre till time were that you should be occupied, least you waxe more rustier than you are. Thus with much laughing of the standers by, she left him with a mocke in his foolish presumption.

He therefore that we seeke for, where the enimies are, shall shew him selfe most fierce, bitter, and evermore with the first. In everie place beside, lowly, sober, and circumspect, fleeing above all things, bragging and unshamefull praysing himselfe: for therewith a man alwaies purchaseth himselfe the hatred of the hearers.

And I, answered the L. Gasper, have known few men excellent in any thing whatsoever it be, but they praise them selves. And me thinke it may wel be borne in them: for he y$^t$ is of skill, when he seeth that hee is not knowne for his workes of the ignorant, hath a disdaine, that his cunning should be buried, and needes must he open it one way, least he should bee defrauded of the estimation that belongeth to it, which is the true rewarde of vertuous travailes.

Therefore among auncient writers, he that much excelleth doth seldome forbeare praysing himselfe.

They in deed are not to be borne withall, that having no skill in them will praise themselves: but we wil not take our Courtier to be such a one.

Then the Count, if you have well understood (quoth he) I blamed the praysing of a mans selfe impudently, and without respect. And surely (as you say) a man ought not to conceive an ill opinion of a skilfull man that praiseth himself discretely, but rather take it for a more certaine witnes, than if it came out of an other mans mouth.

I agree well that hee, which in praysing him selfe falleth not into error, nor purchaseth himselfe lothsomnes or hatred of the hearers, is most discreete: and beside the prayses which he giveth himselfe, deserveth the same of other men also, because it is a verie hard matter.

Then the L. Gasper, this (quoth he) must you teach us.

The Counte answered: among the auncient writers there hath not also wanted that hath taught it. But in mine opinion, all doth consist in speaking such thinges after a sorte, that it may appeare that they are not rehearsed to that end: but that they come so to purpose, that he can not refraine telling them, and alwaies seeming to flee his owne prayse, tell the truth.[1] But not as those lustie lads doe, that open their mouth and thrust out wordes at a venture they care not how. As within these few dayes one of our company, being pusshed through the thigh with a pike at Pysa, thought that it was the byting of a flie. And an other saide that hee occupied no looking glasse in his chamber, because in his rage hee was so terrible to behold, that in looking upon his owne countenance he should put himselfe into much feare.

At this every one laughed. But the L. Cesar Gonzaga saide unto them: at what laugh you?

Know yee not that the great Alexander, hearing a certaine philosophers opinion to be that there were infinite worlds, fel in weeping: And when he was asked the question why hee wept, hee answered: Because I have not yet one in hand, as though his mind was to have them all.

Doe you not thinke that this was a greater braverie, than to speake of a flie byting?

So was Alexander a greater person than hee that so saide, aunswered the Count.

But excellent men in verie deed are to be held excused, when they take much upon them, because hee that undertaketh great enterprises, must have a boldnesse to doe it, and a confidence of himselfe, and not a bashfull or cowardly minde, but yet sober in wordes: shewing as though he tooke lesse uppon him than he doth in deede, so that his taking uppon him doe not extend unto rashnes.

Here the Count respecting a while, M. Bernard Bibiena said merely: I remember you saide before, that this our Courtier ought of nature to have a faire comelinesse of phisnomy[2] and person, with the grace that ought to make him so amiable.

As for the grace and beautie of phisnomy, I thinke not the contrarie but they are in me, and therefore doe so many women burne for the love of me, as you know. But for the comelines of person, I stand somewhat in doubt, and especially by reason of my legges here, for me thinke in deede they are not so well made as I could wish they were: the body and the rest is metely well.

---

[1] "Tell the truth": cf. "achieve it" (praise).
[2] Cf. "beauty of countenance."

Therfore declare somewhat more particularly this comelinesse of person, what it should be, that I may be out of this doubt, and set my hart at rest.

When they had a while laughed at this, the Count saide: Certes, the grace of the Phisonomy may well bee saide to bee in you without any lye. And no other example doe I alledge but this, to declare what maner thing it should be: for undoubtedly wee see your countenance is most acceptable and pleasant to behold unto every man, although the proportion and draughts[1] of it be not verie delicate, but it is manly and hath a good grace withall.

And this qualitie have many and sundry shapes of visages.

And such a countenance as this is, will I have our Courtier to have, and not so soft and womanish as many procure to have, that doe not onely courle the haire, and picke the browes, but also pampre them selves in everie point like the most wanton and dishonest women in the world: and a man would thinke them in going, in standing, and in all their gestures[2] so tender and faint, that their members were readie to flee one from an other, and their wordes they pronounce so drawningly,[3] that a man woulde weene they were at that instant yeelding up the ghost: and the higher in degree that men are they talke withall, the more they use such fashions.

These men, seeing nature (as they seeme to have a desire to appeare and to be) hath not made them women, ought not to bee esteemed in place of good women, but like common Harlots to bee banished, not onely out of princes courtes, but also out of the company of gentlemen.

To come therefore to the qualitie of the person, I say he is well, if he bee neither of the least, nor of the greatest size. For both the one and the other hath with it a certaine spitefull woonder,[4] and such men are marvelled at, almost as much as men marvel to behold monstrous thinges.[5] Yet if there must needes be a default in one of the two extremities, it shall be lesse hurtfull to bee somewhat of the least, than to exceede the common stature of height.

For men so shut up[6] of bodie, beside that many times they are of a dull wit, they are also unapt for all exercise of nimblenesse, which I much desire to have in the Courtier.

---

[1] Cf. "lineaments."
[2] Cf. "in their walk, posture, and every act."
[3] "Drawningly": cf. "mournfully."
[4] Cf. "contemptuous surprise."
[5] Cf. "monsters."
[6] "So shut up": cf. "thus huge."

And therefore wil I have him to bee of a good shape, and well proportioned in his lims, and to shew strength, lightnesse and quicknesse, and to have understanding in all exercises of the bodie that belong to a man of warre.

And herein I thinke the chiefe point is to handle wel all kinde of weapon, both for footeman and horseman, and to know the vantages in it.[1] And specially to bee skilfull on those weapons that are used ordinarily among Gentlemen.

For beside the use that he shall have of them in warre, where peradventure needeth no great cunning, there happen oftentimes variances betweene one gentleman and an other, whereupon ensueth a combat. And many times it shall stand him in steade to use the weapon that he hath at that instant by his side, therefore it is a very sure[2] thing to be skilfull.

And I am none of them which say, that he forgetteth his cunning when hee commeth to the point: for to abide by,[3] who so looseth his cunning at that time, sheweth that hee hath first lost his heart and his spirites for feare.

I thinke also it will serve his turne greatly, to know the feat of wrastling, because it goeth much together with all weapon on foote.

Againe it is behovefull both for himselfe and for his friendes, that he have a foresight in the quarrels and controversies that may happen, and let him beware of the vantages,[4] declaring alwaies in everie point both courage and wisedom.

Neither let him runne rashly to these combats, but when he must needes to save his estimation withall: for beside the great daunger that is in the doubtful lot, he that goeth headlong to these thinges, and without urgent cause, deserveth great blame, although his chaunce bee good.

But when a man perceiveth that he is entred so far that hee can not draw backe without burthen, hee must both in such thinges as hee hath to doe before the combate, and also in the combate, be utterly resolved with him selfe, and alwaies shew a readinesse and a stomacke. And not as some doe, passe the matter[5] in arguing and points.

And having the choise of weapon, take such as have neither point nor edge. And arme themselves as though they should goe against the shotte of a Cannon.

And weening it sufficient not to be vanquished, stand alwaies

[1] Cf. "the advantages of each."  [2] "Sure": cf. "safe."
[3] "For to abide by" (*certamente*): cf. "for he . . . indeed."
[4] Cf. "be quick to seize an advantage."
[5] "Passe the matter": cf. "fritter the affair away."

at their defence and give ground, in so much that they declare an extreame faint hart, and are a mocking stocke [1] to the verie children.

As those two of Ancona: that a while agoe fought a combate beside Perugia, and made them to laugh that looked on.

And what were they, quoth the L. Gasper Pallavicin? The L. Cesar answered: Cousins Germains [2] of two sisters. Then saide the Count: at the combat a man would have thought them naturall bretheren: then hee went forwarde.

Also men occupy their weapon oftentimes in time of peace about sundrie exercises, and gentlemen are seene in open shewes in the presence of people, women and princes.

Therefore will I have our Courtier a perfect horseman for everie saddle. And beside the skill in horses, and in whatsoever belongeth to a horseman, let him set all his delight and diligence to wade in everie thing a little farther than other men, so that he may be knowne among all men for one that is excellent.

As it is redde of Alcibiades, that he excelled all other nations wheresoever hee came. And everie man in the thing hee had most skill in. So shall this our Courtier passe other men, and everie man in his owne profession.

And because it is y$^e$ peculiar praise of us Italians to ride well, to manage with reason, especially rough horses,[3] to runne at the Ring, and at Tilt, he shall be in this esteemed among the best Italians.

At Tournament in keeping a passage, in fighting at Barriers, he shall be [4] good amongst the best Frenchmen.

At *Joco di canne*,[5] running at Bull, casting of Speares and Dartes, hee shall bee among the Spaniards excellent. But principally let him accompanie all his motion with a certaine good judgement and grace, if hee will deserve that generall favor which is so much set by.

There be also many other exercises, the which though they depend not throughly upon Armes, yet have they a great agreement with them, and have in them much manly activitie. And of them me thinke, hunting is one of the chiefest.

For it hath a certaine likenesse with warre, and is truely a

---

[1] "Mocking stocke": cf. "laughing-stock."

[2] "Cousins Germains," etc.: cf. "two cousins."

[3] Cf. "to ride well with the rein, to govern wild horses with consummate skill."

[4] "He shall be": cf. "let him be."

[5] "*Joco di canne*": stick-throwing, a sport introduced by the Moors into Spain, and by the Spaniards into Italy.

pastime for great men, and fit for one living in Court. And it is found that it hath also beene much used among them of olde time.

It is meete for him also to have the arte of swimming, to leape, to runne, to cast the stone: for beside the profit that hee may receave of this in the warres, it happeneth to him many times to make proofe of him selfe in such thinges, whereby hee getteth him a reputation, especially among the multitude, unto whom a man must sometim apply him selfe.

Also it is a noble exercise, and meete for one living in Court to play at Tenise, where the disposition of the bodie, the quicknes and nimblenesse of everie member is much perceived, and almost whatsoever a man can see in all other exercises.

And I reckon vauting of no lesse praise, which for all it is painefull and hard, maketh a man more light and quicker than any of the rest.

And beside the profit, if that lightnes bee accompanied with a good grace, it maketh (in my judgement) a better shew than any of the rest.

If our Courtier then bee taught these exercises more than indifferently well, I believe he may set aside tumbling, climing upon a cord, and such other matters that tast somewhat of Jugglers craft, and doe litle beseeme a gentleman.

But because wee can not alwaies endure among these so painefull doings,[1] beside that the continuance goeth nigh to give a man his fill, and taketh away the admiration that men have of thinges seldom seene, wee must continually alter our life with practising sundrie matters.

Therefore will I have our Courtier to descend many times to more easie and pleasant exercises. And to avoide envie, and to keepe company pleasantly with every man, let him doe whatsoever other men doe: so hee decline not at any time from commendable deedes, but governeth him selfe with that good judgement that will not suffer him to enter into any folly: but let him laugh, dally, jest, and daunce, yet in such wise that he may alwaies declare him selfe to be wittie and discreete, and every thing that hee doth or speaketh, let him doe it with a grace.

Truely, saide then the Lord Cesar Gonzaga, the course of this communication shoulde not bee stopped: but if I should holde my peace, I should not satisfie the libertie which I have to speake, nor the desire that I have to understand one thing. And let me be pardoned, if where I ought to speake against,

[1] Cf. "But since one cannot devote oneself to such fatiguing exercises continually . . ."

I demaund a question: because I suppose I may lawfully doe it after the example of M. Bernard, who for the too great desire he had to bee counted a well favored man, hath offended against the lawes of our pastime, in demaunding without speaking against.

Behold I beseech ye, said then the Dutchesse, how one error bringeth in a great sort. Therefore who so offendeth and giveth evil example, as M. Bernard hath done, deserveth to bee punished, not onely for his owne offence, but for other mens also.

Then answered the Lord Cesar: Therefore must I (Madame) escape punishment, for that M. Bernard ought to be punished for his owne offence and mine both.

Nay (quoth the Dutchesse) you ought both, to have double punishment. He for his offence, and for being an occasion for you to commit the like: and you for your offence, and for taking him for a president that did offend.

I have not hetherto offended Madam, answered the Lord Cesar. Therefore because I will leave the whole punishment for M. Bernard I will keepe silence.

And now hee helde his peace, when the Ladie Emilia answered: say what pleaseth you, for (by the Dutchesse leave) I pardon this fault, and whosoever shall offend in so small a trespasse.

Upon that the Dutchesse saide: I am well pleased. But take ye heede you deceive not your selfe, thinking peradventure to be better reported of for mercy than for justice. For in pardoning the offender too much, ye doe wrong to him that doth not offend.

Yet will not I have my rigour at this time in accusing your mercy to bee the cause that we shall loose the hearing of this the Lord Cesars demaund. So he, after the Dutchesse and the Ladie Emilia had made a signe to him, saide by and by.

If I doe well beare in minde, me thinke (Count Lewis) you have this night often times repeated, that the Courtier ought to accompany all his doings, gestures, demeaners: finally all his motions with a grace.

And this, me thinke, ye put for a sauce to everie thing, without the which all his other properties and good conditions were litle worth.

And I believe verily that every man would soone bee perswaded therein, for by the vertue of the word a man may say, that who so hath grace, is gracious.[1]

But because you have saide sundry times that it is the gift

[1] Cf. "he who has grace finds grace."

of nature and of the heavens, and againe, where it is not so perfect, that it may with studie and diligence be made much more: they that be borne so happie and so welthie with such a treasure (as some that wee see) me thinke therein they have litle neede of any other teacher, because the bountifull favor of heaven doth (as it were) in spite of them, guide them higher than they covet, and maketh them not onely acceptable but marvellous[1] unto all the world.

Therefore I doe not reason of this, because the obtaining of it of our selves lyeth not in our power.

But such as by nature have onely so much, that they be apt to become gracious in bestowing labour, exercise, and diligence,[2] I would faine know with what arte, with what learning, and by what meane they shall compasse this grace, as well in the exercises of the bodie (wherein ye thinke it so necessarie a matter) as in al other things that they doe or speake.

Therefore as you have, in praysing this qualitie to us engendred (I believe) in al a fervent thyrst to come by it, by the charge ye receyved of the Ladie Emilia, so with teaching it us, ye are bound to quench it.

Bound I am not (quoth the Count) to teach you to have good grace, nor any thing els, saving onely to shew you what a perfect Courtier ought to be.

Neither wil I take upon me to teach you this perfection, since a while agoe, I said, that the Courtier ought to have the feate of wrastling and vauting, and such other thinges, the which how should I bee able to teach them, not having learned them my selfe, I am sure ye know it all?

It sufficeth, that as a good souldier can speake his mind to an Armourer, of what fashion, of what temper and goodnes hee will have his harnesse, and for all that can not teach him to make it, nor to hammer or temper it: So perhaps I am able to tell you what a perfect courtier ought to be, but not to teach you how he should doe to be one.

Notwithstanding to fulfill your request in what I am able, although it bee (in maner) in a proverbe, that Grace is not to be learned, I say unto you, who so mindeth to be gracious, or to have a good grace in the exercises of the bodie, (presupposing first that he be not of nature unapt) ought to beginne betimes, and to learne his principles of cunning men.

The which thing how necessarie a matter Philip king of

[1] Cf. "not only pleasing but admirable."
[2] "In bestowing labour" etc.: cf. "by pains, industry, and care."

Macedonie thought it, a man may gather in that his will was, that Aristotle so famous a Philosopher, and perhaps the greatest that ever hath beene in the world, shoulde bee the man that should instruct Alexander his sonne, in the first principles of letters.

And of men whom wee know now adaies, mark how well and with what a good grace Sir Galliazzo Sanseverino maister of the horse to the French king, doth all exercises of the bodie, and that because, beside the naturall disposition of person that is in him, he hath applyed all his studie to learne of cunning men, and to have continually excellent men about him, and of everie one to choose the best of that they have skill in.

For as in wrastling, in vauting, and in learning to handle sundrie kind of weapons, he hath taken for his guide our maister Peter Mount, who (as you know) is the true and onely maister of all artificiall force and sleight[1]: So in ryding, in justing, and in everie other feate, he hath alwaies had before his eyes, the most perfectest that hath beene knowne to be in those professions.

He therefore that will bee a good scholler, beside the practising of good thinges must evermore set all his diligence to be like his maister, and (if it were possible) chaung him selfe into him.

And when hee hath had some entrie,[2] it profiteth him much to behold sundrie men of that profession: and governing him selfe with that good judgement that must alwaies be his guide, goe about to picke out, sometime of one, and sometime of an other, sundrie matters.

And even as the Bee in greene medowes fleeth alwaies about the grasse, choosing out flowers: So shall our Courtier steale his grace from them that to his seeming have it, and from eche one, that parcell that shall be most worthie prayse. And not to do as a friend of ours, whom you all know, that thought he resembled much Ferdinande the younger of Aragon, and regarded not to resemble him in any other point, but in the often lifting up of his heade, wrything therewithall a part of his mouth, the which custome the king had gotten by infirmitie.

And many such there are that thinke that they doe much, so they resemble a great man in somewhat, and take many times the thing in him that worst becommeth him.

But I, imagining with my selfe often times how this grace commeth, leaving apart such as have it from above, finde one

---

[1] Cf. "every form of trained strength and agility."
[2] Cf. "made some progress."

rule that is most generall, which in this part (me thinke) taketh place in all things belonging to a man in word or deede, above all other. And that is to eschue as much as a man may, and as a sharpe and daungerous rocke, too much curiousnesse, and (to speake a new word) to use in everye thing a certaine disgracing to cover arte withall, and seeme whatsoever he doth and saith, to doe it without paine, and (as it were) not minding it.

And of this doe I believe grace is much derived, for in rare matters and well brought to passe, every man knoweth the hardnesse of them,[1] so that a readinesse therein maketh great wonder.

And contrariwise to use force, and (as they say) to hale by the haire, giveth a great disgrace, and maketh everie thing how great so ever it bee, to be litle esteemed.

Therefore that may bee saide to be a verie arte, that appeareth not to be arte, neither ought a man to put more diligence in any thing than in covering it: for in case it be open, it looseth credite cleane and maketh a man litle set by.[2]

And I remember that I have redde in my dayes, that there were some most excellent Orators, which among other their cares, enforced themselves to make everie man believe, that they had no sight in letters, and dissembling their cunning, made semblant their Orations to be made verie simply, and rather as nature and truth ledde them, than studie and arte, the which if it had beene openly knowne, would have put a doubt in the peoples minde, for feare least hee beguiled them.

You may see then, how to shew arte, and such bent studie taketh away the grace of every thing.

Which of you is it that laugheth not when our maister Peter-paul daunceth after his owne fashion, with such fine skippes, and on tipto, without moving his heade, as though he were all of wood, so heedfully, that truly a man woulde weene hee counted his paces. What eye is so blind, that perceiveth not in this the disgrace of curiositie,[3] and in many men and women here present, the grace of that not regarded agility [4] and slight conveyance (for in the motions of the bodie many so terme it) with a kind of speaking or smyling, or gesture, betokening not

---

[1] "For in rare matters," etc.: cf. "because every one knows the difficulty of those things that are rare and well done."

[2] This "covering of art" is instanced by Castiglione's own treatment of this work of his: "the which I accomplished in a few dayes": cf. Epistle of the Author.

[3] Cf. "the ungracefulness of affectation."

[4] Cf. "that nonchalant ease."

to passe[1] upon it, and to minde any other thing more than that, to make him believe that looketh on, that he can not doe amisse.[2]

Here maister Bernard Bibiena not forbearing any longer, said: you may see yet that our maister Robert hath found one to praise his maner of dauncing, though the rest of you set litle by it. For if this excellencie doth consist in disgracing and in shewing not to passe upon,[3] and rather to minde any other thing than that a man is in hand withall, maister Robert hath no peere in the world. For that men should well perceive that hee litle mindeth it, many times his garments fal from his back, and his slippers from his feete, and daunceth on still without taking up againe any of both.

Then answered the Count: Seeing you will needs have me speake, I will say somewhat also of our vices.[4]

Doe you not marke, this that you call in maister Robert disgracing, is a verie curiositie?[5] for it is well knowne that hee enforceth himselfe with all diligence possible to make a shew not to minde it, and that is to minde it too much.

And because hee passeth certaine limits of a meane, that disgracing of his is curious, and not comely, and is a thing that commeth cleane contrary to passe from the drift,[6] (that is to wit) to cover arte.

Therefore I judge it no lesse vice of curiositie to be in dispraysing (which in it selfe is praise worthie) in letting a mans clothes fall off his backe, than in Precisenesse (which likewise of it selfe is praise worthie) to carrie a mans heade very stedfast for feare of ruffling his haire, or to keepe in the bottom of his cappe a looking glasse, and a combe in his sleeve, and to have alwaies at his heeles up and downe the streetes a Page with a Spunge and a Brush.

For this maner of Precisenesse and curiousnesse is too much in extremitie, which is alwaies a vice, and contrarie to that pure and amiable simplicitie, which is so acceptable to mens mindes.

Marke what an ill grace a man at Armes hath, when he enforceth him selfe to goe so bolt upright, setled in saddle (as we use to say after the Venetian phrase[7]) in comparison of an

---

[1] "Not to passe," et c.: cf. "that they have no care."
[2] Cf. "to make the onlooker think they can hardly go amiss."
[3] "Shewing not to passe," etc.: cf. "appearing to take no heed."
[4] "Our vices": cf. "our faults."
[5] "Verie curiositie": cf. "mere affectation."
[6] Cf. "the effect i ntended."
[7] It is not the ph rase, but the stiff manner of riding which Castiglione calls Venetian: the islanders had little chance to learn horsemanship.

other that appeareth not to minde it, and sitteth on horsebacke so nimbly and close as though hee were on foote.

How much more doe we take pleasure in a Gentleman that is a man at armes, and how much more worthy praise is he if he bee modest, of few wordes, and no bragger, than an other that alwaies craketh of himselfe, and blaspheming with a braverie seemeth to threaten the world.

And this is nothing els, but a curiositie to seem to be a roister.[1]

The like happeneth in all exercises, yea in everie thing in the world that a man can doe or speake.

Then said the L. Julian: this in like maner is verified in musicke: where it is a verie great vice to make two perfect cōcordes,[2] the one after the other, so that the verie sense of our hearing abhorreth it, and oftentimes delyteth in a second or in a seventh, which in it selfe is an unpleasant discorde, and not tollerable: and this proceedeth because the countenance in the perfect tunes engendreth irkesomnesse, and betokeneth a too curious harmony, the which in mingling therewithall the unperfect is avoided, with making (as it were) a comparison, whereby our eares stand to listen and greedely attend and tast the perfect, and are otherwhile delited with the disagreement of the second or seventh, as it were with a thing litle regarded.[3]

Behold ye then, answered the Count, that curiousnes hurteth in this, as well as in other things.

They say that also, it hath been a proverbe among some most excellent painters of olde time, that Too much diligence is hurtfull, and that Apelles found fault with Protogenes, because he could not keepe his handes from the table.[4]

Then saide the Lord Cesar. Thē verie same fault (me thinke) is in our Frier Seraphin, that hee can not keepe his handes from the table, especially as long as there is any meate stirring.

The Count laughed, and went forwarde: Apelles meaning was, that Protogenes knew not when it was well, which was nothing els but to reprehend his curiousnes in his workes.

This vertue therefore contrarie to curiositie, which we for this time terme Recklesnesse, beside that it is the true fountaine from the which all grace springeth, it bringeth with it also an other ornament, which accompanying any deede that a man doth, how litle so ever it be, doth not onely by and by open the knowledge of him that doth it, but also many times maketh it

---

[1] "Curiositie . . . roister": cf. "affectation of wishing to appear bold."
[2] Cf. "consonances."       [3] Cf. "unpremeditated."
[4] "Table" for *tavola*, which may mean either "dining-table" or "painter's tablet." A double intent.

to bee esteemed much more in effect than it is, because it imprinteth in the mindes of the lookers on, an opinion, that who so can so sleightly doe well, hath a great deale more knowledge than in deede he hath: and if he will apply his studie and diligence to that he doth, he might do it much better.

And to repeate even the verie examples, marke a man that taketh weapon in hand: If going about to cast a darte, or holding in his hand a sword or any other waster,[1] he setleth him selfe lightsomly (not thinking upon it) in a ready aptnesse, with such activitie, that a man would weene his bodie and all his members were naturally setled in that disposition, and without any paine, though he doth nothing else, yet doth he declare him selfe unto every man to be most perfect in that exercise.

Likewise in dauncing, one measure,[2] one motion of a bodie that hath a good grace, not being forced, doth by and by declare the knowledge of him that daunceth.

A musition, if in singing he rolle out but a plain note, ending in a double relise with a swete tune,[3] so easily that a man would judge hee did it at a venture, in that point alone he doth men to understand, that his knowledge is farre greater than it is in deede.

Oftentimes also in painting, one line not studied upon, one draught with the Pensell sleightly drawne, so it appeareth the hand without the guiding of any studie or art, tendeth to his marke, according to the Painters purpose, doth evidently discover the excellencie of the workeman, about the opinion whereof every man afterwarde contendeth, according to his judgement.

The like happeneth also, in a maner, about everie other thing. Therefore shall our Courtier be esteemed excellent, and in everie thing he shall have a good grace, and especially in speaking, if he avoide curiositie: into which error many men run, and sometime more than other, certaine of our Lumbardes, which after a yeares travaile abroad, come home and beginne by and by to speake the Romane tongue, sometime y^e Spanish tongue or the French, and God woteth how.[4]

And all this proceedeth of an over great desire to shew much knowledge: and in this wise a man applyeth his studie and diligence to get a most odious vice.

And truely it were no small travaile for me, if I should use

---

[1] "Waster": cf. "weapon."

[2] "One measure": cf. "a single step."

[3] Cf. "a single note ending with a sweet tone in a little group of four notes."

[4] So the continentalised Englishman became the jest of Elizabethan playwrights. Cf. *Romeo and Juliet*, II. iv.

in this communication of ours, those auncient Tuskane wordes, that are not in use among the Tuskanes now adaies: and beside that, I believe every man would laugh at me.

Then spake Sir Fredericke. In deede reasoning together as we now doe, peradventure it were not well done to use those auncient Tuskane wordes: for (as you say) they woulde bee a loathsomnesse both to the speaker and to the hearer, and of many they shoulde not be understood without much a doe.

But he that should write, I would thinke he committed an errour in not using them: because they gave a great grace and authoritie unto wrytings, and of them is compact a tongue more grave, and more full of majestie, than of the new.[1]

I know not, answered the Count, what grace and authoritie those wordes can give unto wrytings that ought to be eschued,[2] not only in the manner of speach that wee now use (which you your selfe confesse) but also in any other maner that can be imagined. For if any man, of how good a judgement so ever hee were, had to make an Oration of grave matters in the verie Councell Chamber of Florence, which is the heade of Tuskane: or els to comune privately with a person of estimation in that Citie about waightie affaires: or also with the familiarest friend hee hath about pleasant matters: or with women or Gentlemen about matters of love, either in jeasting or dallying, banketing, gaming, or where ever else: or in any time or place, or purpose, I am assured he would flee the using of those auncient Tuskane words, and in using them, beside that he would be a laughing stocke, hee would bring no small loathsomnesse[3] to him that heard them.

Therefore me thinke it a straunge matter to use those words for good in wryting, that are to bee eschewed for naughtie in every manner of speach: and to have that which is never proper in speach, to bee the properest way a man can use in wryting.

Forsomuch as (in mine opinion) wryting is nothing els, but a maner of speach, that remaineth still after a man hath spoken, or (as it were) an image, or rather the life of the wordes. And therefore in speache, which as soone as the sound is pronounced, vanisheth away, peradventure some things are more to be borne withall, than in writing. Because wryting keepeth the wordes

[1] So also Spenser thought; but Sidney thought otherwise, and that the author of the *Shepheardes Calendar*, in affecting the ancients, writ no language.
[2] The clause is misplaced. Cf. "those words that ought to be avoided."
[3] Cf. "annoyance."

in store, and referreth them to the judgement of the Reader, and giveth time to examine them deeply.

And therefore reason willeth, that greater diligence should bee had therein, to make it more trimme and better corrected: yet not so, that the written wordes should be unlike the spoken, but in wryting to choose out the fairest and proprest of signification that be used in speaking.

And if that should be lawfull in writing which is not lawfull in speaking, there should arise an inconvenience of it (in my judgement) verie greate: namely, that a man might use a greater libertie in the thing, where he ought to use most diligence, and the labour he bestoweth in writing, in steade of furtherance should hinder him.

Therefore it is certaine, whatsoever is allowed in wryting, is also allowed in speaking: and that speach is most beautifull, that is like unto beautifull wrytings.

And I judge it much more behovefull to be understood in wryting than in speaking, because they that write are not alwaies present with them that reade as they that speake with them that speak.

Therefore would I commend him, that beside the eschewing of many auncient Tuskane words, would apply him selfe also to use both in wryting and speaking, such as now adaies are in use in Tuskane and in other partes of Italy, and that have some grace in pronunciation.

And (in my minde) who so followeth any other trade, is not assured not to runne into that curiositie so much blamed, which we have spoken of before.

Then spake Sir Fredericke: I can not deny you, Count Lewis, that wryting is not a maner of speaking. But this I say, if the words that are spoken have any darkenesse in them, that communication pierceth not the minde of him that heareth: and passing without being understood, waxeth vaine and to no purpose: the which doth not happen in writing.

For if the words that the writer useth bring with them a litle (I will not say difficultie) but covered subtiltie,[1] and not so open, as such as be ordinarily spoken, they give a certaine authoritie to writing, and make the Reader more heedefull to pause at it, and to ponder it better, and he taketh a delyte in the wittinesse and learning of him that wryteth, and with a good judgement, after some paines taking, he tasteth the pleasure that consisteth in hard thinges.

---

[1] Cf. "subtlety that is recondite."

And if the ignorance of him that readeth bee such, that he can not compasse that difficultie, there is no blame in the writer, neither ought a man for all that to thinke that tongue not to bee faire.

Therefore in wryting, I holde opinion it is necessarie for a man to use the Tuskan wordes, and onely such as have beene used among the auntient Tuskanes: for it is a great testimoniall, and approved by time, that they be good and of a pithie signification, in that they be applyed to. And beside this, they have that grace and majestie that antiquitie giveth not onely to wordes, but unto buildinges, images, paintings, and to everie thing that is of force to preserve it.[1] And many times with this onely brightnesse and dignitie, they make the forme of sentences verye faire, and through the vertue and elegancie thereof, every matter how base so ever it be, may be so decked out, that it may deserve very great commendation.

But this your custome, that you make so much a doe off, appeareth unto me very daungerous, and many times it may be naught.[2] And if any vice of speech be taken up of many ignorant persons, me thinke for all[3] that it ought not to be received for a rule, nor followed of other.

Besides this, customes be many and diverse, and yee have not a notable Citie in Italie, that hath not a diverse maner of speach from al the rest.

Therefore if ye take not the paines to declare which is the best, a man may as well give him selfe to the Bergamaske tongue, as to the Florentine, and to follow your advise, it were no errour at all.

Me seemeth then, who so will be out of doubt and wel assured, it is requisite for him to determine with him selfe to follow one, that by all mens accorde is judged good, and to take him for a guide alwaies, and for a shield, against such as will goe about to find fault, and that I thinke ought to be none other, (I meane in the vulgar tongue) but Petrarca and Boccacio: and who so swarveth from these two, goeth at all adventure,[4] as he that walketh in the darke without light, and therefore many times strayeth from the right way.

But we are so hardy now adayes, that wee disdaine to doe as other good men of ancient time have done: that is to say, to take diligent heede to following,[5] without the which, I judge no

---

[1] Cf. "everything that is able to attain it."
[2] "Naught": cf. "bad."
[3] "For all": cf. "on this account."
[4] "Goeth at all adventure": cf. "gropes."
[5] Cf. "to imitation."

man can write well. And mee thinke Virgill declareth a great tryall of this, who for all that with his so divine a witte and judgement, hee tooke all hope from his posteritie for any to follow him at any time, yet would he follow Homer.

Then the Lorde Gasper Pallavicin, This disputation (quoth he) of wryting in verie deede is worth the hearing: yet were it more to our purpose, if you woulde teach in what sorte the Courtier ought to speake, for me thinke hee hath more neede of that, and he serveth his turne oftner with speaking than with wryting.

The Lord Julian answered: there is no doubt, but so excellent and perfect a Courtier hath neede to understand both the one and the other: and without these two qualities, peradventure all the rest shoulde not bee much worthie praise.

Therefore if the Count will fulfill his charge, hee shall teach the Courtier not onely to speake, but also to write well.

Then said the Count: I will not (my Lord) undertake this enter-prise, for it should bee a great folly for me to teach an other that I understand not my self. And though I were skilfull in it, yet can I not see howe I should thinke to do the thing in so few wordes, which great Clarkes have scarce done with such great studie and diligence, unto whose wrytinges I would remit our Courtier, if it were so, that I were bound to teach him to write and to speake.

The Lord Cesar then said: the Lorde Magnifico meaneth the speaking and wryting of the vulgar tongue, and not Latin, therfore those wrytings of great Clarkes are not for our purpose.

But you must shew us in this behalfe as much as you know, and for the rest yee shall be held excused.

I have alreadie saide, answered the Count. But in reasoning upon the Tuskan tongue, perhaps it were rather the Ladie Julians parte,[1] than any mans els to give judgement in it.

The L. Magnifico saide: I can not, nor of reason ought to speake against him, that saith the Tuskane tongue is fairer then all the rest.

Truth it is, there are many wordes in Petrarca, and Boccaccio, worne out of use now adaies: and such would I never use, neither in speaking, nor in wryting, and peradventure they themselves, if they were now alive, woulde use them no more.

Then spake Sir Fredericke: no doubt but they would use them still. And you Lordes of Tuskane ought to renew your tongue, and not to suffer it decay, as you doe: for a man may say

_____
[1] L. Julian de Medici was, of course, a Tuscan born and bred.

now, that there is lesse knowledge in Florence, than in many other places of Italie.

Then answered maister Bernard: those words that are no more in use in Florence, doe still continue among the men of the Countrie, and are refused of the Gentlemen for wordes corrupt and decayed by antiquitie.

Then the Dutches, let us not swarve (quoth shee) from our first purpose, but let us marke Count Lewis, teach the Courtier to speake and to write well, bee it Tuskane, or what ever els.

The Count answered: I have alreadie spoken (Madame) what I know. And I suppose the verie same rules that teach the one, may also serve to teach the other. But since you commaund me: I will make answere unto Sir Fredericke what commeth in my head, for I am of a contrarie opinion to him.

And peradventure I shal be driven to answere somewhat more darkely than will be allowed, but it shall be as much as I am able to say.

And first I say, that (to my judgement) this our tongue which we name the vulgar tongue, is tender and new, for all it hath beene now used a long while. For in that Italie hath beene, not onely vexed and spoiled, but also inhabited a long time with barbarous people, by the great resorte of those nations the Latin tongue was corrupted and destroyed, and of that corruption have sprong other tongues. The which like the Rivers that departe from the toppe of the Appennine, and runne abroad towarde the two seas: so are they also divided, and some dyed with the Latin speach have spredde abroad sundrie waies, some into one parte, and some into an other, and one dyed with barbarousnesse hath remained in Italy.

This then hath a long time beene among us out of order, and diverse, because there was none that would bestow diligence about it, nor write in it, ne yet seeke to give it brightnesse, or any grace: yet hath it beene afterwarde brought into better frame in Tuskane, than in the other partes of Italie.

And by that it appeareth, that the flower of it hath remained there ever since those first times, because that Nation hath kept proper and sweete accents in the pronunciation, and an order of Grammer, where it was meete, more than the other. And hath had three noble writers,[1] which wittily both in wordes and tearmes, that custome did allow in their time, have expressed their conceites, and that hath happened (in my minde) with a

[1] Dante, Petrarch, and Boccaccio.

better grace to Petrarca, in matters of love,[1] than to any of the other.

Where there arose afterwarde from time to time, not onely in Tuskane, but in all Italy, among gentlemen brought up in Court, in armes and in letters, some studie, to speake and to write more finely than they did in that first rude age, when the turmoile of the miseries that rose through barbarous nations, was not as yet quieted, many words have beene left out,[2] as well in Florence it selfe, and in all Tuskane, as in the residue of Italie, and other brought in, in their steade, and made in this behalfe the alteration that happeneth in all worldlye thinges: the which also hath evermore chaunced in other tongues.

For in cause these auncient Latin writinges had lasted hetherto, we shoulde see that Evander and Turnus, and the other Latins in those dayes, spake otherwise than did afterwarde the last kings of the Romans, and the first Consules.

You may see the verses sung by the Salii were scantly understood of their posteritie: but because it was so ordeined by the first inventers of it, they were not altered for reverence of religion.

So from time to time Orators and Poets forsooke many wordes that had beene used among their predecessors: for Antonius, Crassus, Hortensius, and Cicero, eschued many that Cato had used, and Virgill many of Ennius and so did the rest. For albeit they had antiquitie in great reverence, yet did they not esteeme them so much, that they would be so bound to them, as you will have us now. Yea, where they thought good, they spake against them, as Horace, that saith his predecessors did foolishlye praise Plautus, which would[3] that we should have the authoritie to bring up new wordes. And Cicero in many places reprehendeth manie of his predecessors.

And to blame S. Gibda, he saith that his Orations smelled of antiquitie. And affirmeth that Ennius also in some pointes set litle by his predecessors, so that if wee will follow them of old time, we shall not follow them.

And Virgill that you say followed Homer, followed him not in the tongue.[4]

Therefore would I (for my parte) alwaies shunne the use of those auncient wordes, except it were in certaine clauses,[5] and in them verie seldom. And (in my judgement) hee that useth

---

[1] Cf. "amorous subjects."    [2] "Left out": cf. "laid aside."
[3] "Which would," etc.: cf. "and thinks he has a right."
[4] Cf. "did not imitate him in language."    [5] "Clauses": cf. "places."

them otherwise, committeth a no lesse error, than who so would, to follow them of old time, feede upon maste,[1] where he hath now abundance of corne found out.

And because you say, the auncient wordes onely with the brightnesse of antiquitie, decke out so highly every matter, how base so ever it be, that it may make it worthie great commendation: I say unto you, that not of these auncient words onely, but of those that bee good in deede, I make no small account, that I suppose without the juice of faire sentences,[2] they ought of reason to be litle set by. For to divide the sentences frō the words, is the deviding of the soule from the bodie, the which can not bee done, neither in the one nor in the other, without destruction ensue upon it.

That therefore which is the principall matter and necessarie for a Courtier to speake, and write well, I believe is knowledge. For he that hath not knowledge and the thing in his minde that deserveth to bee understood, can neither speake nor write it.

Then must hee couch in a good order that hee hath to speake or to write, and afterwarde expresse it well with wordes: the which (if I bee not deceived) ought to bee apt, chosen, cleare, and well applyed, and (above all) in use also among the people: for very such make the greatnesse and gorgeousnesse of an Oration, so he that speaketh have a good judgement and heedfulnesse withall, and the understanding to picke such as be of most proper signification, for that he intendeth to speake and commend, and tempering them like waxe after his owne minde, applyeth them in such part and in such order, that at the first shew they may set forth and doe men to understand the dignitie and brightnesse of them,[3] as tables of painting placed in their good and naturall light.

And this doe I say, as well of writing as of speaking, wherein certain things are requisite that are not necessarie in writing, as a good voice, not too subtill or soft, as in a woman: nor yet so boistrous and rough, as in one of the countrie, but shril, cleare, sweete and well framed with a prompt pronunciation, and with fit maners, and gestures, which (in my minde) consist in certaine motions of all the bodie, not affected nor forced, but tempred with a manerly countenance and with a moving[4] of the eyes that may give a grace and accorde with the wordes,

---

[1] "Maste": cf. "acorns."

[2] Cf. "without the pith of beautiful thoughts."

[3] "And doe men," etc.: cf. "and make known their dignity and splendour."

[4] Cf. "play."

and (as much as he can) signifie also with gestures, the intent and affection [1] of the speaker.

But all these things were in vaine and of small account, if the sentences expressed by the wordes should not be faire, wittie, subtill, fine and grave according to the matter.

I doubt, saide the L. Morello, if this Courtier speake with such finenesse and gravitie among us, there will be some that will not understand him.

Nay, every one shall understand him, answered the Count, for finenes hindreth not the easinesse of understanding.[2]

Neither will I have him to speake alwaies in gravity, but of pleasant matters, of mery conceites, of honest devises, and of jestes according to the time, and in all notwithstanding after a pithy maner, and with readinesse and varietie without confusion, neither shall hee in anie part shew vanitie or childish follie.

And when hee shall then commune of a matter that is darke and hard, I will have him both in words and sentences well pointed, to expresse his judgement, and to make every doubt cleare and plaine after a certaine diligent sorte without tediousnesse.[3]

Likewise (when hee shall see time [4]) to have the understanding to speake with dignitie and vehemencie and to raise [5] those affections which our mindes have in them, and to inflame or stirre them according to the matter [6]: sometime with a simplicitie of such meekenesse of minde, that a man would weene nature her selfe spake to make them tender and (as it were) dronken with sweetnes: and with such conveyance of easinesse, that who so heareth him, may conceive a good opinion of him selfe, and thinke that he also with verie litle adoe, might attaine to that perfection, but when hee commeth to the proofe, shall finde him selfe farre wide.

I would have our Courtier to speake and write in that sorte, and not onely choose gorgeous and fine wordes out of every part of Italie, but also I woulde judge him worthie praise to use some of those termes both French and Spanish, which by our custome have beene admitted.

Therefore it shoulde not mislike me, falling so to purpose, to say *vauntcourrour*, to say, to ascertaine, to aventure, to say, to pearce through a bodie with talke, meaning thereby to use a

---

[1] Cf. "intent and feeling."
[2] Cf. "because facility is no impediment to elegance."
[3] "Without tediousnesse": cf. "with a certain touch of unpedantic care."
[4] Cf. "(where there is occasion)."
[5] "To raise": cf. "to arouse."      [6] "Matter": cf. "need."

familiaritie with him, and grope him to get of him some perfect knowledge: to say, a royall gentleman, a neat man to be about a prince, and such other tearmes, so hee may thinke to be understood.[1]

Sometime I would have him take certaine wordes in an other signification than that is proper to them, and wrasting them to his purpose (as it were) graffe them like a graffe of a tree in a more luckie stocke, to make them more sightly and faire, and (as it were) draw the matters to the sense of the verie eyes, and (as they say) make them felt with hande, for the delite of him that heareth, or readeth.

Neither would I have him to sticke to forge new also, and with new figures of speach, deriving them featly from the Latins, as the Latins in old time derived from the Grecians.

In case then of such learned men both of good witte and judgement, as now adayes may be picked out among us, there were some that would bestow their travell to write after the maner that we have spoken off, in this tongue things worth the reading, we should soone see it in good frame, and following with termes and good phrases, and so copious that a man might as well write in it, as in any other tongue: and though it were not the mere auncient Tuskane tongue, yet shoulde it be the Italian tongue, commune, plentifull, and variable, and (as it were) like a delicious garden full of sundrie flowers and fruites.

Neither should this bee a new matter: for of the foure tongues, that were in use among the Greeke writers, picking out of everie word, moodes and rules as they thought meete,[2] they raised[3] thereby an other, which was named ye Commune tongue, and afterwarde all five they called with one name the Greeke tongue.

And albeit the Athenian tongue was more fine, pure, and eloquenter than the rest, yet did not the good writers that were not of Athens borne, so affect it, but in the stile of writing, and (as it were) in the smacke and propertie of their naturall speach they were wel inough knowne: neither were they any whit the lesse regarded for all that, but rather such as would appeare over mere Athenians were blamed for it.

[1] Cf. "Thus it would not displease me if, on occasion, he were to say, *primor* (excellence); or *accadere* (to succeed), *avventurare* (to run a risk successfully), or *ripassare una persona con ragionamento*, meaning to sound a person and to talk with him in order to gain perfect knowledge of him; or *un cavaliere senza rimproccio* (a cavalier without reproach), *attillato* (elegant), *creato d'un principe* (a prince's creature), and other like terms, provided he might hope to be understood."

[2] Cf. "they culled words, forms, and figures from each as they saw fit."

[3] Cf. "brought forth."

Among the Latin wryters in like case many there were in their dayes much set by that were no Romanes, although there appeared not in them that proper and peculiar purenesse of the Romane tongue, which men of an other nation can verie seldome attaine.

In times past, Titus Livius was not neglected, although some one saide hee found in him mere Padowan: Nor Virgill, for that he was reprehended that hee spake not Romane.

And (as you know) there were also read, and much set by in Rome, many writers of barbarous nations.

But wee more precise a great deale than they of old time, doe binde our selves with certaine new lawes out of purpose: and having the broad beaten way before our eyes, seeke through gappes to walke in unknowne pathes. For in our owne tongue, whose office is (as all others) to expresse well and clearely the conceites of the minde, we delite in darknesse, and calling it the vulgar tongue, will use in it wordes, that are not onely not understood of the vulgar people, but also of the best sorte of men, and those men of learning, and are not used in any part, not regarding that all good writers of olde time blamed such wordes as were refused of custome, the which you (in my mind) do not wel know: forsomuch as you say, if any vice of speach be taken up of any ignorant persons, it ought not to bee called a custome, nor received for a rule of speach.

And (as at other times I have heard you say) ye will have againe in stead of Capitolio, we should say Campidoglio: for Ieronymo, Girolamo: Aldace, for Audace: and for Patrono, padrone: and such corrupt and mangled wordes, because they have bin found so written by some ignorant Tuscane of olde time, and bicause the men of the Countrie speak so in Tuscane now a daies.

The good use of speech therfore I beleeve, ariseth of men that have witte, and with learning and practise have gotten a good judgement, and with it consent and agree to receive the wordes that they thinke good, which are knowen by a certaine naturall judgement, and not by art or any manner rule.

Doe you not knowe, that figures of speech which give such grace and brightnesse to an Oration, are all the abuse of Grammer rules, but yet are received and confirmed by use, because men are able to make no other reason but that they delite, and to the verie sense of our eares it appeareth, they bring a life [1] and a sweetnes.

[1] Cf. "suavity."

And this believe I is good custome, which the Romanes, the Neapolitans, the Lumbards, and the rest are as apt to receive, as the Tuskanes. Truth it is, in everie tongue some things are alwaies good, as easiness to be understood, a good order, varietie, picked sentences, clauses well framed[1]: and on the other side Affectation, and the other contrary to these, are to bee shunned.

But of words some there are that last a good time, and afterwarde waxe stale and cleane lose their grace: other some take force and creepe into estimation.

For as the seasons of the yeare make leaves and fruites to fall, and afterwarde garnish the trees a fresh with other: even so, doth time make those first wordes to fall, and use maketh other to spring a fresh, and giveth them grace and estimation, until they in like sorte consumed by litle and litle with the envyous byting of time, come to their end, because at the last both wee and whatsoever is ours, are mortall.

Consider with our selves, that we have no more knowledge of the Osca tongue. The Provinciall tongue, that (a man may say) the last day[2] was renowmed of noble writers, now is it not understoode of the inhabitants of the Countrey.

I believe therefore (as the Lorde Magnifico hath saide) that were Petrarca and Boccaccio at this present in life, they woulde not use many words that we see in their writings. Therefore (in mine opinion) it is not wel done to follow them therein.

Yet doe I much commend them that can follow that ought to be followed: but notwithstanding I believe it be possible inough to write well without following, and especially in this our tongue, wherein we may bee helped by custome, the which I wil not take upon me in the Latin.[3]

Then Sir Fredericke, why, will you (quoth hee) custome should bee more apprised in the vulgar tongue, than in the Latin?

Nay, both in the one and the other (answered the Count) I judge custome ought to bee the mistresse. But for so much as those men, unto whom the Latin tongue was as proper, as is the vulgar tongue now to us, are no more in the world, we must learne of their writinges that they learned by use and custome: neither doth auncient speach signifie any thing els but an auncient custome of speach: and it were a fond matter to love the auncient speach for nothing els but to speake rather as men did speake, than as men doe speake?

---

[1] Cf. "beautiful sentences, harmonious periods."
[2] "The last day": cf. "but lately."
[3] Cf. "which I should not dare say of Latin."

Did not they then of olde time follow, answered Sir Fredericke?

I believe, (quoth the Count) many did follow, but not in every point.

And if Virgill had altogether followed Hesiodus, hee should not have passed him, nor Cicero Crassus, nor Ennius his predecessors.

Behold Homer, who is so ancient that he is thought of many to be the first heroicall Poete, as well of time, as also of excellencie of phrase: and whom will you have him to have followed?

Some other, answered Sir Fredericke, more auncient than he was, which wee heare not of, by reason of antiquitie.

Whom will you say then Petrarca and Boccaccio followed, said the Count, which (a man may say) were but three dayes agoe in the world?

I know not, answered Sir Fredericke, but it is to bee thought they in like wise bent their minde to following, though we know not of whom.

The Count answered: a man may believe that they that were followed, were better than they that did follow: and it were too great a wonder that their name and renowne, if they were good, should so soone bee cleane lost. But I believe their verie maister was witt, and their owne naturall inclination and judgement. And thereat no man ought to wonder, for (in a manner) alwaies a man by sundrie waies may climbe to the top of all perfection.

And there is no nature, that hath not in manye things of like sorte unlike the one to the other, which for al that among themselves deserve a like praise.

Marke me musike, wherein are harmonies sometime of base sound and slow, and otherwhile verie quicke and of new devises,[1] yet doe they all recreate a man, but for sundrie causes, as a man may perceive in the manner of singing that Bidō useth, which is so artificiall, cunning, vehement, stirred, and such sundrie melodies, that the spirites of the hearers move all and are inflamed, and so listing, a man would weene they were lift up into heaven.

And no lesse doth our Marchetto Cara move in his singing, but with a more soft harmony, that by a delectable way and full of mourning[2] sweetenes maketh tender and perceth the mind, and sweetly imprinteth in it a passion full of great delite.

Sundrie thinges in like manner doe equally please our eyes so

---

[1] Cf. "Consider music, the harmonies of which are now grave and slow, now very fast and of novel moods and means."

[2] "Mourning": cf. "plaintive."

much that a man shall have much a doe to judge in which they most delite.

Behold in painting Lenard Vincio, Mantegna, Raphael, Michelāgelo, George of Castelfranco: they are all most excellent doers, yet are they in working unlike, but in any of them a man would not judge that there wanted ought in his kinde of trade: for everie one is knowne to bee of most perfection after his manner.

The like is of many Poets both Greeke and Latin, which being diverse in writing are alike in prayse.

Orators also have alwaies had such a diversitie among them, as (in a manner[1]) every age hath brought forth and set by one sorte of Orators peculiar for that time, which have beene unlike and disagreeing not onely to their predecessors and followers but also among them selves. As it is written among the Grecians of Isocrates, Lysias, Eschines, and many other excellent, but yet like unto none saving themselves.

And among the Latins, Carbo, Lælius, Scipio Affricanus, Galba, Sulpitius, Cotta, Graccus, Marcus Antonius Crassus, and so many that it should be long to repeate them, all good and most divers one from another. So that who so could consider al the Orators that have beene in the world, he should finde so many Orators, so manie kindes of speach.

Me thinke I remember also that Cicero in a place bringeth in Marcus Antonius to say unto Sulpitius that there are many that follow no man, and yet climbe they to a high degree of excellencie.

And speaketh of certaine that had brought up a new stile and phrase of speaking faire, but not used[2] of Orators of that time wherein they followed none but themselves.

Therefore he affirmeth also that maisters should consider the nature of their scholers, and taking it for their guide, direct and prompt them in the way that their wit and naturall inclination moveth them unto.

For this cause therefore, Sir Fredericke, doe I believe if a man have not an inclination unto some author whatsoever he bee, it were not well done to force him to follow him. Because the vertue of that disposition of his soone fainteth,[3] and is hindred, by reason that it is to stray out of the way in which he would have profited, had he not beene stopped in it.

---

[1] Cf. "almost."

[2] Cf. "a new form and figure of speech, beautiful but not usual . . ."

[3] Cf. "Because the vigour of his faculty languishes."

I know not then how it will stand well, in steade of enriching this tongue, and of giving it majestie and light, to make it poore, slender, bare and darke, and to seeke to shut it up into so narrow a roome, that everye man should bee compelled to follow onely Petrarca and Boccaccio, and that we should not also in that tongue, credite Politian, Laurēce de Medicis, Francis Diaceto, and certain other [1] that notwistanding are Tuskanes, and perhaps of no lesse learning and judgement than Petrarca and Boccaccio.

And truely it should bee a great miserie to stop without wading any further than almost the first that ever wrote: and to dispaire, that so many and so noble wits shall never finde out any moe than one good manner of speach in the tongue that unto them is proper and naturall.

But now adaies there be some so scrupulous, that (as it were) with a religion and high mysteries of this their Tuskan tongue, put as many as heareth in such dread, that they bring in like case many gentlemen and learned men in such awe, that they dare not open their mouth: and confesse plainely, that they can not speake the tongue which they have learned of their nourses, even from their cradle.

But in this point (me think) we have spoken too much. Therefore let us now proceede in our communication of the Courtier.

Then answered Sir Fredericke: but first I will say this litle, which is, that I deny not but the opinions and writers of men are diverse among them selves: neither doe I judge it comely for one that is vehement and quicke of nature to take in hand to write of soft and quiet matters. Nor yet for an other that is severe and grave to write of mery conceites. For in this point, me think, it is reason every man should apply him selfe to his own proper inclination. And of this I believe spake Cicero, when he said that maisters should have a consideration to the nature of their scholars, least they should do like the ill husbandman, that sometime in a soyle that is good onely for vines, will sowe graine.

But it will not sinke into my heade why in a peculiar tongue, that is not so proper unto all men, as are discourses and conceites, and many other operations, but an invention contained under certaine termes,[2] a man may not with more reason followe them that speake best, than speake at all aventure.[3] And that,

---

[1] Cf. "give credence to Poliziano, to Lorenzo de' Medici," etc.

[2] "As are discourses," etc.: cf. "like speech and thought, and many other functions, but an invention of limited use."

[3] Cf. "at random."

as in the Latin tongue a man ought to apply himselfe to be in the tongue like unto Virgill and Cicero rather than Silius and Cornelius Tacitus, so in the vulgar tongue why it were not better to follow the tongue of Petrarca and Boccaccio than any mans else: and therein expresse well his owne conceites, and so apply himselfe as (Cicero saith) to his own naturall inclination. And thus shall the difference which you say is betweene the good Orators, be found to consist in the senses and not in the tongue.[1]

Then the Count, I feare me (quoth he) wee shall enter into a large sea, and leave our first purpose of the courtier. But I would knowe of you, wherein consisteth the goodness of this tongue?

Sir Fredericke answered: in keeping well the propertie[2] of it, and in taking it in the signification (using the same stile and measure)[3] that all such have done as have written well.

I would know then, quoth the Count, whether this stile and measure which you speake of, arise of the sentences[4] or of the wordes?

Of the wordes, answered Sir Fredericke. Doe you not thinke then, quoth the Count, that the wordes of Silius and Cornelius Tacitus, are the verie same that Virgill and Cicero use? and taken in the same signification? Sir Fredericke aunswered: they are the very same in deede, but some ill applyed and diversly taken.

The Count answered: in case a man shoulde picke out of a booke of Cornelius and of Silius, all the wordes placed in other signification than is in Virgill and Cicero, (which shoulde bee very few) would you not then say that Cornelius in the tongue were equall with Cicero, and Silius with Virgill?

Then the Ladie Emilia, me thinke (quoth she) this your disputation hath lasted too long, and hath beene very tedious, therefore it shall be best to deferre it untill an other time.

Sir Fredericke begun stil to make answere, but the Ladie Emilia alwais interrupted him.

At last the Count saide, many will judge of styles: and talke of numbers and measures,[5] and of following, but they can not doe mee to understand what manner a thing stile and measure is, and wherein following consisteth: Nor why thinges taken out of Homer or any other, are so well couched in Virgill, that they

---

[1] Cf. "consist in sense and not in language."
[2] "The propertie": cf. "its proprieties."
[3] Cf. "in giving it that sense, and in using that style and those rhythms."
[4] "The sentences": cf. "the thought."
[5] "Measures": cf. "rhythm."

appeare rather amplified than followed, and peradventure the occasion thereof is, that I am not able to conceive it.

But because a great argument that a man understandeth a thing, is the understanding that hee hath to teache it, I feare mee they themselves have small understanding in it, and praise Virgill and Cicero, because they heare them praysed of many, not for that they know the difference betwene them and others, which out of peradventure consisteth not in the observation of two or three, or of ten wordes [1] used after a diverse manner from other.

In Salust, in Cesar, in Varro, and in other good writers, there are founde some termes applyed otherwise than Cicero applyeth them, and both the one and the other doe well inough. Because in so trifling a matter the goodnesse and perfection of a tongue doth not consist, as Demosthenes answered Eschines well, that had taken him up, demaunding him of certaine wordes which he had used and yet were not auncient, what monsters, or woondrous matters they were? whereat Demosthenes laughed, and answered him, that the fortunes of Greece dependeth not upon them.

Even so woulde I passe full litle, if a Tuskane should reprehend mee for speaking rather *Satisfatto* then *Sodisfatto*: and *Honorevole*, than *Horrevole*: and *Causa*, than *Cagione*: and *Populo*, than *Popolo*, and such other matters.

Then arose Sir Fredericke upon his feete and saide: I beseech ye give the hearing of these few words.

The Ladie Emilia answered laughing, upon my displeasure I forbid any of you to talke anye more in this matter, for I will have you to breake it of until an other night.

But you Count, proceede you in your communication of the Courtier, and let us see how good a memory you have: for I believe if you can knit it againe where you brake of, you shall not doe a litle.

Madam, answered the Count, me thinke the threed is broken in sunder, but if I be not deceived, I trow wee saide that pestilent curiositie doth alwaies give an evill grace [2] unto all thinges: and contrariwise simplicitie and Rechlesnesse a marvailous good grace. In commendation whereof and in dispraise of curiositie, manye other thinges might be saide, yet will I alledge but one moe, and then have done.

---

[1] Cf. "for in truth it does not consist in preserving two or three or ten words . . ."

[2] Cf. "the pest of affectation imparts . . . ungracefulness."

All women generally have a great desire to be, and when they can not be at the least to appeare beawtifull.

Therefore where nature in some part hath not done her devoir, therein they endevour them selves to supply it with arte. Of this ariseth the trimming[1] of the face, with such studie and many times paines, the pilling[2] of the browes and forehead, and the using of all those manner waies, and the abyding of such loth-somnesse[3] that you women believe are kept very secrete from men, and yet doe all men know them.

The Ladie Constance Fregosa laughed at this and saide: you should doe much better to goe forwarde in your communication, and declare how a man may attaine a good grace, and speak of Courting,[4] than to discover the faultes of women without purpose.

Nay it is much to purpose, answered the Count, because these faultes that I talke of, take this grace[5] from you: for they proceede of nothing els, but of curiousnesse,[6] whereby ye discover openly unto every man the over great desire that yee have to be beawtifull.

Doe you not marke how much more grace is in a woman, that if she doth trimme[7] her selfe, doth it so scarcely and so litle, that who so beholdeth her, standeth in doubt whether she bee trimmed or no: than in an other so bedawbed, that a man would wene she had a viser on her face, and dareth not laugh for making it chappe: nor at any time changeth her colour, but when she apparaileth her selfe in the morning and all the rest of the day standeth like an image of woode without moving, shewing her selfe onely in torche light, as craftie marchantmen doe their clothes in their darke lights.

How much more then doth a man delite in one, I meane not foule, that is manifestly seene she hath nothing upon her face, though shee bee not white nor so redde, but with her naturall colour somewhat wan, sometime with blushing, or through other chaunce dyed with a pure rednesse, with her haire by happe out of order and ruffled, and with her simple and naturall gestures, without shewing her selfe to bestow diligence or studie to make her faire?

This is that not regarded purenesse[8] which best pleaseth the

---

[1] Cf. "painting."     [2] Cf. "plucking."
[3] Cf. "and the endurance of that trouble."     [4] Cf. "Courtiership."
[5] "Take this grace": cf. "deprive you of grace."
[6] Cf. "affectation"     [7] Cf. "paint."
[8] Cf. "This is that nonchalant simplicity . . ."

eyes and mindes of men, that stand alwaies in awe to be deceived by arte.

White teeth is a good sight in a woman, for since they are not so in open sight as is the face, but most commonly are hid, a man may thinke she bestoweth not so much labour about them, to make them white, as shee doth in the face.

Yet who so should laugh without cause purposely to shew them, shoulde discover the arte, and for all their faire whitenesse shoulde appeare unto all men to have a verie ill grace, as Egnatius in Catullus.

The like is in the hands, which being delicate, smooth and faire, if they be shewed bare at any time when occasion is to occupie them, and not of purpose to shew the beawtie of them, they leave a very great desire of them selves, and especially after they are covered with gloves againe, for a man woulde judge that in putting them on again she passeth not and litle regardeth whether they be in sight or no, and that they are so faire rather by nature, than by any studie or diligence.

Have ye not had an eye otherwhile, when either in the streetes going to Church, or in any other place, or in sporting, or by any other chaunce it happeneth that a woman lifteth up her clothes so high, that she sheweth her foote, and sometime a litle of her pretie legge unwittingly?

And seemeth she not to you to have a verie good grace, if ye behold her then with a certaine womanly disposition, cleanely and precise,[1] with her shoes of velvet, and her hose sitting cleane to her legge?

Truely it delyteth mee much, and I believe all of you: for every man supposeth that precisenesse in so secrete a place and so seldom seene, to be unto that woman rather naturall and proper, than forced, and that thereby she thinketh to get her no commendation at all.

In such sorte is curiousnesse avoided and covered, the which you may now conceive how contrarie it is, and taketh away the grace of everie operation and deed, as well of the bodie as of the minde, whereof hetherto we have spoken but litle, and yet ought ·t not to bee omitted, for as the minde is much more worthie than the body, so deserveth it also to be better decked and polished.

And how that ought to be in our Courtier (leaving apart the precepts of so manie wise Philosophers that write in this matter, and define the vertues of the mind, and so subtilly dispute of

[1] Cf. "tricked out with a touch of feminine daintiness."

the dignitie of them) we will expresse in fewe wordes, applying to our purpose, that it is sufficient he bee (as they terme it commonly) an honest man and well meaning: for in this is comprehended the goodnesse, the wisedom, the manlinesse and the temperance of the mind, and all other qualities that belong to so worthie a name. And I recken him onely a true morall Philosopher that will be good, and to that he needeth few other precepts than that will of his.

And therefore saide Socrates well, that he thought his instructions had brought forth good fruite, when by them hee had provoked any one to apply his will to the knowledge and learning of vertue. For they that are come to the point that they covet nothing more than to be good, doe easily attaine the understanding of all that belongeth thereto: therefore herein wil we make no more adoe.

But beside goodnesse the true and principall ornament of the minde in every man (I believe) are letters, although y^e Frenchmen know onely the noblenes of armes, and passe for nothing beside: so that they doe not onely set by letters, but they rather abhorre them, and all learned men they doe count very rascalles,[1] and they thinke it a great villany when any one of them is called a Clarke.

Then answered the Lord Magnifico, you say verye true, this error in deed hath longe raigned among the Frenchmen. But if Monseigneur de Angoulesme[2] have so good luke that he may (as men hope) succede in the Crowne, the glory of armes in France doth not so florish nor is had in such estimation, as letters will be, I believe.

For it is not long sins I was in France, and saw this Prince in the Court there, who seemed unto mee beside the handsomnesse of person and bewtie of visage, to have in his countenance so great a majestie, accompanied neverthelesse with a certaine lovely courtesie, that the realme of Fraunce shoulde ever seeme unto him a small matter.

I understood afterwarde by many gentlemen both French and Italian, verie much of the most noble conditions, of the greatnesse of courage, prowesse and liberalitie that was in him: and among other things, it was tolde me, that hee highly loved and esteemed letters, and had in very great reputation all learned men, and blamed the Frenchmen themselves that their mindes were so far wide from this profession, especially having at their

[1] Cf. "most base."
[2] M. d'Angoulême, afterwards Francis I. (born 1494, died 1547).

doores so noble an universitie as Paris is, where all the world resorteth.

Then spake the Count: It is great wonder that in these tender yeares, onely by the provocation of nature, contrarie to the manner of the countrie, he hath given him selfe to so good a way. And because subjectes follow alwaies the conditions of the higher powers, it is possible that it may come to passe (as you say) that ye Frenchmen will yet esteeme letters to be of that dignitie that they are in deede. The which (if they will give eare thereto) they may soone bee perswaded.

Forsomuch as men ought to covet of nature nothing so much, and nothing is more proper for them, than knowledge: which thing it were a great folly to say or to holde opinion that it is not alwaies good.

And in case I might commune with them, or with other that were of a contrary opinion to me, I would doe my diligence to shew them, how much letters (which undoubtedlye have beene graunted of God unto men for a soveraigne gift) are profitable and necessarie for our life and estimation. Neither should I want the examples of so many excellent captaines of old time, which all joyned the ornament of letters with prowesse of armes.

For (as you know) Alexander had Homer in such reverence, that hee laide his *Ilias* alwaies under his beds heade: and hee applyed diligently not these studies onely, but also the speculations of Philosophy under the discipline of Aristotle.

Alcibiades encreased his good conditions, and made them greater with letters, and with the instructions of Socrates.

Also what diligence Cesar used in studie, those thinges which hee had so divinelye writen him selfe, make triall.

It is saide that Scipio Affricanus carried alwaies in his hand the bookes of Xenophon, wherein under the name of Cyrus he instructeth a perfect king.[1]

I coulde recite unto you Lucullus, Sylla, Pompeius, Brutus, and many other Romanes and Grecians, but I woulde doe no more but make mention of Hannibal, which being so excellent a Captaine (yet for all that of a fierce nature and voide of all humanity, an untrue dealer, and a despiser of men and of the Gods) had also understanding in letters, and the knowledge of the Greeke tongue.

And if I bee not deceived (I trow) I have redde in my time, that he left a booke behinde him of his own making in the Greeke tongue. But this kinde of talke is more than needeth:

[1] Cf. "wherein the perfect king is portrayed under the name of Cyrus."

for I knowe all you understand how much the Frenchmen be deceived in holding opinion letters to doe any hurt to armes.

You know in great matters and adventures in wars the true provocation [1] is glory: and who so for lucres sake or for any other consideration taketh it in hande (beside that hee never doth any thing worthie prayse) deserveth not the name of a gentleman, but is a most vile marchant.

And every man may conceive it to be true glory, that is stored up in the holy treasure of letters,[2] except such unluckie creatures as have no taste thereof.

What minde is so fainte, so bashfull, and of so base a courage, that in reading the actes and greatnes of Cesar, Alexander, Scipio, Annibal, and so many other, is not incensed with a most fervent longing to be like them: and doth not preferre the getting of that perpetuall fame, before the rotten [3] life that lasteth two dayes? Which in despite of death maketh him live a great deale more famous than before.

But hee that favoureth not the sweetnes of letters, can not know how much is the greatnesse of glory, which is a long while preserved by them, and onely measureth it with the age of one or two men, for further hee beareth not in minde. Therefore can he not esteeme this short glory so much as he would doe that, which (in a manner) is everlasting, if by his ill happe he were not barred from the knowledge of it. And not passing upon it so much, reason perswadeth, and a man may well believe hee will never hazard himselfe so much to come by it, as hee that knoweth it.

I woulde not now some one of the contrarie parte should alledge unto mee the contrarie effectes to confute mine opinion with all: and tell mee how the Italians with their knowledge of letters have shewed small prowesse in armes from a certaine time hetherto,[4] the which neverthelesse is too true: but in very deed a man may well say that the offence of a few, hath brought (beside the great damage) an everlasting reproch unto all other, and the verie cause of our confusion, and of the neglecting of vertue in our mindes (if it bee not cleane deade) proceeded of them. But it were a more shamefull matter unto us to publish it, than unto the Frenchmen the ignorance in letters.

[1] "Provocation": cf. "stimulus."
[2] Cf. "in the sacred treasure-house of letters."
[3] "Rotten": cf. "frail."
[4] Machiavelli ascribes Italian unsuccess in war to antiquated and bad tactics; Charles VIII.'s officers, according to Montaigne, had an explanation which is akin to Count Lewis's that virtue in their minds was neglected (Opdycke).

Therefore it is better to passe that over with silence that cannot bee rehearsed without sorrow, and leaving this purpose into the which I am entred against my wil, returne againe unto our Courtier, whom in letters I will have to be more than indifferently well seene, at the least in those studies, which they call Humanitie and to have not onely the understanding of the Latin tongue, but also of the Greek, because of the many and sundrie things that with great excellencie are written in it.

Let him much exercise him selfe in Poets, and no lesse in Oratours and Historiographers, and also in writing both rime and prose, and especially in this our vulgar tongue. For beside the contentation [1] that hee shall receive thereby him selfe, hee shall by this meanes never want pleasant intertainements with women which ordinarily love such matters.

And if by reason either of his other businesse beside, or of his slender studie hee shall not attaine unto that perfection that his writings may bee worthy much commendation, let him bee circumspect in keeping them close, least he make other men to laugh at him. Onely hee may shew them to a friende whom he may trust.

For at the least wise hee shall receive so much profit, that by that exercise hee shall be able to give his judgement upon other mens doinges. For it happeneth very seldome, that a man not exercised in writing, how learned soever he be, can at any time know perfectly the labour and toile of writers, or tast of the sweetnesse and excellency of styles, and those inner observations [2] that often times are founde in them of olde time.

And beside that, those studies shal make him copious,[3] and (as Aristippus answered a Tirant) bold to speake upon a good ground with every man.

Notwithstanding I will have our Courtier to keepe fast in his minde one lesson, and that is this, to bee alwaies warie both in this and in everie other point, and rather fearefull than bolde,[4] and beware that hee perswade not himselfe falsly, to know the thing he knoweth not in deede.

Because we are of nature all the sort of us much more greedy of prayse than is requisite, and better do our eares love the melodie of wordes sounding to our praise, than any other song or sound that is most sweete. And therefore many times like the voyces of Marmaidens, they are the cause of drowning of

---

[1] "Contentation": cf. "enjoyment."
[2] "Inner observations": cf. "latent niceties."
[3] "Copious": cf. "fluent."
[4] Cf. "Diffident rather than forward."

him that doth not well stoppe his eares at such deceitfull harmony.

This daunger being perceived, there hath beene among the auncient wise men that have writen bookes, how a man should knowe a true friend from a flatterer. But what availeth it? If there bee many of them (or rather infinite) that manifestly perceive they are flattered, and yet love him that flattereth them, and hate him that telleth them the troth.

And oftentimes (standing in opinion that he that prayseth them is too scarce[1] in his wordes) they them selves helpe him forwarde, and utter such matters of themselves, that the most impudent flatterer of all is ashamed of.

Let us leave these blinde buzzards[2] in their owne errour, and make our Courtier of so good a judgement, that he will not bee given to understand blacke for white, nor presume more of himselfe than what he knoweth very manifestly to be true, and especially in those thinges, which (if yee beare well in minde) the Lorde Cesar rehearsed in his devise of pastimes, that we have many times used for an instrument to make many become foolish.[3] But rather that hee may be assured not to fall into any error, where he knoweth those prayses that are given him to be true, let him not so openly consent to them, nor confirme them so without resistance, but rather with modestie (in a manner) deny them cleane, shewing alwaies and counting in effect,[4] armes to bee his principall profession, and all the other good qualities for an ornament thereof.

And principally among Souldiers, least hee bee like unto them that in learning will seeme men of warre, and among men of warre, learned.

In this wise, for the reasons we have said, he shall avoide curiousnesse, and the meane[5] thinges which he taketh in hand, shall appeare very great.

Here M. Peter Bembo answered: I know not (Count Lewis) how you will have this Courtier, being learned, and of so many other vertuous qualities, to count every thing for an ornament of armes, and not armes, and the rest for an ornament of letters. The which without other addition, are in dignitie so much above armes, as the mind is above the bodie: because the practising of them belongeth properly to the minde, even as the practising of armes doth the bodies.

[1] Cf. "too sparing."   [2] Cf. "blind ones."
[3] Cf. "to bring men's folly to light."   [4] Cf. "really esteeming."
[5] "The meane": cf. "the middling."

The Count answered then: nay the practising of armes belongeth as well to the minde as to the bodie. But I would not have you (maister Peter) a judge in this cause, for you would be too partiall to one of the partes.

And for so much as this disputation hath alreadie beene tossed a long time by most wise men, we need not to renue it, but I count it resolved upon armes side, and wil have our Courtier (since I have the fashioning of him at my will) thinke thus also.

And if you be of a contrarie opinion, tarrie till you heare a disputation, where it may bee as well lawfull for him that taketh part with armes, to use his armes, as they that defend letters, use in the defence the verie same letters, so that if each helpe them selves with their instruments, you shall see that letters shall loose.

Oh (quoth maister Peter) you rebuked the Frenchmen before for setting litle by letters, and declared what a great light of glory they shew unto men, and how they make them immortall: and now it seemeth you are in an other opinion.

Doe you not remember that such verses are taken out of Petrarch.

> The great Macedo, when he proched neare
> Fierce Achylles famous tomb thus saide and sight:
> O happie Prince that found a trumpe so cleare,
> And happie he that praisde so worthie a wight.

And if Alexander envied Achilles, not for his deedes, but for his fortune that gave him so great lucke to have his actes renowmed by Homer, a man may gather hee esteemed more the letters of Homer, than the armes of Achilles.

What other judge then, or what other sentence looke you for, as touching the dignitie of armes and letters, than that which was given by one of the greatest Captaines that ever were?

The Count answered: I blame the Frenchmen because they think letters hurt the profession of armes: and I holde opinion that it is not so necessary for any man to be learned, as it is for a man of warre.

And these two points linked together, and aided the one by the other (which is most fit) will I have to bee in the Courtier. Neither do I thinke my selfe for this to be in an other opinion,[1] but (as I have said) I will not dispute, which of them is most worthie prayse.

It sufficeth that learned men take not in hand at anie time to praise any but great men and glorious actes, which of them selves

[1] Cf. "Nor do I think I have changed my mind in this."

deserve praise by their proper essentiall vertues from whence they arise.

Beside that, they are a most noble Theme for writers, which is a great ornament, and partly the cause of continuance of writinges, that peradventure shoulde not be so much read, and set by, if there wanted in them noble matter, but counted vaine and of small reputation.

And if Alexander envied Achilles, because hee was praised of him that did it, yet doth it not consequently follow, that he esteemed letters more than armes. Wherein he had knowne him selfe so farre wide from Achilles, as in writing hee thought all they would be from Homer that shoulde goe about to write of him, I am sure hee would much sooner have desired well doing in himselfe, than well speaking in an other.

Therefore think I that this was a close praise of him selfe, and a wishing for that he thought he had not, namely the high excellencie of a writer, and not for that hee thought with him selfe hee had alreadie obtained, that is to say, the prowesse of armes, wherein hee counted not Achilles any whit his superior, wherefore he called him happie, as it were signifying, where his fame aforetime was not so renowmed in the worlde,[1] as was the fame that by so divine a Poeme was cleare and excellent, it proceeded not for that his prowesse and deserts were not such, and worthie so much praise: but it arose of fortune, that had before hand prepared for Achilles, that miracle of nature for a glorious renowne and trumpet of his acts.

And peradventure againe he minded thereby to stirre up some noble witt to write of himselfe, declaring thereby how acceptable it would be to him, forsomuch as hee loved and reverenced the holy monuments of letters: about the which we have spoken sufficient.

Nay more than sufficient, answered the Lord Lodovicus Pius, for I believe there is never a vessell in the world possible to be found so bigge, that shall bee able to receive all the thinges that you will have in this Courtier.

Then the Count, abide yet a while (quoth hee) for there be many other thinges to be had in him yet.

Peter of Naples answered: after this manner Crassus de Medicis [2] shall have a great advantage of M. Peter Bembo.

[1] Cf. "as if hinting that although his own fame had hitherto not been so celebrated in the world as Achilles's . . ."
[2] "Crassus de Medicis," *Grasso* or "Fatty," a nickname for some soldier whose size would give him the advantage, in this connection, over Bembo, who was thin.

At this they all laughed. And the Count beginning a fresh, my Lords (quoth he) you thinke I am not pleased with y^e Courtier, if he be not also a Musition, and beside his understanding and cunning upon the booke,[1] have skil in like manner on sundry instruments. For if wee weigh it well, ther is no ease of the labors, and medicines of feeble mindes to be found more honest and more praise worthie in time of leisure than it. And principally in Courtes, where (beside the refreshing of vexations that musike bringeth unto eche man) many things are taken in hand to please women withall, whose tender and soft breastes are soone pierced with melodie, and filled with sweetnesse.

Therefore no marvell, that in olde times and now adayes they have alwaies beene inclined to Musitions, and counted this a most acceptable food of the minde.

Then the L. Gasper, I believe musick (quoth he) together with many other vanities is meet for wome, and peradventure for some also that have the likenesse of men, but not for them that be men in deede: who ought not with such delicacies to womanish their mindes, and bring them selves in that sort to dread death.

Speake it not, answered the Count. For I shall enter in a large sea of the praise of Musicke, and call to rehearsall how much it hath alwaies beene renowmed among them of olde time, and counted a holy matter: and how it hath beene the opinion of most wise Philosophers, that the worlde is made of musike, and the heavens in their moving make a melodie, and our soule is framed after the verie same sort and therefore lifteth up it selfe, and (as it were) reviveth the vertues and force of it selfe with Musicke.

Wherefore it is written that Alexander was so fervently stirred with it, that (in a manner) against his will hee was forced to arise from bankets and runne to weapon, afterward the Musition chaunging the stroke, and his manner of tune, pacified him selfe again, and returned from weapon to banketing.

And I shall tell you that grave Socrates when he was well stricken in yeares, learned to play upon the harpe. And I remember I have understoode that Plato and Aristotle will have a man that is wel brought up, to be also a Musition: and declare with infinite reasons the force of musicke to bee to very great purpose in us, and for many causes (that should be too long to rehearse) ought necessarily to be learned from a mans childhood, not onely for the superficiall melodie that is heard, but to be

[1] Cf. "being able to read notes."

sufficient to bring into us a new habite that is good, and a custome inclining to vertue, which maketh the minde more apt to the conceiving of felicitie,[1] even as bodely exercise maketh the bodie more lustie, and not onely hurteth not civil matters and warrelike affaires, but is a great stay to them.

Also Lycurgus in his sharp lawes allowed musicke. And it is read that the Lacedemoniãs, which were valiant in armes, and the Cretenses used harpes, and other soft instruments: and many most excellent Captaines of olde time (as Epaminondas) gave themselves to musicke: and such as had not a sight in it (as Themistocles) were a great deale the lesse set by.

Have you not reade, that among the first instructions which the good olde man Chiron taught Achilles in his tender age, whom he had brought up from his nurse and cradle, musicke was one? And the wise maister woulde have those handes that should shedde so much Troyan bloud, to bee often times occupied in playing upon the Harpe?

What souldier is there (therefore) that will thinke it a shame to follow Achilles, omitting many other famous Captaines that I could alledge?

Doe ye not then deprive our Courtier of Musicke, which doth not onely make sweete the mindes of men, but also many times wilde beastes tame: and who so savoureth it not, a man may assuredly thinke him not to be well in his wits.[2]

Behold I pray you what force it hath, that in times past allured a fish to suffer a man to ride upon it through the tempestuous sea.

We may see it used in the holy temples, to render laud and thankes unto God, and it is a credible matter that it is acceptable unto him, and that he hath given it unto us for a most sweete lightning of our travailes and vexations.

So that many times the boysterous labours in the fields, in the heat of the sun, beguile their paine with rude and carterly singing.[3]

With this the unmannerly countrie woman, that ariseth before day out of her sleepe to spinne and carde, defendeth her selfe[4] and maketh her labour pleasant.

This is the most sweete pastime after raine, winde and tempest, unto the miserable marriners.

With this doe the verie Pilgrimes comfort themselves in their

[1] Cf. "habitual tendency . . . which renders the soul more capable of happiness."
[2] Cf. "ill attuned in spirit."          [3] Cf. "crude and rustic song."
[4] Cf. "the rude peasant lass . . . wards off her drowsiness."

troublesome and long voyages. And oftentimes prisoners, in adversitie, fetters and in stockes.

In like manner for a greater proofe, that the tunablenesse of musick (though it be but rude) is a verie great refreshing of all worldlye paines and griefes, a man woulde judge that nature hath taught it unto nurses for a speciall remedie to the continuall waylings of sucking babes, which at the sound of their voice fall into a quiet and sweete sleepe, forgetting the teares that are so proper to them, and given us of nature in that age, for a gesse of the rest of our life to come.

Here the Count pausing a while, the L. Julian said: I am not of the Lorde Gaspers opinion, but I believe for the reasons you alledge, and for many other, that musicke is not only an ornament, but also necessarie for a Courtier.

But I would have you declare, how this and the other qualities which you appoint him, are to bee practised, and of what time, and in what sort. Because many thinges that of themselves be worthie praise, oftentimes in practising them out of reason seeme most foolish. And contrariewise, some thinges that appeare to bee of small moment, in the well applying them, are greatly esteemed.

Then said the Count: before we enter into this matter, I will talke of an other thing, which for that it is of importance (in my judgement) I believe our Courtier ought in no wise to leave it out. And that is the cunning in drawing, and the knowledge in the verie arte of painting.

And wonder ye not if I wish this feate in him, which now adayes perhappes is counted an handicraft and full litle to become a gentleman, for I remember I have reade that the men of olde time, and especially in all Greece, would have gentlemens children in the scholes to apply [1] painting, as a matter both honest [2] and necessarie. And this was received in the first degree of liberall artes, afterwarde openly enacted not to bee taught to servants and bondmen.

Among the Romanes in like manner it was in verie great reputation, and thereof sprung the sirname of the most noble family of Fabii, for the first Fabius was sirnamed Pictor, because in deed he was a most excellent Painter, and so addicted to painting, that after hee had painted the walles of the temple of Health, hee writte therein his name, thinking with him selfe, that for all he was borne in so noble a familie, which was honoured with so many titles of Consulshippes and triumphes, and other dignities, and was learned and well seene

[1] "Apply"; cf. "study."  [2] "Honest": cf. "honourable."

in the law, and reckoned among orators, to give also an increase of brightenesse, and an ornament unto his renowne, by leaving behind him a memorie that he had beene a Painter.

There have not in like manner wanted many other of notable families that have beene renowned in this arte, of the which (beside that in it selfe it is most noble and worthie) there ensue many commodities, and especially in warre, to draw out Countries, Platformes, Rivers, Bridges, Castels, Holdes, Fortresses, and such other matters, the which though a man were able to keepe in minde (and that is a hard matter to doe) yet can he not shew them to others.

And in verie deed who so esteemeth not this arte, is (to my seeming) farre wide from all reason: for somuch as the ensigne of the world that we behold with a large skye, so bright with shining starres, and in the middest, the earth, environed with the seas, severed in partes with hilles, dales, and rivers, and so decked with such divers trees, beautifull flowers and herbes, a man may say it to be a noble and great painting, drawne with the hand of nature and of God: the which who so can follow,[1] in mine opinion he is worthie much commendation. Neither can a man attaine to this, without the knowledge of many thinges, as he well knoweth that tryeth it.

Therefore had they of old time in very great estimation, both the arte and the artificers, so that it came to the toppe of all excellencie.

And of this may a man gather a sufficient argument at the auncient Images of Marble and mettall, which at this day are to bee seene.[2] And though painting bee a diverse matter from carving, yet doe they both arise of one selfe fountaine (namely) of a good patterne.[3]

And even as the Images[4] are divine and excellent, so it is to be thought paintinges were also, and so much the more, for that they containe in them a greater workemanship.

Then the Ladie Emilia turning her unto John Christopher Romano, that sate there among the rest, howe thinke you (quoth she) to this judgement, will you graunt that painting containeth in it a greater workemanshipe, than carving?

John Christopher answered: in my minde carving is of more travaile, of more arte, and of more dignitie than painting.

[1] Cf. "imitate."
[2] "The Apollo Belvedere was discovered in 1503, the Laocöon group in 1506, and other famous antique statues only a few years earlier." — Opdycke.
[3] "Patterne": cf. "design."     [4] "Images": cf. "statues."

Then saide the Count, Because Images are more durable, perhaps a man may say that they are of a more dignitie. For sith they are made for a memorie,[1] they better satisfie the effect why they be made, than painting.

But beside memorie, both painting and carving are made also to set out a thing, and in this point hath painting a great deale the upper hand, the which though it be not so long lasting (to terme it so) as carving is, yet doth it for all that endure a long time, and for the while it lasteth, is much more sightly.

Then answered John Christopher: I believe verily you think not as you speake, and all this doe you for your Raphaelles sake.

And peradventure too, you judge the excellencie you know to bee in him in painting, to be of such perfection, that carving in Marble can not come to that degree. But waigh with your selfe, that this is the prayse of the artificer, and not of the arte.

Then he proceeded: and I judge also both the one and the other, to bee an artificiall following of nature. But yet I knowe not how you can say, that the truth and property that nature maketh, can not bee followed better in a figure of Marble or Mettall, wherein the members are all rounde proporcioned and measured as nature her selfe shapeth them, than in a Table, where men perceive nothing but the outwarde sight, and those colours that deceive the eyes: and say not to me, that being, is not nigher unto the truth than seeming.

Againe, I judge carving in Marble much harder, because if yee make a faulte, it can not be amended againe, for marble can not be joyned together, but ye must be driven to make a new Image.

The which happeneth not in painting, for a man may alter, put to, and diminish, alwaies making it better.

The Count saide laughing: I speake not for Raphaelles sake, neither ought you to think me so ignorant a person, but I understand the excellencie of Michaelangelo, of you your selfe, and of other men in carving of Marble, but I speake of the arte, and not of the Artificers.

And you say well, that both the one and the other is following of nature. But for all that, it is not so, that painting appeareth and carving is: for although images are all rounde like the lively patterne, and painting is onely seene in outwarde apparance, yet want there many things in images, that want not in paintinges, and especially lights and shadowes, for flesh giveth one light, and Marble another, and that doth the Painter

[1] Cf. "as memorials."

naturally follow with cleare and darke, more and lesse, as he seeth occasion, which the graver in marble can not doe.

And when the Painter maketh not his figure round he maketh the muscules and members in round wise, so that they goe to meete with the partes not seene, after such a manner, that a man may very well gather the Painter hath also a knowledge in them, and understandeth them.

And in this point he must have an other craft that is greater to frame those members, that they may seeme short, and diminish according to the proportion of the sight by the way of prospective,[1] which by force of measured lines, colours, lights, and shadowes, discover unto you also in the outwarde sight of an upright wall the plainesse and fairenesse, more and lesse as pleaseth him.

Thinke you it againe a trifling matter to counterfeite naturall colours, flesh, cloth, and all other coloured thinges.

This can not nowe the graver in marble doe, ne yet expresse the grace of the sight that is in the blacke eyes, or in azure with the shining of those amorous beames.

Hee can not shew the colour of yellow haire, nor the glistring of armor, nor a darke night, nor a sea tempest, nor those twincklings and sparkes, nor the burning of a Citie, nor the rysing of the morning in the colour of Roses, with those beames of purple and golde. Finally hee can not shewe the skye, the sea, the earth, hilles, woodes, medowes, gardens, rivers, Cities, nor houses, which the Painter doth all.

For this respect (me thinke) painting is more noble, and containeth in it a greater workmanship than graving in Marble. And among them of olde time, I believe it was in as high estimation as other thinges, the which also is to be discerned by certain litle remnants that are to be seene yet, especially in places under ground in Roome.[2]

But much more evidently may a man gather it by olde wrytings, wherein is so famous and so often mention both of the worke and workemen, that by them a man may understande in what high reputation they have beene alwaies with Princes and common weales.

Therefore it is read, that Alexander loved highly Apelles of Ephesus, and so much, that after he had made him draw out a woman of his naked, whome hee loved most dearely, and under-

---

[1] Cf. "And in this another and greater skill is needed to represent those members that are foreshortened and grow smaller in proportion to the distance by reason of perspective."

[2] The Catacombs.

standing that this good Painter, for her marvellous beautie was most fervently in love with her, without any more adoe, hee bestowed her upon him. Truely a worthie liberallitie of Alexander, not to give onely treasure and states, but also his owne affections and desire, and a token of verie great love towarde Appelles, not regarding (to please him withall) the displeasure of the woman that he highly loved, who it is to be thought was sore agreeved to chaunge so great a king for a painter.

There bee many other signes rehearsed also of Alexanders good will towardes Apelles, but he shewed plainly in what estimation he had him, when hee commanded by open Proclamation no other Painter should bee so hardie to drawe out his picture.

Here could I repeat unto you the contentions of many noble Painters, with the greatest commendation and marvaile (in a manner) in the world.

I coulde tell you with what solemnitie the Emperours of olde time decked out their triumphes with paintinges, and dedicated them up in haunted [1] places, and how deare it cost them, and that there were some painters that gave their workes freely, seeming [2] unto them no golde nor silver was enough to value them: And how a table [3] of Protogenes was of such estimation, that Demetrius lying encamped before Rhodes, where hee might have entred the Citie by setting fire to the place, where hee wist this table was, for feare of burning it, stayed to bid them battaile, and so he wunne not the Citie at all.

And how Metrodorus a Philosopher and a most excellent Painter, was sent out of Athens to Lord Paulus, to bring up his children, and to decke out his triumph he had to make.

And also many noble writers have written of this arte, which is a token great inough to declare in what estimation it hath beene. But I will not wee proceede any farther in this communication.

Therefore it sufficeth onely to say that our Courtier ought also to have a knowledge in painting, since it was honest and profitable, and much set by in those dayes when men were of more prowesse than they are now. And though hee never get other profit or delite in it (beside it is a helpe to him to judge of the excellencie of Images both olde and new, of vessels, buildings, old coines, cameses, [4] gravings, and such other matters) it maketh him also understand the beautie of lively bodies, and not onely

---

[1] "Haunted": cf. "public."   [2] Cf. "esteeming."
[3] "A table": cf. "a painting."   [4] "Cameses": cf. "cameos."

in the sweetnesse of the Phisiognomie, but in the propoition of all the rest, as well in men as other living creatures.

See then how the knowledge in painting is cause of verie great pleasure. And this let them thinke that doe enjoy and view the beautie of a woman so throughly, that they thinke themselves in Paradise, and yet have not the feate of painting: the which if they had, they would conceive a farre greater contentation, for then shoulde they more perfectly understand the beauty that in their brest ingendreth such hearts ease.

Here the Lorde Cesar laughed and saide: I have not the arte of painting, and yet I knowe assuredly I have a farre greater delite in beholding a woman in the world,[1] than Apelles himselfe that was so excellent, whom ye named right now, coulde have if he were now in life againe.

The Count answered: this delite of yours proceedeth not wholy of beautie, but of the affection which you perhaps beare unto the woman. And if you will tell the truth, the first time that you beheld that woman, yet felt not the thousandeth part of the delite which you did afterwarde, though her beautie were the verie same.

Therefore you may conceive how affection beareth a greater stroke in your delite than beautie.

I deny not that (quoth the Lord Cesar:) but as delite ariseth of affection, so doth affection arise of beautie, therefore a man may say for all that, that beautie is the cause of delite.

The Count answered: there be many other thinges also, that beside beautie oftentimes inflame our minds as manners, knowledge, speach, gestures, and a thousand moe (which peradventure after a sorte may be called beautie too) and above all, the knowing a mans selfe to be beloved: so that without the beautie you reason of, a man may bee most fervently in love:

But those loves that arise onely of the beautie which we discerne superficially in bodies, without doubt will bring a farre greater delite to him that hath a more skill therein, than to him that hath but a litle.

Therefore returning to our purpose, I believe Apelles conceived a farre greater joye in beholding the beautie of Campaspes, than did Alexander, for a man may easily believe, that the love of them both proceeded of that beautie, and perhaps also for this respect Alexander determined to bestow her upon him, that (in his mind) could know her more perfectly than he did.

[1] "A woman in the world": cf. "a woman"—like enough accompanied with a glance at the Lady Emilia.

Have you not reade of the five daughters of Croton, which among the rest of that people, Zeusis the Painter chose to make of all five one figure that was most excellent in beautie, and were renowned of many Poets, as they that were allowed for beautifull of him that ought to have a most perfect judgement in beautie?

Here the Lorde Cesar declaring him selfe not satisfied, nor willing to consent by any meanes, that anie man could tast of the delite that he felt in beholding the beautie of a certain woman,[1] but hee him selfe began to speake, and then was there heard a great scraping of feet in the flore, with a cherme of loud speaking, and upon that every man turning him selfe about, saw at the chamber doore appeare a light of Torches, and by and by after entred in the Lord Generall[2] with a great and noble traine, who was then returned from accompanying the Pope a peece of the way.

And at the first entrie into the Palace, demaunding what the Dutches did, hee was certified what kinde of pastime they had in hande that night, and howe the charge was committed to Count Lewis, to entreat of courting. Therefore he hasted him as much as he could to come betime to heare somwhat.

And so soone as hee had saluted the Dutches, and setled the rest that were risen up at his comming, he sat him downe in the circle among them, and certaine of the chief of his traine, among which were the Marques Phebus of Ceva and Ghirardin brethren, Maister Hector of Rome, Vincent Calmeta, Horace Floridus, and many other. And when all was whist, the Lord Generall said.

My Lordes, my comming should bee too hurtfull if I shoulde hinder such good communication as I gesse was even now among you.

---

[1] "Beautie of a certain woman": cf. "a woman's beauty."

[2] "Lord Generall": cf. "Lord Prefect." Francesco della Rovere, heir adoptive of the Duchy, nephew of Julius II., and Prefect of Rome. The state of his entrance and mature dignity of his speech in this passage require Castiglione's further comment, a little later, to assure us that it is a boy of seventeen who has entered—all the more so when it is recalled that the boy was a firebrand: the next year he killed his sister's lover or "seducer" (Castiglione elsewhere passes over it very lightly), and a few years later killed Cardinal Alidosi for smiling at him. Admittedly the time was inopportune for smiling. Francesco had just come hot from the presence of Julius II., who had violently belaboured him with words for having been defeated by the French Marshal Trivulzio, and having lost Bologna for the Pontiff. Micheal Angelo's great statue of Julius II. was in that city; we may add, they made a cannon out of it, and, crowning the insult, named the piece La Giulia.

Therefore doe you me not this injurie, to deprive both your selves and mee of this pleasure.

Then answered Count Lewis, I believe (my Lord) silence ought rather to please all parties than speaking. For seeing it hath beene my lot this night before all other to take this travaile in hand, it hath now wearied me in speaking, and I weene all the rest in hearing, because my talke hath not beene worthie of this company, nor sufficient inough for the waightinesse of the matter I have beene charged withall, wherein since I have litle satisfied my selfe, I recken I have much lesse satisfied others.

Therefore (my Lorde) your lucke hath beene good to come at the latter end, and now shall it be well done to give the entreprise of that is behinde to an other that may succeede in my rowme. For whosoever hee be, I knowe well he will much better acquite him selfe than I should do, if I went forward with it, being thus wearie as I am.

This will I in no wise permit, answered the Lorde Julian, to be deceived of the promise ye have made. And I know well the Lorde Generall will not be against the understanding of that point.

And what promise was that, quoth the Count? The Lord Julian answered: To declare unto us in what sort the Courtier ought to use those good conditions and qualities which you say are meete for him.

The Lorde Generall, although he were but a childe in yeares, yet was hee wise and discrete, more than a man would thinke belonged unto those tender yeares of his, and in every gesture hee declared with a greatnesse of mind, a certaine quicknesse of wit, which did sufficiently prognosticate the excellent degree of honor and vertue, whereunto afterwarde he ascended.

Wherefore he saide incontinently[1]: if all this be behind yet to bee spoken of[2] (mee thinke) I am come in good season. For understanding[3] in what sort[4] the Courtier must use his good conditions and qualities, I shall know also what they are, and thus shall I come to the knowledge of all that have beene spoken hitherto.

Therefore sticke not (Count) to pay this debt, being alreadie discharged of one part thereof.

I should not have so great a debt to discharge, answered the Count, if the paines were equally devided, but the fault hath

[1] "Incontinently": cf. "quickly."
[2] Cf. "if all this is to be told."
[3] "For understanding": cf. "For by hearing."
[4] "Sort": cf. "way."

beene in giving a Ladie authoritie to command, that is too partiall: and so smyling he beheld the Ladie Emilia, which said immediately.

You ought not to complaine of my partialitie, yet since you doe it against reason, we will give one part of this honour, which you call paines, unto an other: and turning her unto Sir Fredericke Fergoso.

You (quoth she) propounded this devise of the Courtier, therefore reason willeth ye should say somewhat in it: and that shall be to fulfil the Lord Julians request, in declaring in what sort, manner and time the Courtier ought to practise his good conditions and qualities, and those other thinges which the Count hath saide are meete for him.

Then Sir Fredericke, Madame (quoth he) where ye will sever the sort, the time, and the manner of good conditions and qualities, and the well practising of the Courtier, ye will sever that can not be sundred: for it is these thinges that make the conditions and qualities good, and the practising good.

Therefore since the Count hath spoken so much and so well, and also saide somwhat of these circumstances, and prepared for the rest in his minde that he had to say, it were but reason he should go forwarde untill hee came to the end.

The Ladie Emilia answered: Set the cause you were the Count your selfe, and spake that your mind giveth you he would doe, and so shal all be well.

Then said Calmeta, my Lordes, since it is late, least Sir Fredericke should finde a scuse to utter that hee knoweth, I believe it were well done to defere the rest of the communication untill to morrow, and bestow the small time that remaineth about some other pastime without ambition.[1]

The which being agreed upon of all hands, the Dutchesse willed the Lady Margaret and the Ladie Constance Fregosa, to shew them a daunce.

Wherefore Barletta immediately, a very pleasant Musition, and an excellent dauncer, who continually kept all the Court in mirth and joy, began to play upon his Instruments, and they hand in hand shewed them a daunce or two,[2] with a very good grace and great pleasure to the lookers on.

That done, because it was farre in night, the Dutchesse arose upon her feete, and so every man taking his leave reverently of her, departed to his rest.

[1] Cf. "in some other quiet diversion."
[2] Cf. "danced first a basset and then a *roegarze*."

# SECOND BOOK

## THE SECOND BOOKE OF THE COURTIER, OF COUNT BALDESSER CASTILION, UNTO MAISTER ALFON-SUS ARIOSTO

NOT without marvel manie a time and often have I considered with my selfe, how one errour shoulde arise, the which because it is generallye seene in olde men, a man may beleve it is proper and naturall unto them: and that is, how (in a manner) al of them commend the times past, and blame the times present: dispraysinge our doings and maners, and whatsoever they did not in their youth:

Affirming moreover every good custome and good trade[1] of living, every vertue, finally each thinge to decline alwaies from evil to worse.

And in good sooth it seemeth a matter verie wide from reason, and worthie to be noted, that ripe age which with long practise is wont to make mens judgementes more perfect in other things, should in this behalfe so corrupt them, that they shoulde not discerne, y$^t$ if the world waxed worse and worse, and the fathers were generally better than the children, we shoulde long ere this time have beene come to that utmost degree of ill that can not waxe worse. And yet doe we see not onely in our dayes, but also in times past that this hath alwaies beene the peculiar vice of that age.[2]

The which is to be manifestly gathered by the wrytings of many most auncient authors, and especially Comedie writers, which expresse better than the rest, the trade of mans life.

The cause therfore of this false opinion in olde men, I believe (in mine opinion) is, for that, yeares wearing away, carry also with them many commodities, and among other take away from the bloud a great part of the lively spirites that altereth the complexion, and the instruments waxe feeble, whereby the soule worketh her effects.[3]

Therefore the sweete flowers of delyte vade away in that

---

[1] "Trade": cf. "manner."          [2] "That age": cf. "old age."
[3] Cf. "exerts its powers."

season out of our harts, as the leaves fall from the trees after harvest, and in steade of open and cleare thoughts, there entreth cloudie and troublous heavinesse accompanied with a thousand heart griefes: so that not onely the bloud, but the minde is also feeble: neither of the former pleasures receiveth it any thing els but a fast memorie, and the print[1] of the beloved time of tender age, which when wee have upon us, the heaven, the earth, and each thing to our seeming rejoyceth and laugheth alwaies about our eyes, and in thought (as in a savorie and pleasant Garden) flourisheth the sweete spring time of mirth, so that peradventure it were not unprofitable, when now in the colde season, the Sunne of our life (taking away from us our delites) beginneth to draw towarde the West, to lose in like case therewithall the mindfulnes of them, and to finde out (as Themistocles saith) an arte to teach us to forget: for the senses of our bodies are so deceivable, that they beguile many times also the judgement of the minde.

Therefore (me thinke) olde men be like unto them, that sayling in a vessell out of an haven, beholde the ground with their eyes, and the vessell to their seeming standeth still and the shore goeth: and yet is it cleane contrarie, for the haven, and likewise the time and pleasures continue still in their estate, and we with the vessel of mortalitie fleing away, go one after another through the tempestuous sea, that swalloweth up and devoureth all thinges, neither is it graunted us at any time to come on shore againe, but alwaies beaten with contrarie windes, at the ende wee breake our vessell at some rocke.

Because therefore the minde of old age is without order subject to many pleasures,[2] it can not taste them: and even as to them that bee sicke of a Fever, when by corrupt vapours they have lost their taste, all wines appeare most bitter, though they be precious and delicate in deede: so unto olde men for their unaptnesse, (wherein notwithstanding desire faileth them not) pleasures seeme without tast and cold, much differing from those that remember they have proved in foretime, although the pleasures in themselves be the selfe same.

Therefore when they feele them selves voide of them, it is a griefe, and they blame the time present for ill, not perceiving that this chaunce proceedeth of them selves, and not of the time.

And contrariwise, when they call to minde the pleasures past, they remember therewithall the time they had them in, and

---

[1] "Print": cf. "image."
[2] Cf. ". . . the senile mind is an unfit subject for many pleasures."

therefore commend it for good, because to their weening[1] it carrieth with it a savour of it, which they felt in them when it was present.[2]

By reason that in effect our mindes conceive an hatred against all thinges that have accompanied our sorrowes, and love such as have accompanied our pleasures.

Upon this it commeth, that unto a lover it is most acceptable, sometime to beholde a windowe though it be shut, because otherwhiles[3] it may be his chaunce to see his maistresse there: in like manner to see a ring, a letter, a garden, or any other place, or what ever other thing he supposeth hath beene a witting testimoniall of his pleasures.

And contrariwise, oftentimes a faire trimmed and well decked Chamber is abhorred of him that hath been kept prisoner in it, or abidden therin any other sorrow.

And in my dayes I have knowne some that will never drinke of a cup like unto that wherein in their sicknes they had taken a medicine. For even as that window, ring, or letter, doth bring to the minde a sweete remembrance unto the one, that so much pleaseth him, for that he imagineth it was a parcell[4] of his pleasures, so unto the other the chamber or cup seemeth to bring with the memorie, his sicknesse or imprisoning againe.

The verie same cause (I believe) moveth olde men to prayse the times past, and discommend the present.

Therefore as they talke of other thinges, so doe they also of Courtes, affirming such as have beene in their memory to be much more excellent and farre better furnished with notable men, than we see them to bee that are now adayes.

And immediately when they enter into this kinde of talke, they beginne to extoll with infinite prayses the Courtiers of Duke Philip, of Duke Borso,[5] and declare the sayings of Nicholas Piccininus,[6] and rehearse that in those times a man shoulde verie seldome have heard of a murther committed, and no combates, no crafts nor deceites, but a certaine faithfull and loving good meaning[7] among all men, and an upright dealing. And in Courtes at that time there raigned such good conditions,

---

[1] ". . . weening,": cf. "because it seems."
[2] "When it," etc.: cf. "when these were enjoyed."
[3] "Otherwhiles," etc: cf. "once, it may have been."
[4] Cf. "part."
[5] Duke Filippo Maria Visconti, of Milan (born 1391, died 1447). Duke Borso d'Este, of Ferrara (born 1413, died 1471).
[6] Niccolo Piccinino (born 1380, died 1444), a famous *condottiere*, friend and general of Duke Federico of Urbino, celebrated also for his wit.
[7] Cf. "a certain frank and kindly good will."

and such honestie, that the Courtiers were (in a manner) religious folke[1]: and woe unto him that shoulde have spoken an evil word of an other, or made but a signe otherwise than honestie to a woman.

And on the other side, they say in these dayes every thing is cleane contrary, and not onely that brotherly love and manerly conversation is lost among Courtiers, but also in Courtes there raigneth nothing els but envy and malice, ill manners, and a most wanton life in every kinde of vice: the women enticefull,[2] past shame, and the men womanish.

They dispraise also the apparrell to be dishonest[3] and too soft. To be short, they speake against infinit things, among the which many in very deede deserve to be discommended, for it can not be excused, but there are many evil and naughtie men among us, and this our age is much more full of vices, than was that which they commend.

But (me thinke) they do ful ill scanne the cause of this difference, and they be fonde persons, because they would have all goodnesse in the world without any ill, which is unpossible.

For since ill is contrarie to good, and good to ill, it is (in a manner) necessarie by contrarietie and a certaine counterpeise[4] the one shoulde underproppe and strengthen the other, and where the one wanteth or encreaseth,[5] the other to want or increase also: because no contrarie is without his other contrarie.

Who knoweth not that there should bee no justice in the worlde, were it not for wronge? no stoutnesse of courage, were there not faint harted? nor continencie, were there not incontinencie? nor health, were there not sicknesse? nor truth, were there not lyes? nor happinesse were there not mischaunces?

Therefore Socrates saith well in Plato,[6] that hee marvaileth that Esope made not an Apologus or fable, wherin he might have fained that God, since hee coulde never couple pleasure and sorrow together, might have knit them with an extremitie,[7] so that the beginning of the one should have beene the end of the other. For wee see no pleasure can delite us at any time if sorrow goeth not before.

Who can love rest well, unlesse hee have first felt the griefe of wearinesse? Who favoureth meate, drinke, and sleepe, if hee have not first felt hunger, thirst, and watching?

[1] Cf. "were like monks."  
[2] "Enticefull": cf. "lascivious."  
[3] "Dishonest": cf. "indecorous."  
[4] Cf. "by force of opposition and counterpoise."  
[5] Cf. "wanes or waxes."  
[6] Cf. *Phædo*, c. 3.  
[7] Cf. "joined them by their extremities."

I believe therefore passions and diseases are given to men of [1] nature, not principally to make them subject to them, for it were not meete that she which is the mother of all goodnesse, shoulde by her owne purposed advise give us so many evils, but since nature doth make health, pleasure and other goodnesse, consequently after these, were joyned diseases, sorrowes and other evils.

Therefore since vertues were graunted to the world for favor and gift of nature, by and by were vices by that linked contrarietie necessarily accompanied with them: so that the one encreasing or wanting, the other must in like manner encrease or want.

Therefore when our olde men prayse the Courtes of times past because there were not in them so vitious men, as some that are in ours, they do not know that there were not also in them so vertuous men, as some that are in ours.

The which is no wonder, for no ill is so evil, as that which ariseth of the corrupt seede of goodnesse.

And therefore where nature nowe bringeth forth much better wittes than she did tho, even as they that be given to goodnesse doe much better than did those of their time, so also they that bee given to ill doe much worse.

Therefore it is not to bee saide, that such as abstained from doing ill, because they knewe not how to doe it, deserve in that case any prayse: for although they did but a litle ill, yet did they the worst they knew.

And that the wittes of those times were generally much inferiour to these now adayes, a man may judge by all that hath proceeded from them, as letters, painting, statutes, buildings and all other things.

Againe these olde men discommend many things in us, which of them selves are neither good nor badde, onely because they did them not: and say it is no good sight to see yong men on horsebacke about the streetes, and especially upon Mules,[2] nor to weare furres nor side garments in winter, nor to weare a cappe befor a man bee at the least eighteene yeares of age, and such other matters, wherein truely they be much deceived. For these fashions (beside that they be commodious and profitable [3]) are brought up by custome, and generally men delite in them, as at

[1] "Of": cf. "by."
[2] "Especially upon Mules": cf. (!) "still less in pumps." In Italian, "massimamente nelle mula"—"mula" means both "mule" and "slipper"; hence Hoby's slip.
[3] Cf. "convenient and useful.'

that time they were contented to goe in their jacket, in their breechlesse hose, and in their lowe shoes with latchets,[1] and (to appeare fine) carry all daye long a Hauke upon their fist, without purpose, and daunce without touching a womans hand, and used many other fashions, the which as they are now stale, so were they at that time much set by.

Therefore may it be lawfull for us also to follow the custome of our times, without controlement of these olde men, which going about to prayse themselves, say.

When I was twentie yeares olde I lay with[2] my mother and sisters, nor a great while after wist I what women ment: and now children are not so soone crept out of the shell, but they know more naughtinesse, than they that were come to mans state did in those dayes.

Neither be they aware in so saying, that they confirme our children to have more wit than their old men.

Let them leave therefore speaking against our times, as full of vices: for in taking away them, they take also away the vertues. And let them remember that among the good men of auntient time, when as the glorious wits florished in the world, which in very deede were of most perfection in every vertue, and more than manly,[3] there were also many most mischievous, which if they had still lived, shoulde have excelled our ill men so much in ill, as those good men in goodnes: and of this doe all Histories make full mention.

But unto these olde men I weene I have made a sufficient answere. Therefore we will leave apart this discourse, perhaps too tedious, but not altogether out of purpose: and being sufficient to have declared that the Courtes of our time are worthie no lesse praise than those that old men commend so much, we will attend to our communication that was had about the Courtier, whereby a man may easily gather in what degree the Court of Urbin was among the rest, and what manner a Prince and Ladie they were that had such noble wittes attending upon them, and how fortunate all they might call them selves that lived in that familiar fellowship.

When the day following therefore was come, there was great and sundrie talke betweene the gentlemen and Ladies of the Court upon the disputation of the night before: which arose a

---

[1] Cf. "in gala dress with open breeches and polished pumps."

[2] Cf. "still slept with."

[3] "Good men of auntient time," etc.: cf. "the worthies of old, in the ages when there lived those spirits who were glorious and truly divine in every virtue, and those more than human minds . . ."

great part of it, upon the Lorde Generalles greedy desire, to understand as much as had beene said in the matter, who had enquired it almost of every man: and (as it is alwaies wont to come to passe) it was reported unto him sundrie waies, for some praysed one thing, some an other.

And also among many, there was a contention of the Countes own meaning,[1] for every man did not so fully beare in mind the matters that had been spoken. Therfore almost the whole day was spent about talking in this, and as soone as night drew on, the Lord Generall commanded meat to bee set on the borde, and tooke all the Gentlemen with him.

And immediatly after supper hee repayred to the Dutchesse chamber: who, beholding so great a company assembled sooner than they had done at other times, saide.

Me thinke, it is a great waight, Sir Fredericke, that is laide upon your shoulders, and a great expectation that you must satisfie.

Here not tarrying for Sir Frederickes aunswere, and what great waight (I beseech ye) is it, saide then Unico Aretino:

Who is so foolish that when he can doe a thing, wil not doe it in a fitte and due time? Reasoning in this wise about the matter everie man sat him downe in his wonted place and manner[2] with very heedfull expectation of the propounded talke.

Then Sir Fredericke turning him to Unico, doe you not thinke then M. Unico (quoth he) that I am laden this night with a great and painefull burden, since I must declare in what sorte, manner and time, the Courtier hath to practise his good conditions and qualities, and to use those other things that are alreadie saide to bee meete for him?

Me thinke it is no great matter, answered Unico: and I believe a good judgement in the Courtier is sufficient for all this, which the Count saide well yesterday night that he ought to have: and in case be so, without any other precepts, I suppose hee may practise wel inough the thing that hee knoweth, in due time and after a good sorte.

The which to bring more particularly into rule, were too hard a matter, and perhaps more than needeth, for I know not who is so fond to goe about his fence,[3] when the rest bee in their musicke: or to goe about the streetes dancing the morisco, though he could doe it never so well: or going about to comfort

---

[1] Cf. "disagreement as to the Count's real opinion."
[2] "Manner": cf. "order."
[3] Cf. "I know no man so stupid as to wish to fence . . ."

a mother that had buried her childe, to begin to talke with her of pleasant matters and merie conceites. I believe surely no gentleman will doe this, unlesse hee were cleane out of his wits.

Me thinke (M. Unico) quoth sir Fredericke then, ye harpe too much upon your extremities.[1] For it happeneth otherwhile, a man is so fond, that hee remembreth not him selfe so easily,[2] and oversights are not all alike.

And it may be, that a man shall abstaine from a common folly which is too manifest, as that is you speake of, to goe daunce the Morisco in the market place, and yet shall he not refraine from praysing him selfe out of purpose, from using a noysome sawsinesse, from casting out otherwhile a word thinking to make men laugh, which for that it is spoken out of time will appeare colde and without grace.

And these oversights oftentimes are covered with a certaine veile that suffereth a man not to forget who doth them, unlesse hee take no heede to them.[3]

And although for many causes our sight discerneth but litle, yet for ambitions sake it is darkened in especiall, for every man willingly setteth forth him selfe in that he perswadeth himselfe he knoweth whether this perswasion of his be true or false.

Therefore the well behaving of a mans selfe in this case (me thinke) consisteth in certaine wisedome and judgement of choice, and to know more and lesse what encreaseth or diminisheth in thinges, to practise them in due time, or out of season.[4]

And for all the Courtier bee of so good a judgement that he can discerne these differences, yet shall he the sooner compasse that he seeketh, if this imagination be opened with some rule,[5] and the waies shewed him, and (as it were) the places where he should ground himselfe uppon, than if hee should take him selfe onely to the generallitie.

For so much as therefore the Count yesterday night entreated upon Courtiership so copiously and in so good a manner, hee hath made me (truely) conceive no small feare and doubt that I shall not so throughly satisfie this noble audience in the matter that lyeth upon me to discourse in, as he hath doone in that was his charge. Yet to make my selfe partener in what I may of his

---

[1] "Harpe . . . extremities": cf. "run too much to extremes."

[2] Cf. "For sometimes one may be silly in a way that is not so easily seen."

[3] Cf. "that does not suffer them to be seen by him who commits them, unlesse he searches for them with care."

[4] i.e. from being practised unseasonably or seasonably.

[5] Cf. "if he were to broaden his mind by a few precepts."

praise, and to be sure not to erre (at the least in this parte) I will not contrarie him in any point.

Wherefore agreeing to his opinions, and beside the rest, as touching noblenesse of birth, wit and disposition of person, and grace of countenance, I say unto you that to get him worthie prayse and a good estimation with all men, and favour with such great men as he shal attend upon, me thinke it is behoveful he have the understanding to frame all his life and to set forth his good qualities generally in company with all men without purchasing him selfe envy.[1]

The which how hard a matter it is of it selfe, a man may consider by the seldomnesse of such as are seene to attaine to that point: because we are all the sorte of us in very deede more inclined of nature to dispraise faultes, than to commend thinges well done. And a man would thinke that many by a certaine rooted malice, although they manifestly discerne the goodnesse, enforce them selves with all studie and diligence to finde in things either a fault, or at the least the likenesse of a fault.

Therefore it behoveth our Courtier in all his doings to be charie and heedfull, and what so he saith or doth to accompany it with wisedom,[2] and not onely to set his delite to have in him selfe partes and excellent qualities, but also to order the tenor of his life after such a trade,[3] that the whole may be answerable unto these parts, and see the selfe same to bee alwaies and in every thing such, that it disagree not from it selfe, but make one bodie of these good qualities, so that every deede of his may bee compact and framed of all the vertues, as the Stoikes say the duetie of a wise man is: although notwithstanding alwaies one vertue is the principall, but all are so knit and linked one to another, that they tende to one end, and all may be applyed and serve to every purpose.

Therefore it behoveth hee have the understanding to set them forth, and by comparison, and (as it were) contrarietie of the one, sometime to make the other better knowne: as the good painters with a shadow make the lights of high places to appeare, and so with light make low[4] the shadowes of plaines, and meddle[5] divers colours together, so that through that diversitie both the one and the other are more sightly to beholde, and the placing of the figures contrarie the one to the other is

---

[1] "Purchasing . . .": cf. "exciting envy."
[2] Cf. "to mingle good sense" with it.
[3] "Trade": cf. "fashion."
[4] Cf. "deepen."
[5] "Meddle": cf. "assemble."

a helpe to them to doe the feate that the painters mind is to bring to passe.

So that lowlinesse [1] is much to be commended in a gentleman that is of prowesse and well seene in armes: and as that fiercenesse seemeth the greater when it is accompanied with sober mood,[2] even so doth sober moode encrease and shew it selfe the more through fiercenesse.

Therefore litle speaking, much doing, and not praysing a mans owne selfe in commendable deedes, dissembling them after an honest sorte,[3] doth encrease both the one vertue and the other in a person that can discretely use this trade: and the like is to be saide in all the other good qualities.

Therefore will I have our Courtier in that he doth or saith to use certaine generall rules, the which (in my minde) containe briefly as much as belongeth to mee to speake.

And for the first and chiefe let him avoid (as the Count saide well in that behalfe yesternight) above all thinges curiositie.[4]

Afterwarde let him consider well what the thing is he doth or speaketh, the place where it is done, in presence of whom, in what time, the cause why he doth it, his age, his profession, the end wherto it tendeth, and the meanes that may bring him to it: and so let him apply him selfe discretely with these advertisements to what soever hee mindeth to doe or speake.

After Sir Fredericke had thus saide, he seemed to stay a while. Then saide M. Morello of Ortona: mee thinke these your rules teach but litle. And I for my part am as skilfull now as I was before you spake them, although I remember I have heard them at other times also of ye Friers with whom I have beene in confession, and I ween they terme them circumstances.[5]

Then laughed Sir Fredericke and saide: if you doe well beare in minde, the Count willed yesternight that the chiefe profession of the Courtier shoulde bee in armes, and spake very largely in what sort he should doe it, therefore will we make no more rehearsall thereof.

Yet by our rule it may bee also understood, that where the Courtier is at skirmish, or assault, or battaile upon the lande, or in such other places of enterprise, he ought to worke the matter wisely in separating him selfe from the multitude, and undertake notable and bolde feates which hee hath to doe, with as litle company as he can, and in the sight of noble men that

---

[1] Cf. "gentleness."
[2] "Fiercenesse . . . sober mood": cf. "boldness . . . modesty."
[3] Cf. "tactfully."      [4] "Curiositie": cf. "affectation."
[5] Cf. "who called them 'the circumstances.'"

be of most estimation in the campe, and especially in the presence and (if it were possible) before the very eyes of his king or great personage he is in service withall: for in deede it is meete to set forth to the shew things wel done.

And I believe even as it is an evil matter to seeke a false renowne, and in the thing he deserveth no prayse at all, so is it also an ill matter to defraud a mans selfe of his due estimation, and not to seeke that prayse, which alone is the true rewarde of vertuous enterprises.

And I remember I have knowne of them in my time, that for all they were of prowesse, yet in this point they have shewed them selves but grosse headed, and put their life in as great hazarde to goe take a flocke of sheepe, as in being the formost to scale the walles of a battered towne, the which our Courtier will not doe if hee beare in mind the cause that bringeth him to warre, which ought to be onely his estimation.[1]

And if he happen moreover to be one to shew feates of Chivalrie in open sights, at tilt, turney, or *Joco di canne*, or in any other exercise of the person, remembring the place where he is, and in presence of whom, hee shall provide before hand to be in his armour no lesse handsom and sightly than sure, and feede the eyes of the lookers on with all thinges that hee shall thinke may give a good grace, and shall doe his best to get him a horse set out with faire harnesse and sightly trappings, and to have proper devises, apt posies, and wittie inventions that may draw unto him the eyes of the lookers on as the Adamant stone doth yron.

He shall never be among the last that come forth into the listes to shew themselves, considering the people, and especially women take much more heede to the first than to the last: because the eyes and mindes that at the beginning are greedy of that noveltie, note every lite matter, and printe it[2]: afterwarde by continuance they are not onely full, but wearie of it.

Therefore was there a noble Stageplayer in olde time that for this respect would alwaies be the first to come forth to play his part.

In like manner also if our Courtier doe but talke of armes, he shall have an eye to the profession of them hee talketh withall, and according to that frame himselfe, and use one maner of talke with men, and an other with women: and in case hee will touch any thing sounding to his owne praise, he shall doe it so

---

[1] "Estimation": cf. "honour."
[2] Cf. "observe and are impressed by every trifle."

dissemblingly as it were a chaunce and by the way, and with the discretion and warinesse that Count Lewis shewed us yesterday.

Doe you not now thinke (M. Morello) that our rules can teach somewhat? Trow you not that that friend of ours I tolde you of a few daies ago had cleane forgotten with whom hee spake, and why? When to entertaine a gentle woman whom he never saw before, at his first entring in talke with her, he began to tell how many men he had slaine, and what a hardie felow hee was, and how hee coulde play at two hand sword.

And had never done until he had taught her how to defend certaine strokes with a Pollaxe[1] being armed, and how unarmed, and to shew how (in a mans defence) to laye hand[2] upon a dagger, so that the poore gentlewoman stood upon thornes, and thought an houre a thousand yeare till she were got from him, for feare least he would goe nigh to kill her as hee had done those other.

Into these errours runne they that have not an eye to the circomstances which you say you have heard of Friers.

Therefore I say of the exercises of the bodie, some there are that (in a manner) are never practised but in open shew, as running at tilt, barriers, *Joco de canne*, and all the rest that depende uppon Armes.

Therefore when our Courtier taketh any of these in hand, first he must provide to bee so well in order for Horse, harnesse, and other furnitures belonging thereto, that he want nothing. And if he see not him selfe throughly furnished in all pointes, let him not meddle at all. For if he be not well, it can not be excused that it is not his profession.

After this, he ought to have a great consideration in presence of whome hee sheweth him selfe, and who be his matches. For it were not meet that a gentleman should be present in person and a doer in such a matter in the countrey,[3] where the lookers on and the doers were of a base sorte.

Then said the Lorde Gasper Pallavicin. In our countrey of Lumbardy these matters are not passed upon,[4] for you shall see the yong gentleman upon the holy dayes come daunce all the day long in the sunne with them of the countrey, and passe the time with them in casting the barre, in wrastling, running and leaping. And I believe it is not ill done. For no comparison

---

[1] Cf. "how certain blows of the battle-axe ought to be parried."
[2] Cf. "to show the different ways of grasping the handle."
[3] "A matter in the countrey": cf. "a rustic festival."
[4] Cf. "we do not make these distinctions."

is there made of noblenesse of birth, but of force and sleight,[1] in which thinges many times the men of the countrey are not a whit inferiour to gentlemen, and it seemeth this familiar conversation conteyneth in it a certaine lovely freenesse.[2]

This dauncing in the sunne, answered Sir Fredericke, can I in no case away with all[3] : and I can not see what a man shall gaine by it.

But who so will wrastle, runne and leape with men of the countrey, ought (in my judgement) to doe it after a sorte: to prove himselfe[4] and (as they are wont to say) for courtisie, not to try maistry[5] with them: and a man ought (in a manner) to be assured to get the upper hand, else let him not meddle withall, for it is too ill a sight and too foule a matter and without estimation, to see a gentleman overcome by a carter, and especially in wrastling.

Therefore I believe it is well done to abstaine from it, at the least wise in presence of many, because if hee overcome his gaine is small, and his losse in being overcome very great.

Also they play at tenise (in manner) alwaies in open sight, and this is one of the common games, which the multitude with their presence much set forth.

I will have our Courtier therefore to doe this and all the rest beside handling his weapon, as a matter that is not his profession: and not to seeme to seeke or looke for any prayse for it.

Nor yet will I have him to be acknowne that he bestoweth much studie or time about it, although he doe it excellently well. Neither shall he bee like unto some that have a delite in musicke, and in speaking with whom soever, alwaies when he maketh a pause in their talke, beginne in a voice as though he would sing. Other walking in the streetes or in the Churches, goe alwaies dansing. Other meeting in the market place or wheresoever any friend, make a gesture as though they would play at fence, or wrastle according as their delite is.

Here saide the Lord Cesar Gonzaga, we have in Rome a young Cardinall that doth better than so, which feeling him selfe lustie of person, leadeth as many as come to visite him (though hee never saw them before) into a garden, and is very instant uppon them to strip themselves into their doublet to leape with him.

[1] Cf. "strength and agility."
[2] "Lovely freenesse": cf. "pleasant touch of generosity."
[3] "I . . . with all": cf. "pleases me not in any way."
[4] Cf. "for practice."   [5] "Maistry": cf. "rivalry."

Sir Fredericke laughed, afterwarde hee proceeded on. There be some other exercises that may be done both openly and privately, as dancing: and in this I believe the Courtier ought to have a respect,[1] for if he daunceth in the presence of many, and in a place full of people, he must (in my minde) keepe a certaine dignitie, tempered notwithstanding with a handsome and sightly sweetenesse of gestures.

And for all he feeleth him selfe very nimble and to have time and measure at will, yet let him not enter into that swift-nesse of feet and doubled footinges, that we see are very comely in our Barletta, and peradventure were unseemely for a gentle-man: although privately in a chamber together as we be now, I will not say but hee may doe both that, and also dance the Morisco, and braulles,[2] yet not openly unlesse hee were in a maske.

And though it were so that all men knew him, it skilleth not, for there is no way to that, if a man will shew him selfe in open sights about such matters,[3] whether it be in armes, or out of armes. Because to be in a maske bringeth with it a certaine libertie and licence, that a man may among other thinges take upon him the forme of that he hath better skill in, and use bent studie and precisenesse about the principall drift of the matter[4] wherein he will shew himselfe, and a certaine recklesnesse[5] about that is not of importance, which augmenteth the grace of the thing, as it were to disguise a yong man in an olde mans attier, but so that his garments be not a hindrance to him to shew his nimblenesse of person. And a man at armes in forme of a wilde[6] shepeheard, or some other such kinde of disguising, but with an excellent horse and well trimmed for the purpose, because the minde of the lookers on runneth forthwith to imagin the thing that is offered unto the eyes at the first shew, and when they behold afterwarde a far greater matter to come of it than they looked for under that attire, it delyteth them, and they take pleasure at it.

Therefore it were not meete in such pastimes and open shewes, where they take up counterfeiting of false visages, a prince should take upon him to bee like a prince in deede, because in so doing, the pleasure that the lookers on receive at the noveltie

---

[1] "A respect": cf. "a care."
[2] "Braulles": *brandi*, a dance something like the *cotillon*.
[3] "For there is no way to that," etc.: cf. "indeed there is no better way of displaying oneself in such matters at public sports" (than to be masked).
[4] Cf. "care and elaboration upon the chief point of the thing."
[5] "Recklesnesse": cf. "nonchalance."   [6] "Wilde": cf. "rustic."

of the matter shoulde want a great deale, for it is no noveltie at all to any man for a prince to bee a prince. And when it is perceyved that beside his being a prince, he will also beare the shape of a prince, he loseth the libertie to doe all those things that are out of dignitie of a prince.

And in case there any contentiō happen especially with weapon in these pastimes, he might easily make men believe that he keepeth the person of a prince because hee will not be beaten but spared of the rest: beside that, doing in sporte the verie same hee should doe in good earnest when neede required, it would take away his authoritie in deede, and would appeare in like case to be play also.

But in this point the prince stripping himselfe of the person of a prince, and mingling him selfe equally with his under-linges (yet in such wise that hee may bee known) with refusing superioritie, let him chalenge a greater superioritie, namely, to passe other men, not in authoritie, but in vertue, and declare that the prowesse is not encreased by his being a prince.

Therefore I say that the Courtier ought in these open sights of armes to have the selfe same respect according to his degree.

But in vauting, wrastling, running and leaping, I am well pleased he flee the multitude of people, or at the least be seene very seldome times. For there is no thing so excellent in the world, that the ignorant people have not their fil of, and smally regard it [1] in often beholding it.

The like judgement I have to Musicke: but I woulde not our Courtier should doe as many doe, that as soone as they come to any place, and also in the presence of great men with whome they have no acquaintance at all, without much entreating set out them selves to shew as much as they know, yea and many times that they know not, so that a man would weene they came purposely to shewe themselves for that, and that it is their principall profession.

Therefore let our Courtier come to shew his musick as a thing to passe the time withall, and as he were enforced to doe it, and not in the presence of noble men, nor of any great multitude.

And for all hee be skilfull and doth well understand it, yet will I have him to dissemble the studie and paines that a man must needes take in all thinges that are well done. And let him make semblance that he esteemeth but litle in himselfe that qualitie, but in doing it excellently well, make it much esteemed of other men.

[1] Cf. "and hold it of small account."

Then saide the Lord Gasper Pallavicin. There are many sortes of musike, as well in the brest as upon instruments,[1] therefore would I gladly learne which is the best, and at what time the Courtier ought to practise it.

Me thinke then answered Sir Frederieke, pricksong is a faire musicke, so it be done upon the booke surely and after a good sorte.[2] But to sing to the lute is much better, because all the sweetnes consisteth in one alone,[3] and a man is much more heedfull and understandeth better the feat manner, and the aire or veyne[4] of it, when the eares are not busied in hearing any moe than one voice: and beside every litle errour is soone perceived, which happeneth not in singing with company, for one beareth out an other.

But singing to the lute with the dittie[5] (me thinke) is more pleasant than the rest, for it addeth to the wordes such a grace and strength, that it is a great wonder.

Also all Instrumentes with freats are full of harmony, because the tunes of them are very perfect,[6] and with ease a man may doe many thinges upon them that fill the mind with sweetnesse of musicke.

And the musicke with a sette of Violes doth no lesse delite a man: for it is verie sweet and artificiall.[7]

A mans brest[8] giveth a great ornament and grace to all these instruments, in the which I will have it sufficient that our Courtier have an understanding. Yet the more cunninger he is upon them, the better it is for him, without medling much with the instruments that Minerva and Alcibiades refused, because it seemeth they are noysome.[9]

Now as touching the time and season when these sortes of musicke are to bee practised: I believe at all times when a man is in familiar and loving company, having nothing else adoe. But especially they are meete to be practised in the presence of women, because those sights sweeten the mindes of the hearers, and make them the more apt to bee pierced with the pleasantnesse of musicke, and also they quicken the spirits of the very doers.

[1] Cf. "vocal as well as instrumental."
[2] Cf. "to sing well by note, with ease and in a beautiful style."
[3] Cf. "lies in the solo part."
[4] Cf. "fine manner and the melody."
[5] Cf. "by way of recitative."
[6] Cf. "All keyed instruments also are pleasing to the ear, because they produce very perfect consonances."
[7] "Artificiall": cf. "exquisite."
[8] "Brest": cf. "the human voice."          [9] Cf. "ungraceful."

I am well pleased (as I have saide) they flee the multitude, and especially of the unnoble.

But the seasoning of the whole must be discretion, because in effect it were a matter unpossible to imagine all cases that fall. And if the Courtier bee a righteous judge of[1] him selfe, hee shall apply him selfe well inough to the time, and shall discerne when the hearers minds are disposed to give eare and when they are not. He shall know his age, for (to say the truth) it were no meete matter, but an ill sight to see a man of any estimation being old, hore-headed and toothlesse, full of wrinkles, with a lute in his armes playing upon it, and singing in the middest of a company of womē, although he coulde doe it reasonably well. And that because such songes containe in them wordes of love, and in olde men love is a thing to be jested at: although otherwhile he seemeth among other miracles of his to take delite in spite of yeares to set a fire frosen heartes.

Then answered the Lord Julian: doe you not barre poore olde men from this pleasure (Sir Fredericke) for in my time I have knowne men of yeares have very perfect brestes[2] and most nimble fingers for instruments, much more than some yong men.

I goe not about (quoth Sir Fredericke) to barre old men from this pleasure, but I wil barre you and these Ladies from laughing at that follie.

And in case olde men will sing to the lute, let them doe it secretely, and onely to rid their mindes of those troublesome cares and grievous disquieting that our life is full of: and to taste of that excellencie[3] which I believe Pythagoras and Socrates savoured in musicke.

And set case they exercise it not at all: for that they have gotten a certaine habite and custome of it, they shall favour it much better in hearing, than he that hath no knowledge in it: For like as the armes of a Smith that is weake in other thinges, because they are more exercised, bee stronger than an other bodies that is sturdie, but not exercised to worke with his armes: even so the armes that bee exercised in musicke, doe much better and sooner discerne it, and with much more pleasure judge of it, than other, how good and quicke soever they be, that have not beene practised in yᵉ variety of pleasant musicke: because those musical tunes pearce not, but without leaving any tast of themselves passe by yᵉ eares not accustomed to

---

[1] Cf. "rightly understands."
[2] "Brestes," etc.: cf. "right perfect voices."
[3] Cf. "rapture."

heare them, although the verie wilde beastes feele some delite in melodie.

This is therefore the pleasure meete for olde men to take in musicke.

The selfe same I say of dauncing, for in deede these exercises ought to be left off before age constraineth us to leave them whether we will or no.

It is better then, answered here M. Morello halfe chafed,[1] to except all old men, and to say that onely yong men are to be called Courtiers.

Then laughed Sir Fredericke and saide: Note (maister Morello) whether such as delite in these matters, if they bee not yong men, doe not studie to appeare young, and therefore dye their haire and make their bearde grow[2] twice a weeke, and this proceedeth upon that nature saith to them in secrete, that these matters are not comely but for yong men.

All these Ladies laughed, because they knewe these wordes touched maister Morello, and he seemed somwhat out of patience at the matter.

Yet are there other entertainementes with women, saide immediatly Sir Fredericke, meete for olde men.

And what be these (quoth maister Morello) to tell fables ?[3]

And that too, answered Sir Fredericke. But every age (as you know) carrieth with him his thoughts, and hath some peculiar vertue and some peculiar vice. And olde men for all they are ordinarilye wiser than yong men, more continent, and of a better foresight, yet are they withall more lavish in wordes, more greedy, harder to please, more fearefull, alwaies chafing in the house, sharpe to their children, and wil have every man wedded to their will.

And contrariwise, yong men are hardy, easie to be entreated,[4] but more apt to brawling and chiding, wavering and unstedfast, that love and unlove all at a time: given to all their delites, and enimies to them that tell them of their profit.

But of all the other ages, mans state is most temperate, which hath now done with the curst prankes of youth,[5] and not yet growne to auncientnes.[6]

---

[1] "Halfe chafed": cf. "with a little heat."
[2] "Make their bearde grow": cf. (!) "shave."
[3] "Fables": cf. "stories" —a thrust at Sir Frederick, so employed.
[4] Cf. "spirited, generous, frank . . ."
[5] Hoby at twenty-four is much sterner than Castiglione at twice those years. "Curst prankes . . .": cf. "the faults of youth."
[6] Cf. "to those of age."

These then that bee placed (as it were) in the extremities, it is behovefull for them to know how to correct the vices with reason, that nature hath bredde in them.

Therefore ought old men to take heede of much praysing them selves, and of the other vices, that wee have saide are proper to them, and suffer the wisedom and knowledge to beare stroke in them that they have gottē by long experience, and to be (as it were) Oracles, to the which every man should haunt for counsaile, and have a grace in uttering that they know, applying it aptly to the purpose, accompanying with grace of yeares a certaine temperate and merry pleasantnesse.

In this wise shall they be good Courtiers, and be well entertained with men and women, and every man will at all times be glad of their company, without singing or dauncing: and when need requireth they shall shewe their prowesse in matters of waight.

The very same respect and judgement shall yong men have, not in keeping the fashion of olde men (for what is meete for the one, were not in all pointes so fit for the other: and it is a common saying, To much gravitie in yong men is an ill signe) but in correcting the naturall vices in them.

Therefore delight I in a yong man, and especially a man at armes, if hee have a certaine sagenesse in him and few wordes, and somewhat demure, without those busie gestures and unquiet manners which wee see so many times in that age: for they seeme to have a certaine gift above other yong men.

Beside that, this milde behaviour containeth in it a kind of sightly fiercenesse,[1] because it appeareth to be stirred, not of wrath but of judgement, and rather governed by reason than appetite: and this (in manner) alwaies is knowne in all men of stomacke.

And we see it likewise in brute beastes, that have a certaine noble courage and stoutnesse above the rest: as the Lion and the Egle: neither is it voide of reason,[2] for so much as that violent and sodaine motion without wordes or other token of choler which with all force bursteth out together at once (as it were the shot of a gunne) from quietnes, which is contrarie to it, is much more violent and furious, than that which increaseth by degrees and waxeth hotte by litle and litle.

Therfore such going about some enterprise, are so full of wordes, they so leape and skip and can not stand still, that it appeareth they be ravished [3] in those matters, and (as our maister

---

[1] Cf. "impressive boldness."　　　　　[2] Cf. "strange."
[3] Cf. "exhaust their powers."

Peter Mount saith well) they doe like children, that going in the night sing for feare, as though yᵗ singing of theirs should make them plucke up their spirits to bee the bolder.

Even as therefore in a yong man a quiet and ripe youth is to be commended, because it appeareth that lightnesse (which is the peculiar vice of that age) is tempred and corrected: even so in an olde man a greene and lively old age is much to be esteemed, because it appeareth that the force of the mind is so much, that it heateth and giveth a certaine strength to that feeble and colde age, and maintaineth it in that middle state, which is the better parte of our life.

But in conclusion all these good qualities shall not suffise our Courtier to purchase him the generall favour of great men, gentlemen and Ladies, if he have not also a gentle and loving behaviour in his dayly conversation.

And of this I believe verily it is a hard matter to give any manner rule, for the infinite and sundrie matters that happen in practising one with an other: for so much as among all men in the worlde, there are not two to be found that in every point agree in minde together.

Therefore he that must be plyable to bee conversant with so many, ought to guide himselfe with his own judgement. And knowing the difference of one man and an other, every day alter, fashion and manner according to the disposition of them he is conversant withall.

And for my part I am not able in this behalfe to give him other rules than the aforesaide, which our maister Morello learned of a childe in confessing himselfe.[1]

Herein L. Emilia laughed and saide, you would ridde your hands of paines taking (Sir Fredericke) but you shall not escape so, for it is your part to minister talke untill it be bedtime.

And what if I have nothing to say (madam) how then, answered Sir Fredericke?

The Ladie Emilia saide: we shall now trye your wit. And if all be true I have hearde, there have beene men so wittie and eloquent, that they have not wanted matter to make a booke in the prayse of a flie, other in the praise of a quartaine Fever, an other in the prayse of baldnesse: doth not your hart serve you to finde out somewhat to say for one night of Courting?

We have alreadie, answered Sir Fredericke, spoken as much as will goe nigh to make two bookes. But since no excuse shall

[1] "In confessing": cf. "at the confessional."

serve, I will speake until you shall thinke I have fulfilled though not my dutie, yet my power.

I suppose the conversation which ye Courtier ought chiefly to bee plyable unto, with all diligence to get him favor, is the very same that he shall have with his prince. And although this name of conversation bringeth with it a certaine equalitie, that a man would not judge can raigne betweene the maister and the servant, yet will we so terme it for this once.

I will have our Courtier therefore (beside that he hath and doth dayly give men to understand that he is of the prowesse which wee have said ought to be in him) to turne all his thoughts and force of minde to love, and (as it were) to reverence the prince hee serveth above all other thinges, and in his wil, manners and fashions, to bee altogether plyable to please him.

Here without any longer stay, Peter of Naples said: of these Courtiers now adayes ye shall finde ynow, for (me thinke) in few words ye have painted us out a joly flatterer.

You are farre deceived, answered Sir Fredericke, for flatterers love not their Lordes, nor their friendes, the which I say unto you I will have principally in our Courtier.

And to please him, and to obey his commandements whom he serveth, may bee done without flatterie, for I meane the commandements that are reasonable and honest, or such as of themselves are neither good nor bad, as in gamming and pastime, and giving him selfe more to some one exercise than to an other. And to this will I have the Courtier to frame him selfe, though by nature he were not enclined to it: so that when-soever his Lord looketh upon him, hee may thinke in his minde that hee hath to talke with him of a matter that he wil be glad to heare. The which shall come to passe if there bee a good judgement in him to understande what pleaseth his prince, and a wit and wisedom to knowe how to apply it, and a bent will to make him pleased with the thing which perhaps by nature should displease him.

And having these principles, he shall never be sadde before his prince, nor melancholy, nor so soleyn as many, that a man would weene were at debate with their Lordes, which is truely a hatefull matter.

He shal not be ill tongued, and especially against his superi-ours which happeneth oftentimes: for it appeareth that there is a storme in courtes that carrieth this condition with it, that alwaies looke who so receiveth most benefits at the Lordes hands,[1] and is promoted from very base degree to high estate, hee is evermore complayning and reporteth worst of him: which is an uncomely thing, not onely for such as these be, but even for such as be ill handled in deed.

Our Courtier shall use no fond saucinesse. He shall be no carrier about of tryfling newes. He shall not be overseene[2] in speaking otherwhile wordes that may offend, where his intent was to please.

He shall not be stubborne and full of contention, as some busie bodies that a man would weene had none other delyte but to vexe and stirre men like flies, and take upon them to contrarie every man spitefully without respect. He shall be no babler, not given to lightnesse, no lyar, no boaster, nor fond flatterer, but sober, and keeping him alwaies within his boundes, use continually, and especially abroad, the reverence and respect that becommeth the servant toward the maister.

And shall not doe as many that meeting a prince how great soever he be, if they have once spoken with him before come towarde him with a certaine smyling and friendlye countenance, as though they would make of one their equall, or shew favour to an inferiour of theirs.

Very seldom or (in manner) never shall he crave any thing of his Lorde for him selfe, least the Lorde having respect to deny it him for him selfe, should not graunte it him without displeasure, which is farre worse.[3] Againe, in suing for others, he shall discretely observe the times, and his sute shall bee for honest and reasonable matters,[4] and he shal so frame his sute, in leaving out those points that he shall knowe will trouble him, and in making easie after a comely sort the lettes, that his Lorde wil evermore graunt it him and though he deny it, hee shall not thinke to have offended him whom he meant not to doe, for because great men oftentimes after they have denyed a request to one that hath sued to them with great instance, think the person that laboured to them so earnestly for it, was verie greedy of it, and therefore in not obtaining it, hath cause to beare him ill will that denyed him it, and upon this suspition they conceive an hatred against that person and

[1] Cf. "that those who have been most favoured . . ."
[2] "Overseene": cf. "thoughtless."
[3] Castiglione's frequent letters to his mother requiring money, clothes, and food, are good proof that he followed this counsel.
[4] It was a reasonable matter for Castiglione to try to have his young brother made a cardinal.

can never afterwarde brooke him nor afforde him good countenance.[1]

He shal not covet to presse into the chamber or other secrete places where his Lord is withdrawne, unlesse hee be bid, for all he bee of great authoritie with him: because great men oftentimes when they are privately gotten alone, love a certaine libertie to speake and doe what they please, and therefore will not bee seene or heard of any person that may lightly deeme of them, and reason willeth no lesse.

Therefore such as speake against great men for making of their chamber persons of no great qualitie in other thinges, but in knowing how to attend about their person (me thinke) commit an error: because I can not see why they should not have the libertie to refresh their mindes, which we our selves would have to refresh ours.

But in case the Courtier that is inured with waightie affaires, happen to be afterwarde secretly in chamber with him, he ought to change his coate, and to deferre grave matters till an other time and place, and frame him selfe to pleasant communication, and such as his Lord will be willing to give eare unto, least hee hinder that good moode of his. But herein and in all other thinges, let him have an especiall regarde, that he bee not combrous to him.

And let him rather looke to have favour and promotion offered him, than crave it so openly in the face of the world, as many doe, that are so greedie of it, that a man would weene, the not obtaining it greeveth them as much as the losse of life: and if they chaunce to enter into any displeasure, or els see other in favour, they are in such anguish of mind, that they can by no meanes dissemble the malice, and so make all men laugh them to scorne, and many times they are the cause that great men favour some one, onely to spite them withall.

And afterwarde if they happen to enter into favor, then passing a meane, they are so dronken in it, that they know not what to doe for joy: and a man would weene that they wist not what were become of their feete and handes, and (in a manner) are readie to call company to behold them, and to rejoyce with them, as a matter they have not been accustomed withall. Of this sorte I will not have our Courtier to be.

[1] Castiglione suffered for long on account of a request granted. He was first attached to the court of Mantua, and suing and obtaining permission to serve Guidobaldo of Urbino instead, won the almost relentless dislike of his first, and natural, lord, Federico Gonzaga. This was unfortunate, for his estates were in Mantuan territory, and at times he dared not visit them nor his mother who resided on them.

I woulde have him to esteeme favour and promotion, but for all that not to love it so much, that a man should thinke hee coulde not live without it. And when he hath it, let him not shew him selfe new or straunge in it, nor wonder at it when it is offered him.

Nor refuse it in such sort as some, that for very ignorance receive it not, and so make men believe that they acknowledge themselves unworthie of it.

Yet ought a man alwaies to humble him selfe somewhat under his degree, and not receive favor and promotions so easily as they be offered him, but refuse them modestly, shewing he much esteemeth them, and after such a sort, that he may give him an occasion that offereth them, to offer them with a great deale more instance.

Because the more resistance [1] a man maketh in such manner to receive them, the more doth he seeme to the prince that giveth them to be esteemed,[2] and that the benefit which hee bestoweth is so much the more, as he that receiveth it, seemeth to make of it, thinking him selfe much honoured thereby.

And these are the true and perfect promotions,[3] that make men esteemed of such as see them abroad [4]: because when they are not craved, every man conjectureth they arise of true vertue, and so much the more, as they are accompanied with modestie.

Then saide the Lord Cesar Gonzaga, me thinke ye have this clause out of the Gospel, where it is writen: When thou art bid to a mariage, goe and sit thee down in the lowest roome, that whē he commeth that bid thee, he may say, Friend come higher, and so it shall bee an honour for thee in the sight of the guestes.[5]

Sir Fredericke laughed and saide: it were too great a sacriledge to steale out of the Gospel. But you are better learned in scripture than I was aware of: then he proceeded.

See into what daunger they fall sometime, that rashly before a great man enter into talke unrequired, and many times that y^t Lord, to scorne them withall, maketh no answere, and turneth his head to the other hand: and in case hee doth make answere, every man perceiveth it is done full scornefully.

Therefore to purchase favour at great mens handes, there is no better way than to deserve it. Neither must a man hope when he seeth an other in favor with a prince, for whatsoever matter,

[1] "Resistance": cf. "reluctance."
[2] Cf. "the more highly will the prince who gives them think himself esteemed."
[3] "True and perfect promotions": cf. "true and solid favours."
[4] Cf. "from without."
[5] St. Luke iv. 8 and 10.

E 807

in folowing his steps to come to the same, because every thing is not fitte for every man. And ye shall finde otherwhile some one that by nature is so readie in his mery jestes, that what ever he speaketh, bringeth laughter with it, and a man would weene that he were borne onely for that: and if another that hath a grave fashion in him, of how good a wit soever he be, attempt the like, it will be very cold and without grace, so that hee will make a man abhore to heare him, and in effect will be like the Asse,[1] that to counterfeite the dogge, would play with his maister.

Therefore it is meete eche man know him selfe, and his owne disposition, and apply him selfe thereto, and consider what thinges are meete for him to follow, and what are not.

Before you goe any further, saide here maister Vincent Calmeta, if I have well marked, me thought ye saide right now, that the best way to purchase favour, is to deserve it: and the Courtier ought rather to tarry til promotions be offred him, than presumptuouslye to crave them.

I feare me least this rule be litle to purpose, and mee thinke experience doth us manifestly to understand the contrary: because now adaies very few are in favour with princes, but such as be malapert. And I wote well you can be a good witnesse of some, that perceiving themselves in small credite with their princes, are come up onely with presumption.

As for such as come to promotion with modestie, I for my part know none, and if I give you respite to bethinke your selfe, I believe ye will find out but few.

And if you marke the French court which at this day is one of the noblest in all Christendom, ye shal find that all such as are generally in favor there, have in them a certaine malapertnesse,[2] and that not onely one with an other, but with the king him selfe.

Doe you not so say, answered Sir Fredericke, for in Fraunce there are very modest and curteous gentlemen. Truth it is, that they use a certaine libertie and familiaritie without ceremonies, which is proper and natural unto them, and therfore it ought not to bee termed malapertnesse. For in that manner of theirs, although they laugh and jeast at such as be malapert, yet doe they set much by them that seeme to them to have any prowesse[3] or modestie in them.

---

[1] "The Asse," in Æsop's fable.
[2] "Have . . . malapertnesse": cf. "are somewhat presumptuous."
[3] "Prowesse": cf. "worth."

Calmeta answered: marke the Spaniards that seeme the very maisters of Courtly fashions, and consider how many ye find that with women and great men are not most malapert,[1] and so much worse [2] than the Frenchmen, in that at the first shew they declare a certaine modestie? And no doubt but they bee wise in so doing, because (as I have said) the great men of our time doe all favour such as are of these conditions.

Then answered Sir Fredericke: I can not abide (maister Vincent) that yee should defame in this wise the great men of our time, because there be many notwithstanding that love modestie: the which I doe not say of it selfe is sufficient to make a man esteemed.

But I say unto you, when it is accompanied with great prowesse, it maketh him much esteemed that hath it. And though of it selfe it lye still,[3] the worthie deedes speake at large, and are much more to be wondred at, than if they were accompanied with presumption or rashnesse.

I will not now deny, but many Spaniards there bee full of malapertnesse: but I say unto you, they that are best esteemed, for the most part are very modest.

Againe some other there be also so cold, that they flee the company of men too out of measure, and passe a certaine degree of meane: so that they make men deeme them either too fearefull, or to high minded.[4] And this do I in no case allowe, neyther would I have modestie so drie and withered, that it should become rudenesse. But let the Courtier, when it commeth to purpose, bee well spoken, and in discourses upon states, wise and expert: and have such a judgement that he may frame him selfe to the manners of the Countrey where ever hee commeth.

Then in lower matters, let him be pleasantly disposed, and reason well upon every matter, but in especiall tende alwaies to goodnesse.[5] No envious person, no carrier of an evil tongue in his head: nor at any time given to seeke preferment or promotion any naughtie way, nor by the meane of any subtill practise.

Then saide Calmeta: I will assure you all, the other waies are much more doubtfull and harder to compasse, than is that you discommend: because now adayes (to rehearse it againe) great men love none but such as be of that condition.

Doe you not so say, answered then Sir Fredericke, for that

[1] Cf. "not very presumptuous."    [2] Cf. "and even more so."
[3] "Lye still": cf. "be silent about itself."
[4] "High minded": cf. "proud."
[5] Cf. "speak well about everything."

were too plaine an argument, that the great men of our time were all vicious and naught, which is untrue, for some there be that be good.

But if it fell to our Courtiers lot to serve one that were vicious and wicked, as soone as he knoweth it, let him forsake him, least hee tast of the bitter paine that all good men feele that serve the wicked.

We must pray unto God, answered Calmeta, to helpe us to good, for when we are once with them, wee must take them with all their faultes, for infinite respectes constraine a gentleman after he is once entred into service with a Lord, not to forsake him.[1] But the ill lucke is in the beginning: and Courtiers in this case are not unlike unluckie foules bred up in an ill vale.[2]

Me thinke, quoth Sir Fredericke, duetie ought to prevaile before all other respects, but yet so that a gentleman forsake not his Lord at the warre, or in any other adversitie, and be thought to doe it to follow fortune, or because hee seemed then to want the meane to profitte by: at all other times I believe hee may with good reason, and ought to forsake that service that among good men shall put him to shame, for all men will imagine that he that serveth the good, is good, and he that serveth the ill is ill.

I woulde have you to cleare me of one doubt that I have in my head, quoth then the Lorde Lodovicus Pius, namely whether a gentleman be bound or no, while he is in his princes service, to obey him in all thinges which he shall commaund, though they were dishonest and shameful matters.

In dishonest matters we are not bound to obey any bodie, answered Sir Fredericke.

And what? (replyed the Lord Lodovicus Pius) if I be in service with a prince who handleth me well, and hopeth that I will doe any thing for him that may bee done, and he happen to command me to kill a man, or any other like matter, ought I to refuse to doe it?

You ought, answered Sir Fredericke, to obey your Lord in all thinges that tend to his profit and honour, not in such matters as tende to his losse and shame.

Therefore if he shoulde command you to conspire treason, ye are not onely not bound to doe it, but yee are bound not to doe

---

[1] This was Castiglione's own manner: Federico's two murders did not shake the loyalty of the "perfect courtier." In next paragraph is sufficient excuse for his leaving the Gonzagas.

[2] Cf. "unhappy birds hatched in a gloomy valley."

it, both for your owne sake, and for being a minister of the shame of your Lord.

Truth it is, many things seeme at the first sight good, which are ill: and many ill, that notwithstanding are good.

Therefore it is lawful for a man somtime in his Lords service, to kill not one man alone, but ten thousand, and to doe many other thinges, which if a man waigh them not as he ought, wil appeare ill, and yet are not so in deede.

Then answered the Lord Gasper Pallavicin. Ah by your faith talke somewhat in this case, and teach us howe wee may discerne things good in deede, from such as appeare good.

I pray you pardon mee, quoth Sir Fredericke, I wil not at this time enter into that, for there were too much to be saide in it: but all is to be referred to your discretion.

Cleare ye me at the least of an other doubt, replyed the Lord Gasper. And what doubt is that, quoth Sir Fredericke?

This answered the Lorde Gasper: I woulde knowe where I am charged by my maister in expresse wordes in an enterprise of businesse what ever it bee, what I have to doe therein: if I, at the deed doing thinking with my selfe in doing it more or lesse, or otherwise than my commission, to bring it more prosperously to passe, and more for his profit that gave mee that commission, whether ought I to governe my selfe according to the first charge, without passing the bounds of the commission, or els doe the thing that I judge to be best?

Then answered Sir Fredericke: in this point I would give you the judgement with the example of Manlius Torquatus, which in that case for over much affection slue his sonne, if I thought him worthie great prayse, (which to saye the truth) I doe not: although againe I dare not discommend him, contrarie to the opinion of so many hundred yeares.[1] For out of doubt, it is a daungerous matter to swarve from the commandements of a mans superiors, trusting more in his owne judgement than in theirs, whom of reason he ought to obey.

Because if his imagination faile him, and the matter take ill successe, he runneth into the error of disobedience, and marreth that hee hath to doe, without any manner of excuse or hope of pardon. Againe, in case the matter come well to passe according to his desire, he must thanke his fortune, and no more adoe. Yet in this sorte a custome is brought up, to set litle by the commandement of the superior powers. And by his example

[1] Cf. p. 126. Private judgment is subordinated to general custom. See also Montaigne.

that bringeth the matter to good passe, which peradventure is a wise man, and hath discoursed with reason and also aided by fortune, afterwarde a thousande other ignorant persons, and light headed, will take a stomacke to adventure in matters of most importance to doe after their owne way, and to appeare wise and of authoritie, will swarve from the commission of their heads, which is a very ill matter, and oftentimes the cause of infinit errors.

But I believe in this point, the person whom the matter toucheth, ought to skanne it deepely, and (as it were) put in a balance the goodnesse and commoditie that is like to ensue unto him in doing contrarie to that he is charged, admitting his purpose succeed according to his hope.

And counterpeise on the other side the hurt and discommoditie that ariseth, if in doing otherwise than hee is cōmanded, the matter chance to have ill successe: and knowing that the hurt may bee greater and of more importance, if it succeed ill, then the profit, if it happen well, hee ought to refraine, and in every point to observe his commission.

And contrariwise, if the profit be like to bee of more importance, if it succeed well, than the hurt, if it happen amisse, I believe he may with good reason take in hande to doe the thing that reason and judgement shall set before him, and leave somewhat aside the very forme of the commission,[1] after the example of good merchant men, that to gaine much, adventure a litle, and not much, to gaine a litle.

I allow well that he have a regarde to the nature of the Lord he serveth, and according to that, frame himselfe. For in case he be rigorous (as many such there are,) I woulde never counsaile him, if he were my friend, to vary in any parcell from the appointed order, least it happen unto him, as a maister Inginner of Athens was served, unto whom P. Crassus Mutianus, being in Asia, and going about to batter a towne, sent to demaund of him one of yᵉ two shipmastes that he had seene in Athens to make a Ram to beat downe the walles, and saide, hee woulde have the greater.

This Inginner, as he that was very cunning in deede, knew the greater would not very well serve for this purpose, and because the lesser was more easie to be carried, and also fitter to make that ordinance, he sent that to Mutianus. And after he had understood how the matter passed, he sent for the poore Inginner, and asked him why he obeyed him not, and not

[1] Cf. "the very letter of his orders."

admitting any reason he could alledge for himselfe, made him to be stripped naked, beaten and whipped with rods, so that he dyed, seeming to him in steade of obeying him, he would have counsailed him: therefore with such rigorous men, a man must looke well to his doings.

But let us leave a part now this practise of the superiours, and come downe to the conversation that a man hath with his equalles or somewhat inferiors, for unto them also must a man frame himselfe, because it is more universally frequented, and a man findeth himselfe oftner among them, than among his superiors.

Although there be some fond persons, that being in company with the greatest friende they have in the world, if they meete with one better apparrelled, by and by they cleave unto him: and if an other come in place better than he, they doe the like altogether unto him.

And againe when the prince passeth through the market place, through Churches or other haunted[1] places, they make all men give them roome with their elbowes, till they come to their heeles,[2] and though they have nothing to say to him, yet will they talk with him, and keepe him with a long tale, laugh, clappe the handes, and nod the heade, to seeme to have waightie businesse, that the people may see they are in favour.

But because these kind of men vouchsafe not to speake but with great men, I will not we should vouchsafe to speake of them.

Then the Lorde Julian, Since ye have (quoth he) made mention of these that are so readie to felowshippe themselves with the wel apparreled, I would have you to shew us in what sort the Courtier shoulde apparrell himselfe, what kinde of garment doth best become him, and how he should fit himself in all his garments about his bodie: because we see infinit varietie in it.

And some are araied after the French fashion, some after the Spanish attyre, another will seeme a Dutchman. Neither want we of them also that will clothe themselves like Turkes: Some weare beardes, other doe not.

Therefore it were a good deed in this varietie, to shew how a man should choose out the best.

Sir Fredericke saide: In very deede, I am not able to give any certaine rule about rayment, but that a man should frame himselfe to the custome of the most. And since (as you say) this custome is so variable, and Italians are so desirous to take up

---

[1] "Haunted": cf. "public."
[2] "Come to their heeles": cf. "reach his side."

other mens fashions, I believe every man may lawfully apparrell him selfe at his pleasure.

But I know not by what destinie it commeth, that Italie hath not as it was wont to have, a fashion of attire, known to be the Italian fashion: for although the bringing up of these new fashions maketh the first [1] to appeare very grosse, yet were they peradventure a token of libertie, where these have beene a prognosticate of bondage, the which (me thinke) now is plainely inough fulfilled.

And as it is writtē, when Darius, the yeare before hee fought with Alexander, had altered his sword he wore by his side, which was a Persian blade, into the fashion of Macedonie, it was interpreted by the Soothsayers, how this signified, that they into whose fashion Darius had altered the forme of his Persian blade, shoulde become rulers of Persia: even so where wee have altered our Italian fashions into straunge, me thinke it signified, that all they into whose fashions ours were chaunged, should come in to overcome us: the which hath beene too true: for there is not now a nation left that hath not left us their pray, so that there remaineth litle behinde to pray upon, and yet for all that cease they not to pray still.

But I will not enter into communication of sorrow: therefore it shall be well to speake of the raiment of our Courtier, the which so it be not out of use, nor contrary to his profession, in the rest (I thinke) it will doe well inough, so as the wearer be satisfied withall.

Truth it is, that I would love it the better, if it were not extreme in any part, as the Frenchman is wont to be sometime over long, and the Dutchman over short,[2] but as they are both the one and the other amended and brought into better frame by the Italians.

Moreover I will holde alwaies with it, if it bee rather somewhat grave and auncient,[3] than garish. Therfore me thinke a blacke colour hath a better grace in garments than any other, and though not throughly blacke, yet somewhat darke, and this I meane for his ordinarie apparrell.

For there is no doubt, but upon armor it is more meete to have sightly and merrie colours,[4] and also garments for pleasure,[5] cut, pompous and rich.

---

[1] "The first": cf. "the former ones."

[2] Cf. "over-amplitude . . . over-scantiness."

[3] "Auncient": cf. "sober."

[4] Cf. "bright and cheerful colours."

[5] "For pleasure," etc.: cf. "for gala use also dress may be fringed, showy, and magnificent."

Likewise in open shewes about triumphes, games, maskeries, and such other matters, because so appointed there is in them a certain livelinesse and mirth, which in deede doth well set forth feates of armes and pastimes.

But in the rest I coulde wish they should declare the solemnitie[1] that the Spanish nation much observeth, for outwarde matters many times are a token of the inwarde.

Then said the Lord Cesar Gonzaga, I would not stick much at this, for so a gentleman be of worthinesse in other matters, his garments neither encrease nor minish reputation.

Sir Fredericke answered: ye say true. Yet which of us is there, that seeing a gentleman goe with a garment upon his backe quartered with sundrie colors, or with so many pointes tied together, and all about with laces and fringes set overthwart, will not count him a verie dizarde, or a common jeaster?

Neither dizard, quoth maister Peter Bembo, nor a jeaster[2] would a man count him, that had lived any while in Lumbardy, for there they goe all so.

Why then, answered the Dutchesse smyling, if they goe all so, it ought not to be objected to them for a vice, this kinde of attire being as comely and proper to them, as it is to the Venetians, to weare their long wyde sleeves, and to the Florentines their hoodes.[3]

I speake no more of Lombardy quoth sir Fridericke, than of other places, for in every nation yee shall finde both foolish and wise.

But to speake that I thinke is most requisite as touching apparell, I will have the Courtier in all hys garmentes handsome and cleanely,[4] and take a certaine delight in modest precisenes,[5] but not for all that after a womanish or light manner, neyther more in one poynte than in another, as wee see many so curious about their haire, that they forget all the rest.

Other delite to have their teeth faire: other in their beard: other in buskins: other in caps: other in coiffes. And so it commeth to passe, that those few things which they have clenly in them, appeare borrowed ware, and all the rest which is most fond,[6] is knowne to be their owne. But this trade will I have our Courtier to flie by my counsaile, with an addition also, that he ought to determine with him selfe what he will

---

[1] "Solemnitie": cf. "sobrietie."
[3] Bembo was a Venetian.
[5] Cf. "elegance."

[2] Cf. "fool or a buffoon."
[4] Cf. "neat and dainty."
[6] Cf. "very tasteless."

*E 807

appeare to be, and in such sort as he desireth to be esteemed, so to apparrel himselfe, and make his garments helpe him to bee counted such a one, even of them that heare him not speake, nor see him doe any manner thing.

I thinke it not meet, quoth the Lord Pallavicin, neither is it used amongst honest men, to judge mens conditions by their garments, and not by their wordes and deeds, for many a man might bee deceived: and this proverbe ariseth not without cause: The habite maketh not The Monke.

I say not, answered Sir Fredericke, that men shoulde give a resolute judgement by this alone, of mens conditions, and that they are not knowne by words and deedes, more than by the garments. But I say that the garment is withal no small argument of the fancy of him that weareth it, although otherwhile it appeare not true.[1] And not this alone, but all the behaviour, gestures and manners, beside wordes and deeds, are in a judgement of inclination of him in whom they are seene.

And what things be those, answered the Lorde Gasper, that you finde we may give judgement upon, that are neither wordes nor deeds?

Then saide Sir Fredericke: You are too subtill a Logitian, but to tell you as I meane, some operations[2] there are that remaine after they are done, as building, writing, and such other: some remaine not, as these that I meane now. Therefore doe I not count in this purpose, going,[3] laughing, looking, and such matters to bee operations, and notwithstanding outwardly doe give many times a knowledge of that in writing.

Tell me, did you not give your judgement upon that friend of ours we communed off this morning past, to be a foolish and light person, as soone as you saw he wryed his head, and bowed his bodie, and invited with a chearefull countenance the company to put off their caps to him.

So in like manner, when you see one gaze earnestly wh his eies abashed,[4] like one that hath litle wit: or that laugheth so fondly as doe those dumbe men, with the great wennes in their throat,[5] that dwell in the mountaines of Bergamo, though hee neither speake ne doe any thing els, will you not count him a very foole?

Ye may see then, that these behaviours, manners, and gestures,

---

[1] Cf. "although it may be sometimes wrong."
[2] Cf. "acts."
[3] Cf. "walking."
[4] Cf. "gazing too intently with dull eyes."
[5] Cf. "goitrous mutes."

which I minde not for this time to terme Operations, are a great matter to make men knowne.

But me thinke there is an other thing that giveth and diminisheth much reputation: namely, the choise of friends, with whom a man must have inwarde conversation.[1] For undoubtedly reason willeth, that such as are coupled in strayte amitie, and unspeakable company, should be also alike in will, in minde, in judgement, and inclination.

So that who so is conversant with the ignorant or wicked, he is also counted ignorant and wicked. And contrariwise, he that is conversant with the good, wise, and discrete, hee is reckened such a one. For it seemeth by nature, that every thing doeth willingly felowshippe[2] with his like.

Therefore I believe that a man ought to have respect in the first beginning of these friendships, for of two neare friendes, who ever knoweth the one, by and by he imagineth the other to bee of the same condition.

Then answered maister Peter Bembo: To be bound in friendship with such agreement of minde as you speake of, me thinke in deede a man ought to have great respect, not onely for getting or loosing reputation, but because now adayes ye finde verie few true friendes.

Neither doe I believe that there are any more in the world, those Pylades and Orestes, Theseus and Perithous, nor Scipio and Lælius, but rather it happeneth dayly, I wote not by what destinie, that two friendes, which many yeares have lived together with most hartie love, yet at the ende beguile one an other, in one manner or other, either of malice or envy, or for lightnesse, or some other ill cause: and each one imputeth the fault to his fellow, of that which perhaps both the one and the other deserveth.

Therefore because it hath happened to mee more than once to be deceived of him whom I loved best, and of whom I hoped I was beloved above any other person, I have thought with my selfe alone otherwhile to bee well done,[3] never to put a mans trust in any person in the worlde, nor to give him selfe so for a pray to friende how deare and loving soever he were, that without stoppe a man should make him partaker of all his thoughts, as he would his owne selfe: because there are in our minds so many dennes and corners, that it is unpossible for the wit of man to know the dissimulations that lye lurking in them.

---

[1] "Inwarde conversation": cf. "intimate relations."

[2] Cf. "join."

[3] "To bee well done": cf. "that it would be well for us."

I believe therefore that it is well done to love and beare with [1] one more than an other, according to their deserts and honestie: but not for all that so to assure a mans selfe, with this sweete baite of friendship, that afterward it should bee too late for us to repent.

Then Sir Fredericke, Truely (quoth he) the losse should be much more than the gaine, if that high degree of friendship should be taken from the fellowship of man, which (in mine opinion) ministreth unto us al the goodnesse contained in our life: and therefore will I in no case consent to you, that it is reasonable, but rather I can finde in my hart to conclude, and that with most evident reasons, that without this perfect friendship, men were much more unluckie than all other living creatures.

And albeit some wicked and prophane taste of this holy name of friendship, yet is it not for all that to bee so rooted out of mens mindes, and for the trespasse of the ill, to deprive the good of so great a felicitie. And I believe verily for my part, there is here among us moe than one couple of friends, [2] whose love is indissoluble and without any guile at all, and to endure untill death, with agreement of will, no lesse than those men of old time, whom you mentioned right now. And so is it alwaies, when beside the inclination that commeth from above, a man chooseth him a friende like unto him selfe in conditions. And I meane the whole to consist among the good and vertuous men, because the friendshippe of the wicked, is no friendship.

I allow well that this knot, which is so strayte, knit or binde no moe than two, els were it in hazarde: for (as you know) three Instrumentes of musicke are hardlier brought to agree together than two.

I would have our Courtier therefore to finde him out an especiall and hartie friend, if it were possible, of that sorte wee have spoken off. Then according to their deserts and honestie, love, honour and observe all other men, and alwaies doe his best to fellowshippe himselfe with men of estimation that are noble and knowne to bee good, more than with the unnoble and of small reputation, so he bee also beloved and honoured of them. And this shall come to passe, if he be gentle, lowly, freeharted, easie to bee spoken to, and sweete in companie, humble and diligent to serve, and to have an eye to his friendes profit and estimation, as wel absent as present, bearing with

---

[1] Cf. "serve."

[2] Castiglione and Raphael (the latter absent at the time) are good examples.

their naturall defaults that are to be borne withall, without breaking with them upon a small ground, and correcting in himselfe such as lovingly shall bee tolde him, never preferring himselfe before other men in seeking the highest and chiefe roomes of estimation, neither in doing as some that a man would weene despised the worlde, and with a noysome sharpenesse[1] will tell every man his duetie, and beside that they are full of contention in every tryfling matter, and out of tune, they controll[2] whatsoever they do not themselves, and alwaies seeke cause to complaine of their friendes, which is a most hatefull thing.

Here when Sir Fredericke had made a stay, the Lorde Gasper Pallavicin saide: I would have you to expresse somewhat more particularly this cōversatiō with friends, than you doe, for in deede you keepe your selfe too much in the general, and touch unto us things (as it were) by the way.

How by the way? answeryd Sir Fredericke, Would you have me to tell you also the very wordes that a man must use? Suppose you not then we have sufficiently communed of this?

I thinke yea, answered the Lord Gasper. Yet doe I desire to understande also some particular point of the manner of entertainement among men and women, which (me thinke) is very necessarie matter, considering the most part of mans time is spent therein in Courtes, and if it were alwaies after one manner wise, a man would soone waxe wearie of it.

Me thinke, answered Sir Fredericke, we have given the Courtier a knowledge in so many thinges, that hee may well varie his conversation, and frame himselfe according to the inclination of them he accompanieth him selfe withall, presupposing him to be of a good judgemēt, and otherwhile to guide him selfe. And according to the time otherwhile, have an eye to great matters, and sometime to pastimes ánd games.

And what games, quoth the Lord Gasper?

Sir Fredericke answered: let us aske counsaile of Frier Seraphin that dayly inventeth new.

But in good earnest, replyed the Lorde Gasper, doe you not thinke it a vice in the Courtier to play at Dice and Cardes?

I thinke it none, quoth Sir Fredericke, unlesse a man apply it too much, and by reason of that, setteth aside other thinges more necessarie, or els for none other intent but to get money

---

[1] Cf. "kind of tiresome preciseness."
[2] Cf. "censure."

and to beguile his fellow, and in his losse fume and take on so, that it might bee thought a token of covetousnesse.

The Lord Gasper answered: and what say you to the game at Chests?

It is truly an honest kind of entertainment and wittie, quoth Sir Fredericke. But me thinke it hath a faulte, which is, that a man may be too cunning at it, for who ever will bee excellent in the play of Chests, I believe he must bestow much time about it, and apply it with so much studie, that a man may as soone learne some noble science, or compasse any other matter of importance, and yet in the ende in bestowing all that labour, hee knoweth no more but a game.

Therefore in this I believe there happeneth a verie rare thing, namely, that the meane [1] is more commendable, than the excellencie.

The Lord Gasper answered: there be many Spaniards excellent at it, and in many other games, which for all that bestow not much studie upon it, nor yet lay aside the compassing of other matters.

Believe not the contrarie answered Sir Fredericke, but they bestow much studie upon it, although fainingly.

As for those other games ye speake of beside Chestes, peradventure they are like many which I have seene that serve to small purpose, but onely to make the common people wonder.

Therefore (in mine opinion) they deserve none other praise or rewarde, than the great Alexander gave unto him, that standing a far off, did so well broch Chiche peason upon [2] a needle.

But because fortune, as in many other thinges, so in the opinion of men seemeth to beare a great stroke, it is sometime seene that a gentleman how well conditioned soever he be, and endewed with many qualities, shall be litle set by of a great man, and (as they say) groweth not in favour [3] with him, and without any cause why, that a man may discerne.

Therefore when he commeth into his presence without any acquaintance before hand, with the rest about him, though he be wittie and readie in his answeres, and sheweth himselfe handsomely in his behaviors, in his conditions and wordes, and in what ever belongeth unto him, yet will that Lord set light by him, and rather give him an ill countenance, than esteeme him: and of this will arise that the rest immediatly will frame

---

[1] "The meane," moderate skill.
[2] Cf. "impale chick-peas on . . ."
[3] Cf. "and (as we say) goes against the grain."

themselves to their Lords minde, and it shall seeme unto every man that he is litle worth, neither will any man regard him, or make of him, or laugh at his pleasant sayings, or set anie thing by him, but will begin all to serve him sluttish pranckes, and make him a Cousin.[1]

Neither shall good answeres suffise the poore soule, nor yet the taking of thinges as spoken in jest, for even the very Pages will bee at him, so that were he the fairest conditioned man in the world, he can not choose but bee thus baited and jeasted at.

And contrariwise, if a prince be inclined to one that is most ignorant, that can neither do nor say any thing, his manners and behaviors, (be they never so fonde and foolish) are many times commended with acclamation and wonder of all men, and it seemeth that all the Court beholdeth and observeth him, and every man laugheth at his boording and certaine carterly jestes,[2] that shoulde rather move a man to vomit[3] than to laugh: so addicted and stiffe men be in the opinions that arise of the favorers and disfavorers of great men.

Therefore will I have our Courtier the best he can (beside his worthinesse) to helpe himselfe with wit and arte, and when ever he hath to goe where he is straunge and not knowne, let him procure that there goe first a good opinion of him, before he come in person, and so worke, that they may understand there, how he is in other places with Lordes, Ladies, and gentlemen in good estimation: because that fame, which seemeth to arise of the judgements of many, engendreth a certaine assured confidence of a mans worthinesse, which afterwarde finding mens mindes so setled and prepared, is easily with deedes maintained and encreased, beside that a man is eased of the trouble that I feele, when I am asked the question Who I am, and what is my name.

I can not see what this can helpe, answered maister Bernard Bibiena, for it hath sundrie times happened unto me, and I believe to many moe, after I had grounded in my mind by report of many men of judgement a matter to be of great perfection before I had seene it, when I had once seene it, I fainted much,[4] and I was much deceived in mine imagination, and this proceeded of nothing els, but of giving too much credit to fame and report, and of conceiving in my minde so great an opinion, that measuring it afterwarde with the truth, the effect, though it

[1] "Serve him sluttish pranckes," etc.: cf. "deride and persecute him."
[2] Cf. "at his jests and at certain rustic and stupid jokes."
[3] Cf. "excite to disgust."
[4] Cf. "I found it paltry."

were great and excellent, yet in comparison of that I had imagined of it, seemed very slender unto me.

Even so (I feare me) may also come to passe of that Courtier. Therefore I can not see how it were wel done to give these expectations, and to send that fame of a man before: because our mindes many times fashion and shape thinges, which is unpossible afterwarde to answere to and fulfill, and so doth a man lose more than he gaineth by it.

Here Sir Fredericke said: Thinges that come to you and many moe being lesse in effect than the fame is of them, are for the most part of that sorte, that the eye at the first sight may give a judgement of them. As if you have never beene at Naples or at Rome, when you heare men commune of it, you imagine much more of it, than perhaps you finde afterwarde in sight. But in the conditions of men it is not alike, because that you see outwardly is the least part.

Therefore in case the first day you heare a gentleman talke, you perceive not the worthinesse in him that you had before imagined, you doe not so soone lose the good opinion of him, as you do in the thinges wherein your eye is by and by a judge. But you will looke from day to day, to have him disclose some other hid vertue, keeping notwithstanding alwaies the stedfast imprinting which you have risen by the words of so many.

And this man then being (as I set case our Courtier is) of so good qualities, hee will every houre strengthen you more and more, to give credence to that fame, for that with his doinges hee shall give you a cause, and you will ever surmise somewhat more to be in him, than you see.

And certainly it can not be denyed, but these first imprintinges have a very great force, and a man ought to take much heede to them.

And that you may understand of what waight they be, I say unto you, that I have knowne in my dayes a gentleman, who albeit hee was of sufficient mannerly behaviour and modest conditions and well seene in armes, yet was he not in any of these qualities so excellent, but there were many as good and better.

Notwithstanding (as lucke served him) it befell that a gentlewoman entred most fervently in love with him, and this love dayly encreasing through declaration that the yong man made to agree with her in that behalfe, and perceiving no manner meane howe they might come to speake together, the gentlewoman provoked with too great passion opened her desire unto another gentlewoman, by whose meane she hoped upon some commoditie: this woman neither in bloud nor in beautie was a whit inferior to the first.

Upon this it came to passe, that she perceyving her talke so effectually of this yong man, whom she never sawe, and knowing how that gentlewoman, whom she wist well was most discrete and of a very good judgement, loved him extremely, imagined forthwith that hee was the fairest, the wisest, the discreetest, and finally the worthiest man to be beloved that was in the worlde: and so without seeing him, fell so deepe in love with him, that she practised what she coulde come by to him, not for her friend, but for her own selfe, and to make him answerable to her in love, the which she brought to passe without any great adoe, for (to say the truth) she was a woman rather to be sought upon than to seeke upon others.[1]

Now heare a pretie chance. It happened not long time after, that a letter which this last gentlewoman writ unto her lover, came to the hands of an other, that was a noble woman of excellent qualities and singular beautie, who being (as the most part of women are) inquisitive and greedy to understande secrets, and especially of other women, opened the letter, and in reading it, perceived it was written with an extreme affection of love.

And the sweete words full of fire that shee read, first moved her to take compassion on that Gentlewoman: for she knew verye well from whom the letter came, and to whom it went.

Afterwarde they had such force, that scanning them in her minde, and considering what manner a man this was like to bee, that coulde bring that woman into such love, by and by she fell in love with him, and that letter was more effectuall to worke in this case, than peradventure it woulde have beene if it had beene sent her from the yong man him selfe.

And as it chanceth sometime, poyson prepared in a dish of meate for some great man, killeth him that tasteth first of it,[2] so this poore gentlewoman because she was too greedy, dranke of the amorous poison that was ordained for another.

What shall I say to you? the matter was verie open, and spred so abroad that many women beside these, partly in despite of the other, and partly to doe as the other did, bent all their studie and diligence to enjoy his love, and for a season played as

[1] Cf. "rather to be wooed than to woo others."

[2] As was probably the occasion of the death of Pope Alexander VI.: the poison he had prepared for another came accidentally to him first.

children doe at Chopcherie,[1] and the whole proceeded of the first opinion which that woman conceived that heard him so praysed of an other.

Now the Lorde Gasper Pallavicin [2] answered her smiling: You to confirme your judgement with reason, alleage unto me womens doinges, which for the most part are voide of all reason. And in case you woulde tell all, this good fellow so favored of so many women was some doult, and a man in deede not to be regarded, because the manner of them is alwaies to cleave to the worst, and like sheepe to doe that they see the first doe, bee it well or ill.

Beside that, they be so spitefull among themselves, that if he had beene a monstrous creature they would surely have stolen him one from another.

Here many beganne and (in manner) all, to speake against the Lord Gasper, but the Dutchesse made them all to holde their peace. Afterwarde she saide smyling.

If the ill which you speak of women were not so farre wide from the truth, that in speaking it, it hurteth and shameth rather the speaker than them, I woulde suffer you to be answered. But I will not have you, in speaking against you with a number of reasons, forsake this your ill custome, because you may bee sharpely punished,[3] for this offence of yours: which shall be with the ill opinion that all they will conceive of you that heare you talke in this wise.

Then answered Sir Fredericke: Say not, my Lord Gasper, that women are so void of reason, though sometime they apply them selves to love more through the judgement of others than their owne.

For great men and many wise men, doe often times the like. And if it be lawful to tell the truth, you your selfe and all wee here have many times, and doe at this present credite the opinion of others,[4] more than our owne.

And that it is true, not long agoe there were certain verses shewed here, that bore the name of Senazarus, and were thought of every body very excellent, and praysed out of reason, afterwarde when they were certainely knowne to be an other mans

---

[1] Cf. "contended for it . . . as boys contend for cherries."

[2] L. Gaspar, who so speaks against women and who yet seems popular with them, may be the original of Shakespeare's Benedick; see M. Scott, *The Book of the Courtyer.*

[3] That is: "I am not willing you should be cured by argument—as is easy. You must suffer."

[4] Recall how Benedick was brought into love.

doing, they lost by and by their reputation, and seemed worse than meane.

And where there was song in the Dutchesse presence here a certaine Antheme, it never delyted nor was reckned good, until it was knowne to be the doing of Josquin de Pris.

But what token wil you have more plainer of opinion? Doe you not remember where you your selfe dranke of one selfe wine, sometime ye said it was most perfect, and another time, without all taste? and that because you had beene perswaded they were two sortes, the one of the coast of Genua, and the other of this soile.

And when the error was opened, by no meanes you would believe it: that false opinion was grounded so stifly in your head, which arose notwithstanding of other mens words.

Therfore ought the Courtier diligently to apply in the beginning to give a good opinion of him selfe, and consider what a harmefull and deadly thing it is, to run in the contrarie. And in this danger more than other men doe they stand, that will make profession to bee very pleasant and with this their merry fashion, purchase them a certaine libertie, that lawfully they may say and doe what commeth in their minde, without thinking upon it.

For such men many times enter into certaine matters, which when they can not get out againe, will afterwarde helpe them selves with raising laughter, and it is done with so ill a grace, that it will in no wise frame,[1] whereby they bring a very great lothsomnesse upon as many as see or heare them, and they remaine very colde and without any grace or countenance.

Sometime thinking therby to be subtill witted and full of jestes, in the presence of honourable women, yea, and oftentimes to themselves, they thrust out filthy and most dishonest wordes: and the more they see them blush at it, the better Courtiers they recken themselves and still they laugh at it, and rejoyce among them selves at this goodly vertue they thinke they have gotten them.

But they practise this beastlinesse[2] for none other cause, but to be counted good fellowes.

This is the name alone which they deeme worthie praise, and which they brag more of, than of any thing els, and to get it them, they speake the foulest and shamefullest villanies in the world.

Many times they shoulder one an other downe the stayers, and hurle billets and brickes, one at anothers heade.

---

[1] "Frame": cf. "succeed."     [2] Cf. "folly."

They hurle handfuls of dust in mens eyes. They cast horse and man into ditches, or downe on the side of some hill.

Then at table, potage, sauce, gelies, and what ever commeth to hand, into the face it goeth. And afterward laugh: and who so can doe most of these tricks, he counteth him selfe the best and gallantest Courtier, and supposeth that he hath wonne great glory.

And in case otherwhile they get a Gentleman in their pleasaunt pastimes, that will not give himselfe to such horse play, they say by and by[1]: He is too wise, we shall have him a Counseller, he is no good fellow.

But I will tell you a worse matter. Some there be that contend and lay wager, who can eate and drinke more unsaverie and stinking[2] thinges, and so abhorring and contrarie to mans senses, that it is not possible to name them without very great lothsomnesse.[3]

And what thinges bee those, quoth the Lord Lodovicus Pius?

Sir Fredericke answered: Let the Marquesse Phebus tell you, for hee hath often seene it in Fraunce, and peradventure felt it.

The Marquesse Phebus answered: I have seene none of these thinges done in Fraunce more than in Italie. But looke what good things the Italians have in their garments, in feasting, in banketing, in feates of armes and in every other thing that belongeth to a Courtier, they have it all of the Frenchmen.

I deny not answered Sir Fredericke, but there are also among the Frenchmen very honest and sober gentlemen, and for my part I have knowne many (without peradventure) worthie all prayse. But yet some there are of litle good manner. And to speake generally (me thinke) the Spaniardes agree more with Italians, in conditions, than Frenchmen: because (in my minde) the peculiar quiet gravitie of the Spaniardes is more agreeable to our nature than the quicke livelinesse that is perceived in the French nation almost in everie gesture: which is not to be discommended in them, but is rather a grace, for it is so naturall and proper to them, that there is no manner affection or curiositie in it.

There are many Italians that woulde faine counterfaite their fashion, and can doe nought els but shake the heade in speaking, and make a legge with an ill grace,[4] and when they come out of their doores into the Citie, goe so fast that good footemen can

---

[1] "By and by": cf. "at once."
[2] Cf. "vilest and most offensive."    [3] Cf. "without disgust."
[4] Cf. "make clumsy crosswise bows."

scant overtake them, and with these manners they weene them selves good Frenchmen, and to have of that libertie: which (I wis) chaunceth very seldome saving to such as are brought up in Fraunce, and have learned that fashion from their childhood.

The like is to be saide in the knowledge of sundrie tongues, which I commend much in our Courtier, and especially Spanish and Frēch, because the entercourse of both the one nation and the other is much haunted in Italy, and these two are more agreeable unto us than unto any of the rest, and those two Princes for that they are very mightie in warre and most royall in peace, have their Court alwaies furnished with valiant gentlemen, which are dispersed[1] throughout the worlde, and againe we must needes practise with them.

I will not now proceede to speake any more particularlye of matters too well knowne, as that our Courtier ought not to professe to be a glutton nor a drunkard, nor riotous and unordinate in any ill condition, nor filthie and unclenly in his living, with certaine rude and boysterous[2] behaviors that smell of the plough and cart[3] a thousand mile off, for hee that is of that sorte, it is not onely not to be hoped that he will make a good Courtier, but he can be set to no better use than to keepe sheepe.

And to conclude, I say that (to doe well) the Courtier ought to have a perfect understanding in that wee have saide is meete for him, so that every possible thing may be easie to him, and all men wonder at him, and hee at no man: meaning notwithstanding in this point that there bee not a certaine loftie and unmannerly stubbornesse,[4] as some men have that shew themselves not to wonder at the things which other men doe, because they take upon them that they can doe them much better: and with their silence doe commend them as unworthy to bee spoken of, and will make a gesture (in a manner) as though none beside were (I will not say their equal) but able to conceive the understanding of the prowesse of their cunning.

Therfore ought the Courtier to shunne these hatefull manners, and with gentlenesse and courtesie prayse other mens good deedes.

And though hee perceive himselfe excellent and farre above others, yet shew that he esteemeth not himselfe for such a one.

But because these so full perfections are very seldome found in the nature of man, and perhaps never, yet ought not a man

[1] "Which are dispersed": cf. "who spread."
[2] "Rude and boysterous": cf. "peasant."
[3] "Plough and cart": cf. "hoe and plough."
[4] "Stubbornesse": cf. "indifference."

that perceiveth himselfe in some part to want, to lay aside his hope to come to a good passe, though he can not reach to that perfect and high excellencie which hee aspireth unto.

Because in every arte there bee many other places beside the best, all praise worthie, and he that striveth to come by the highest, it is seldome seene that hee passeth not the meane.

I will have our Courtier therefore, if he finde himselfe excellent in any thing beside armes, to set out himselfe, and get estimation by it after an honest sorte, and be so discrete and of so good a judgement, that he may have the understanding after a comely manner, and with good purpose to allure men to heare or to looke on that hee supposeth himselfe to be excellent in, making semblant alwaies to doe it, not for a bragge and to shewe it for vaine glory, but at a chance, and rather praied by others,[1] than comming of his owne free will.

And in every thing that he hath to doe or to speake, if it be possible, let him come alwaies provided and thinke on it before hand, shewing notwithstanding the whole to be done *ex tempore*, and at the first sight.

As for the things he hath but a meane skill in, let him touch them (as it were) by the way, without grounding[2] much upon them, yet in such wise that a man may believe he hath a great deale more cunning therein, than he uttereth: as certaine Poets sometime that harped upon very subtil pointes of Philo-sophie, or rather sciences, and peradventure had small under-standing in the matter.

And in that hee knoweth himselfe altogether ignorant in, I will never have him make any profession at all, nor seeke to purchase him any fame by it: but rather when occasion serveth, confesse to have no understanding in it.

This, quoth Calmeta, woulde Nicholetto never have done, which being a very excellent Philosopher, and no more skilfull in the lawe than in fleeing, when a governour of Padoa, was minded to give him one of the Lectures in ye law, he would never yeeld at the perswasion of many scholers, to deceive the opinion which the governour had conceived of him, and confesse that he had understanding in it: but said still that he was not in this point of Socrates opinion, for it is not a Philosophers part to say at any time, that he hath no understanding.

I say not, answered Sir Fredericke, that the Courtier should of himselfe goe say hee hath no understanding, without it be

---

[1] Cf. "by chance and at others' request."
[2] "Grounding": cf. "dwelling."

required of him: for I allow not this fondnesse to accuse and debase him selfe. Againe I remember some otherwile that in like sorte do willingly disclose some matters, which although they happened perhaps without anie fault of theirs, yet bring they with them a shadow of slander, as did a gentleman (whom you al know) which alwaies when he heard any mention made of the battaile beside Perna against king Charles, he would by and by declare how he fled away, and a man would weene that hee saw or understood nothing els in that journey.[1]

Afterwarde talking of a certaine famous justing, he rehearsed still how hee was overthrowne: and manye times also hee seemed in his talke to seeke howe hee might bring into purpose to declare that [2] upon a night as hee was going to speake with [3] a gentle-woman, hee was well beaten with a cudgel.

Such trifling follies I will not have our Courtier to speake off. But me think when occasion is offered to shew his skill in a matter he is altogether ignorant in, it is well done to avoide it. If necessitie compel him, let him rather confesse plainely his lacke of understanding in it, than hazarde himselfe, and so shall he avoide a blame that many deserve now adayes, which I wote not through what corrupt inwarde motion or judgement out of reason, doe alwaies take upon them to practise the thing they know not, and lay aside that they are skilfull in.

And for a confirmation of this, I know a very excellent musition, which leaving his musicke a part hath wholy given himselfe to versifying, and thinketh himselfe a great clarke therin, but in deede he maketh every man to laugh him to scorne, and now hath he also cleane lost his musicke.

An other, one of the chiefest painters in the worlde,[4] neglecting his arte wherein he was very excellent, hath applied himself to learn Philosophy, wherein he hath such straunge conceits and monstrous fansies, that withall the painting he hath [5] he can not paint them.

And such as these there be infinite. Some there be that knowing themselves to have an excellencie in one thing, make their principall profession in an other, in which notwithstanding they are not ignorant, but when time serveth to shew themselves in that they are most skilfull in, they doe it alwaies very per-

---

[1] "In that journey": cf. "that day."
[2] Cf. "seemed to seek an opportunity to tell how."     [3] Cf. "meet."
[4] "The reference here is plainly to Leonardo da Vinci" (Opdycke). What to us seems his marvellous anticipation of modern discoveries or inventions seemed to his contemporaries as Castiglione writes.
[5] Cf. "all his painter's art."

fectly: and otherwhile it commeth so to passe, that the company perceiving them so cunning in that which is not their profession, they imagine them to bee much better in that they professe in deed.

This arte in case it bee coupled with a good judgement, discontenteth me nothing at all.

Then answered the Lord Gasper Pallavicin. I thinke not this an arte, but a very deceite, and I believe it is not meet for him that will be an honest man to deceive at any time.

This quoth Sir Fredericke, is rather an ornament that accompanieth the thing he doth, than a deceite: and though it be a deceite, yet it is not to be disalowed.

Will you not say also, that he that beateth his fellow, where there be two playing at fence together, beguileth him, and that is because hee hath more arte than the other.

And where you have a jewell that unset seemeth faire, afterwarde when it commeth to a goldsmithes handes that in well setting it maketh it appeare much more fairer, will you not say that the goldsmith deceiveth the eyes of them that looke on it? And yet for that deceite, deserveth he prayse, for with judgement and arte a cunning hand doth many times adde a grace and ornament to Ivorie, or to silver, or to a stone that is faire in sight, setting it in gold.

We say not then that this arte or deceite (in case you will so terme it) deserveth any manner blame.

Also it is not ill for a man that knoweth himselfe skilfull in a matter, to seeke occasion after a comely sorte to shew his feate therein, and in like case do cover the partes hee thinketh scant worthie prayse, yet notwithstanding after a certaine warie dissimulation.

Doe you not remember how king Ferdinande without making any shew to seek it, tooke occasion very well to strippe himselfe sometime into his doublet? and that because he knew he was very well made and nimble withall. And because his handes were not all of the fairest, he seldom plucked of his gloves, and (in manner) never. And few there were that tooke heede to this warinesse of his.

Me thinke also I have reade, that Julius Cæsar ware for the nonce a garland of Laurell, to hide his baldnesse withall. But in these matters a man must be very circumspect and of a good judgement, least he passe his boundes: for to avoide one errour oftentimes a man falleth into an other, and to get him prayse, purchaseth blame.

Therefore the surest way in the world, is, for a man in his living and conversation to governe himselfe alwaies with a certaine honest meane, which (no doubt) is a great and most sure shield against envie, the which a man ought to avoid in what he is able.

I will have our Courtier also to take heede he purchaseth not the name of a lyar, nor of a vaine person, which happeneth many times, and to them also that deserve it not. Therefore in his communicatiō let him be alwaies heedfull not to goe out of the likelihood of truth, yea and not to speake too often those truthes that have the face of a lye, as many do that never speake, but of wonders, and will bee of such authoritie, that every incredible matter must bee believed at their mouth.

Other, at the first entring into friendship with a new friend, to get favor with him, the first thing that they speake, sweare that there is not a person in the worlde whom they love better, and they are willing to jeoparde their life for his sake, and such other matters out of reason, and when they part from him, make wise to weepe, and not to speake a word for sorrow. Thus because they would be counted to be loving wormes,[1] they make men count them lyers, and fond flatterers.

But it were too long a matter and tedious to recken up all vices that may happen in conversation. Therefore, for that I desire in ye Courtier, it sufficeth to say (beside the matters rehearsed) that he bee such a one that shall never want good communication and fitte for them hee talketh withall, and have a good understanding with a certaine sweetnesse to refresh the hearers minds, and with merry conceites and jestes to provoke them to solace and laughter, so that without being at any time lothsome or satiate, he may evermore delite.

Now I hope my Ladie Emilia will give me leave to holde my peace, which in case she deny me, I shall by mine owne wordes be convicted not to be ye good Courtier I have told you of: for not onely good communication, which neither at this time nor perhaps at any other ye have heard in me, but also this I have, such as it is, doth cleane faile me.

Then spake the Lord Generall: I will not have this false opinion to sticke in the heade[2] of any of us, that you are not a very good Courtier: for (to say the truth) this desire of yours to hold your peace proceedeth rather because you would be ridde of your paine, than for that ye want talke.

Therefore that it may not appeare in so noble assembly as

---

[1] Cf. "very loving."  [2] Cf. "rest in the mind."

this is, and in so excellent talke, any parcel be left out, say you
not nay to teach us how wee shoulde use these jestes you have
made mention of, and shew us the arte that belongeth to all this
kinde of pleasant speach to provoke laughter and solace after
an honest sorte, for (in mine opinion) it is verie necessarie and
much to purpose for a Courtier.

My Lord, answered Sir Fredericke, jestes and merrie conceites
are rather a gift, and a grace of nature, than of arte, but yet
there are some nations more redier in it than other some, as the
Tuscanes, which in deed are very subtill.

Also it appeareth proper to the Spaniardes to invent merry
conceits. Yet are there many notwithstanding both of this
nation and other also, that in too much babling[1] passe sometime
their boundes and were unsavery and fond, because they have
no respect to the condition of the person they commune withal,
to the place where they bee, to the time, to the great gravitie
and modesty which they ought to have in themselves.

Then aunsweared the L. Generall: You deny that there is any
arte in jeastes, and yet in speaking against such as observe them
not with modestie and gravitie, and have not respect to the
time and to the person they commune withall, me thinke ye
declare that this may also be taught and hath some doctrine in it.

These rules my Lord, answered Sir Fredericke, be so generall,
that they may bee applyed to every matter, and helpe it forwarde. But I have saide there is no arte in jeastes, because (me
thinke) they are onely of two sortes: whereof the one is enlarged
in communication that is long and without interruption[2]: as is
seene in some men that with so good an utterance and grace and
so pleasantly declare and expresse a matter that happened unto
them or that they have seene and heard, that with their gesture
and wordes they set it before a mans eyes, and (in manner)
make him feele it with hand, and this peradventure for want of
an other terme we may call Festivitie or els Civilitie.[3]

The other sorte of jeastes[4] is verie briefe, and consisteth onely
in quicke and subtill[5] sayinges,[6] as many times there are heard
among us, and in nickes: neither doth it appeare that they are
of any grace, without some litle byting, and these among them
of olde time were also called Sayinges, now some terme them
Privie tauntes.

[1] Cf. "over-loquacity."
[2] Cf. "one . . . stretches out in long and continuous talk."
[3] "Festivitie," etc.: cf. "the humorous or urbane manner."
[4] Cf. "witticism."                          [5] "Subtill": cf. "sharp."
[6] "Sayinges": cf. "apophthegms."

I say therefore in the first kind, which is a merry manner of expressing, there needeth no arte, because very nature her selfe createth and shapeth men apt to expresse pleasantly, and giveth them a countenance, gestures, a voice, and wordes for the purpose to counterfeite what they lust.

In the other of Privie tauntes, what can arte doe? Since that quippe ought to be shot out and hit the pricke [1] before a man can discerne that he that speaketh it can thinke upon it, els it is colde and litle worth.

Therefore (thinke I) all is the worke of witte and nature.

Then tooke maister Peter Bembo the matter in hand, and said: The Lord Generall denieth not that you say: namely that nature and wit beare not the chiefest stroke, especially as touching invention, but it is certaine that in each mans minde, of how good a wit soever he be, there arise conceites both good and bad, and more and lesse, but then judgement and arte both polish and correct them, and chooseth the good and refuseth the bad.

Therefore laying aside that which belongeth to wit, declare you unto us that consisteth in arte: that is to wit of jeasts and merry conceites that move laughter, which are meete for y^e Courtier and which are not: and in what time and manner they ought to bee used: for this is that the Lord Generall demaundeth of you.

Then Sir Frederick saide smiling: there is never a one of us here that I will not give place unto in everie matter, and especially in jeasting, unlesse perhaps follies, which make men laugh many times more than wittie sayings, were also to be allowed for jeastes.

And so turning him to Count Lewis and to maister Bernard Bibiena, hee saide unto them. These bee the maisters of this facultie, of whom in case I must speak of merry sayings, I must first learne what I have to say.

Count Lewis answered: me thinke you begin now to practise that you say yee are not skilfull in, which is, to make these Lordes laugh in mocking maister Bernarde and me, because every one of them woteth well that the thing which you prayse us for, is much more perfectly in you.

Therefore in case you be wearie, it is better for you to sue to the Dutchesse that it would please her to deferre the remnant of our talke till to morrow, than to goe about with craft to ridde your handes of paines taking.

[1] "The pricke": cf. "the mark."

Sir Fredericke began to make answere, but the Ladie Emilia interrupted him immediatly and saide: It is not the order that the disputation should be consumed upon your prayse, it sufficeth yee are verie well knowne all. But because it commeth in my minde that you (Count) imputed to me yesternight, that I devided not y<sup>e</sup> paines taking equally, it shall bee well done that Sir Fredericke rest him a while and the charge of speaking of jeastes wee will commit to maister Bernarde Bibiena, for we doe not onely know him very quicke witted in talking without intermission, but also it is not out of our memory that hee hath sundrie times promised to write of this matter. And therefore we may thinke he hath very wel thought upon it all this while, and ought the better to satisfie us in it. Afterwarde when there shal be sufficiently spoken of jeastes, Sir Fredericke shall proceed forwarde againe with that he hath yet behinde concerning the Courtier.

Then saide Sir Fredericke: Madam, I know not what I have left behinde any more, but like a travailer on the way now wearie of the painefulnesse of my long journey at [1] noone tide, I will rest me in maister Bernardes communication at the sowne of his wordes, as it were under some faire tree that casteth a goodly shadow at the sweete roaring of a plentifull and living spring [2]: afterwarde (may happe) being somewhat refreshed, I may have somewhat els to say.

Maister Bernarde answered laughing: If I shew you the toppe, [3] ye shall see what shadow may be hoped for at the leaves of my tree.

To heare the roaring of the lively spring ye speake of, it may happen be your chance so to doe, for I was once turned into a spring: not by anie of the Goddes of olde time, but by our Frier Marian. And from that time hetherto I never wanted water.

Then began they all to fall in a laughing, because this pleasant matter which maister Bernard ment happened to him in Rome in the presence of Galeotto Cardinall of S. Petro in Vincula, was well knowne to them all.

After they had ceased laughing, the Ladie Emilia saide: Leave now making us laugh with practising of jeastes, and teach us how we should use them, and whence they are derived, and whatever els ye know in this matter. And for losing any more time, beginne out of hand.

---

[1] "At": cf. "and."
[2] Cf. "with the soft murmur (*mormorar sueve*) of a plashing spring."
[3] "Toppe": cf. "head." Bibbiena was bald.

I doubt me, quoth maister Bernard, it is late, and least my talke of pleasant matters should seeme unpleasant and tedious, perhaps it were good to deferre it till to morrow.

Here incontinently many made answere that it lacked yet a good deale of the houre when they were wont to leave of reasoning.

Then maister Bernarde turning to the Dutchesse and the Ladie Emilia, I will not refuse this labour (quoth he) although I be wont to marvell at the boldnesse of them that dare take upon them to sing to the Lute, when our James Sansecondo standeth by, even so ought not I in the presence of hearers that have much better understanding in that I have to say, than I my selfe, take upon me to entreat of jeastes. Neverthelesse least I should shew a president to any of these Lordes to refuse that they shall bee charged withall, I will speake as briefly as I can possible what commeth in my minde as touching matters that cause laughter, which is so proper to us, that to describe a man, the common saying is, He is a living creature that can laughe: because this laughing is perceived onely in a man, and (in manner) alwaies is a token of a certaine jocondnesse and merry moode that he feeleth inwardly in his minde, which by nature is drawne to pleasantnesse,[1] and coveteth quietnesse and refreshing.

For which cause we see men have invented manie matters, as sportes, games and pastimes, and so many sundrie sortes of open shewes.

And because wee beare good will to such as are the occasion of this recreation of ours, the manner was among the kings of olde time, among the Romanes, the Athenians and many other, to get the good will of the people withall, and to feede eyes and mindes of the multitude, to make great Theaters, and other publike buildinges, and there to shew new devices of pastimes, running of horses and Charets, fightinges of men together, straunge beastes, Comedies, Tragedies, and daunces of Antique.[2] Neither did the grave Philosophers shun these sights, for manie times both in this manner and at bankets they refreshed their wearisome mindes,[3] in those high discourses and divine imaginations of theirs.

The which in likewise all sortes of men are willing to doe, for not onely Ploughmen, Mariners, and all such as are inured with hard and boysterous exercises with hand, but also holy religious

---

[1] "Pleasantnesse": cf. "amusement."
[2] "Daunces of Antique": cf. "mimes."
[3] Cf. "minds . . . fatigued by lofty discourse," etc.

men and prisoners that from houre to houre waite for death, goe about yet to seeke some remedie and medicine to refresh themselves.

Whatsoever therfore causeth laughter, the same maketh the mind jocunde and giveth pleasure, nor suffereth a man in that instant to mind the troublesome griefes that our life is full off.

Therefore (as you see) laughing is very acceptable to all men, and hee is much to be commended that can cause it in due time and after a comely sort.

But what this laughing is, and where it consisteth, and in what manner, sometime it taketh the veines, the eyes, the mouth and the sides, and seemeth as though it would make us burst, so that what ever resistance we make, it is not possible to keepe it, I will leave it to be disputed of Democritus, the which also in case he would promise us, hee shoulde not performe it.

The place therefore and (as it were) the head spring that laughing matters arise of, consisteth in a certaine deformitie, or ill favourednesse,[1] because a man laugheth onely at those matters that are disagreeing[2] in themselves, and (to a mans seeming) are in ill plight, where it is not so in deed.[3] I wote not otherwise how to expound it.

But if you will bethinke your selfe, ye shall perceive the thing that a man alwaies laugheth at, is a matter that soundeth not well, and yet is it not in ill sitting.

What kind of waies therefore those be that the Courtier ought to use in causing laughter, and of what scope, I will assay in what I can to utter unto you as farre as my judgement can give me, because to make men laugh alwaies is not comely for the Courtier, nor yet in such wise as frantike, dronken, foolish and fond men and in like manner common jeasters doe: and though to a mans thinking, Courtes can not be without such kind of persons, yet deserve they not the name of a Courtier, but each man to be called by his name, and esteemed such as they are.

The scope and measure to make men laugh in taunting, must also be diligently considered: who he is that is taunted, for it provoketh no laughter to mocke and scorne a sillie soule in miserie and calamitie, nor yet a naughtie knave and common ribauld, because a man would thinke that these men deserved to be otherwise punished, than in jeasting at. And mens minds are not bent to scoffe them in miserie, unlesse such men in their

---

[1] "Deformitie," etc.: cf. "a kind of distortion."
[2] "Disagreeing," etc.: cf. "that have incongruity."
[3] Cf. "seem amiss without being so."

mishappe bragge and boast of themselves, and have a proud and hautie stomacke.

Againe, a respect must be had to them that are generally favoured and beloved of every man, and that beare stroke, because in mocking and scorning such a one, a man may sometime purchase himselfe daungerous enimitie. Therefore it is not amisse to scoffe and mocke at vices that are in persons not of such miserie that it should move compassion, nor of such wickednesse that a man would thinke they deserved not to goe on the ground, nor of such authoritie, that any litle displeasure of theirs may be a great hinderance to a man.

You shall understande moreover, that out of the places[1] jeasting matters are derived from, a man may in like manner picke grave sentences to praise or dispraise. And otherwhile with the selfe same words, as to praise a liberall man that partaketh his goods in common with his friendes, the common saying is, That he hath, is none of his owne.

The like may bee saide in dispraise of one that hath stolen or compassed that hee hath by other ill meanes. It is also a common saying, She is a woman of no small price, when a man will prayse her for the vertues, for her wisedom and goodnesse. The verie same may be saide of a woman that looketh to be kept sumptuously.

But it commeth oftner to purpose, that a man in this case serveth his turne with the selfe same places, than with the selfe same wordes. As within these few dayes three gentlemen standing at masse together in a Church where was a gentlewoman one of the three was in love withall, there came a poore begger and stood before her requiring her almes, and so with much instance and lamenting with a groning voice repeated many times his request: yet for all that did she not give him her almes, nor deny it him in making signe to depart in Gods name, but stood musing with her selfe as though she minded an other matter.

Then saide the gentleman that loved her, to his two companions, see what I may hope for at my mistresse hands, which is so cruel, that she will neither give the poore naked soule dead for hunger, that requireth her with such passion and so instantly, her almes, ne yet leave to depart, so much she rejoyceth to behold with her eyes one that is brought lowe with miserie, and that in vaine requireth her rewarde.

One of the two answered: it is no crueltie, but a privie admoni-

[1] "Out of the places": cf. "from the same occasion."

tion for you to doe you to wit, that your mistresse is not pleased with him that requireth her with much instance.

The other answered: Nay, it is rather a lesson for him, that although she give not that is required of her, yet she is willing inough to be sued to.

See here, because the gentlewoman sent not the poore man away, there arose one saying of great dispraise, one of modest praise, and another of nipping boord.[1]

To returne therefore to declare the kindes of jeastes appertaining to our purpose, I say (in mine opinion) there are of three sortes, although Sir Fredericke hath made mention but of two. The one a civill and pleasant declaration without interruption, which consisteth in the effect[2] of a thing. The other a quick and subtil readinesse, which consisteth in one saying alone.[3]

Therefore will we adde a third sorte to these, which we call Boordes or merrie Pranckes, wherein the processe is long, and the sayings short, and some deedes withall.[4]

The first therefore that consisteth in communication without interruption, are in that sorte (in a maner) as though a man would tell a tale. And to give you an example, when Pope Alexander ye sixt dyed and Pius the third was created, being then in Rome, and in the Palaice, your Sir Anthonie Agnello of Mantua, my Ladie Dutchesse, and communing of the death of the one, and creation of the other, and therein making sundrie discourses with certaine friends of his, he saide.

Sirs, in Catullus time, gates began to speake without tongues, and to heare without eares, and in that sorte discovered Advouteries.[5]

Now although men bee not of such worthinesse as they were in those dayes, yet perhaps the gates that are made, a great sort of them especially here in Rome, of auncient Marble, have the same vertue they had then.

And for my part I believe that these two will cleare us of all our doubtes, in case wee will aske counsaile of them.

Then those Gentlemen mused much at the matter, and attended to see to what end it would come, when sir Anthony following on still[6] up and down lift up his eies, as at a sodaine, to one of the two gates of the Hall where they walked: and

---

[1] "Nipping boord": cf. "biting satire."
[2] "In the effect": cf. "in rendering the effect."
[3] "One saying": cf. "a single phrase."
[4] Cf. "called practical joking, in which long narratives and short sayings have place, and also some action."
[5] "Advouteries": cf. "adulteries."          [6] Cf. "continuing to walk."

staying a while, with his finger hee shewed his company the inscription over it, which was Pope Alexanders name, and at the end of it was V, and I, because it should signifie (as ye know) the sixt.

And said: See here, this gate saith Alexander Papa VI., which signifieth, he hath beene Pope through the force he hath used, and hath prevailed more thereby than with right and reason.

Now let us see if we may of this other understand any thing of the new Bishop: and turning him as at adventure to the other gate, pointed to the inscription of one N, two P P, and one V, which signifieth Nicolaus Papa quintus, and immediately he said.

Good Lord, ill newes, see here this gate saith *Nihil Papa valet*.

See now how this kinde of jeastes is proper and good, and how fitting it is for one in Court, whether it be true or false a man saith, for in this case it is lawfull to feigne what a man lusteth [1] without blame: and in speaking the truth, to set it forth with a feate lye, augmenting or diminishing according to the purpose.

But the perfect grace and very pith of this, is to set forth so well and without paine,[2] not onely in wordes, but in gestures, the thing a man purposeth to expresse, that unto the hearers he may appeare to doe before their eyes the thinges he speaketh of.

And this expressed manner in this wise hath such force, that otherwhile it setteth forth and maketh a matter delite very much, which of it selfe is not very merrie nor wittie.

And although these protestations neede gestures, and the earnestnesse that a lively voice hath, yet is the force of them knowne also otherwhile in writing.

Who laugheth not when John Boccaccio in the eight journey of his hundreth tales [3] declareth how the Priest of Varlungo strained himselfe to sing a Kyrie and a Sanctus, when he perceived Belcolore was in the Church.

There be also pleasant declarations in his tales of Calandrino,[4] and manie other.

After the same sort seemeth to be the making of a man laugh in counterfeiting [5] or imitating (how ever wee list to terme it) of a mans manners, wherein hetherto I have seene none passe our maister Robert of Bari.

---

[1] Cf. "to fabricate as much as he pleased."
[2] "Without paine": cf. "with such ease."
[3] Cf. "the Eighth Day of his *Decameron*" (tale two).
[4] "Calandrino": see *Decameron*, Eighth Day, tales three and six; Ninth Day, tale five.
[5] Cf. "by mimicry."

This were no small praise quoth maister Robert, if it were true, for then woulde I surely goe about to counterfeite rather the good than the bad: and if I could liken my selfe to some I know, I would thinke my self a happie man. But I feare me I can counterfeite nothing but what maketh a man laugh, which you saide before consisteth in vice.[1]

Maister Bernard answered. In vice in deede, but that that standeth not in ill plight.[2] And weete ye well that this counterfeiting yee speake of, can not be without wit, for beside the manner to apply his wordes and his gestures, and to set before the hearers eyes the countenance and manners of him he speaketh of, he must bee wise, and have great respect to the place, to the time and to the persons with whom hee talketh, and not like a common jeaster passe his boundes, which thinges you wonderfully well observe, and therefore I believe yee are skilfull in all.

For undoubtedly it is not meete for a gentleman to make weeping and laughing faces, to make soundes and voices, and to wrastle with him selfe alone, as Berto doth, to apparrel himselfe like a lobbe of the Countrie, as doth Strascino, and such other matters, which doe well become them, because it is their profession.

But we must by the way and privily steale this counterfeiting,[3] alwaies keeping the estate of a gentleman, without speaking filthie wordes, or doing uncomely deedes, without making faces and antiques, but frame our gestures after a certaine manner, that who so heareth and seeth us, may by our wordes and countenances imagine much more than he seeth and heareth, and upon that take occasion to laugh.

He must also in this counterfeiting take heede of too much taunting in touching a man, especially in the ill favourednesse of visage, or ill shape of bodie. For as the mishaps and vices of the bodie minister many times ample matter to laugh at, if a man can discretely handle it, even so the using of this manner too bytingly, is a token not onely of a common jeaster, but of a plaine enimie.

Therefore must a man observe in this point (though it be hard) the fashion of our maister Robert, as I have saide, which counterfeiteth all men, and not without touching them in the matters wherein they be faultie, and in the presence of them selves, and yet no man findeth himselfe agreed, neither may a man thinke

---

[1] "In vice": cf. "in the imperfect."
[2] Cf. "Imperfect, yes; but not unpleasantly so."
[3] "By the way," etc.: cf. "give only a fleeting and covert imitation."

that he can take it in ill part. And of this I will give you no example, because we all see infinite in him dayly.

Also it provoketh much laughter (which neverthelesse is contained under declaration [1]) when a man repeateth [2] with a good grace certaine defaults of other men, so they be meane and not worthie greater correction: as foolish matters sometime simply of them selves alone, sometime annexed with a litle readie nipping fondnesse. Likewise certaine extreame curious matters. Otherwhile a great and well forged lye: as few dayes agoe our maister Cesar declared a pretie foolish matter, which was, that being with the Maior of this Citie, hee saw a Countrieman come to him, to complaine that hee had an asse stolen from him, and after he had tolde him of his povertie, and how the thiefe deceived him, to make his losse the greater he saide unto him.

Sir if you had seene mine Asse you should have known what a cause I have to complaine, for with his pad on his backe a man would have thought him verie Tully him selfe.

And one of our traine meeting a herde of Goates before the which was a mightie great Ram Goate, he stayed, and with a marvellous countenance saide: Marke me the Goate, he seemeth a Saint Paul.

The Lord Gasper saith, he knew an other, which for that he was an olde servant to Hercules Duke of Ferrara, did offer him two pretie boyes which he had, to be his pages, and these two died both before they came to his service. The which when the Duke understood, he lamented lovingly with the father, saying that he was verie sorie, bycause when he sawe them upon a time, hee thought them handsome and wittie children. The father made answere.

Nay my Lord, you sawe nothing, for within these few daies they were become much more handsome and of better qualities than I woulde ever have thought: and song together like a couple of Haukes.

And one of these dayes a Doctour of ours beholding one that was judged to bee whipped about the market place, and taking pittie upon him, because the poore soules shoulders bledde sore, and went so soft a pace, as though he had walked about for his pleasure to passe the time withall, he saide to him: Goe on a pace poore fellow, that thou maist be the sooner out of thy paine.

Then he turning about, and beholding him that so saide (in a manner) with a wonder, staied a while without any word,

---

[1] "Under declaration": cf. "under the head of narrative."
[2] Cf. "describes."

afterwarde he saide: When thou art whipped, goe at thy pleasure, for now will I goe as I shall thinke good.[1]

You may remember also the foolish matter that not long agoe the Duke rehearsed of the Abbot, that being present upon a day when Duke Fredericke was talking where he shoulde bestow the great quantitie of rubbish that was cast up to lay the foundation of this Pallace, working dayly uppon it, saide: My Lorde, I have well bethought mee where you shall bestow it, let there be a great pitte digged, and into that may you have it cast without any more adoe.

Duke Fredericke answered him not without laughter: And where then shall we bestowe the quantitie of earth that shall be cast out of that Pitte? The Abbot saide unto him: Let it be made so large, that it may wel receive both the one and the other. And so for all the Duke repeated sundrie times the greater the Pitte was, the more earth should be cast out of it, yet could he never make it sinke into his braine, but it might be made so large, that it might receive both the one and the other: and he answered him nothing else, but, make it so much the larger. Now see what a good forecast this Abbot had.

Then saide maister Peter Bembo: And why tell you not that, of your great Captaine of Florence, that was beseeged of the Duke of Calabria within Castellina? Where there were founde upon a day in the towne certaine quarels poysoned, that had beene shotte out of the campe, hee wrote unto the Duke, if the warre shoulde proceede so cruelly, he would also put a medicine upon his Gunstones, and then he that hath the worst, hath his mendes in his hands.[2]

Maister Bernarde laughed and saide: If you holde not your peace (maister Peter) I will tell whatsoever I have seene my selfe, and heard of your Venetians, which is not a litle, and especially when they play the ryders.

Doe not I beseech ye, answered maister Peter, for I will keepe to my selfe two other verie pretie ones that I know of your Florentines.

Maister Bernarde saide: They are rather of the Seneses,[3] for it often happeneth among them. As within these few dayes one of them hearing certaine letters read in the Councell Chamber, in which for avoiding too often repetition of his name y[t] was spoken of, this tearme was many times put in, *il Prelibato,*

[1] Cf. "when . . . you will go your own gait; so I choose to go mine now."
[2] Cf. "then woe to the one who had the worst of it."
[3] "Seneses": Sienese.

(which signifieth the aforenamed) he saide unto them that read them: soft, stay there a litle, and tell me this Prelibato what is he? A friende to our Communaltie?

Maister Peter laughed: then he proceeded: I speake of Florentines, and not of Seneses. Speake it hardly, quoth the Ladie Emilia, and bash not for that matter.

Maister Peter saide, when the Lords of Florence were in warre against the Pisanes they were otherwile out of money, by reason of their great charges and laying their heades together upon a day in the councell chamber, what way were best to make provision to serve their turne withall, after manie devises propounded, one of the auncientest Citizens saide.

I have found two waies, whereby without much travel we may in a small while come by a good portion of money. Whereof the one is (because we have no readier rent than the custome at the gates of Florence) where we have XI. gates, let us with speede make a XI. moe, and so shall we double our revenue.

The other way is to set up a Mint in Pistoia, and an other in Prato, no more nor lesse [1] than is here within Florence, and there doe nothing els day and night but coine money, and all Ducats of golde: and this devise (in mine opinion) is the speedier and lesse chargeable.

They fell a laughing a pace at the subtil device of the Citizen, and when laughing was ceased, the Ladie Emilia said: Will you (maister Bernarde) suffer maister Peter thus to jeast at Florentines without a revenge?

Maister Bernarde answered smiling: I pardon him this offence, for where hee hath displeased me in jeasting at Florentines, he hath pleased me in obeying of you, the which I would alwaies doe my selfe.

Then saide the Lord Cesar: I heard a Brescian speak a joly grosse matter, [2] which being this yeare in Venice at the feast of the Ascension, rehearsed in a place where I was to certaine mates of his, the goodly matters hee had seene there, what sundrie marchandise, what plate, what sortes of spices, and what cloth and silke there was, then how the Signoria issued out with a great pompe in the Bucentoro to wedde the Sea, in which were so many gentlemen well apparayled, so manye sortes of instruments and melodies, that a man would have thought it a Paradise.

And when one of his companions demaunded him what kinde of Musicke did please him best of all that he had hearde there,

---

[1] "No more," etc.: cf. "just the same."
[2] Cf. "a delightful blunder."

hee saide: All were good, yet among the rest I saw one blow on a straunge Trumpet, which at every push thrust it into his throate more than two handfull, and then by and by drew it out againe, and thrust it in a fresh, that you never saw a greater wonder.

Then they all laughed, understanding the fond imagination of him that thought the blower thrust into his throat that part of y^e Shagbut that is hid in putting it backe againe.

Then maister Bernarde went forwarde: Those affections and curiosities that are but meane, bring a lothsomnesse with them,[1] but when they bee done out of measure, they much provoke laughter. As otherwhile when some men are heard to speake of their auncientrie and noblenesse of birth: some time women of their beautie and handsomnesse.

As not long ago a gentlewoman did, which at a great feast being verie sad, and musing with her selfe, it was demanded of her what she thought upō, that should make her so sad. And she made answere, I thought upon a matter, which as oft as it commeth into my mind doth much trouble me, and I can not put it out of my hart: which is, where in the day of generall judgement, all bodies must arise againe and appeare naked before the judgement seat of Christ, I can not abide the griefe I feele in thinking that mine must also be seene naked.

Such affections as these be, because they passe the degree, doe rather provoke laughter than lothsomnesse.

Those feate lyes now that come so well to purpose, how they provoke laughter yee all know.

And that friend of ours that suffereth us not to want, within these fewe dayes rehearsed one to me that was verie excellent.

Then saide the Ladie Julian, What ever it were, more excellenter it can not be, nor more subtiler, than one that a Tuskane of ours, which is a merchant man of Luca, affirmed unto me the last day for most certaine.

Tell it us, quoth the Dutchesse. The Lord Julian saide smyling: This merchant man (as he saith) being upon a time in Polonia, determined to buye a quantitie of Sables, minding to bring them into Italie, and to gaine greatly by them. And after much practising in the matter, where he could not himselfe goe into Moscovia, because of the warre betwixt the king of Polonia, and the Duke of Moscovia, he tooke order by the meane of some of the Countrie, that upon a day appointed, certain merchant men of Moscovia should come with their Sables into the borders

---

[1] "Those affections . . . lothsomnesse": cf. "Moreover common affections are tedious."

of Polonia, and he promised also to be there himselfe to bargaine with them.

This merchant man of Luca travailing then with his company toward Moscovia, arrived at the river of Boristhenes, which he found hard frozen like a marble stone, and saw the Moscovites which for suspicion of the warre were in doubt of the Polones, were on the other side, and nearer came not than the breadth of the river.

So after they knew the one the other, making certain signes, the Moscovites beganne to speake aloude, and tolde the price howe they would sell their Sables, but the colde was so extreme, that they were not understood, because the wordes before they came on the other side where this merchant of Luca was and his interpreters, were congeled in the ayre, and there remained frozen and stopped. So that the Polones that knew the manner, made no more adoe, but kindled a great fire in the middest of the river (for to their seeming that was the point whereto the voyce came hote before the frost tooke it) and the river was so thicke frozen, that it did well beare the fire.

When they had thus done, the wordes that for space of an houre had beene frozen, beganne to thaw, and came downe, making a noyse as doth the snow frō the mountaines in May, and so immediately they were well understood: but the men on the other side were first departed[1]: and because he thought that those wordes asked too great a price for the Sables, he woulde not bargaine, and so came away without.

Then they laughed all. And maister Bernard, Truely (quoth hee) this that I will tell you is not so subtill, yet is it a pretie matter, and this it is.

Where talke was a few dayes agoe of the Countrie or world newly found out by the Mariners of Portugal,[2] and of straunge beastes and other matters brought from thence, that friende I tolde you of, affirmed that he had seene an Ape, very divers in shape from such as wee are accustomed to see that plaied excellently well at Chestes.

And among other times upon a day before the king of Portugal the gentleman that brought her plaied at Chestes with her, where the Ape shewed some draughtes[3] very subtil, so that she put him to his shifts, at length she gave him Checkemate. Upon this the gentleman being somewhat vexed (as commonly they

---

[1] "First departed": cf. "already gone."
[2] The reference is to Vasco da Gama's voyage to India.
[3] "Some draughtes": cf. "some moves."

are all that lose at the game) toke the king in his hand which
was good and bigge (as the fashion is among the Portugales) and
reached yᵉ Ape a great knocke on the heade. She forthwith
leaped aside complaining greatly, and seemed to require justice
at the kinges handes for the wrong done her.

The gentleman afterward called her to play with him again,
the which with signes she refused a while, but at last was contented to playe another game, and as she had done the other
time before, so did she now drive him to a narrow point.

In conclusion: the Ape perceiving she could give the gentleman the mate, thought with a new devise she would be sure to
escape without any moe knockes, and privily conveyed her
right hand without making semblant what her intent was,
under the gentlemans left elbowe, leaning for pleasure upon a
litle taffata coushin, and snatching it slightly away, at one
instant gave him with her left hand a mate with a paune,[1] and
with her right hand cast the coushing upon her head to save
her from strokes: then she made a gamboll before the king
joyfully, in token (as it were) of her victory. Now see whether
this Ape were not wise, circumspect, and of a good understanding.

Then spake the Lord Cesar Gonzaga: It must needs be that
this Ape was a doctour among other Apes, and of much authoritie: and I believe the common weale of the Apes of India sent
her into Portugal to get a name in a straunge Countrie.

At this every man laughed, both for the lye and for the
addition made to it by the Lord Cesar: so proceeding on in this
talke, maister Bernard saide: you have understood therefore
what jeastes are that be of effect and communication without
interruption as much as commeth to minde: therefore it shall
be well now we speake of such as consist in one saying alone,
and have a quick sharpnesse that lyeth briefly in a sentence or
in a worde. And even as in the first kinde of merrie talke a man
must in his protestation and counterfeiting take heede that hee
be not like common jeasters and parasites, and such as with
fond matters move men to laugh, so in this briefe kinde the
Courtier must be circumspect that he appeare not malicious
and venemous, and speake tauntes and quippes onely for spite
and to touch the quicke, because such men oftentimes for offence
of the tongue are chastised in the whole bodie.

Of those readie jeastes therefore that consist in a short saying,
such are most lively that arise of doubtfulnesse,[2] though alwaies

---

[1] Cf. "checkmated him with a pawn."
[2] "Doubtfulnesse": cf. "ambiguity."

they provoke not laughing: for they bee rather praysed for wittie, than for matters of laughter. As few dayes it is that our maister Anniball Palleotto saide to one that appointed him a maister to teach his children the Grammer, and after that hee had praysed him, to be a man very well learned, coming to wages, saide, that besides the money he would have a chamber furnished to dwell and sleepe in, for that he had not *letto*, that is a bedde.

Then maister Anniball answered presently: and how can he be learned, if he have not *letto*, that is, read.

See how well he tooke a vantage at the diverse signification of *haver letto* (which is interpreted both to have a bedde, and to have read.) But because those doubtfull wordes have a pretie sharpenesse of wit in them, being taken in a contrarie signification to that all other men take them, it appeareth (as I have saide) that they rather provoke a man to wonder than to laugh, except when they be joyned with other kindes of sayinges.

The kinde therefore of wittie sayinges that is most used to make men laugh, is when we give eare to heare on thing, and he that maketh answere, speaketh an other, and is alledged contrarie to expectation, and in case a doubt be annexed therewithall, then it is verie wittie and pleasant. As the last night disputing to make a faire *mattonato*, that is, paviment in the chamber of the Ladie Dutchesse, after many wordes. You maister John Christopher saide, If we could have the bishop of Potentia, and make him flat, it should be very fit, for that he is the fairest *matto nato*, that is naturall foole, that ever I did see.[1]

Every one laughed greatlye for that dividing that worde *matto nato* you made the doubt, afterwarde saying that if they had to make flat a bishop and place him for paviment of a chamber it was farre from the opinion of the hearers, thus the sentence came to bee verie sharpe and worthie the laughing.

But of doubtfull wordes there be many sortes, therefore must a man bee circumspect, and choose out termes very artificiall, and leave out such as make the jeast colde, and that a man would weene were haled by the haire, or els (as wee have saide) that have too much bitternesse in them. As certain cōpanions being in a friends house of theirs, who had but one eye, after he had desired the companie to tarrie dinner with him, they departed all saving one, that saide.

And I am well pleased to tarrie, for I see a voide roome for

---

[1] A pavement (*mattonato*) was required. Bring the bishop, said one, for he is the craziest creature born (*il più bel matto nato*).

one, and so with his finger pointed to the hole where his eye had beene.

See how bitter and discourteous this is passing measure, for he nipped him without a cause, and without being first pricked himselfe: and he saide the thing that a man might speake against blinde men. Such generall matters delite not, because it appeareth they are thought upon of purpose.

And after this sorte was the saying to one without a nose: And where dost thou fasten thy spectacles? Or wherewithall doest thou smell Roses at the time of the yeare?

But among other merry sayings, they have a verie good grace, that arise when a man at the nipping talke of his fellow, taketh the verie same words in the selfe same sense, and returneth them backe againe, pricking him with his owne weapon. As an Attorney in the law, unto whom in the presence of the Judge his adversarie saide, what barkest thou? Forthwith he answered: Because I see a thiefe.

And of this sorte was also, when Galeotto of Narni passing through Siena stayed in a streete to enquire for an Inne, and a Senese seeing him so corpulent as he was, saide laughing: Other men carrie their Bougettes behind them, and this good fellow carrieth his before him. Galeotto answered immediately: So must men doe in the Countrie of theeves.

There is yet an other sorte called in Italian _Bischizzi_ and that consisteth in chaunging or increasing, or diminishing of a letter or sillable. As he that said: Thou shouldest be better learned in the Latin tongue than in the Greeke.

And to you (madam) was written in the superscription of a letter, To the Ladie Emilia Impia.

It is also a merrie devise to mingle together a verse or moe, taking it in an other meaning than the Author doth, or some other common saying. Sometime in the verie same meaning, but altering a worde, as a gentleman that had a foule and scouling wife: when he was asked the question how hee did, he answered.

Thinke thou thy selfe, for _Furiarum maxima juxta me cubat._[1]

And maister Hierom Donato going a visiting the Stations of Rome in Lent in companie with many other gentlemen, met with a knotte of faire Romane Ladies, and when one of these gentlemen had said:

Quot cœlum stellas, tot habet tua Roma Puellas.[2]

[1] He changed Virgil's "accubat" ("lies hard by"), to "cubat" —"the greatest of the Furies couches with me."

[2] "As many stars as heaven has, so many girls has Rome."

By and by he added:

Pascua quotque hædos, tot habet tua Roma cinædos.[1]

Shewing a rout of yong men that came on the other side.

And Marcantonio della Torre said after the manner to the bishop of Padoa, Where there was a Nunrie in Padoa, under the charge of a religious person, much esteemed for his good life and learning, it happened that this Father haunting much to the Nunrie very familiarly, and confessing often the sisters, begatte five of them with childe, where there were not passing five mo in all. And when the matter was knowne, the Father would have fledde, and wist not how.

The bishoppe caused him to be apprehended, and upon that, he confessed that he had gotten those five Nunnes with childe through ye temptations of the divel, so that the bishoppe was fully bent to chastice him sore. And because this man was learned, hee had made manie friendes, which altogether assayed to helpe him, and among the rest there went also maister Marcontonio, to entreate for him.

The bishop woulde in no wise give eare to them. At length they being instant upon him, and commending the guiltie, and excusing him through the commoditie of place, frailtie of man, and many other causes, the bishop saide.

I will doe nothing for you, because I must make account unto God of this. And when they had replied againe, the bishop said: what answere shall I make unto God at the day of judgemēt, when he shall say unto me, *Redde rationem villicationis tuæ?*[2]

Maister Marcantonio answered him immediatelye: Mary my Lorde, the verie same that the Gospel saith[3]: *Domine quinque talenta tradidisti mihi, ecce alia quinque superlucratus sum.*

Then could not the bishop abstaine laughing, and hee asswaged much his anger and the punishment that hee had ordained for the offender.

It is likewise verie pretie to allude to names and to faine somewhat, wherfore he yt the talke is of is so called, or els because he doth some thing: as not long since the provost of Luca (which as you know is one merrilie disposed) asking the bishoprik of Caglio, the Pope answered him.

Dost thou not know that Caglio, in ye Spanish tongue is as much to say as, I holde my peace, and thou art a great prater.

---

[1] "As many kids has pasture, so many sodomites has your Rome."
[2] "Give an account of thy stewardship," etc. —St. Luke xvi. 2.
[3] See St. Matthew xxv. 20.

Therefore it were unfitting for a bishop at any time in naming his title to make a lye, now Calia, hold thy peace then.

To this yᵉ provost gave an answere, the which although it were not in this sorte, yet was it no lesse pretie than this. For after he had often put him in remembrance of this his sute and saw it of none effect, at last hee saide, Holy father, in case your holinesse doe give me this bishoprike, it shall not be without profit to you, for then will I surrender two offices into your hands.

And what offices hast thou to surrender into my handes, quoth the Pope? the provost answered: I shall surrēder unto you *Officium principale* and *Officium beatæ Mariæ.*[1]

Then could not the Pope though he were a very grave person, abstaine from laughing. An other also in Padoa saide, Calphurnius was so named because he was wont to heate furnaces.

And upon a day when I asked Phedra how it happeneth, where prayer is made in the Church upon good Fryday not onely for Christians, but also for Paganes and for Jewes, there was no mention made of the Cardinalles, as there was of bishops and other prelates. He answered me, that the Cardinalles were contained in the Collect, *Oremus pro hæreticis et Schismaticis.*

And our Count Lewis saide, that I reprehended a ladie of love for occupying a certaine kinde of lye[2] that shined much, because when she was trimmed therewithall, I might see my selfe in her face, and for that I was ill favoured I could not abide to looke upon my selfe.

In this manner was that maister Camillo Paleotto said unto maister Anthonio Porcaro, which reasoning of a companion of his that under confession had saide unto the Priest that he fasted with all his hart, and went to Masse and to holy service, and did all the good deedes in the world, saide: This fellow in stead of accusing praiseth him selfe. Unto whom maister Camillo answered nay, he rather confesseth him selfe of these matters, because he reckoneth the doing of them great sinne.

Doe you not remember how well the Lord Generall saide the last day, when John Thomas Galeotto wondred at one that demaunded two hundred Ducats for a horse? for when John Thomas said that he was not worthie a farthing, because among other ill properties he had, he coulde not abide weapons, neither was it possible to make him come nigh where he saw any, the Lord Generall saide (willingly to reprehend him of cowardise)

[1] The play is on the word "officium" (*ufficio*), meaning employment and, here, prayer book. The "Officium principale" is complete, the "Officium Mariæ" abbreviated.
[2] Cf. "for using a certain cosmetic."

if the horse hath this propertie that hee can not abide weapons, I marvell hee asketh not a thousand Ducates.

Also sometime a man speaketh the very same word, but to another ende than the common use is. As, when the Duke was passing over a verie swift river, he saide to the trumpeter: goe on. The trumpeter turned him backe with his cappe in his hand and after a reverent manner, saide: It shall bee yours my Lord.[1]

It is also a pleasant manner of jeasting, when a man seemeth to take the wordes and not the meaning of him that speaketh. As this yeare a Dutchman in Rome meeting in an evening our maister Phillip Beroaldo whose scholler he was, saide unto him *Domine magister, Deus det vobis bonum sero*. And Beroaldo answered incontinently *Tibi malum cito*.[2]

And another Spaniard sitting at the table with the great Captaine, Diego de Chignognes saide, *Vino dios*[3] (calling for wine) Diego answered him againe: *Vino, y no lo conocistes*, to nip him for a chesnut.[4]

Also maister James Sadoleto saide unto Beroaldo, that had tolde him how hee would in any wise goe to Bolonia, what is the cause that maketh you thus to leave Rome where there are so many pleasures, to goe to Bolonia, full of disquietnesse?

Beroaldo answered: I am forced to goe to Bolonia for three Counts. And now he had lift up three fingers of his left hand to alledge three causes of his going, when maister James sodainly interrupted him and saide: The three countes that make you goe to Bolonia are, Count Lewis da San Bonifacio, Count Hercules Rangon and the Count of Pepoli.

Then they all laughed because these three Countes had been Beroaldoes scholers and were proper young men and applyed their studie in Bolonia.

This kinde of merry jeasting therfore maketh a man laugh much, because it bringeth with it other manner answeres than a man looketh for to heare, and our own errour doth naturally delite us in these matters, which when it deceiveth us of that we looke for, wee laugh at it.

---

[1] Cf. "turned cap in hand . . . and said . . . 'After your Lordship.'"

[2] "Master, God give you good evening." He used *sero* in the Low Latin sense (evening). His master twisted it to the classical sense (late), and replied in kind, "Evil to you, soon."

[3] *Dios* is omitted in other versions. *Vino* may mean "wine," or "he came." In this latter sense Diego answered it: "He came (Christ) and you knew Him not."

[4] Hoby seems to have confused *marrone*, which means a large chestnut, with *marrano* (or *marrané*), a traitor, a heretic. "Heretic" is meant.

But the termes of speach and figures that have any grace and grave talke, are likewise (in a manner) alwaies comely in jeastes and merrie pleasantnesse.

See how wordes placed contrariwise give a great ornament, when one contrarie [1] clause is set against an other.

The same manner is oftentimes verie merrie and pleasant. As a Genuese that was verie prodigall and lavish in his expences being reprehended by an usurer, who was most covetous that saide unto him: And when wilt thou leave casting away thy substance? Then answered he: when thou leavest stealing of other mens.

And because (as we have alreadie saide) of the places that wee derive jeastes from, that touch a man, wee may many times from the very same take grave sentences to praise and cōmend: It is a very comely and honest manner both for the one and the other purpose, when a man consenteth to and confirmeth the selfe same thing that the other speaketh, but interpreteth it otherwise thā he meaneth.

As within these few daies a Priest of the countrie saying Masse to his parishioners, after he had told them what holy dayes they should have that weeke, he beganne the generall confession in the name of all the people, and saide: I have sinned in ill doing, in ill speaking, in ill thinking, and the rest that followeth, making mention of all the deadly sins. Then a Gossippe of his and one that was very familiar with the Priest to sporte with him, saide to the standers by.

Beare recorde, Sirs, what he confesseth with his owne mouth he hath done, for I entend to present him to the bishop for it.

The very same manner used Sallazza della Pedrad to honour a Ladie withall, with whom entring in talk, after he had praysed her, beside her vertuous qualities, for her beautie also, she answered him that she deserved not that praise, because she was now well striken in yeares. And he then saide to her: That is in you of age,[2] is nothing els but to liken you unto the Angels which were first, and are the auncientest creatures that ever God made.

Also merry sayinges are much to the purpose to nippe a man, as well as grave sayinges to praise one, so the metaphors be well applyed, and especially if they be answered, and he that maketh answere continue in the selfe same metaphor spoken by the other.

And in this sorte was answered to M. Palla Strozzi, which

---

[1] Cf. "contrasting."    [2] Cf. "Your only sign of age."

banished out of Florence, and sending thither one of his about certaine affaires, saide unto him after a threatening manner.

Tel Cosmus de Medicis in my name, that the henne sitteth[1] a brood. The messenger did the errand to him, as hee was willed. And Cosmus without any more deliberation, answered him immediately.

Tell maister Palla in my name againe, that Hens can full ill sit a brood out of the nest.

With a metaphor also maister Camillo Parcaro commended honorably the Lord Marcantonia Colonna, who understanding that maister Camillo in an Oration of his had extolled certaine noble men of Italy that were famous in marciall prowesse, and among the rest had made most honourable mention of him, after rendring due thankes, he saide to him: you (maister Camillo) have done by your friendes as some marchant men play by their money, which finding a counterfeite Ducate, to dispatch him away, cast him into a heape of good ones and so utter him.

Even so you, to honour me withall, where I am litle worth, have set me in companie with so excellent and vertuous personages, that through their prowesse, I may peradventure passe for a good one. Then maister Camillo made answere.

They that use to counterfeite Ducates, gylt them so that they seeme to the eye much better than the good: therefore if there were to be found counterfeiters of men, as there be of Ducates, a man might have a just cause to suspect you were false, being (as you are) of much more faire and brighter mettall than anie of the rest.

You may see that this place is common both for the one and the other kinde of jeastes, and so are many moe, of the which a man might give infinite examples, and especially in grave sayinges. As the great captaine saide, (which being set at table and every roome filled) saw two Italian gentlemen standing by that had done him verie good service in the warre, sodainly he start up and made all the rest to arise to give place to those two, and saide.

Make roome Sirs for the gentlemē to sit at their meat, for had not they beene, wee shoulde not have had now wherewithall to feede our selves. He saide also to Diego Garzia that perswaded him to remove out of a dangerous place that lay open upon gunshot: Since God hath not put feare into your minde, put not you it into mine.

---

[1] "Sitteth": cf. "is hatching."

And king Lewis, which is now French king, where it was saide unto him soone after his creation, that then was the time to be even with the enimies that had done him much injurie while hee was Duke of Orleans. Hee made answere: That the French king hath nothing adoe to revenge the wronges done to the Duke of Orleans.

A man toucheth also in jeast manie times with a certaine gravitie without moving a man to laugh. As Gein Ottomani brother to the great Turke, when hee was prisoner in Rome, he saide: Justing (as wee used it in Italie) seemed to him over great a daliance, and a trifle to that should be in deede.

And he saide, when it was told him that king Ferdinande the younger was nimble and quicke of person in running, leaping, vauting, and such matters, in his countrey slaves used these exercises, but great men learned from their childhood liberalitie, and were renowmed for that.

And in a manner after that sorte, saving it had a litle more matter to laugh at, was that the Archbishop of Florence saide unto Cardinall Alexandrino, That men have nothing but Substance, a bodie and a soule. Their Substance is at Lawiers disposing,[1] their bodie at Phisitions, and their soule at Divines.

Then answered the Lord Julian: A man might adde unto this y$^e$ saying of Nicholetto: which is, that it is seldom seene a Lawier to goe to law, nor a Phisition take medicin, nor a Divine a good Christian.

Maister Bernarde laughed, then hee proceeded: Of this there bee infinite examples spoken by great Princes and very grave men. But a man laugheth also many times at comparisons. As our Pistoia wrote unto Seraphin: I send thee backe againe thy great male [2] which is like thy selfe. If ye remember well Seraphin was much like a male.

Againe, there be some that have a pastime to liken men and women to horses, to dogges, to birdes, and often times to coffers, to stooles, to cartes, to candelstickes, which sometime hath a good grace, and otherwhile very stale.

Therefore in this point a man must consider the place, the time, the persons, and the other thinges wee have so manie times spoken of.

Then spake the Lord Gasper Pallavicin: The comparison that the Lorde John Gonzaga made of Alexander the great to maister Alexander his sonne, was very pleasant. I wote not what it was, answered maister Bernarde.

[1] Cf. "put in peril by."        [2] "Male": cf. "wallet."

The Lord Gasper saide: The Lord John was playing at dice (as his use is) and had lost a number of Ducats and was still on the losing hand, and maister Alexander his sonne, which for all hee is a childe, deliteth no lesse in play than his Father, stoode very still to behold him, and seemed very sad.

The Count of Pianella, that was there present with manie other gentlemen, said: See (my Lord) maister Alexander is verie heavie for your losse, and his hart panteth waiting when lucke wil come to you that he may get some of your winninges: therfore rid him of his griefe, and before yee lose the rest, give him at least one Ducate that he may goe play him too, among his companions.

Then saide the Lord John: You are deceived, for Alexander thinketh not upon such a trifle, but as it is writen of Alexander the great while he was a childe, understanding that Philip his father had discomfitted a great armie, and conquered a certaine kingdom, he fell in weeping, and when he was asked the question why he wept, hee answered, because he doubted that his father woulde conquere so many Countreyes, that he woulde have none left for him to conquere: Even so now Alexander my sonne is sory and readie to weepe in seeing me his father lose, because he doubted that I shall lose so much, that I shall leave him nothing at all to lose. When they had a while laughed at this, maister Bernarde went forwarde.

A man must take heed also his jeasting be not wicked, and that the matters extend not to appeare quicke witted, to blaspheme, and studie therein to invent new waies.

Least herein, where a man deserveth not onely blame, but also sharpe punishment, he should appeare to seeke a prayse, which is an abhominable matter. And therefore such as these be, that goe about to shew their pregnant witte with small reverence to Godwarde, deserve to bee excluded out of everie gentlemans company.

And no lesse, they that be filthie and baudie in talke, and that in the presence of women have no manner respect, and seeme to take none other delite, but to make women blush for shame, and uppon this go seeking out merrie and jeasting words.

As this yeare in Ferrara at a banket in presence of many Ladies, there was a Florentine and a Senese, which for the most part (as you know) are enimies together. The Senese saide to nip the Florentine: We have marryed Siena to the Emperour and given him Florence to dowrie. And this he spake because the talke was abroad in those dayes, that the Seneses had given a certaine quantitie of money to the Emperour, and he tooke the protection of them upon him.

The Florentine answered immediately: But Siena shall be first ridden (after the French phrase, but hee spake the Italian word) and then shall the dowrie afterwarde be pleaded for at good leasure.

You may see the taunt was wittie, but because it was in presence of women, it appeared bawdie and not to be spoken.

Then spake the Lord Gasper Pallavicin: Women have none other delite but to heare of such matters, and yet will you deprive them of it. And for my part I have beene readie to blush for shame at wordes which women have spoken to mee oftner than men.

I speake not of such women as these be, quoth maister Bernard, but of the vertuous that deserve to be reverenced and honoured of all gentlemen.

The Lorde Gasper saide: It were good we might find out some pretie rule how to know them, because most commonly the best in apparance are cleane contrarie in effect.

Then saide maister Bernard smiling: were not the Lorde Julian here present, that in every place is counted the protector of women, I would take upon me to answere you, but I will not take his office from him.

Here the Ladie Emilia in like manner smyling, saide: Women neede no defender against an accuser of so small authoritie. Therefore let the Lorde Gasper alone in this his forward opinion, risen more because he could never finde woman that was willing to looke upon him, than for any want that is in women, and proceed you in your communication of jeastes.

Then maister Bernarde, truely Madam (quoth hee) me thinke I have named unto you many places, out of the which a man may picke pleasaunt and wittie sayinges, which afterwarde have so much the more grace, as they are set forth with a comelye protestation.

Yet may there bee alleaged manie other also, as when to increase or diminish, thinges be spoken that uncredibly passe the likelihood of truth. And of this sorte was that Marius de Volterra saide by a prelate that thought him selfe so tall a person, that as he went into Saint Peters, hee stouped for hitting his heade against the great beame over the porch.

Also the Lord Julian here saide, that Golpino his servant was so leane and drye, that in a morning as he was blowing the fire to kindle it, the smoke bore him up the chimney unto the fonnel, and had gone away with him had he not stuck on the crosse at one of the holes above.

And maister Augustine Bevazzano tolde, that a covetous man which woulde not sell his corne while it was at a high price, when he saw afterwarde it had a great fall, for desperation hee hanged him selfe upon a beame in his chamber, and a servant of his hearing the noise, made speede, and seeing his maister hang, forthwith cut in sunder the rope and so saved him from death: afterwarde when the covetous man came to him selfe, hee would have had his servant to have paide him for his haulter that he had cut.

Of this appeareth to bee also that Laurence de Medicis saide unto a colde jeaster: thou shouldest not make me to laugh if thou tickledst me. The like he answered unto an other foolish person, who in a morning had found him in bed very late, and blamed him for sleeping so much, saying unto him: I have now beene in the newe and olde market place, afterwarde I went out at the gate of San Gallo to walke about the walles, and have done a thousand other matters, and you are yet in bedde. Then saide Laurence: that I have dreamed in one houre, is more worth, than all that you have done in foure.

It is also pretie when one reprehendeth a thing which a man would not thinke hee minded to reprehend. As the marquesse Fredericke of Mantua our Dutchesse father being at table with many gentlemen, one of them after he had eaten up his dish of broth, saide: by your leave my Lorde marquesse. And when he had so saide, he began to suppe up the rest that remained in the dish. Then saide the marquesse by and by: Aske leave of the swine, for thou doest me no wrong at all.

Also maister Nicholas Leonicus saide, to touch a noble man that was falsly reported to be liberall: Gesse you what liberalitie is in him, that doth not onely give away his owne good but other mens also.

That is in like manner an honest and comely kinde of jeasting, that consisteth in a certaine dissimulation, when a man speaketh one thing and privily meaneth another. I speake not of the manner that is clean contrarie, as if one shoulde call a dwarfe a giant: and a blacke man, white: or one most ill favored, beawtifull: because they be too open contraries, although otherwhile also they stirre a man to laugh. But when with a grave and drie speach in sporting a man speaketh pleasantly that hee hath not in his mind.

As when a gentleman tolde maister Augustine Folietto a loud

lye and earnestly did affirme it, because he thought he scarse believed it. At last maister Augustine saide: Gentleman, if you will ever doe me pleasure, be so good to me as to quiet your selfe in case I doe not believe any thing you say.

Yet when he replyed againe and bound it with an oth to be true, at length hee saide: Since you will have me, I am content to believe it for your sake, for to say the truth I would doe a greater thing for you than this commeth too.

In a manner after the same sorte Don Giovanni di Cardona saide of one that woulde forsake Rome: in mine opinion this fellow is ill advised, for hee is so wicked, that in abiding in Rome it may be his chaunce in time to be made a Cardinall.

Of this sorte is also that Alfonsus Santocroce saide, which a litle before having certaine injuries done him by the Cardinall of Pavia, and walking without Bolonia with certaine gentleman nigh unto the place of execution, and seeing one newly hanged there, turned him that way with a certaine heavie looke, and saide so loude that everie man might heare him: Thou art a happie man that hast nothing adoe with the Cardinall of Pavia.

And the kinde of jeasting that is somewhat grounded upon scoffing seemeth verie meete for great men, because it is grave and wittie and may be used both in sporting matters and also in grave.

Therefore did many of olde time and men of best estimation use it: As Cato, Scipio Affricanus minor. But above all they say Socrates the Philosopher excelled in it. And in our time king Alphonsus the first of Aragon: which upon a time as he went to dinner tooke many rich jewels from his fingers, for wetting them in washing his handes, and so gave them to him that stood next him as though hee had not minded who it was. This servant had thought sure the king marked not to whom he gave them, and because his heade was busied with more waightie affaires, woulde soone forget them cleane, and thereof hee tooke the more assurance when hee saw the king asked not for them againe. And when that matter was passed certaine dayes, weekes, and monthes without hearing any worde of it, he thought surely he was safe.

And so about the yeares end after this matter had happened, an other time as the king was in like manner going to dinner, he stepped forth and put out his hand to take the kinges ringes. Then the king rounding him in the eare, saide: The first is well[1] for thee, these shal be good for another.

[1] "Is well": cf. "will do."

See this taunt how pleasant, wittie, and grave it is, and worthie in verie deede for the noble courage of an Alexander.

Like unto this manner grounded upō scoffing there is also an other kinde, when with honest wordes, a man nameth a vicious matter or a thing that deserveth blame. As the great Captaine saide unto a gentleman of his, that after the journey of Cirignola and when all things were alreadie in safetie, met him as richly armed as might be, readie to fight. Then the great Captaine turning him to Don Ugo di Cardona, saide: Feare ye not now any more Sea tempest,[1] for S. Hermus [2] hath appeared. And with this honest worde hee gave him a nicke. Because you know Saint Hermus doth alwaies appeare unto Mariners after a tempest, and giveth a token of calme.

And the meaning of the great Captaine was, that when this gentleman appeared, it was a signe the daunger was alreadie cleane past.

Againe maister Octavian Ubaldino being in Florence in companie with certaine of the best Citizens, and reasoning together of souldiers, one of them asked him whether he knew Antonello da Forli which was then fledde out of the state of Florence. Maister Octavian answered: I have no great knowledge of him, but I have heard him alwaies reported to be a quicke souldier. Then saide an other Florentine, It appeareth he is quicke, for he tarried not so long as to aske leave to depart.

They be also pretie taunts when a man of the very communication of his fellow taketh that he would not, and my meaning is in that sort, as our Duke answered the Captaine that lost Saint Leo. When this state was taken by Pope Alexander, and given to Duke Valentin.

The Duke being in Venice at that time I speake of, many of his subjects came continually to give him secrete information how the matters of state passed, and among the rest, thither came also the Captaine: which after hee had excused himselfe the best he coulde, laying the fault in his unluckinesse, hee saide.

My Lord doubt ye not, my hart serveth mee yet to worke a mean that Saint Leo may be recovered again. Then answered the Duke: trouble not thy self any more about it, for in losing it thou hast wrought a meane that it may be recovered againe.[3]

Certaine other sayinges there are, when a man that is knowne to be wittie speaketh a matter that seemeth to proceede of

---

[1] "Sea tempest": cf. "storm."

[2] "Saint Hermus": cf. "Saint Elmo."

[3] Cf. "for the mere loss of it was a measure that rendered its recovery possible.

follie. As the last day maister Camillo Paleotto saide by one: that foole, as soone as hee began to waxe rich, died.

There is like unto this matter a certaine wittie and kinde dissimulation, when a man (as I have saide) that is wise maketh semblant not to understand that hee doth understand.

As the marquesse Fredericke of Mantua, which being sued to by a prating felow that complained upon a certaine of his neighbours taking the Pigions of his Dovehouse with snares, and held one continually in his hand hanging by the foote in a snare, which he had found so deade, hee answered him that there would be a remedie for it.

This fellow never satisfied, not once but many a time repeated unto him his losse, shewing alwaies the Pigion so hanged, and saide still: But I beseech you, how think ye (my Lorde) what shoulde a man doe in this matter?

The marquesse at length saide: By mine advise the Pigion ought in no wise to be buried in the Church, for since he hath so hanged him selfe, it is to be thought that he was desperate.

In a manner after the same sorte was that Scipio Nasica saide unto Ennius. For when Scipio went unto Ennius house to speake with him and called to him in the streete, a maiden of his made him answere that he was not at home. And Scipio heard plainely Ennius him self speak unto his maiden to tell him that he was not at home, so he departed.

Within a while after Ennius came unto Scipioes house, and so likewise stoode beneath, and called him. Unto whom Scipio himselfe with a loude voice made answere, that hee was not at home.

Then saide Ennius: What, doe not I know thy voice? Scipio answered: Thou hast small courtesie in thee, the last day I believed thy maiden, that thou wast not at home, and now wilt not thou believe me my selfe?

It is also pretie when one is touched in the verie same matter that he hath first touched his fellow.

As Alonso Carillo being in the Spanish Court, and having committed certaine youthfull partes, that were of no great importance, was by the kings commandement carried to prison, and there abode for one night. The next day he was taken out againe, and when he came to the pallace in the morning, he entred into the chamber of presence, that was full of gentlemen and Ladies, and jeasting together at this his imprisonment, maistresse Boadilla saide.

Maister Alonso, I tooke great thought for this mishap of

yours, for all that knew you were in feare lest the king would have hanged you.

Then saide immediatly Alonso: In deede maistresse, I was in doubt of the matter my selfe too, but yet I had a good hope that you would have begged me for your husband.

See how sharpe and wittie this is. Because in Spaine (as in many other places also) the manner is when a man is lead to execution, if a common harlot will aske him for her husband, it saveth his life.

In this manner also Raphaell the painter answered two Cardinals (with whom he might be familiar) which to make him talke, founde fault in his hearing with a table he had made, where S. Peter and S. Paule were: saying, that those two pictures were too redde in the face. Then saide Raphael by and by.

My Lordes, wonder you not at it, for I have made them so for the nonce, because it is to be thought that S. Peter and S. Paule are even as red in Heaven as you see them here, for very shame, that their Church is governed by such men as you be.

Also those jeasts are pleasant that have in them a certaine privy semblāt of laughter.[1] As when a husband lamented much and bewailed his wife that had hanged her selfe upon a figge tree, an other came to him and plucking him by the sleeve, saide.

Friende, may I receive such pleasure as to have a graffe of that figge tree to graffe in some stocke of mine Orchard?

There be certaine of other jeastes that bee patient and spoken softly with a kinde of gravitie. As a man of the Countrie carrying a coffer upon his shoulders, chaunced therewithall to give Cato a hard push, and afterwarde saide: Give roome: Cato answered: hast thou any thing upon thy shoulders beside that coffer?

It is also a matter of laughter when a man hath committed an errour, and to amend it speaketh a matter purposely that appeareth foolish, and yet is applyed to the end that he hath appointed, and serveth his turne therewithal that he seeme not out of countenance and dismayed.

As not longe since two enemies being together in the counsel chamber of Florence, (as it happeneth often in those Common weales) the one of them which was of the house of Altoviti, slept, and he that satte next unto him for a sport, where his adversarie that was of the house of Alamanni, had saide nothing neither then nor before, stirring him with his elbow made him

[1] Cf. "a certain latent spice of fun."

awake, and saide unto him: Hearest thou not what such a one saith? make answere, for the Lords aske for thine advise.

Then did Altoviti all sleepie arise upon his feete and without any more deliberation saide: My Lordes, I say the cleane contrarie to that Alamanni hath spoken.

Alamanni answered, what? I have saide nothing: Altoviti saide immediatly: To that thou wilt speake.

In this manner also did your maister Seraphin the Phisition here in Urbin say unto a man of the Countrie, which had received such a stroke upon the eye, that in very deede it was out, yet thought he best to goe seeke to maister Seraphin for remedie. When hee saw it, though he knew it was past cure, yet to plucke money out of his handes as that blow had plucked the eye out of his heade, he promised him largely to heale it. And so he was in hand with him every daye for money, putting him in comfort that within sixe or seven dayes, he should beginne to see with it againe.

The poore Countrie man gave him the litle he had, but when he saw him so prolong the matter, he began to finde himselfe agreeved with the Phisition, and saide that he was nothing the better, neither coulde he see any more with that eye, than if he had none at all in his head.

At length maister Seraphin perceiving there was no more to be gotten at his handes, saide: Brother mine, thou must have patience, thou hast cleane lost thine eye, and no remedie is there for it, pray God thou lose not thine other withall.

The Countrie man seeing this, fell in weeping, and lamented much, and saide, maister mine, you have pilled me and robbed me of my money, I will complaine to the Duke, and made the greatest outcries in the world.

Then saide maister Seraphin in a rage, and to cleare himselfe: ah thou villaine knave: thou wouldest then have two eyes as Citizens and honest men have, wouldest thou? Get thee hence in the divels name. And those words were thrust out with such fury, that the poore sillie man was dismayed, and held his peace, and soft and faire departed in Gods name, thinking that hee himselfe had beene in the wrong.

It is also pretie when a man declareth or interpreteth a matter merrily. As in the Spanish Court in a morning there came into the palace a knight who was very ill favoured, and his wife, that was verye beautifull, both apparrelled in white Damaske, and the Queene saide unto Alonso Carillo, How thinke yee Alonso by these two?

Madam, answered Alonso, me thinke the Ladie is the Dame, and he the Aske, which signifieth a foule person and uglesome.[1] Also when Raphael de Pazzi saw a letter that the Priour of Messina had writen to a maistresse of his, the superscription whereof was: *Esta carta s' ha dar a qui en causa mi penar*, that is, This letter be given to the cause of my griefe[2]: me thinke (quoth he) this letter is directed to Paul Tholossa.

Imagine you howe the standers by laughed at it, for they all knew that Paule Tholossa had lent ten thousand Ducates to the Priour of Messina, and because he was verie lavish in his expences, he coulde finde no way to pay his debt.

It is like unto this, when a man giveth familiar admonition in manner of counsel, but dissemblingly. As Cosmus de Medicis saide unto a friend of his that had more riches than witte, and by Cosmus meanes had compassed an office[3] without Florence, and at his setting forth asking Cosmus what way he thought best for him to take to execute this office well.

Cosmus answered him: Apparrel thy selfe in scarlet, and speake litle. Of this sort was that Count Lewis saide unto one that woulde passe for an unknowne person in a certaine daungerous place, and wist not how to disguise him selfe, and the Count being demaunded of his advise therein, answered: Apparrell thy selfe like a Doctor, or in some other raiment that wise men use to weare.

Also Jannotti de Pazzi saide unto one that minded to make an arming coate of as many divers colours as might be invented: Take[4] the wordes and deedes of the Cardinall of Pavia.

A man laugheth also at certaine matters disagreeing. As one saide the last day unto maister Antony Rizzo of a certaine Forlivese.

Gesse[5] whether he be a foole or no, for his name is Bartholomew. And an other: Thou seekest a rider and hast no horses. And this man wanteth nothing but good and a horse.[6]

And at certaine other that seeme to agree. As within these few dayes where there was a suspition that a friend of ours had caused a false advousion of a benefice to bee drawne out, afterward when an other Priest fell sicke, Antony Torello saide unto

[1] They were clad in *damasco*: she, the *dam(a)* (beauty); he, the *asco* (beast).
[2] Cf. "This missive is to be delivered to the author of my woes."
[3] "An office": cf. "a mission."
[4] "Take": cf. "Imitate."
[5] "Gesse," etc.: cf. "you may know . . ."
[6] Cf. "all the fellow lacks is money and brains."

him: What dost thou linger the matter? Why dost thou not send for thy Clarke and see whether thou canst hit upon this other benefice?

Likewise at certaine that doe not agree. As the last day when the Pope had sent for maister John Luke of Pontremolo and maister Dominick da la Porta, which (as you know) are both crookebacked, and made them Auditours, saying that hee intended to bring the Rota into a right frame. Maister Latin Juvenal saide: Our holy father is deceived, if he thinke that he can bring the Rota into a right frame with two crooked persons.[1]

Also it provoketh laughter, when a man graunteth the thing that is tolde him and more, but seemeth to understand it otherwise. As Captaine Peralta being brought into the lists to fight the combat with Aldana, and Captaine Molart that was Aldanas patrone, requiring Peralta to sweare, whether he had about him any Saint Johns Gospel or charme and inchauntment, to preserve him from hurt. Peralta swore that he had about him neither Gospel nor inchantment, nor relike, nor any matter of devotion wherein he had any faith.

Then saide Molart, to touch him to be a Marrane: Well no mo wordes in this, for I believe without swearing that you have no faith also in Christ.

It is pretie moreover to use metaphors at a time in such purposes. As our maister Marcantonio that saide to Botton de Cesena, who had vexed him with wordes: Botton, Botton, thou shalt one day be the button, and the haulter shall be the buttonhole.

And also when Marcantonio had made a Comedy which was very long and of sundrie actes, the very same Botton saide in like manner to Marcantonio: to play your Comedie ye shall neede for preparation as much woode as is in Sclavonia. Maister Marcantonio answered, and for preparation of thy Tragedie three trees[2] is inough.

Againe a man speaketh a word many times wherein is a privie signification farre from that appeareth hee would say. As the Lord Generall here being in companye where there was a communication of a Captaine that in deede all his life time for the more part had received the overthrow, and as then by a chaunce wan the victorie: and when hee that ministred this talke saide: When he made his enterie into that towne he was apparelled in a very faire crimosin velvet coate, which he wore

---

[1] Cf. "set (the Rota) right with two wrongs."
[2] "Three trees": cf. "three sticks"; i.e. a gallows.

alwaies after his victories. The Lord Generall saide, Belike it is verie new.

And no lesse doth it provoke laughter, when otherwhile a man maketh answere unto that which the other he talketh withall hath not spoken: or els seemeth to believe he hath done that which he hath not done, and should have done it.

As Andrew Cosia, when he went to visit a gentleman that discourteously suffered him to stand on his feete and he himselfe sate, saide: Since you commande me Sir, to obey you, I will sit, and so sate him downe.

Also a man laugheth when one accuseth himself of some trespasse. As the last day when I saide to the Dukes Chaplaine, that my Lordes grace had a Chaplaine that could say masse sooner[1] than he: He answered me, it is not possible. And rounding mee in the eare, saide. You shall understand that I say not the third part of the secretes.[2]

Also Biagin Crivello, when a Priest was slaine at Millane, he required his benefice of the Duke, the which he was minded to bestow upon another. At length Biagin perceiving no other reason would prevaile, and what (quoth he) if I were the cause of his death,[3] why will you not give me his benefice?

It hath also many times a good grace to wish those thinges that can not be. As the last day one of our company beholding all these gentlemen here playing at fence, and he lying upon a bedde, saide: O what a pleasure it were, were this also a valiant mans and a good souldiers exercise.

In like manner it is a pretie and wittie kinde of speaking, and especially in grave men and of authoritie, to answere contrarie to that he woulde with whom he talketh, but drily and (as it were) with a certaine doubting and heedfull consideration.

As in times past Alphonsus the first king of Aragon, giving unto a servant of his, horse, harnesse and apparrell, because he told how the night before he had dreamed that his highnesse had given him all those kinde of matters, and not long after, the verie same servant saide againe how he dreamed that night, that he had given him a good sorte of royalles, hee answered him: Henceforth believe dreames no more, for they are not alwaies true.

In this sorte also did the Pope answere the Bishop of Cervia, that to grope his mind saide unto him: Holy father, it is noysed

---

[1] "Sooner": cf. "faster."
[2] Cf. "You must know, I do not recite a third of the silent prayers."
[3] Cf. "what! after I have had the priest killed . . ."

all Rome over and in the Palace too, that your holinesse maketh me governour.

Then answered the Pope: Let the knaves speake what they lust, doubt you not, it is not true I warrant you. I coulde (my Lordes) beside these gather many other places, from which a man maye draw merrie and pleasant jeastes, as matters spoken with feare, with marvaile, with threatnings out of order, with overmuch furiousnesse: Beside this, certaine newly happened cases provoke laughter: sometime silence with a certaine wonder: at other times verie laughter it selfe without purpose. But me thinke I have now spoken sufficient: for the jeastes that consist in wordes (I believe) passe not these boundes we have reasoned of.

As for such as be in operation,[1] though there be infinite partes of them, yet are they drawne into few principles. But in both kindes the chiefe matter is to deceive opinion, and to answere otherwise than the hearer looketh for: and (in case the jeast shall have any grace) it must needs be seasoned with this deceite, or dissimulation, or mocking, or rebuking, or comparison, or what ever other kinde a man will use.

And although all kinde of jeastes move a man to laugh, yet doe they also in this laughter make diverse effects. For some have in them a certaine cleannesse and modest pleasantnesse. Other bite sometime privily, otherwhile openly. Other have in them a certaine wantonnesse. Other make one laugh as soone as he heareth them. Other the more a man thinketh upon them. Other in laughing make a man blush withall. Other stirre a man somewhat to anger. But in all kindes a man must consider the disposition of the mindes of the hearers, because unto persons in adversity oftentimes merry toyes augment their affliction: and some infirmities ther be, that the more a mā occupieth medicine about them, the worse they waxe.

In case therefore the Courtier in jesting and speaking merry conceites have a respect to the time, to the persons, to his degree, and not use it too often (for pardye it bringeth a lothsomnesse if a man stand evermore about it all day in all kinde of talke and without purpose) hee may be called pleasant and feate conceited.[2] So hee be heedfull also that he be not so bitter and byting, that a man might conjecture hee were an envious person, in pricking without a cause, or for plaine malice, or men of too great authoritie (which is lacke of discretion) or of too much miserie (which is crueltie)[3] or too mischievous (which

---

[1] Cf. "shown in action."　　　[2] Cf. "called a man of humour."
[3] "Or . . . or": cf. "either . . . or."

is vanitie) or els in speaking matters that may offend them whom he would not offend (which is ignorance.) For some there bee that thinke they are bound to speake and to nip without regarde, as often as they can, how ever the matter goe afterwarde.

And among these kinde of persons are they, that to speake a word which should seeme to come of a readines of wit, passe not for staining of a worthie gentlewomans honestie, which is a verie naughtie matter and worthy sore punishment. Because in this point women are in the number of sillie soules [1] and persons in misery, and therefore deserve not to be nipped in it, for they have not weapon to defend themselves.

But beside these respects, he that will be pleasant and full of jeasting, must be shaped of a certaine nature apt to all kinde of pleasantnesse, and unto that frame his fashions, gestures, and countenance, the which the more grave, steadie and set it is, so much the more maketh it the matters spoken to seeme wittie and subtil.

But you (Sir Frederick) that ought to rest your selfe under this my tree without leaves, and in my withered reasonings, I believe you have repented your selfe, and you recken ye are entred into a bayting place [2] of Montefiore.

Therefore it shall be well done for you like a wel practised Courtier (to avoid an ill hosterie) to arise somewhat before your ordinarie houre and set forwarde on your journey.

Nay, answered Sir Fredericke, I am come to so good an hosterie, that I minde to tarrie in it longer than I had thought at ye first. Therfore I will rest mee yet a while, untill you have made an end of al the talke ye have begun withall. Whereof ye have left out one parcel that ye named at the beginning: which is merrie pranckes,[3] and it were not well done to deceive the companie of it.

But as you have taught us many pretie matters concerning jeastes, and made us hardie to use them through example of so many singular wittes, great men, Princes, Kinges and Popes, I suppose ye will likewise in merie pranckes so bolden us, that we may take a courage to practise some against your selfe.

Then saide maister Bernarde smyling: you shall not be the first, but perhaps it will not be your chaunce, for I have so many times beene served with them, that it maketh me looke

---

[1] Cf. "are to be numbered among the weak."

[2] "Bayting place," etc.: cf. "inn." "A proverbial expression for a bad hostelry" (Opdycke).

[3] Cf. "practical jokes."

well about me: As dogs, after they have beene once scaulded with hote water, are afeard of the colde.

Howbeit since you will have me to speake somewhat of this too, I believe I may rid my handes of it in fewe wordes.

And in mine opinion a merrie prancke is nothing els, but a friendly deceite in matters that offend not at al or very litle. And even as in jeasting to speake contrarie to expectation moveth laughter, so doth in merrie pranckes, to doe contrarie to expectation. And these doe so much the more delite and are to be practised, as they be wittie and modest. For he that will worke a merrie prancke without respect, doth many times offend, and then arise debates and sore hatred.

But the places that a man may derive merrie pranckes from, are (in a manner) the verie same that be in jeasts. Therefore to avoid repetition of them, I will say no more but that there bee two kindes of merrie pranckes every one of which may afterward be devided into moe partes.

The one is, when any man whosoever he be, is deceived wittily, and after a feate manner and with pleasantnesse.[1] The other, when a man layeth (as it were) a nette, and sheweth a peece of a baite so, that a man runneth to bee deceived of himselfe.

The first is such, as the merrie prancke was, that within these few dayes was wrought unto a couple of great Ladies (whom I will not name) by the meane of a Spaniarde called Castilio.

Then the Dutchesse, and why, (quoth she) will you not name them? maister Bernarde answered: because I would not have them to take it in ill part.

Then saide the Dutchesse againe, smyling: it is not against good manner sometime to use merrie pranckes with great men also. And I have heard of many that have beene played to Duke Fredericke, to king Alphonsus of Aragon, to Queene Isabel of Spaine, and to many other great Princes, and not onely they tooke it not in ill part, but rewarded verie largely them that played them those partes.

Maister Bernarde answered: neither upon this hope doe I entende to name them. Say as pleaseth you, quoth the Dutchesse. Then proceeded maister Bernarde and saide: Not manie dayes since in the Court that I meane, there arrived a man of the Countrey about Bergamo, to be in service with a gentleman of the Court: which was so well set out with garments and so finely clad, that for all his bringing up was alwaies in keeping oxen

[1] Cf. "cleverly tricked in a fine amusing manner."

and could doe nothing els, yet a man that had not heard him speake woulde have judged him a worthie gentleman.

And so when those two Ladies were enformed that there was arrived a Spaniarde, servant to Cardinall Borgia whose name was Castilio, a very wittie man, a musition, a dauncer, and the best Courtier in all Spaine, they longed verie much to speake with him, and sent incontinently for him, and after they had received him honourably, they caused him to sit down, and began to entertaine him with a very great respect in the presence of all men, and few there were present that knew him not to be a Bergamaske Cowheard.

Therefore seeing those Ladies entertaine him with such respect, and honour him so much, they fell all in a laughing, the more because the sillie fellow spake still his native language the mere Bergamaske tongue.

But the gentlemen that devised this prancke, had first tolde those Ladies that among other thinges he was a great dissembler, and spake all tongues excellently well, and especially the Countrie speach of Lumbard, so that they thought he fained, and many times they beheld the one the other with certaine marvellings, and saide: what a wonderfull matter is this, how he counterfaiteth this tongue?

In conclusion, this communication lasted so long, that every mans sides aked for laughing, and he coulde not choose him selfe but utter so many tokens of his noblenesse of birth,[1] that at length those Ladies (but with much adoe) believed hee was the man that he was in deed.

Such merrie pranckes we see dayly, but among the rest they be pleasant that at the first make a man agast, and after that, end in a matter of suretie, because he that was deceived laugheth at himself when he perceiveth he was afeard of nothing.

As lying upon a time in Paglia, there chanced to be in the verie same Inne three other good fellowes, two of Pistoia and one of Prato, which after supper (as the manner is for the most part) fell to gaming. And not long after, one of the Pistoians losing his rest,[2] had not a farthing left him to blesse him selfe, but beganne to chafe, to curse, and to banne and to blaspheme terribly, and thus tearing of God he went to bedde. The other two after they had played a while, agreed to worke a merrie prancke with him that was gone to bed.

And when they perceived that he was fallen in sleepe, they

---

[1] Cf. "giving so many tokens of his gentility."
[2] "Rest": cf. "all he had."

blewe out the candels and raked up the fire and beganne to speake aloud, and to make the greatest hurly burly in the world, making wise to contend together about their game. The one saide: Thou tookest the card underneath.[1] The other denying it saide: Thou hast vied upon flush, let us mount [2]: and such other matters, with such noise, that he that slept awoke, and hearing them at play and talking even as though they had seene the cardes, did a litle open his eyes: when hee saw there was no manner light in the chamber, he saide: What a divel meane you to cry thus all night?

Afterwarde hee laide him downe againe to sleepe. The other two companions gave him no manner answere: but still continued in their purpose untill he awoke better, and much wondred, and when he sawe for certaintie that there was neither fire nor any kinde of light, and perceived they played still and fell in contention, he said.

And how can ye see the cardes without light? The one of the two answered, I weene thou hast lost thy sight as well as thy money. Seest thou not that wee have here two candles?

He that was in bedde lift up himselfe upō his elbowes, and in a manner angred, said: Either I am dronken or blinde, or els you make a lye. The two arose and went to yᵉ bed darkelong, laughing and making wise to believe that he went about to mocke them. And he againe saide to them: I tell you truth I see you not. At length the two began to wonder much, and the one said to the other. By good Lord, I believe he speaketh in good earnest, reach me the candle, and let us see lest perhaps hee have some impediment in his sight.

Then thought the poore wretch surely that hee had beene blinde, and weeping downe right, saide: oh sirs, I am blind, and forthwith hee beganne to call upon our Ladie of Loreto and to beseech her to pardon him his blasphemies and cursing for the losse of his money.

But his two companions put him in good comfort and saide: it is not possible but thou shouldest see us. It is some fancie that thou hast conceived in thine head. Oh good Lorde answered the other, it is no fancie, nor I see no more than if I had never had eyes in my head. Thy sight is cleare inough, quoth the two. And the one saide to the other.

Marke how well he openeth his eyes: and how faire they be

---

[1] "The card underneath": cf. "the under card."
[2] Cf. "And you have wagered on four of a suit; let us deal again."

to looke to: and who would believe but he coulde see? The pore soule wept faster, and cryed God mercie.

In conclusion they saide unto him: see thou make a vow to goe devoutly to our Ladie of Loreto barefooted and bare legged, for that is the best remedie that may be had. And in the mean space we will goe to Aquapendente and the other townes here about to seeke for some Phisition, and will helpe thee in what we can.

Then did the sillie soule kneele upon his knees in the bed, and with aboundance of teares and very bitter repentance for his blaspheming, made a solemne vow to goe naked to our Ladie of Loreto and to offer unto her a paire of eyes of silver, and to eate no flesh upon the wednesday, nor egges upon Friday, and to fast breade and water every Saterday in worship of our Ladie, if she give him the grace to receive his sight againe.

The two companions entring into an other chamber, lighted a candel, and came with the greatest laughter in the world before this poore soule, who for all he was rid of so great an anguish as you may thinke he had, yet was he so astonied with his former feare, that he could not only not laugh, but not once speake a word, and the two companions did nothing else but stur him, saying that hee was bounde to perfourme all those vowes, for that hee had received the grace he asked.

Of the other kinde of merrie pranckes when a man deceiveth himselfe, I will give you none other example, but what happened unto me my selfe not long since. For this shroftide that is past, my Lordes grace of Saint Peter ad vincula, which knoweth full well what a delite I have when I am in maskerie to playe merrie pranckes with Friers, having first given order as hee devised the matter, came uppon a day with my Lorde of Aragon and certaine other Cardinals, to ye windowes, making wise to stand there to see maskers passe to and fro, as the manner of Rome is.

I being in maskerie passed by, and when I behelde on the one side of the streete a Frier standing (as it were) in a studie with himselfe, I judged I had found that I sought for, and forthwith ranne to him, like a greedie hauke to her pray, and when I had asked him and he told me who hee was, I made semblant to knowe him, and with many wordes beganne to make him believe that the marshall went about to seeke him for certaine complaintes against him, and perswaded him to goe with me to the Chauncerie and there I would save him.

The Frier dismaied and all trembling seemed as though he

G 807

wist not what to doe, and saide that he doubted taking, in case he shoulde goe farre from Saint Celso.[1] Stil I put him in good comfort, and said so much to him, that he leaped up behind me, and then me thought my devise was fully accomplished. And I beganne to ride my horse by and by up and downe the merchants streete, which went kicking and winsing.

Imagine with your selves now what a faire sight it was to beholde a Frier on horsebacke behind a masker, his garments flying abroad, and his head shaking too and fro, that a man would have thought he had been alwaies falling.

With this faire sight, the gentlemen began to hurle egges out at the windowes, and afterwarde all the bankers and as many as were there, so that the haile never fell with a more violence from the skye, than there fell egges out from yᵉ windowes, which for the most part came all upō me. And I for that I was in mas-kerie, passed not upon the matter,[2] and thought verily that all the laughing had beene for the Frier and not for me, and upon this went sundrie times up and downe the bankes, alwaies with that furie of hel[3] behind me. And though the Frier (in manner) weeping besought mee to let him goe downe, and not to shew such shame to the weede, yet did the knave afterwarde privily cause egs to be given him by certaine Lackies set there for the nonce, and making wise[4] to gripe me hard for falling,[5] squised them in my bosom, and many times on my heade, and other-while on my forehead, so that I was foule arrayed.

Finally, when every man was wearie both of laughing and throwing egges, he leaped downe from behinde me, and plucking his hoode backwarde, shewed a great bush of haire,[6] and saide: maister Bernarde I am a horsekeeper in the stable of Saint Peter ad vincula, and am hee that looketh to your Mulet.

Then wist I not which prevailed most in me, griefe, anger, or shame. Yet for the lesse hurt, I fled toward my lodging, and the next morning I durst not shew my heade abroad. But the laughing at that merrie prancke did not endure the day following onely, but also lasteth (in manner) untill this day. And so when they had a while renewed the laughing at rehearsing this againe, maister Bernard proceeded.

It is also a good and pleasant kinde of merrie prancks, from

---

[1] "Saint Celso": the name of a street, and of a church, near the Bianchi.
[2] "Passed not": cf. "I did not care."
[3] Cf. "fury."
[4] Cf. "pretending."
[5] "For falling": cf. "to keep from falling."
[6] "Great bush," etc.: cf. "his long hair."

whence in like manner jeastes are derived, when one believeth that a man will doe a matter which he will not in deed.

As when I was in an evening after supper upon the bridge of Leo, and going together with Cesar Beccadello sporting one with another, we beganne to take holde fast the one of the others armes, as though we would have wrastled, because then wee perceived no man about the bridge, and being in this manner together, there came two French men by, which seeing us thus striving, demaunded what the matter meant, and staied to part us, thinking we had beene at debate in good earnest.

Then said I incontinently: Helpe sirs, for this poore gentleman at certaine times of the Moone is frantike, and see now how he striveth to cast himselfe off the bridge into the river.

Then did the two runne and laide hand upon Cesar with me and held him straight. And he (saying alwaies that I was out of my wit) struggled the more to winde himselfe out of their handes, and they griped him so much the harder. At this the people assembled to beholde our ruffling together, and everie man ran, and the more poore Cesar laide about him with his handes and feete (for he beganne now to enter into choller) the more resort of the people there was, and for the great strength he put, they believed verily that hee would have leaped into the river, and therefore held they him the straiter, so that a great throng of people carried him to the Inne above ground, all turmoiled and without his cappe, pale for wrath and shame, that nothing hee spake coulde prevaile, partly because those Frenchmen understood him not, and partly because I also carrying him to the Inne did alwaies bewaile the poore soules ill lucke, that was so waxed out of his wit.

Now (as we have saide) of merrie prancks a man may talke at large, but it sufficeth to repeat that the places whence they are derived bee the verie same which wee have saide of jestes.

As for examples, we have infinite which wee see dayly and among the rest there are many pleasant in the tales of Boccaccio, as those that Bruno and Buffalmacco plaied[1] to their Calandrino, and to maister Symon: and many other of women, which in verie deede are wittie and pretie.

I remember also I have knowne in my dayes many that have beene merrily disposed in this manner, and among the rest a scholer in Padoa borne in Sicilia, called Pontius, which seeing upon a time a man of the Countrie have a couple of fat Capons,

---

[1] See *Decameron*, Eighth Day, tales three, six, nine; Ninth Day, tale five.

faining himselfe to buye them, was at a point with him for the price, and bid him come with him to his lodging, for beside his price hee woulde give him somewhat to breake his fast withall. And so brought him to a place where was a steeple that stood by him selfe alone severed frō the Church, that a man might goe round about him, and directly over against one of the foure sides of the steeple was a lane.

Here Pontius, when he had first bethought himself what he had to doe, saide unto the man of the Countrie: I have laide these Capons on a wager with a fellow of mine, who saith that this Toure compasseth fortie foote, and I say no, and even as I met with thee, I had bought this packthreed to measure it.

Therefore before we goe to my lodging, I will trye which of us hath wonne the wager. And in so saying, he drew the pacthreed out of his sleeve, and put the one end of it into the man of the Countries hand, and saide: give here, and so tooke the Capons: and with the other end he began to goe about the bell toure, as though hee would have measured it, making first the man of the Countrie to stand still, and to holde the pacthreed directly on the contrarie side of the toure to that, that was at the head of the lane, where as soone as he came, he drove a naile into the wall, to the which hee tyed the packthreede, and leaving it so, went his wayes without any more adoe downe the lane with the Capons.

The man of the countrey stood still a good while, allwayes lookinge when hee would have done measuring. At length after hee had sayde many times, what do you so long? he thought hee would see, and founde that Pontius held not the line, but a naile that was drivē into the wal, which onelye remayned for payment of his Capons.

Of this sorte Pontius played many Merry Pranckes. And ther have bene also manye other pleasaunt men in this maner, as Gonella Meliolo in those dayes, and now our Frier Seraphin and Frier Marian here, and many well knowen to you all. And in very deede this kind is to bee praysed in men that make profession of nothinge els. But the merry prankes that the Courtier oughte to use, must (by myne advise) bee somewhat wide from immoderate jesting.

He ought also to take heed that his mery prankes turne not to pilferinge, as wee see many naughty packes, that wander about the worlde with divers shifts to get money, fayninge now one matter, now another. And that they be not yet bitter, and above all that hee have respect and reverence, as well in this, as in all other thinges, to women, and especially where the stayning of their honesty shall consist.

Then the L. Gaspar, truely, M. Bernard (quoth hee) you are too partiall to these women. And why will you that men shoulde have more respect to women than women to men? Set not you as much by your honestye, as they do by theirs?

Thinke you the that women ought to nip men both with wordes and mockes, in everye matter without anye regard, and men should stand with a flea in their eare, and thanke them for it[1]?

M. Bernard aunsweared: I say not the contrary, but women in their Jestes and merry pranckes, ought to have the respectes to menne which wee have spoken of. Yet I say, with more liberty may they touch men of small honesty, then men may them. And that beecause wee our selves have established for a law, that in us wanton life is no vice, nor default, nor any slaunder, and in women it is so great a reproach and shame, that shee that hath once an ill name, whether the reporte that goeth of her be true or false, hath lost her credite for ever.

Therefore since talking of womens honesty is so daungerous a matter to offende them sore. I say that wee ought to touch them in other matters, and refraine from this. For when the Jest or merry prancke, nippeth too sore, it goeth out of ye bounds which we have allready said is fit for a gentleman.

Here M. Bernard making a little stop, the L. Octavian Fregoso saide smyling: My L. Gaspar can make you an aunsweare to this law, which you alledge that wee our selves have made, that it is not perchance so out of reason, as you thinke. For since women are so unperfit creatures, and of litle or no worthinesse in respect of men, it behoved for that they were not apt to worke any vertuous deede of themselves, that they should have a bridle put upon them with shame and feare of infamie, that should (in manner) by force bring into them some good condition. And continencie was thought more necessarie in them than any other, to have assurance of children.

So that verie force hath driven men with all inventions, pollicies, and waies possible, to make women continent, and (in manner) graunted them in all thinges beside to be of small worthinesse, and to doe the cleane cotrarie alwaies to that they ought to doe.

Therefore since it is lawfull for them to swarve out of the way in al other things without blame, if we should touch them in those defaults, wherein (as we have saide) they are to be

---

[1] Cf. "should quietly endure it."

borne withall,[1] and therefore are not unseemely in them, and passe full litle upon it, we shoulde never move laughter. For you have alreadie saide, that laughter is provoked with certaine thinges that are disagreeing.[2]

Then spake the Dutchesse: speake you (my Lord Octavian) of women thus, and then complaine that they love you not?

The Lorde Octavian answered: I complaine not of it, but rather I thanke them for it, since in not loving of me, they binde not me to love them. Neither doe I speake after mine owne opinion, but I say that the Lorde Gasper might alleage these reasons.[3]

Maister Bernarde saide: truely women should make a good bargaine, if they could make attonements with such two great enimies as you and the Lord Gasper be.

I am not their enimie answered the Lord Gasper, but you are an enimie to men. For in case you wil not have women touched in this honestie of theirs, you ought as well to appoint them a law not to touch men, in that which is as much shame to us, as incontinencie to women.

And why was it not as meete for Alonso Carillo to make the answere which hee gave mistresse Boadilla of the hope that hee had to save his life, in that she would take him to husband, as it was for her to say first: All that knew him thought the king woulde have hanged him?[4]

And why was it not as lawfull for Richard Minutoli to beguile Phillippellos wife, and to traine her to that baite, as it was for Beatrice to make Egano her husband arise out of his bedde, and Anichin to beswadele him with a cudgell, after she had lyen a good space with him?

And the other that tyed the packthreede to her great toe, and made her owne husband believe that hee was not himselfe,[5] since you saye those merrie pranckes of women in Boccaccio are so wittie and pretie?

Then saide maister Bernarde smiling: my Lordes, for so much as my part hath beene to entreate onely of jeastes, I entend not to passe my boundes therein, and I suppose I have alreadie shewed why I judge it not meete to touch women neither in

---

[1] "Are to be borne withall": cf. "are all permitted them."

[2] Cf. "incongruous."

[3] Cf. "Nor am I speaking my own mind, but saying that my Lord Gaspar might use these arguments."

[4] See the *Decameron*, Third Day, tale six; Seventh Day, tales seven and eight.

[5] Cf. "that she was not herself."

worde nor deede above their honestie, and I have also given them a rule not to nip men where it greeveth them.

But I say, that those merrie pranckes and jeastes which you (my Lord Gasper), aleage, as that Alonso saide unto maister Boadilla, although it somewhat touch honestie: yet doth it not discontent mee, because it is set farre inough,[1] and is so privie, that it may be seemely[2] understood, so, that hee might have dissembled the matter, and affirmed that he spake it not to that end.

He spake an other (in mine opinion) verie unseemely, which was: when the queene passed by maister Boadillas house, Alonso saw painted with coales all the gate over such kind of dishonest beasts,[3] as are painted about Innes in such sundrie wise, and comming to the Countesse of Castagneto saide unto her.

See (madam) the heads of the wilde beasts[4] that maister Boadilla killeth every day in hunting. Marke you this, though it were a wittie metaphor, and borrowed of hunters, that count it a glorie to have many wilde beastes heades nailed at their gates, yet is it dishonest and shamefull jeasting. Beside that, it was not in answering, for an answere hath much more courtesie in it,[5] because it is thought that a man is provoked to it, and it must needes bee at a sodaine.

But to returne to our matter of the merrie pranckes of women, I say not that they doe well to beguile their husbands: But I say that some of the deceites which Boccaccio reciteth of women, are pretie and wittie inough, and especially those you have spoken of your selfe.

But in mine opinion the prancke that Richard Minutoli wrought, doth passe the boundes, and is much more bitterer than that Beatrice wrought. For Richard Minutoli tooke much more from Philippellos wife, than did Beatrice from Egano her husband: because Richard with that privie pollicie enforced her, and made her to doe of her selfe that she woulde not have done: And Beatrice deceived her husband to doe of her selfe that she lusted.

Then saide the Lorde Gasper: for no other cause can a man excuse Beatrice but for love, which ought to be allowed as well in men as in women.

Then answered maister Bernard: Truely the passions of love bring with them a great excuse of everie faulte, yet judge I

---

[1] Cf. "very remote."   [2] Cf. "innocently."
[3] Cf. "indecencies."   [4] "Wilde beasts": cf. "game."
[5] Cf. "for it is far less rude to say a thing by way of retort . . ."

(for my part) that a gentleman that is in love, ought as well in this point as in all other thinges, to be voide of dissimulation, and of an upright meaning. And if it be true that it is such an abhominable profit and trespasse to use tradiment against a mans verie enimie[1]: consider you how much more hainous that offence is against a person whom a man loveth. And I believe each honest lover sustaineth such veines, such watchinges, hazardeth him selfe in such dangers, droppeth so many teares, useth so many meanes and waies to please the woman whom he loveth, not chiefely to come by her body, but to win the fortresse of that minde, to breake in peeces those most hard Diamonds, to heate that colde yce, that lye manie times in the tender breasts of these women.

And this doe I believe is the true and sound pleasure, and the end whereto the intent of a noble courage is bent. And for my part truely (were I in love) I would like it better to know assuredly that she whom I loved and served, loved me againe with hart, and had bent her minde towarde me, without receiving any other contentation, than to enjoy her, and to have my fill of her against her owne wil, for in that case I shoulde thinke my selfe maister of a deade carkase.

Therefore such as compasse their desires by the meane of these merrie präcks, which may perhaps rather be termed Tradiments[2] than merrie pranckes, doe injurie to other, and yet receive they not for all that the contentation which a man shoulde wish for in love, possessing the bodie without the will.

The like I say of certaine other that in love practise enchantments, sorceries, and otherwhile plaine force, sometimes meanes[3] to cast them in sleepe and such like matters. And know for a sooth, that gifts also diminish much the pleasures of love, because a man may stande in doubt whether he be beloved or no, but that the woman maketh a countenance to love him, to fare the better by him.

Therefore ye see that the love of Ladies and great women is esteemed, because it appeareth that it can arise of none other cause, but of perfect and true love: neither is it to be thought that a great Ladie will at any time shew to beare good will to her inferiour, unlesse she love him in verie deede.

Then answered the Lord Gasper: I denye not that the intent, the paines and daungers of lovers ought not principally to have

---

[1] ". . . that to betray even an enemy is such a vile act . . ."
[2] Cf. "treachery."
[3] "Meanes," etc.: cf. "sleeping-potions."

their end directed to the victorie rather of the minde than of the bodie of the woman beloved. But I say, that these deceites which you in men terme Tradiments, and in women merrie prannckes, are a verie good meane to come to this end, because alwaies he that possesseth the bodie of women, is also maister of the minde: And if you bethinke you well, Philippellos wife after her great lamentation for the deceite wrought her by Richard, knowing how much more savorie the kisse of a lover were than her husbands, turning her rigour into tender affection towarde Richard, from that day forwarde loved him most dearely.

You may perceive now that his continual haunting, his presents, and his so many other tokens, which had beene so long a proofe of his good will towards her, were not able to compasse that, that his being with her a small while did. Now see this merrie prancke or Tradiment (how ever you will terme it) was a good way to win the fortresse of that minde.

Then maister Bernarde, you (quoth he) make a surmise, which is most false, for in case women shoulde alwaies give their minde to him that possesseth their bodie, there shoulde bee none found that woulde not love their husbandes more than any person in the world beside, where it is seene not to be so. But John Boccaccio was (as you bee) without cause an enimie to women.

The Lord Gasper answered: I am no enimy of theirs, but (to confesse the truth) few men of worthinesse there bee that generally set anie store by women, although otherwhile, to serve their turne withall, they make wise to the contrarie.

Then answered maister Bernard: You doe not onely injurie to women, but to all men also that reverēce them. Notwith-stāding (as I have saide) I will not swarve from my first purpose of merrie pranckes, and undertake such an enterprise so hard, as is the defence of women against you that are a valiant Champion.

Therefore I will end this my cōmunication which perhaps hath beene longer than needed, but out of peradventure not so pleasant as you looked for. And since I see the Ladies so quiet, and beare these injuries at your handes so paciently as they doe, I will henceforth believe that some part of that which the Lord Octavian hath spokē is true: namely, That they passe not to be evil reported of in every other matter, so their honestie be not touched.

Then a great part of the women there, for that the Dutchesse had beckoned to them so to doe, arose upon their feete, and ran all laughing toward the Lord Gasper, as they would have buffeted him, and done as the wood women did to Orpheus, saying continually: Now shall you see whether we passe to be ill spoken off or no.

Thus partly for laughing, and partly for the rising of every one from his seate, it seemed the sleepe that now beganne to enter into the eyes and heade of some of them departed, but the Lord Gasper saide.

See I pray you where they have not reason on their side, they will prevaile by plaine force, and so end the communication, giving us leave to depart with stripes.[1]

Then answered the Ladie Emilia: No (quoth she) it shall not be so: for when you perceived maister Bernarde was wearie of his long talk, you began to speake so much ill of women, thinking you shoulde finde none to gainesay you. But wee will set into the field a fresher knight that shall fight with you, because your offence shall not bee long unpunished. So turning her to the Lord Julian, that hetherto had saide litle, she saide unto him.

You are counted the protector of the honour of women, therefore it is now high time to shew that you come not by this name for nothing, and in case yee have not beene worthily recompensed at any time for this professiõ hetherto, now must you thinke that in putting to flight so bitter an enimie, you shall binde all women to you much more, and so much, that where they shall doe nothing els but reward you, yet shall the bondage still remaine fresh,[2] and never cease to be recompensed.

Then answered the L. Julian: me thinke (madam) you shew great honour to your enimie, and verie litle to your defender: for undoubtedly the Lorde Gasper hath saide nothing against women, but it hath beene fully answered by maister Bernard. And I believe every one of us knoweth, that it is meete the Courtier beare verie great reverence towarde women, and a discrete and courteous person ought never to touch their honestie neither in jeast, nor in good earnest. Therefore to dispute of this so open a truth, were (in manner) to put a doubt in manifest matters.

I thinke well that the Lorde Octavian passed his boundes somewhat in saying that women are most unperfect creatures,

[1] "To depart with stripes": cf. "giving us Braccesque leave"—which amounts to the same thing.

[2] "Yet shall the bondage," etc.: cf. "yet the obligation must always stand."

and not apt to worke any vertuous deede, and of litle, or no worthinesse in respect of men. And because many times credite is given to men of great authoritie, although they speake not the ful truth, and when they speake in jest, the Lord Gasper hath suffered himselfe to be led by the Lord Octavians words, to say that men of wisedom set no store by them, which is most false. For I have knowne few men of worthinesse at any time that doe not love and observe women, the vertue and consequently the worthinesse of whom I deeme not a jotte inferiour to mens.

Yet if we should come to this contention, the cause of women were like to quaile greatly, because these Lords have shaped a Courtier that is so excellent and of so many devine qualities, that who so hath the understanding to consider him to bee such a one as he is, will imagine that the deserts[1] of women can not attaine to that point. But in case the matter should bee equally devided, we shall first neede of so wittie and eloquent a person as is Count Lewis and Sir Fredericke, to shape a gentlewoman of the Pallace with all perfections due to a woman, as they have shaped the Courtier with the perfections belonging to a man. And then if he that defended their cause were any thing wittie and eloquent, I believe (because the truth will be a helpe to him) hee may plainely shew that women are as full of vertues as men be.

The Ladie Emilia answered: Nay a great deale more, and that it is so, ye may see, vertue is the female, and vice the male.[2] The Lord Gasper then laughed, and turning him to maister Nicholas Phrisio, what is your judgement Phrisio (quoth he.)

Phrisio answered: I am sorie for the Lord Julian that he is so seduced with the promises and flattering wordes of the Ladie Emilia to runne into an errour to speake the thing which for his sake I am ashamed of.

The Ladie Emilia answered smiling: you will surely bee ashamed for your owne sake when you shall see the Lord Gasper after he is convicted, confesse his owne errour, and yours too, and demaund that pardon which we will not graunt him.

Then spake the Dutchesse: Because it is verie late, I will wee deferre the whole untill to morrow, the more for that I think it well done we follow the Lorde Julians counsel, that before he come to this disputation we may have a gentlewoman of the Palace so fashioned in all perfections, as these Lordes have fashioned the perfect Courtier.

[1] "Deserts": cf. "merits."  [2] *La virtù, il vizio.*

Madam, quoth the Ladie Emilia then, I pray God it fall not to our lotte, to give this enterprise to any confederate with the Lord Gasper, least he fashion us for a gentlewoman of the Court, one that can doe naught els but looke to the kitchin and spin.

Then saide Phrisio: In deed that is an office fit for her. Then the Dutchesse, I have a good hope in the Lord Julian (quoth she) who will (for the good wit and judgement I know he is of) imagin the greatest perfection that may be wished in a woman, and in like manner expresse it well in wordes, and so shall we have somewhat to confound the Lorde Gaspers false accusation withall.

Madam, answered the L. Julian, I wot not whether your devise be good or no, to commit into my handes an enterprise of so great waight, for (to tell you the truth) I thinke not my selfe able inough. Neither am I like the Count and Sir Fredericke, which with their eloquence have shaped such a Courtier as never was: nor I believe ever shall be. Yet if your pleasure be so, that I shall take his burden upon me, let it be at the least with those conditions that the other have had before me: namely that everie man, where hee shall thinke good, may reply against mee, and this shall I reckon not overthwarting, but aide, and perhaps in correcting mine errours wee shal finde the perfectiõ of a gentlewomã of the palace which we seeke for.

I trust, answered the Dutchesse, your talke shall be such, that litle may be saide against you. Therefore settle your minde to thinke upon onely this, and fashion us such a gentlewoman, that these our adversaries may be ashamed to say, that she is not equall with the Courtier in vertue: of whom it shall be well done Sir Fredericke speake no more, for he hath but too well set him forth, especially since we must compare a woman to him.

I have (madam) answered Sir Fredericke, litle or nothing now left to speake of the Courtier, and that I did thinke upon maister Bernardes jestes have made mee forget.

If it be so, quoth the Dutchesse, assembling together to morrow betimes, wee shall have leisure to accomplish both the one and the other. And when she had so saide, they arose all upon their feet, and taking their leave reverently of the Dutchesse, every man withdrew him to his lodging.[1]

---

[1] "His lodging": cf. "his own room."

# THIRD BOOK

THE THIRDE BOOKE OF THE COURTIER, OF
COUNT BALDESSER CASTILION, UNTO MAISTER
ALFONSUS ARIOSTO

It is read that Pythagoras verie wittily and after a subtill
manner found out the measure of Hercules bodie, in that he
knew that the space where every five yeares they kept the
games or prises of Olympus[1] in Achaia nigh unto Elis before
Jupiter Olympicus Temple, was measured by Hercules himselfe:
and appointed a furlong of ground there of sixe hundreth and
five and twentie of his own feete[2]: and the other furlongs which
after his time were cast out in diverse partes of Greece by his
successors, were also of sixe hundreth and five and twentie
of their feete, but for all that somewhat shorter than his. Pythagoras knew forthwith by that proportion how much Hercules
foot was bigger than all the other mens feete, and so the measure
of his foote once known, he gathereth that all Hercules bodie
proportionally in greatnesse exceeded all other mens, so much,
as that furlong, all other furlongs.

You may then (gentle maister Alphonsus) by the verie same
reason easily gather by this least part of all the rest of the bodie
how farre the Court of Urbin excelled all the other in Italy.
For if the sportes and pastimes (that are used to none other end
but to refresh the wearisom mindes after earnest labours)
farre passed all such as are commonly used in the other Courts
of Italy.

What (gesse you) were all the other vertuous practises, whereunto all men had their mindes bent, and were fully and wholy
addicted. And of this I may be bolde to make my vaunt, nothing
mistrusting but to be credited therin, considering I goe not
about to prayse so auncient antiquities wherein I might, if I
were disposed, faine what I lusted[3]: but of this I speake, I am
able to bring forth many men of worthie credence, for sufficient

[1] Cf. "the Olympic games."
[2] Cf. "and a Stadium made 625 times the length of his own foot."
[3] Cf. "I am not praising things so ancient that I might be allowed to
invent."

triall, which as yet are in life, and have themselves seene and marked well the living and conversation of such as in times past excelled in that Court. And I reckon my selfe bound (for that lyeth in me to doe) to stretch forth my force with all diligence to defend this famous memorie from mortall oblivion, and with my penne to make it live in the mindes of our posteritie.

Whereby perhaps in time to come, there shall not want that will envie this our time. For there is no man that readeth of the wonderfull families of times past, but in his mind hee conceiveth a certaine greater opinion of them that are written upon, than it appeareth those bookes can expresse, though they have beene written with perfection.

Even so doe wee desire, that all the readers of this our travaile (if at the least wise it shall deserve so much favor, that it may come to the sight of noble men and vertuous Ladies) will cast in their minde and thinke for a suretie, that the Court of Urbin hath beene much more excellent and better furnished with notable men, than wee are able to expresse in writing. And in case so much eloquence were in mee, as there was prowesse in them, I should need none other testimonie to make such give full credence to my wordes, as have not seene it.

When therefore the companie was assembled in the accustomed place, the daye following at the due houre, and set with silence, every man turned his eyes to Sir Fredericke and to the Lorde Julian, waiting when the one of them woulde beginne to speake his minde.

Wherefor the Dutchesse, after she had beene still a while, my Lord Julian (quoth she) every mans desire is to see this your gentlewoman wel set forth, and if you shew us her not in such manner, that all her beauties may bee discerned, wee will suspect that you are jealous over her.

The Lord Julian answered: Madam, if I reckoned her beautiful, I would shew you her without any other setting forth,[1] and in such wise as Paris did beholde the three goddesses. But in case these Ladies bee not a helpe to me to trim her (who can doe it right well) I doubt me, that not onely the Lord Gasper and Phrisio, but all the other Lordes here shall have a just cause to speake ill of her.

Therefore since she is yet in some part deemed beautifull,[2] perhaps it shall be better to keepe her close[3] and see what Sir

---

[1] "Without . . .": cf. "all unadorned."
[2] Cf. "while still she stands in some repute for beauty."
[3] "Close": cf. "hidden."

Fredericke hath yet behinde to speake of the Courtier, which (no doubt) is much more beautifull than my woman can be.

That I had in minde, answered Sir Fredericke, is not so necessarie for y^e Courtier, but it may be left out, and no hurt done: yea, it is a contrarie[1] matter almost to that hetherto hath beene reasoned of.

And what matter is it then, quoth the Dutchesse? Sir Fredericke answered, I was purposed in what I could, to declare the causes of these companies and orders of knights brought up by great Princes, under divers standers, as is that of Saint Michael in the house of Fraunce, the order of the Garter under the title of Saint George in the house of England,[2] the golden Fleece in the house of Burgony, and how these dignities be given, and in what sorte they that deserve are disgraded from them, how they first came up, who were the founders of them, and to what end they were ordained, because we see that these knights in great Courtes are alwaies highly esteemed.

I minded also, if time had sufficed me, beside the diversitie of manners used in the Courtes of christian Princes in feasting and appearing in open shewes, to speak somewhat also of the great Turke, but much more particularly of the Sophy[3] king of Persia.

For when I understood by merchant men a long time trafficked in that countrie, the noble men there be verie full of prowesse and well mannered, and use in their conversation one with another, and in womens service, and in all their practisinges much courtesie and great sobrietie, and when time serveth, in martiall feates, in sportings, and undertaking enterprises, much sumptuousnesse, great liberalitie and braverie: I delited to know what order they take in these thinges which they set most store by, wherein their pomps consist, and braveries of garments and armour, wherein they differ from us, and wherein we agree, what kinde of entertainement their women use, and with what sober moode[4] they shew favour to who so is in their love service, but to say the truth, it is no fit time now to enter into this talke, especiallye since there is other to be said, and much more to our purpose than this.

Yes, quoth the Lorde Gasper, both this and many other things bee more to the purpose, than to fashion this gentle-

---

[1] "Contrarie": cf. "rather different."

[2] It will be remembered that Castiglione had returned from England only a few days before, bringing with him the dignity and insignia of Companion of the Order of the Garter to Duke Guidobaldo.

[3] Cf. "Sophi."  [4] "Sober moode": cf. "modesty."

woman of the pallace, forsomuch as the verie same rules that are given for the Courtier, serve also for the woman, for aswell ought she to have respect to times and places, and to observe (as much as her weakenesse is able to beare) all the other properties that have beene so much reasoned upon, as the Courtier.

And therefore in stead of this it were not perhaps amisse to teach to me particular points that belong to the service about a Princes person: for no doubt the Courtier ought to knowe them, and to have a grace in doing them. Or els to speake of the way that hee ought to take in the bodily exercises, how to ride, to handle weapon, and wrastle, and wherein consisteth the hardnes of these feates.

Then spake the Dutchesse, smiling: Princes are not served about their persons with[1] so excellent a Courtier as this is. As for the exercises of bodie and strength, and slightnesse[2] of person, we will leave them for maister Peter Mount here to take charge to teach them when he shall thinke most meet, for presently the Lorde Julian hath nothing els to speake of, but of this womā, whom (me thinke) you now begin to have a feare of, and therefore would bring us out of our purpose.

Phrisio answered: certaine it is, that now it is needles and out of purpose to talke of women, especiall being yet behinde somewhat to be spoken of the Courtier, for the one matter ought not to be mingled with the other.

You are in a great errour, answered the Lorde Cesar Gonzaga: for like as no Court, how great soever it be, can have any sightlinesse or brightnesse in it, or mirth without women, nor any Courtier can bee gracious, pleasant or hardie, nor at any time undertake any galant enterprise of Chivalrie, unlesse he be stirred with the conversation and with the love and contentatiō[3] of women, even so in like case, the Courtiers talke is most unperfect evermore, if the entercourse of women give them not a part of the grace wherwithall they make perfect and decke out their playing the Courtier.[4]

The Lorde Octavian laughed and saide: Beholde a peece of the baite that bringeth men out of their wits. Then the Lorde Julian turning him to ye Dutchesse, Madam (quoth he) since it is so your pleasure, I will speak that commeth to mind, but with verie great doubt to satisfie. And I wis a great deale lesse paine it were for mee to fashion a Ladie that shoulde deserve

[1] Cf. "Princes do not employ the personal service of . . ."
[2] Cf. "agility."          [3] Cf. "pleasure."
[4] "A part of the grace," etc.: cf. "a touch of that grace wherewith they perfect Courtiership and adorn it."

to bee Queene of the world, than a perfect gentlewoman of the Court, for of her I wot not where to fetch any patterne, but for a Queene I shoulde not neede to seeke farre, and sufficient it were for me onely to imagine the heavenly conditions of a Ladie whom I know, and through seeing them, direct all my thoughts to expresse plainelye with wordes the thing, that many see with their eyes, and where I coulde doe no more, yet should I fulfill my duetie in imagining[1] her.

Then saide the Dutchesse: Passe not your bounds (my Lord Julian) but minde the order taken, and fashion the gentlewoman of the pallace, that this so worthie a maistresse may have him that shall so worthily serve her.

Then the Lord Julian proceeded: for a proofe therefore (Madam) that your commandement may drive me to assay to doe, yea the thing I have no skill in, I will speake of this excellent woman, as I woulde have her. And when I have fashioned her after my minde, and can afterwarde get none other,[2] I will take her as mine owne, after the example of Pigmalion.

And whereas the Lorde Gasper hath said, that the verie same rules that are given for the Courtier serve also for the woman. I am of a contrarie opinion. For albeit some qualities are common and necessarie as well for the woman as the man, yet are there some other more meete for the woman than for the man, and some again meete for the man, that she ought in no wise to meddle withall.

The verie same I say of the exercises of the bodie: But principally in her fashions, manners, wordes, gestures and conversation (me thinke) the woman ought to be much unlike the man. For right as it is seemely for him to shew a certaine manlinesse full and steadie, so doth it well in a woman to have a tendernesse, soft and milde, with a kinde of womanlye sweetenesse in every gesture of hers, that in going, standing, and speaking what ever she lusteth, may alwaies make her appeare a woman without anye likenesse of man.

Adding therefore this principle to the rules that these Lords have taught the Courtier, I thinke well, she may serve her turne[3] with manie of them, and be endued with verie good qualities, as the Lorde Gasper saith. For many vertues of the minde I recken be as necessarie for a woman, as for a man.

Likewise noblenesse of birth, avoiding affectation or curiositie, to have a good grace of nature in all her doings, to be of

[1] Cf. " by merely naming."　　　[2] Cf. "have (none) other such."
[3] Cf. "profit by."

good conditions, wittie, foreseeing,[1] not haughtie, not envious, not ill tongued, not light, not contentious, not untowardly,[2] to have the knowledge to winne and keepe the good will of her Ladie and of all others, to doe well and with good grace the exercises comely for a woman.

Me thinke well beautie is more necessary in her than in the Courtier, for (to say the truth) there is a great lacke in the woman that wanteth beautie.

She ought also to be more circumspect, and to take better heede that she give no occasion to bee ill reported of, and so behave her selfe, that she be not onely not spotted with any fault, but not so much as with suspition. Because a woman hath not so manie waies to defend her selfe from slanderous reportes, as hath a man.

But for somuch as Count Lewis hath verie particularly expressed the principal profession of the Courtier, and willeth it to bee in Martiall feates, me thinke also behovefull to utter (according to my judgement) what the gentlewoman of the Palace ought to be: in which point when I have throughly satisfied, I shal thinke my selfe rid of the greatest part of my duetie.

Leaving therefore a part the vertues of the minde that ought to be common to her with the Courtier, as wisedom, noblenesse of courage, staiednesse,[3] and many moe, and likewise the conditions that are meet for all women, as to be good and discreete, to have the understanding to order her husbands goodes and her house and children[4] when she is married, and all those partes that belong to a good huswife: I' say that for her that liveth in Court, me thinke there belongeth unto her above all other thinges, a certaine sweetenesse in language[5] that may delite, wherby she may gently entertain all kinde of men with talke worthie the hearing and honest, and applyed to the time and place, and to the degree of the person she cōmuneth withal. Accompanying with sober and quiet manners,[6] and with the honestie[7] that must alwaies be a stay to her deedes, a readie livelinesse of wit,[8] whereby she may declare her selfe far wide

---

[1] "Good conditions," etc.: cf. "mannerly, clever, prudent."
[2] "Not light," etc.: cf. "not vain, not quarrelsome, not silly."
[3] Cf. "such as prudence, magnanimity, continence . . ."
[4] Cf. "such as kindness, discretion, ability to manage her husband's property . . ."
[5] "Certaine sweetenesse," etc.: cf. "pleasant affability."
[6] Cf. "calm and modest manners."     [7] Cf. "seemliness."
[8] Cf. "a quick vivacity of spirit."

from all dulnesse [1]: but with such a kinde of goodnesse,[2] that she may bee esteemed no lesse chaste, wise and courteous, than pleasant, feate conceited and sober [3]: and therefore muste she keepe a certaine meane verie hard, and (in a manner) derived of contrary matters, and come just to certaine limittes, but not to passe them.

This woman ought not therefore (to make her selfe good and honest [4]) be so squeimish [5] and make wise [6] to abhorre both the company and the talke (though somewhat of the wantonest [7]) if she bee present, to get her thence by and by,[8] for a man may lightly gesse that she fained to be so coye to hide that in her selfe which she doubted others might come to the knowledge of: and such nice fashions are alwaies hatefull.

Neither ought she againe (to shew her selfe free and pleasant) speake wordes of dishonestie, nor use a certaine familiaritie without measure and bridle, and fashions to make men believe that of her that perhaps is not: but being present at such kinde of talke, she ought to give the hearing with a litle blushing and shamefacednesse.

Likewise to eschew one vice that I have seene raigne in many: namely, to speake and willingly to give eare to such as report ill of other women: for such as in hearing the dishonest behaviors of other women disclosed, are offended at the matter, and make wise not to credit and (in manner) to thinke it a wonder that a womã should leade an uncleane life, they make proofe that since this fault seemeth unto them so foule a matter, they commit it not. But those that goe alwaies harking out the loves of others [9] and disclose them so point by pointe, and with such joy, it seemeth that they envy the matter, and that their desire is to have all men knowe it, that the like may not bee imputed them for a trespace.

And so they tourne it to certaine laughters with a kind of gesture, wherby they make men to suspecte at the very same instant that they take great contentation at it. And of this ariseth, that men although to their seeminge they give diligente eare to it, for the most part conceive an ill opinion of them, and have them in very small reputatiõ, and (to their weening) with these behaviours are entised to attempt them farther.

[1] "Dulnesse": cf. "indelicacy."
[2] "Goodnesse," etc.: cf. "such a kindly manner."
[3] Cf. "agreeable, witty, and discreet."
[4] "To make herself," etc.: cf. "to be thought good and pure."
[5] Cf. "coy."    [6] "Make wise": cf. "seem."    [7] Cf. "a little free."
[8] "By and by," etc.: cf. "as soon as she finds herself therein."
[9] Cf. "continually prying into other men's intrigues."

And many times afterward they runne so farre[1] at rovers that it purchaseth them worthely an ill name, and in conclusion are so little regarded, that men passe not for their company, but rather abhorre them. And contrarywise, there is no man so shamelesse and high minded,[2] but beareth greate reverence toward them that be counted good and honest, because that gravity tēpered with knowledge and goodnes, is (as it were) a shielde againste the wanton pride and beastlinesse of sawsie merchants.[3] Wherefore it is seene that one worde, a laughter or a gesture of good will (howe litle soever it bee) of an honest woman, is more set by of every man, than all the toyes and wanton gestures[4] of them that so lavishly shew small shame-fastnesse. And where they leade not in deede an uncleane life,[5] yet with those wanton countenances, babling, scornfulnes, and such scoffing conditions, they make men to think they doe.

And forsomuch as words that are not grounded upon some pithy foundation, are vain and childish, the gentlewoman of the palace, beside her descretion[6] to understand the condition of him she talketh withall, to entertaine him honestly, must needes have a sight in many things, and a judgement in her communication to picke out such as be to purpose for the condition of him she talketh withall, and be heedfull that she speake not otherwhile where she would not, words that may offend him.

Let her beware of praising her selfe undiscretely, or being too tedious, that she make him not wearie. Let her not go mingle with pleasant and laughing talke matters of gravitie: nor yet with grave jestes and feat conceites.

Let her not foolishly take upon her to know that she knoweth not, but soberly seeke to be esteemed for that she knoweth, avoyding (as is saide) Curiositie in all thinges.

In this manner shall she be indued with good conditions, and the exercises of the bodie comely for a woman shall she do with an exceeding good grace, and her talke shall bee plenteous and full of wisedom, honestie, and pleasantnesse: and so shall she be not onely beloved but reverenced of all men, and perhaps worthy to be compared to this great Courtier, as well for the qualities of the minde as of the bodie.

---

[1] Cf. "go such lengths."
[2] "High minded": cf. "insolent."
[3] "Wanton pride," etc.: cf. "the insolence and coarseness of the presumptuous."
[4] "Toyes and wanton gestures": cf. "endearments and caresses."
[5] Cf. "And if they are not immodest."　　　[6] Cf. "good sense."

When the Lord Julian had hetherto spoken, and he held his peace, and setled himselfe as though hee had made an end of his talke. Then saide the Lord Gasper, no doubt my Lord Julian but you have decked gayly out this gentlewoman, and made her of an excellent condition: yet me seemeth that you have gone generally inough to worke, and named in her certaine things, so great, that I think in my mind you are ashamed to expound them, and have rather wished them in her, after the manner of them that sometimes wish for things unpossible and above nature, than taught them.

Therefore would I that you declared unto us a litle better, what exercises of the bodie are meet for a gentlewoman of the Palace, and in what sorte she ought to entertaine,[1] and what those many thinges be, which you say she ought to have a sight in: and whether wisedom, noblenesse of courage, staiednesse,[2] and those many other vertues that you have spoken of, your meaning is should helpe her about the overseeing only of her house, children and housholde (the which neverthelesse you wil not have her principall profession) or els to entertaine, and to doe these exercises of the bodie with a good grace: and in good felowshippe take heede yee put not these sillie vertues to so vile an occupation,[3] that they may be ashamed of it.

The Lord Julian laughed, and saide: you can not choose (my Lord Gasper) but still you must utter your ill stomacke[4] against women. But certes, mee thought I had spoken sufficient, and especially before such audience, that I believe none here, but understandeth concerning the exercises of the bodie, that it is not comely for a woman to practise feates of armes, ryding, playing at tenise, wrastling, and many other thinges that belong to men.

Then said Unico Aretino: Among them of old time the manner was, that women wrastled naked with men, but wee have lost this good custome together with many moe.

The Lord Cesar Gonzaga replyed to this. And in my time I have seene women play at tenise, practise feates of armes, ride, hunt, and doe (in a manner) all the exercises beside, that a gentleman can doe.

The Lord Julian answered: Since I may fashion this womā after my mind, I will not only have her not to practise these manly exercises so sturdie and boisterous, but also those that

---

[1] Cf. "converse."  [2] Cf. "prudence, magnanimity, continence."
[3] Cf. "these poor virtues to such a menial duty."
[4] Cf. "your ill will."

bee meete for a woman, I will have her to doe them with heede-fulnesse and with the short mildenes that we have saide is comely for her. And therefore in daunsing I would not have her use too swift and violent trickes,[1] nor yet in singing or playing upon instruments those hard and often divisions[2] that declare more cunning than sweetenes. Likewise the instruments of Musicke which she useth (in mine opinion) ought to bee fit for this purpose.

Imagin with your selfe what an unsightly matter it were to see a woman play upon a tabour or drum, or blow in a flute or trumpet, or any like instrument: and this because the boistrous-nesse of them doth both cover and take away that sweete mild-nesse which setteth so forth everie deede that a woman doth.

Therefore when she commeth to daunce, or to shew any kind of musicke, she ought to be brought to it with suffring her selfe somewhat to be prayed, and with a certain bashfulnesse, that may declare the noble shamefastnesse that is contrarie to headinesse.

She ought also to frame her garments to this entent, and so to apparrell her selfe, that she appeare not fonde and light.

But for so much as it is lawfull and necessarie for women to set more by their beawtie than men, and sundrie kindes of beautie there are, this woman ought to have a judgement to know what manner garments set her best out, and be most fitte for the exercise, that she entendeth to undertake at that instant, and with them to aray her selfe. And where she per-ceiveth in her a sightly and chearefull beautie, she ought to farther it with gestures, words and apparel, that all may betoken mirth. In like case an other that feeleth her selfe of a milde and grave disposition, she ought also to accompany it with fashions of the like sorte, to encrease that that is the gift of nature.

In like manner where she is somewhat fatter or leaner[3] than reasonable sise, or wanner, or browner, to helpe it with garments but fainingly as much as she can possible, and keeping her selfe clenly, and handsom,[4] shewing alwaies that she bestoweth no paine nor diligence at all about it.

And because the Lord Gasper doth also aske what these many thinges bee she ought to have a sight in, and how to entertaine, and whether the vertues ought to bee applyed to this enter-

---

[1] "Trickes": cf. "movements."
[2] Cf. "abrupt and oft-repeated diminutions."
[3] Cf. "a little more stout or thin."          [4] Cf. "dainty and neat."

tainement, I say that I will have her to understād that yᵗ these Lordes have willed yᵉ Courtier to know: and in those exercises that wee have saide are not comely for her: I will at the least she have that judgement, that men can have of the thinges which they practise not, and this to have knowledge to praise and make of Gentlemenne more and lesse according to their deserts.

And to make a briefe rehersall in few wordes of that is alreadie saide, I will that this woman have a sight in letters, in musicke, in drawing, or painting, and skilfull in dauncing, and in devising sports and pastimes, accompanying with that discrete sober moode,[1] and with the giving a good opinion of her selfe, the other principles also that have beene taught the Courtier.

And thus in conversation, in laughing, in sporting, in jesting, finally in everie thing she shal be had in great price, and shall entertaine accordingly both with jestes, and feate conceites meete for her, every person that commeth in her company.

And albeit stayednesse, noblenesse of courage, temperance, strength of the minde, wisedom, and the other vertues, a man would thinke belonged not to entertaine, yet will I have her endowed with them all, not so much to entertaine (although notwithstanding they may serve thereto also) as to be vertuous: and these vertues to make her such a one, that she may deserve to bee esteemed, and all her doings framed by them.

I wonder then quoth the Lorde Gasper smyling, since you give women both letters, and stayednesse, and noblenesse of courage, and temperance, ye will not have them also to beare rule in cities, and to make lawes, and to leade armies, and men to stand spinning in the kitchin.

The Lord Julian answered in like manner smiling: Perhaps too this were not amisse: then he proceeded. Do you not knowe that Plato (which in deed was not verie friendly to women) giveth them the overseeing of Cities, and all other martiall offices hee appointed to men? Thinke you not there were many to be found that could as well skill in ruling Cities and armies, as men can? But I have not appointed them these offices, because I fashion a waiting gentlewoman of the Court, not a Queene.

I see well you would covertly have up againe the slaunderous report that the Lord Octavian gave women yesterday: namely, that they be most unperfect creatures and not apt to worke any vertuous deede, and of verie litle worthinesse, and of no value

[1] "Sober moode": cf. "modesty."

in respect of men: But surely both he and you shoulde be in verie great errour if ye thought so.

Then saide the Lord Gasper: I will not have up againe matters alreadie past, but you woulde faine presse me to speake some word that might offend these Ladies mindes, to make them my foes, as you with flattering them falsely will purchase their good will. But they are so wise above other,[1] that they love truth better (although it make not so much with them [2]) than false prayses: Neither take they it in ill part for a man to say, that men are of a more worthines, and they will not let to confesse [3] that you have spoken great wonders, and appointed to the gentlewoman of the Pallace certaine fonde unpossible matters, and so manie vertues, that Socrates and Cato and all the Philosophers in the world are nothing to her.

For to tell you the plaine truth, I marvell you were not ashamed so much to passe your bounds, where it ought to have suffised ye to make this gentlewoman of the pallace beautifull, sober, honest, well spoken,[4] and to have the understanding to entertaine without running in slaunder, with dauncing, musicke, sportes, laughing, jestes, and the other matters that wee see dayly used in Court. But to goe about to give her the knowledge of all thinges in the world, and to appoint her the vertues that so seldome times are seene in men, yea and in them of olde time, it is a matter that can neither be held withall, nor scantly heard.

Now that women are unperfect creatures, and consequently of lesse worthinesse than men, and not apt to conceive those vertues that they are, I purpose not to affirme it, because the prowes of these Ladies were inough to make me a lyar. Yet this I say unto you, that most wise men have left in writing, that nature, because she is alwaies set and bent to make things most perfect, if she could, would continually bring forth men, and when a woman is borne, it is a slackenesse or default of nature, and contrarie to that she would doe. As it is also seene in one borne blinde, lame, or with some other impediment, and as in trees many fruites that never ripen.

Even so may a woman bee saide to bee a creature brought forth at a chaunce and by happe, and that it is so, marke me the workes of the man and the woman, and by them make your proofe of the perfection of each of them. Howbeit since these

---

[1] "Other": cf. "other women."
[2] Cf. ("even if it be little in their favour").
[3] "And will not let," etc.: cf. "and will admit."
[4] Cf. "beautiful, discreet, chaste, gracious . . ."

defaults of women are the defect of nature that hath so brought them forth, wee ought not for this to hate them, nor faint in having lesse respect to them than is meete: but to esteeme them above that they are, me thinketh a plaine errour.

The Lorde Julian looked the Lord Gasper would have proceeded on still, but when he saw now that hee held his peace, he saide.

Of the unperfectnes of women me thinke you have alleaged a verie colde reason, whereunto (albeit may hap it were not now meete to enter into these subtil pointes) I answere according to the opinion of him that is of skill, and according to the truth, that substance in what ever thing it be, can not receive into it more or lesse: for as no stone can bee more perfectly a stone than an other, as touching the being of a stone: nor one blocke more perfectly a blocke, than an other: no more can one man be more perfectly a man than an other: and consequently the male kinde shall not be more perfect, than the female, as touching his formall [1] substance, for both the one and the other is conteined under the Species of *Homo*, and that wherein they differ is an Accidentall matter and no Essentiall.

In case you will then tell me that the man is mor perfecter than yᵉ woman though not as touching the Essentiall, yet in the Accidents, I answere that these accidents must consist either in the bodie, or in the minde: if in the bodie, because the man is more sturdier, nimbler, lighter, and more able to endure travaile, I say that this is an argument of smal perfection: for among men themselves such as abounde in these qualities above other, are not for them the more esteemed: and in warre, where the greatest part of painefull labours are and of strength,[2] the stoutest are not for all that the most set by.

If in the minde, I say, what ever thinges men can understand, the selfe same can women understand also: and where it pearceth the capacitie of the one,[3] it may in likewise pearce the others.

Here after the Lord Julian had made a litle stoppe, hee proceeded smiling: Doe you not know that this principle is helde in Philosophye, who so is tender of flesh, is apt of minde: Therefore there is no doubt, but women being tenderer of flesh, are also apter of mind, and of a more inclined wit to musings and speculations, than men. Afterwarde he folowed on.

But leaving this apart, because you saide that I should make

---

[1] "Formall": cf. "essential."
[2] Cf. "where the greater part of the work is laborious."
[3] Cf. "where the intellect of the one penetrates."

my proofe of the perfection of eche of them by the workes, I say unto you, if you consider effects of nature, you shall finde, that she bringeth women forth as they be, not at a chaunce, but fitly necessarie for the end. For albeit she shapeth them of bodie not stout and of a milde mind, with manie other qualities contrarie to mens, yet doe the conditions of each of them stretch unto one selfe end, concerning the selfe same profit. For even as through that weake feeblenesse, women are of a lesser courage, so are they also by the verie same more wary. Therefore mothers nourish up children, and fathers instruct them, and with manlines provide [1] for that abroad, that they with careful diligēce store up in the house which is no lesse praise.

In case you will then consider the auncient histories (albeit men at all times have beene verie sparing in writing the prayses of women) and them of latter daies, ye shall finde that continually vertue hath raigned as well among women as men: and that such there have beene also that have made warre and obtained glorious victories, governed Realmes with great wisedome and justice, and done what ever men have done.

As touching sciences, doe you not remember yee have reade of so many that were well seene in Philosophie? Other that have beene most excellent in Poetrie? Other, that have pleaded, and both accused and defended before Judges most eloquently?

Of handicrafts, long it were to rehearse, neither is it needfull to make any rehersall thereof. If then in Essentiall substance, the man is no more perfect than the woman, nor yet in the Accidents (and of this beside reason, the experiences are seene) I wot not wherein this his perfection should consist.

And because you said that Natures entent is alwaies to bring forth thinges most perfect, and therefore if she could, would alwaies bring forth a man, and that the bringing a woman forth is rather a default and slacknesse of nature, than her entent. I answere you that this is full and wholy to be denyed, neither can I see why you may say that nature entendeth not to bring forth women, without whom mankinde can not be preserved, whereof nature her selfe is more desirous than of any thing els.

Because through ye means of this felowship of male and female she bringeth forth children, that restore the received benefits in their childhood to their fathers in their old dayes, in that they nourish them: afterwarde they renue them, in begetting themselves also other children, of whom they looke in their olde age to receive it, that being young they bestowed upon their fathers:

1 "Provide": cf. "earn."

whereby nature (as it were) turning her about in a circle, ful-filleth an everlastingnesse, and in this wise giveth an immortalitie to mortall men.

Since then to this, the woman is as needfull as the man, I can not discerne for what cause the one is made by hap more than the other.

Truth it is, that Nature entendeth alwaies to bring forth matters most perfect, and therefore meaneth to bring forth the man in his kind, but not more male than female. Yea were it so that she alwaies brought forth male, then should it without peradventure bee an unperfectnesse: for like as of the bodie and of the soule there ariseth a cōpound more nobler than his partes, which is man: Even so of the felowship of male and female there ariseth a compound preserving mankinde, without which the partes were in decay, and therefore male and female by nature are alwaies together, neither can the one be without the other: right so he [1] ought not to bee called the male, that hath not a female (according to the definition of both the one and the other) nor she the female that hath not a male.

And for so much as one kinde alone betokeneth an imperfection, the Divines of olde time referre both the one and the other to God: Wherefore Orpheus saide that Jupiter was both male and female: And it is read in scripture that God fashioned male and female to his likenesse. And the Poets many times speaking of the Gods, meddle the kindes together.

Then the Lord Gasper, I would not (quoth hee) wee should enter into these subtill pointes, for these women will not understand us. And albeit I answere you with very good reasons, yet will they believe, or at the least make wise to believe that I am in the wrong, and forthwith will give sentence as they list. Yet since wee are entred into them, onely this will I say, (as you know, it is the opinion of most wise men) that man is likened to the Forme, the woman to the Matter, and therefore as the Forme is perfecter than the Matter yea it giveth him his being, so is the man much more perfect than the woman.

And I remember that I have heard (when it was) that a great Philosopher [2] in certaine Problemes of his, saith: Whence commeth it that naturally the woman alwaies loveth the man, that hath been the first to receive of her amorous pleasures? And con-trariwise the man hateth the woman that hath beene the first to couple in that wise with him? And adding thereto the cause, affirmeth it to be this: For that in this act, the woman receiveth

[1] "He": cf. "that."     [2] Aristotle, I. *Physics*, xviii.

of the man perfection, and the man of the woman imperfection: and therefore every man naturally loveth the thing that maketh him perfect, and hateth that maketh him unperfect.

And beside this, a great argument of the perfection of the man, and of the imperfection of the woman, is, that generally every woman wisheth she were a man, by a certain provocatiõ of nature that teacheth her to wish for her perfection.

The Lorde Julian answered sodainely: The silly poore creatures wish not to bee a man to make them more perfect, but to have libertie, and to be rid of the rule that men have of their owne authoritie chalenged over them. And the similitude which you give of the Matter and Forme, is not alike[1] in everie point: because the woman is not made so perfectly by the man, as is the Matter by yᵉ Forme; for the Matter receiveth his being of the Forme, and can not stand without it.

Yea the more Matter Formes have, the more imperfection they have withall, and severed from it, are most perfect: but the woman receiveth not her being of the man, yea as she is made perfect by the man, so doth she also make him perfect: whereby both the one and the other come together to beget children: the which thing they can not doe any of them by themselves.

The cause then of the continuall love of the woman toward the first that she hath beene with, and of the hatred of the man towarde the first woman, I will not affirme to be that your Philosopher alleageth in his Problemes, but I impute it to the surenesse and stablenesse of the woman, and wavering of the man, and that not without naturall reason: for since the male is naturally hote, by that qualitie he taketh lightnesse, stirring and unstedfastnesse: and contrariwise the woman through colde quietnesse, steadie waightinesse, and more earnest imprintings.

Then the Ladie Emilia turning her to the Lorde Julian, for love of God (quoth she) come once out of these your Matters and Formes and males and females, and speake so that you may bee understood: for we have heard and verie well understood the ill that the Lord Octavian and the Lord Gasper have spoken of us: but since wee understand not now in what sorte you stand in our defence, me thinke therefore that this is a straying from the purpose, and a leaving of the ill imprinting in every mans mind that these our enimies have given of us.

Give us not this name answered the Lorde Gasper, for more

[1] "Is not alike": cf. "does not apply."

meeter it were for the Lord Julian, which in giving women false prayses declareth that there are none true for them.

The Lorde Julian saide then: doubt ye not (madam) all shall be answered to. But I will not raile upon men so without reason, as they have done upon women. And if perchance there were any one here that meant to pen this our talke, I would not that in place where these Matters and Formes were understood, the arguments and reasons which the Lord Gasper alleageth against you should be seene unanswered to.

I wote not, my Lord Julian, quoth then the Lorde Gasper, how in this you can deny, that the man is not through his naturall qualities more perfect than the woman, which of complexion is cold and the man hote, and much more nobler and perfecter is heate than colde, because it is active and forth bringing: and (as you know) the element [1] poureth downe here among us onely heate, and not colde, which pearceth not [2] the workes of nature.

And therfore because women are colde of complexion, I thinke it is the cause of their faint-hartednesse and fearfulnesse.

Will you still, answered the Lord Julian, enter into subtill pointes? You shall perceive your selfe at everie time to come into a greater pecke of troubles: and that it is so, hearken to.

I graunt you, that heate in it selfe is more perfect thā colde, but this followeth not in medled matters and compounded, for in case it were so, the bodie that were most hote should be most perfect: which is false, because temperate bodies bee most perfect.

I doe you to wete moreover, that the woman is of complexion colde in comparison of the mans, which for overmuch heate is farre wide from temper [3]: but as touching her selfe, she is temperate, or at the least nearer to temper than the man, because she hath that moisture within her of equall portion with the naturall heat, which in the man through overmuch drouth doth sooner melt and consume away.

She hath also such a kind of colde, that it resisteth, and comforteth the naturall heat, and maketh it nearer to temper, and in the man overmuch heate doth soone bring the naturall warmth to the last degree, the which wanting nourishment, consumeth away: and therefore, because men in generation sooner waxe drye than women, it happeneth oftentimes that they are of a shorter life. Wherefore this perfection may also

---

[1] "The element": cf. "the heavens."
[2] Cf. "does not enter into . . ."
[3] "Wide from temper": cf. "far from temperate."

be given to women, that living longer than men they accomplish it, that is the entent of nature more than men.

Of the heate that the element poureth downe upon us. we talke not now, because it is diverse in signification to it which wee entreat upon: the which since it is nourisher of all thinges under the sphere of yᵉ moone, as well hote as colde, it can not be contrarie to colde.

But the fearefullnesse in women although it betokeneth an imperfection, yet doth it arise of a praise worthie cause, namely the subtilnesse and readinesse of the spirits,[1] that convey speedely the shapes [2] to the understanding, and therefore are they soone out of patience, for outwarde matters.[3]

Full well shall you see many times some men that dread neither death nor any thing els, yet are they not for all that to bee called hardie, because they know not the daunger, and goe forth like harebraines where they see the way open, and cast no more with themselves, and this proceedeth of a certaine grossenes of the dulled spirites.

Therefore a fond person can not be saide to be stoute harted, but verie courage in deede commeth of a proper advisement and determined will so to doe, and to esteeme more a mans honestie and duetie, than all the perils in the world, and although he see none other way but death, yet to be of so quiet an hart and minde that his senses be not to seeke [4] nor amazed, but doe their duetie in discoursing and bethinking,[5] even as though they were most in quiet.

Of this guise and manner we have seene, and heard say many great men to be, likewise many women, which both in old time and presently have shewed stoutnesse of courage, and brought matters to passe in the worlde worthie infinite prayse, no lesse than men have done.

Then said Phrisio: these matters began, when the first woman in offending, made others to offend also against God, and for inheritance left unto mankinde death, affections, sorrowes, and all other miseries and calamities, that be felt now a daies in the world.

The Lord Julian answered: Since you will also farther your purpose with entring into scripture, doe you not know that the same offence was in like manner amended by a woman? which hath profited much more than she hindred us, so that that

---

[1] Cf. "their wits."　　　　　　　　　　　[2] "Shapes": cf. "images."
[3] "Out of patience," etc.: cf. "disturbed by things external."
[4] "To seeke": cf. "clogged."
[5] "Discoursing," etc.: cf. "in speech and thought."

trespasse acquited with so worthie a deede, is counted most happie. But I purpose not now to tell you, how much in dignitie all humane creatures bee inferiour to the virgin our Lady, for meddling holy matters with these our fond reasonings: Nor rehearse how manie women with infinite stedfastnesse have suffered cruel death under Tyrants for the name of Christ: nor them that with learning in disputation have confuted so many Idolaters.

And in case you will answer mee, that this was a miracle and the grace of the holy Ghost, I say unto you that no vertue deserveth more prayse, than that which is approved by the testimony of God.

Many other also of whom there is no talke, you your selfe may looke upon, especially in reading Saint Hierom, which setteth out certaine of his time with such wonderful prayses, that they might suffice the holiest man that can be.

Imagin then how many there have beene of whom there is made no mention at all: because the sillie poore soules are kept close without the pompous pride, to seeke a name of holinesse among the people, that now a daies many men have, accursed Hipocrites, which not minding, or rather setting small store by the doctrine of Christ, that willeth a man when he fasteth, to annoint his face that he may appeare not to fast, and commandeth prayer, almes deedes, and other good works, to be done, not in the market place, nor Sinagogues, but in secrete, so that the left hand know not of the right: they affirme no treasure in the world to be greater, than to give a good example, and thus hanging their heade aside, and fastning their eyes upon the ground, spreading a report about, that they will not once speake to a woman, nor eate any thing but rawe hearbes, smoky,[1] with their side garments all to ragged and torne, they beguile the simple.

But for all that, they abstaine not from falsifying willes, sowing mortall hatred betweene man and wife, and otherwhile poison: using sorcerie, inchauntments, and all kinde of ribaldrie, and afterwarde alleage a certaine authoritie of their own head, that saith: *Si non castè, tamen cautè*, and with this weene to heale every great sore, and with good reason to perswade him that is not heedfull that God forgiveth soone all offences, how hainous soever they be, so they be kept close, and no evil example ariseth of them.

Thus with a veile of holinesse, and this mischievous devise,

---

[1] Cf. "dirty."

many times they turn all their thoughtes to defile the chaste mind of some woman, oftentimes to sow variance betweene brethren, to governe states, to set up the one and plucke down the other, to chop off heades, to imprison and banish men, to be the ministers of wickednesse, and (in a manner) the storers and hoorders up of the roberies that manie Princes commit.

Other past shame, delight to seeme delicate and smoth, with their crowne minionly[1] shaven, and well clad, and in their gate lift up their garment to shew their hose sit cleane, and the handsomnesse of person in making curtesie. Other use certaine bylookes ánd gestures even at masse, which they hold opinion become them well, and make men to behold them: mischievous and wicked men, and cleane voide not onely of all religion, but of all good manner. And when their naughtie life is laide to them, they make a jest at it, and give them a mocke that telleth them of it, and (as it were) count their vices as praise.

Then saide the Ladie Emilia. Such delight you have to speake ill of Friers, that are fallen into this talke without all purpose. But you commit a great offence to murmure against religious persons, and without any profit ye burden your conscience: for were it not for them, that they pray unto God for us, we shoulde yet have farre greater plagues than we have.

Then laughed the Lorde Julian, and saide: How gessed you so eaven (madam) that I speake of Friers, since I named them not? But forsooth this that I say, is not called murmuring, for I speake it plaine and openly. And I meane not the good, but the bad and wicked, of whom I have not yet spoken the thousandeth part of that I know.

Speake you not now of Friers, answered the Ladie Emilia: for I thinke it (for my part) a grievous offence to give eare to you, and for hearing you any more, I wil get me hence.

I am well pleased, quoth the Lord Julian, to speake no more of this. But to return to the prayses of women, I say that the Lord Gasper shal not finde me out any notable man, but I will finde his wife, or sister or daughter of like merite, and otherwhile above him. Beside that, many have beene occasion of infinite goodnesse to their men, and sometime broken them of many errours.

Therefore since women are (as wee have declared) naturally as apt for the selfe same vertues, as men be, and the proofe thereof hath beene often seene, I wote not why, in giving them that is possible they may have, and sundrie times have

[1] "Minionly": cf. "well."

had, and still have, I ought to [1] bee deemed to speake wonders, as the L. Gasper hath objected against me: Considering that there have ever beene in the world, and still are, women as nigh the woman of the Pallace, whom I have fashioned, as men nigh the man whome these Lordes have fashioned.

Then saide the Lord Gasper: those reasons that have experience against them (in my minde) are not good. And I wis, if I should happen to aske you what these great women are, or have beene, so worthie praise, as the great men whose wives, sisters, or daughters they have beene, or that have beene occasion of any goodnesse, or such as have broken them of their errors, I believe it woulde comber you shroudly.

Surely answered the Lord Juliā, none other thing could comber me, but the multitude of them. And if time served me, I would tell you to this purpose the Historie of Octavia wife to Marcus Antonius, and sister to Augustus: of Porcia daughter to Cato and wife to Brutus: of Caia Cecilia wife to Tarquinius Priscus: of Cornelia daughter to Scipio, and of infinite other, which are most known. And not onely these of our countrie, but also Barbarians, as that Alexandra, which was wife to Alexander king of the Jewes, who after the death of her husband, seeing the people in an uproare, and alreadie runne to weapon to slea the two children which he had left behinde him, for a revenge of the cruel and straight bondage that their father had alwaies kept them in, she so behaved her selfe, that sodainly she aswaged that just furie, and in a moment, with wisedom made those mindes favourable to the children, . which the father in many yeares with infinite injuries, had made their most enimies.

Tell us at the least, answered the Ladie Emilia, how she did. The Lorde Julian saide: she perceiving her children in so great a jeopardie, immediatly caused Alexanders bodie to be cast out into the middest of the market place, afterwarde calling unto her the Citizens, she saide, that she knew their mindes were set on fire with most furie against her husband: for the cruel injuries which he wickedly had done them, deserved it: and even as when he lived, she did her best alwaies to withdrawe him from so wicked a life, so now she was readie to make a tryall thereof, and to helpe them to chastice him even dead, as much as she might, and therefore shoulde take that bodie of his and give it to be devoured of dogs, and rent it in peeces in the cruellest manner they coulde imagine. But she desired them to take pittie

[1] Cf. "should."

upon the innocent children, that could not onely be in no fault, but not so much as weeting of their fathers ill doings.

Of such force were these words, that the raging fury once conceived in all that peoples mindes, was sodenly aswaged, and turned into so tender an affection, that not onely with one accord, they chose those children for their heades and rulers, but also to the deade corps they gave a most honourable buriall.

Here the Lord Julian made a litle pause, afterwarde hee proceeded. Know you not that Mithridates wife and sisters shewed a farre lesse feare of death, than Mithridates himselfe? And Asdruballes wife, than Asdrubal himselfe?

Know you not that Harmonia daughter to Hiero the Siracusan, woulde have died in the burning of her Countrie?

Then Phrisio, where obstinacie is bent,[1] no doubt (quoth he) but otherwhile ye shall find some women that will never chaunge purpose, as she that could no longer call her husband pricklouse,[2] with her handes made him a signe.[3]

The Lord Julian laughed and saide: Obstinacie that is bent to a vertuous ende, ought to bee called stedfastnesse, as in Epicaria a libertine of Rome, which made privie to a great conspiracie against Nero, was of such stedfastnesse, that being rent with all the most cruel torments that could be invēted, never uttered any of the partners: And in like perill many noble gentlemen and Senators, fearefully accused brethren, friendes, and the dearest and best beloved persons to them in the world.

What say you of this other, called Leona? In whose honour the Athenians dedicated before the Castle gate, a Lionesse of mettall without a tongue, to betoken in her the steadie vertue of silence. For she being in like sorte made privie to a conspiracie against Tirants, was not agast at the death of two great men her friendes, and for all she was torne with infinite and most cruel torments, never disclosed any of the conspiratours.

Then said the Ladie Margaret Gonzaga: Me seemeth that you make too briefe rehersall of these vertuous acts done by women. For although these our enimies have heard them and read them, yet they make wise not to know them, and woulde faine the memorie of them were lost. But in case ye will doe us to understand them, they will at the least be honourable to us.

Then answered the Lorde Julian: With a good will. Now will

---

[1] "Is bent": cf. "is concerned."
[2] "Call her husband," etc.: cf. "say 'scissors' to her husband."
[3] Cf. "the sign of them."

I tell you of one, that did such a deed, as I believe the Lorde Gasper himselfe will confesse that verie few men doe. And began.

In Massilia there was in times past an usage which is thought came out of Greece, and that was, that openly there was poyson laide up meddled with Cicuta, and it was lawfull for him to take it that alledged to the Senate that he ought to bee rid of his life for some discommoditie that hee felt therein, or els for some other just cause: to the entent that who so had suffered too much adversitie, or tasted over great prosperitie, hee might not continue in ye one, or change the other. In the presence therefore of Sextus Pompeius.

Here Phrisio not tarrying to have the Lord Julian proceede further, this mee seemeth (quoth he) is the beginning of some long tale.

Then the Lord Julian turning him to the Ladie Margaret said: See Phrisio will not suffer me to speake. I would have tolde you of a woman, that after she had shewed the Senate that she ought of right to dye, glad and without any feare, tooke in the presence of Sextus Pompeius the poyson with such stedfastnesse of minde, and with such wise and loving exhortations to hers, that Pompeius, and the rest that beheld in a woman such knowledge and steadinesse in the trēbling passage of death, remayned (not wythout teares) astonied wyth great wonder.

Then the L. Gaspar smiling, and I againe remember (quoth hee) that I have red an Oration, wherein an unfortunate husband asketh leave of the Senate to dye, and alledgeth that hee hath a just cause, for that he can not abide the continuall wearysomnesse of hys wifes chatting, and had lieffer drinke of that poyson which you say was laid up openly for these respectes, than of his wives scoldinges.

The L. Julian aunsweared: Howe many seely poore women shoulde have a juste cause to aske leave to dye, for abidinge, I will not say the ill wordes, but the most evill deedes of their husbandes? For I know some my selfe, that in this world suffer the paynes which are sayd to bee in hell.

Be there not againe, trow you, aunswered the L. Gaspar, many husbandes that are so tormented wyth their wives, that every houre they wish for death?

And what displeasure, quoth the L. Julian, can women do their husbands, that is so wythout remedye, as those are which husbands do their wives? whiche though not for love, yet for feare are obedient to their husbandes.

Sure it is indeede (quoth the L. Gaspar, that the little they doo well otherwhile, commeth of feare, for fewe there are in the worlde that secretely in their minde hate not their husbandes.

Nay, cleane contrarie, answered the Lorde Julian: and in case you will remember what you have reade, it is to be seene in all histories, that alwaies (in a manner) wives love their husbandes better than they their wives.

When have you ever seene or red that a husband hath shewed such a token of love towarde his wife, as did Camma towarde her husband?

I wot not, answered the Lord Gasper, what she was, nor what token she shewed. Nor I, quoth Phrisio.

The Lorde Julian answered: Give eare. And you (my Ladie Margaret) looke ye beare well away. This Camma was a most beautifull young woman, indowed with such modestie, and honest conditions, that no lesse for them, than for her beautie she was to be wondred at: and above other thinges, with all her hart she loved her husband, who had to name Synattus.

It happened that an other gentleman of greater authoritie than Synattus, and (in a manner) heade ruler and Tyrant of the Citie where they dwelled, fell in love with this young woman: and after hee had long attempted by all waies and meanes to compasse her, and all but lost labour, bethinking him selfe that the love she bore her husband, was the onely cause that withstood his desires, hee caused this Synattus to be slaine.

Thus instant upon her afterward continually, other fruite could he never get of her, than what hee had before. Wherefore this love dayly encreasing, hee was fully resolved to take her to wife, for all in degree she was much inferiour to him.

So sute being made to her friendes by Sinoris (for so was the lover named) they tooke in hand to perswade her to bee contented with it: Declaring that to agree thereto, was verie profitable, and to refuse it, perillous for her, and them all. She after she had a while gainesayed them, at length made answere that she was contented.

Her kinsfolke brought this tydinges to Synoris, which passing measure glad, gave order to have this marriage made out of hand.

After they were then both come for this purpose solemnly into the Temple of Diana, Camma had caused to be brought to her a certaine sweete drinke which she had made, and so before the image of Diana, in the presence of Sinoris she dranke the one moitie.[1] Afterwarde with her owne hand (for this was the

---

[1] "Moitie": cf. "half."

usage in mariages) she gave the remaine to the bridegroome, which dranke it cleane up.

Camma as soone as she saw her devise take effect, kneeled her downe very joyfull before the image of Diana, and saide.

Oh Goddesse, thou that knowest the bottom of my hart, bee a good witnesse to me, how hardly after my deare husband deceased, I have refrained from killing my selfe, and what paines I have sustained to endure the griefe to live in this bitter life, in which I have felt none other joy or pleasure, but the hope of the revenge, which I perceive now is come to effect.

Therefore with gladnes and contentation, I goe to finde out the sweete company of that soule, which in life and death I have alwaies more loved than mine owne selfe.

And thou caitife, that weenedst to have beene my husband, in stead of a marriage bed, give order to prepare thee a grave, for of thee doe I here make a sacrifice to the shadow of Synattus.

Synoris amazed at these wordes, and alreadie feeling the operation of the poyson within him, that put him to great paine, proved many remedies, but all prevailed not. And Camma had fortune so favourable on her side, or what ever els, that before she dyed, she had knowledge that Synoris was dead.

When she heard of that, with verie great contentation she laid her upon her bed, with her eyes to heaven, continually calling upon the name of Synattus and saying: O most sweete mate, since now I have bestowed for the last tokens upon thy death, both teares and revenge, and perceive not that I have any thing yet behind to doe for thee here, I flee the world, and this without thee a cruel life, which for thy sake onely in times past was deare to mee. Come therefore and meete me (oh my Lorde) and embrace as willingly this soule, as she willingly commeth to thee.

And speaking these words with her armes spread, as though she would at that instant have embraced him, dyed. Say now Phrisio, what thinke you by this? Phrisio answered.

Me thinke you woulde make these Ladies weepe. But let us set case this was true, I say unto you, that we finde no more such women in the world.

The Lord Julian said: yes, that there be, and that it is so, give eare. In my dayes there was in Pisa a gentleman whose name was maister Thomas, of what house, I remember not, for all I heard my father often times tell it, which was his great friend.

This maister Thomas then, passing upon a day in a litle vessell from Pisa towarde Sicilia about his affaires, was over-

takē with certaine foistes[1] of Moores, that were on the backe
of him unawares, and before the governours of the vessell had
espied them: and for all the men within, defended themselves
well, yet because they were but few, and the enimies many,
the vessel with as many as were on borde was taken by the
Moores, some hurt, some whole, as fell to their lot, and among
them maister Thomas, which had plaied the man and slaine
with his owne hand a brother of one of the Captains of those
foists.

For which matter the Captaine full of wrath, as you may
conjecture by the losse of his brother, woulde have him for his
prisoner, and beating and buffeting him dayly, brought him
into Barbary, where in great miserie hee determined to keepe
him alive his captive and with much drudgery.

All the rest, some one way, some another, within a space
were at libertie, and returned home, and brought tidinges to
his wife, called maistresse[2] Argentine, and children, of the hard
life and great afliction which maister Thomas lived in, and was
like without hope to live in continually, unlesse God wonderfully helped him. The which matter when she and they understood for a certaintie, attempting certaine other waies for his
deliverance, and where he himselfe was fully resolved to end his
life, there happened a carefull affection and tender pittie so to
quicken the witte and courage of a sone of his called Paule,
that he had respect to no kinde of daunger, and determined
either to dye, or to deliver his father. The which matter he
brought to passe, and with such privie conveyance, that hee[3]
was first in Ligurno before it was knowne in Barbary, that he
was parted thence.

Here hence maister Thomas (being arived in safety) writte
to his wife, and did her to weete his setting at libertie, and
where hee was, and how the next day he hoped to see her.

The honest gentlewoman filled with so great and sodaine joy,
that she should so shortly aswell through the zeale as prowesse
of her sonne, see her husband whom she loved so much, where
she once surely believed never to have seene him againe, after
she had read the letter, she lifted her eyes to heaven, and calling
upon the name of her husband, fell starke dead to the ground,
and with no remedie done to her, did the departed soule returne
to the bodie againe. A cruel sight, and inough to temper the
willes of men and to withdraw them from coveting too fervently
superfluous joyes.

[1] "Foistes": cf. "galleys."    [2] Cf. "Madonna."    [3] Cf. "the father.

Then saide Phrisio smiling: What know you whether she dyed for sorrow or no,[1] understanding her husband was comming home?

The Lord Julian answered: Because the rest of her life was nothing agreeable thereto.[2] But I weene rather the soule could not tarry the lingring to see him with the eyes of her body, and therefore forsooke it, and drawne out thence with coveting, fled by and by where in reading the letter, her thought was fled.

The Lorde Gasper saide: it may be that this woman was over loving, because women in every thing cleave alwaies to the extremitie, which is ill. And see for that she was over loving she did ill to her selfe, to her husband, and to her children, in whom she turned into bitternesse the pleasure of that dangerous and desired libertie of his. Therefore you ought not to alleage her for one of the women that have beene the cause of so great goodnesse. The Lorde Julian answered.

I alleage her for one of them that make tryall[3] that there are wives which love their husbands. For of such as have beene occasion of great profits in the worlde, I could tell you of an infinit number, and rehearse unto you so auncient, that wellnigh a man woulde judge them fables. And of such as among men, have beene the inventers of such kinde of matters, that they have deserved to be deemed Goddesses, as Pallas, Ceres, the Sybilles, by whose mouth God hath so often times spoken and discovered to the world matters to come.

And such as have taught verie great men, as Aspasia and Diotima, the which also with sacrifice drove of a plague tenne yeares that shoulde have fallen in Athens.

I could tell you of Nicostrata mother to Evander, which shewed the Latins their letters. And of another woman also that was maistresse[4] to Pindarus Liricus. And of Corinna and Sappho which were most excellent in Poetrie: but I will not seeke matters so far off.

I say unto you, that leaving the rest apart, of the greatnesse of Rome perhaps women were a no lesse cause than men.

This quoth the Lord Gasper, were good to understand. The Lord Julian answered: Hearken to it then. After Troy was wonne, many Trojans, that in so great a destruction escaped, fled some one way, some another: of which, one part, that by many Sea stormes were tossed and tumbled, came into Italy in the coast where the Tever entreth into the sea.

---

[1] Cf. "How do you know that she did not die of grief?"
[2] "Agreeable," etc.: cf. "did not comport with this."
[3] "Make tryall": cf. "bear witness."          [4] Cf. "preceptress."

So landing, to provide for their necessaries, began to goe a forraging about the Countrie. The women that tarried behinde in the ships, imagined among themselves a profitable devise, y⁺ shoulde make an end of their perillous and long sea-wandering, and in stead of their lost countrie recover them a new.

And after they had laide their heades together, in the mens absence, they set fire on the ships, and the first that began this worke was called Roma.

Yet standing in feare of the mens displeasure that were retyring backe againe, they went to meete with them, and embracing, and kissing in token of good will, some their husbandes, some their next a kin, they asswaged that first brunt[1]: Afterwarde they disclosed to them quietly the cause of their wittie enterprise.[2]

Wherefore the Trojans on the one side, for neede, and on the other for being courteously received of the inhabitants, were very wel pleased with that the women had done, and there dwelled with the Latins in the place where afterward was Rome. And of this arose the auncient custome among the Romans, that women meeting their kinsfolke, kissed them. Now ye see what a helpe these women were to give the beginning to Rome.

And the Sabine women were a no lesse helpe to the encrease of it, than were the Trojane to the first beginning: for when Romulus had purchased him the generall hatred of all his neighbours, for the ravin[3] that he made of their women, hee was assailed with warre on all sides, the which for that he was a valiant man, hee soone rid his handes of with victorie: onely the war with the Sabines excepted, which was verie sore, because Titus Tatius king of the Sabines was verie puisant and wise.

Whereupon after a sore bickering betweene the Romanes and Sabines, with verie great losse on both sides, preparing for a fresh and cruell battaile, the Sabine women clad in blacke, with their haire scattered and haled, weeping, comfortlesse, without feare of weapons now bent to give the onset, came into the middest betweene their fathers and husbands, beseeching them not to sile their hands with the bloud of their fathers in law, and sonnes in law, and in case it were so that they repined at this aliance, they should bend their weapons against them: for much better it were for them to dye, than to live widowes or fatherlesse, and brotherlesse, and to remember that their children

[1] "Brunt": cf. "impulse of anger."
[2] "Wittie enterprise": cf. "wise device."     [3] Cf. "seizure."

had beene begotten of such as had slaine their fathers, or they themselves of such as had slaine their husbands.

With these pitifull wailings many of them carried in their armes their young babes, of whom some began alreadie to lose their tongue, and seemed to call and sport with their grand-fathers, unto whom the women shewing forth their nephewes,[1] and weeping saide.

Behold your owne bloud that in such rage ye seeke to shed with your owne hands.

Of such force was in this case the affection and wisedom of the women, that there was not onely concluded betweene the two kinges enimies together, an indissoluble friendship and league, but also (which was a more wonderfull matter) the Sabins came to dwel in Rome, and of two peoples was made one, and so did this accorde much encrease the strength of Rome: thanked be the wise and couragious women which were so rewarded of Romulus, that parting the people into thirtie bandes,[2] gave them the names of the Sabine women.

Here the Lord Julian pausing a while, and perceiving that the Lord Gasper spake not, trow you not (quoth he) that these women were occasion of goodnesse to their men, and helped to the greatnesse of Rome.

The Lord Gasper answered: No doubt, they were worthie much praise. But in case you woulde as well tell the faultes of women, as their well doing, you woulde not have kept hid, that in this warre of Titus Tatius, a woman betrayed Rome, and taught the enimies the way to take the Capitolium, whereby the Romans were well nigh all undone.

The Lorde Julian answered: You mention me one ill woman, and I tell you of infinit good. And beside the afore named, I could apply to my purpose a thousand other examples of the profit done to Rome by women, and tell you why there was once a temple builded to Venus armata, and an other to Venus calva, and how the feast of handmaidens was instituted to Juno, because the handmaidens once delivered Rome from the guiles of the enimies.

But leaving all these thinges apart, that couragious acte for discovering the conspiracie of Catilina, for which Cicero is so praysed, had it not chiefly his beginning of a common woman, which for this may be saide to have beene the occasion of all the good that Cicero boasteth hee did the common weale of Rome?

---

[1] "Their nephewes": cf. "the little ones."     [2] "Bandes": cf. "wards."

And in case I had sufficient time, I woulde (may hap) shew you also, that women have oftentimes corrected men of many vices: but (I feare me) my talke hath alreadie beene overlong and combrous. Therefore since I have according to my power fulfilled the charge that these Ladies have given me, I meane to give place to him that shall speake more worthier matters to bee heard, than I can.

Then the Ladie Emilia, Doe you not deprive (quoth she) women of the true praises due unto them? And remember though the Lorde Gasper and perchaunce the Lord Octavian too, heare you with noysomnesse, yet do we, and these other Lords harken to you with pleasure.

Notwithstanding the L. Julian would there have ended, but all the Ladies began to entreat him to speake.

Wherefore he said laughing: Least I should provoke my Lord Gasper to bee mine enimie any more than he is, I will but briefly tell you of a certaine that come into my minde, leaving many that I could recite unto you. Afterwarde he proceeded.

When Philip, Demetrius sonne, was about the Citie of Scio, and had laide siege to it, he caused to be proclamed, that what ever bondmen would forsake the Citie and fle to him, he promised them libertie and their maisters wives.

The spite of women for this so shamefull a proclamation was such, that they came to the walles with weapon, and fought so fiercely, that in a small time they drove Philip awaye with shame and losse, which the men could not doe.

These selfe same women being with their husbands, Fathers and brethren that went into banishment, after they came into Leuconia, did an act no lesse glorious, than this was. For the Erythrians that were there with their federates, made warre against these Sciotes, which not able to hold out, came to accord, with composition to depart onely in their doublet and shirt out of the Citie.

The women hearing of this so shamefull a composition, were much offended, reviling them, that leaving their weapons, they woulde issue out like naked men among their enimies. And when they made answere that it was alreadie so condicioned, they willed them to carrie their shield and speare, and leave their clothes, and answere their enimies that this was their aray.

And in so doing, by their womens counsell, they covered a great part of the shame, which they could not cleane avoide.

Likewise when Cirus had discomfited in a battaile the armie of the Persians, as they ranne away, in their fleeing they met with their women without their gates, who comming to them, said: whither flee ye you cowards? Entend ye perhaps to hide you in us, from whence ye came? These and such like words the men hearing, and perceiving how much in courage they were inferiour to their women, were ashamed of them selves, and returning backe againe to their enimies fought with them a fresh, and gave them the overthrow.

When the Lorde Julian had hetherto spoken, he stayed, and turning him to the Dutchesse, saide: Now (madame) you will licence me to hold my peace.

The Lord Gasper answered: it is time to holde your peace, when you know not what to saye more. The Lorde Julian saide smyling: You provoke mee so, that ye may chance bee occupied all night in hearing the prayses of women. And ye shall understand of many Spartane womē that much rejoyced at the glorious death of their children: and of them that forsooke them, or slew them with their owne hands when they heard they used dastardlinesse.

Againe, how the Saguntine women in the destruction of their Countrie, tooke weapō in hand against Hanniballes souldiers. And how the armie of the Dutchmen vanquished by Marius, their women not obtaining their sute to live free in Rome in service with the virgins Vestalles, killed them selves everie one with their young children. And a thousand moe that all auncient Histories are full of.

Then saide the Lord Gasper: tush (my Lord Julian) God wotteth how these matters passed, for these times are so farre from us, that many lyes may be tolde, and none there is that can reprove them.

The Lord Julian said: In case you will measure in everie time the worthinesse of women with mens, ye shall finde that they have never beene, nor yet presently are any whit inferior to men.

For leaving apart those so auncient, if ye come to the time when the Gothes raigned in Italy, ye shall finde that there was a Queene among them Amalasunta, that ruled a long while with marvellous wisedom. Afterward Theodelinda queene of the Longobardes, of singular vertue, Theodora empresse of Greece. And in Italy among many other was a most singular Ladie the Countesse Matilda, whose prayses I leave to be told of Count Lewis, because she was of his house.

Nay quoth the Count, it is your part, for you know it is not meete that a man should praise his owne.

The Lord Julian continued on. And how many famous in times past find you of this most noble house of Montefeltro? How many of the house of Gonzaga, of Este and Pii? In case wee will then speake of the time present, we shall not neede to seeke examples far fet, for we have them in the house.

But I will not serve my purpose with them, whom wee see in presence, lest yee should seeme for courtesie to, graunt me it, that in no wise ye can deny me. And to goe out of Italy, remember ye, in our dayes we have seene Anne French Queene, a verie great Ladie, no lesse in vertue than in state: and if in justice and mildnesse, liberalitie and holinesse of life, ye lust to compare her to the kinges Charles and Lewis (which had been wife to both of them) you shall not find her a jotte inferiour to them.

Behold the Ladie Margaret, daughter to the Emperor Maximilian, which with great wisedom and justice hetherto hath ruled, and still doth her state.

But omitting all other, tell me (my Lorde Gasper) what king or what prince hath there beene in our daies, or yet many yeares before in Christendom, that deserveth to be compared to Queene Isabel of Spaine.

The Lord Gasper answered king Ferdinande her husband. The Lorde Julian said: This will I not deny. For since the Queene thought him a worthie husband for her, and loved and observed him so much, it can not bee said nay, but he deserved to be compared to her. And I thinke well the reputation he got by her, was a no lesse dowrie than the kingdom of Castilia.

Nay, answered the Lorde Gasper, I believe rather of many of king Ferdinandes actes Queene Isabell bore the prayse.

Then saide the Lorde Julian: In case the people of Spaine, the nobles, private persons, both men and women, poore and rich, be not all agreed together to lye in her prayse, there hath not beene in our time in the worlde a more cleare example of true goodnesse, stoutnesse of courage, wisedom, religion, honestie, courtesie, liberalitie: to be briefe, of al vertue, than Queene Isabel. And where the renowne of that Ladie in every place, and in all nations is very great, they that lived with her, and were present at all her doings doe all affirme this renowne to bee sprong of her vertue and deserts.

And who so will waigh her actes, shall soone perceive the truth to be so. For leaving apart infinite thinges that make tryall of this, and might be tolde, if it were our purpose, every man knoweth that in the first beginning of her raigne, she found ye greatest part of Castilia possessed by great estates [1]: yet recovered she the whole again, so justly and in such sort, that they dispossessed themselves, continued in a great good affection, and were willing to make surrender of that they had in possession.

It is also a most knowne thing with what courage and wisedome she alwaies defended her realmes from most puissant enimies. And likewise to her alone may be given the honour of the glorious conquest of the kingdom of Granado, which in so long and sharpe a warre against stubborne enimies, that fought for their livelode, for their life, for their law, and to their weening in Gods quarrell, declared evermore with counsell and with her owne person so much vertue and prowesse, as perhaps in our time few princes have had ye stomacke, not only to follow her steps, but to envy her.[2]

Beside this, all that knew her, report that there was in her such a divine manner of government, that a man would have weened that her will only was almost inough to make everie man without any more businesse,[3] to doe that he ought: so that scarse durst a man in his owne home and in secrete commit any thing that hee suspected would displease her. And of this a great part, was cause the wonderfull judgement which she had in knowing and choosing ministers meete for the offices she entended to place them in.

And so well coulde she joine the rigour of justice with the mildenesse of mercie and liberallitie, that there was no good person in her dayes that could complaine he had beene smally rewarded, ne any ill, too sore punished.

Wherefore among her people towarde her, there sprang a verie great reverence derived of love and feare, which in all mens mindes remaineth still so setled, that a man woulde thinke they looked that she shoulde beholde them from heaven, and there above either prayse or dispraise them.

And therefore with her name, and with the waies which she ordained, those realmes are still ruled, in wise that albeit her life wanteth, yet her authoritie liveth, like a wheele long swinged about with violence,[4] keeping the same course a good while after of it selfe, though no man move it any more.

Consider you beside this (my Lorde Gasper) that in our time

---

[1] "Great estates": cf. "the grandees."
[2] "Not only," etc.: cf. "I will not say to imitate, but even to envy her."
[3] "Without . . . businesse": cf. "quietly."
[4] Cf. "like a wheel which, long revolved with force . . . "

al y^e men of Spaine renowmed in what ever thing, have beene made so by Queene Isabel.

And the great Captaine Consalve Ferdinando was more set by for it, than for all his famous victories, and excellent and couragious actes, that in peace and war have made him so notable and famous.

That in case fame bee not unkinde, she will for ever spread abroad to the worlde his immortall prayses, and make proofe that in our age we have had few kinges or great Princes, that by him have not beene surmounted in noble courage, knowledge, and all vertue.

To returne therefore to Italy, I say unto you that we have not wanted here most excellent Ladies. For in Naples wee have two Queenes, and not long agoe in Naples likewise dyed the other Queene of Hungarie, as excellent a Ladie as you know any, and to bee compared well inough to the mightie and glorious king Mathew Covin her husband.

Likewise the Dutchesse Isabel of Aragon most worthie sister to king Ferdinande of Naples which as gold in the fire, so in the stormes of fortune hath she shewed her vertue and prowesse.

If you will come into Lumbardie, you shall marke the Ladie Isabel marquesse of Mantua, whose most excellent vertues shoulde receive great wrong in speaking of them so temperately, as who so will speake of them in this place, must be driven to doe.

I am sory morever that you all knew not the Dutchesse Beatrice of Millane her sister, that you might never againe wonder at a womans wit.

And the Dutchesse Elionor of Aragon, Dutchesse of Ferrara, and mother to both these Ladies whom I have named, was such a one, that her most excellent vertues gave a good tryall to all the world, that she was not onely a worthy daughter to a king, but also deserved to be a Queene over a far greater state than all her auncestors possessed.

And to tell you of an other: How many men know you in the world, woulde abide the bitter strokes of fortune so patiently, as Queene Isabel of Naples hath done? Which for all the losse of her kingdome, banishment and death of king Fredericke her husband, and two sonnes, and imprisonment of the Duke of Calabria her eldest, yet still sheweth her selfe a Queene: and so beareth out the miserable inconveniences of wretched poverty, that every man may see, though she hath chaunged fortune, yet hath she not altered condition.

I omit the naming unto you of infinit other great Ladies, and also women of low degree, as many Pisanes that in defence of their countrie against the Florentines, have declared that noble courage without any feare of death, that the most invincible courages could doe that ever were in the world: Wherefore certaine of them have beene renowmed by many noble Poets.

I could tell you of certain most excellent in letters, in musicke, in painting, in carving, but I will not anie more goe searching out among these examples, which are most knowne to you all.

It sufficeth, that if in your minds you thinke upon women whom you your selves know, it shal be no hard matter for you to understand, that they are not most commonly in prowesse or worthinesse inferiour to their fathers, brethren, and husbands: and that many have beene occasion of goodnesse to men, and many times brokē them of many of their vices. And where presently there are not found in the world those great Queenes that goe to conquere farre Countries, and make great buildinges, Piramides and Cities, as Thomiris Queene of Scithia, Artemisia, Zenobia, Semiramis or Cleopatra, no more are there also men like unto Cæsar, Alexander, Scipio, and the other noble Romane Captaines.

Say not so, answered then Phrisio laughing, for presently there are more found like Cleopatra or Semiramis, than ever there were. And though they have not so manye states, powers and riches, yet there wanteth not in them good will to counterfeite them at the least in giving themselves to pleasure, and satisfying all their lusts as much as they may.

The Lorde Julian saide: You will ever Phrisio passe your boundes. But in case there be found some Cleopatres, there want not for them infinite Sardanapalles, which is much worse.

Make not this comparison quoth the Lorde Gasper then, and believe not that men are so incontinent as women be: and where they were so, yet shoulde it not be worse. For of the incontinencie of women arise infinite inconveniences, that doe not of mens. And therefore (as it was well saide yesterday) they have wisely ordained that it may bee lawfull for them to be out of the way without blame in all other thinges, that they may apply their force to keepe themselves in this one vertue of chastitie, without the which children were uncertain, and the bond that knitteth all the worlde together by bloud, and by the love that naturally each man hath to that is borne him, shoulde be loosed.

Therefore a wanton life in women is lesse to be borne withall

than in men, that carrie not their children nine monthes in
their bodie.

Then answered the Lorde Julian: Doubtlesse these be pretie
arguments that yee make, I marvel you put them not in writing
But tell me, for what cause is it ordained that a wanton life
should not be so shamefull a matter in men, as in women?
Considering if they bee by nature more vertuous and of greater
prowesse, they may also the easier keepe them selves in this
vertue of continencie, and children shoulde be no more nor lesse
certaine: for if women were given to wanton living, so men were
continent, and consented not to the wantonnesse of women,
they among themselves and without any other helpe could
not beare children.

But if you will tell the truth, you your selfe know, that wee
have of our owne authoritie claimed a libertie, whereby wee
will have the selfe same offences in us very light, and otherwhile
worthie prayse, and in women not sufficiently to bee punished,
but with a shamefull death, or at the least everlasting slaunder.

Therefore since this opinion hath taken roote, me thinketh
it a meete matter to punish them in like manner sharpely, that
with lies bring up a slaunder upon women. And I believe that
every worthie gentleman is bound to defend alwaies with weapon,
where neede requireth, the truth, and especiallye when he
knoweth any woman falsely reported of to be of litle honestie.

And I, answered the Lord Gasper smiling, doe not onely
affirme to bee every worthie gentlemans duetie, that you say,
but also take it for great courtesie and honestie to cover some
offence, that by mishap or overmuch love a woman is runne
into. And thus you may see that I am more on womens side,
where reason beareth me out, than you be.

I deny not that men have taken a litle libertie, and that
because they know by the common opinion, that to them wanton
living is not so slanderous as to women, which through the
weakenesse of their kinde, are much more enclined to appetites,
than men: and in case they abstaine otherwhile from satisfying
their lusts, they doe it for shame, not that will is not most readie
in them.

And therefore have men laide upon them feare of slaunder
for a bridle, to keepe them (in a manner) whether they will or
no in this vertue, without the which (to say the truth) they were
litle to be set by: for the worlde hath no profit by women, but
for getting of children.

But the like is not of men, which governe Cities, armies, and doe so many other waightie matters, the which (since you will so have it) I will not dispute how women could doe, it sufficeth they doe it not. And when it was meet for men to make tryall of their continencie, as well how they passed women in this vertue as in the rest, although you graunt it not. And about this, will not I rehearse unto you so many Histories or fables, as you have done, I remit you to the continencie onely of two most mightie personages, youthful and upon their victory,[1] which is wont to make hautie men of lowest degree.[2]

And the one is, the great Alexander toward the most beautifull women of Darius his enimie and discomfited. The other, Scipio, unto whom being twentie and foure yeares of age, and having wonne by force a Citie in Spaine, there was brought a most beautifull and noble Damsel taken among many other. And when Scipio understood that she was affianced to a Lorde of the Countrie, he did not onely abstaine from al dishonest acte toward her, but undefiled restored her to her husband, and a large gift withall.

I could tell you of Xenocrates, which was so continent, that a most beautifull woman lying naked by his side and dallying with him, and using all the waies she could (in which matters she was very well practised) she had never the power to make him once shew the least signe of wantonnesse, for all she bestowed a whole night about it.

And of Pericles that did no more but heare one praise with overmuch earnestnesse the well favourednesse of a boye, and he tooke him up sharpely for it. And of many other most continent of their owne free will, and not for shame or feare of punishment, that compelleth the greatest part of women to keepe themselves upright in this vertue, which notwithstanding deserve much praise withall: and who so falsely bringeth up of them a slaunderous report of uncleannesse of living, is worthie (as you have saide) very sore punishment.

Then spake the Lord Cæsar which had held his peace a good while: judge you in what sort the Lorde Gaspar speaketh in the dispraise of women, when these are the matters that hee speaketh in their prayse.

But if the Lorde Julian will give mee leave, that I may in his stead answere him certaine few matters, as touching where (in mine opinion) he hath falsely spoken against women, it shall

---

[1] "I remit you," etc.: cf. "I refer you to the continence . . ., and to their victory."

[2] Cf. "makes even men of lowest rank insolent."

be good for him and mee both. For he shall rest him a while, and shall afterwarde the better goe forwarde to speake of some other perfection of the gentlewoman of the pallace, and I shall have a good turne that I have occasion to execute jointly with him this duety of a good knight, which is to defend the truth.

Mary I beseech ye, answered the Lord Julian: for me thinke I have alreadie fulfilled according to my power, that I ought, and this communication now is out of the purpose that I went about.

The Lorde Cesar then began: I will not now speake of the profit that the worlde hath by women beside the bearing of children: for it is well inough declared how necessarie they be, not onely to our being, but also to our well being. But I say (my Lorde Gasper) that in case they be as you affirme, more enclined to appetites, than men, and notwithstanding abstaine more than men (which you your selfe grant) they are so much the more worthie praise, as their kind is lesse able to withstand naturall appetites.

And if you saye they doe it for shame, I can not see but for one vertue you give them two. For in case shame can doe more in them than appetite, and through it refraine from ill doing, I esteeme this shame (which in conclusion is nothing els but feare of slaunder) a most seldome vertue and raigning in verie fewe men. And if I coulde without infinite reproch to men, tell how many of them bee drowned in unshamefastnes, and impudencie (which is the vice contrarie to this vertue) I should infect these devoute eares that heare me. And for most part these kinde of injurious persons both to God and nature, are men well striken in yeares, which professe some priesthood, some Philosophie, some divinitie, and rule common weales with such Catoes gravitie in countenance, that it maketh an outwarde shew of all the honestie in the world, and alwaies alleage womenkinde to be most incontinent, where they at no time finde themselves more agreeved, than at the want of their naturall lustinesse, that they may satisfie their abhominable desires, which still abide in the minde after nature hath taken them from their bodie, and therefore manye tymes finde out waies, where force prevaileth not.[1]

But I will not tell farther. It sufficeth for my purpose ye graunt that women abstaine more from uncleane living, than men. And sure it is, that they are not kept short with any other bridle, than what they put upon themselves. And that it is

[1] Cf. "is not necessary."

true, the most part of them that be kept under with over straight looking to, or beaten of their husbands or fathers, are lesse chaste, than they that have some libertie.

But generally a great bridle to women, is the zeale of true vertue, and the desire of good name, which many that I have knowne in my dayes more esteeme, than their owne life. And in case you will tell the truth, every one of us have seene most noble yong men, discreete, wise, of prowesse, and well favoured spend many yeares in loving, sparing for nothing that might entice, tokens, sutes, teares [1]: to bee short whatsoever may bee imagined, and all but lost labour.

And if it might not bee tolde me that my conditions never deserved I shoulde be beloved, I woulde alleage my selfe for a witnesse, which more than once through the unchaungeablenes and over stedfast honestie of a woman, was nighe deathes doore.

The Lord Gasper answered: marvell you not thereat, for women that are sued to, alwaies refuse to fulfil his request, that sueth to them, but those that are not sued to, sue to others.

The Lord Cæsar saide: I never knew them that have beene sued to by women, but many there bee that perceiving they have attempted in vaine, and spent their time fondly, runne to this noble revenge, and say that they had plentie of y'e thing which they did but cast in their minde. And to their weening, to report ill, and to studie for inventions how to bring up slaunderous tales of some worthie gentlewoman, is a kinde of Courtiers trade.[2]

But these kinde of persons that knavishly make their vaunt of any woman of price, be it true or false, deserve very sore correction and punishment. And if it be otherwhile bestowed upon them it can not be saide, how much they are to be commended that doe this office.

For in case they tell lyes, what mischiefe can be greater than to take from a worthie woman with guile the thing which she more esteemeth than her life? And no other cause but that [3] ought to make her renowmed with infinite prayses. If againe it bee true they say, what paine can suffise so traiterous a person, that rendreth such ingratitude in recompence to a gentlewoman, which wonne with his false flatterings, fained teares, continuall sutes, bewailings, crafts, deceites, and perjuries, hath suffered her selfe to be led to love overmuch, afterwarde without respect,[4]

---

[1] "Sparing," etc.: cf. "without omitting augh of care, of gifts, of prayers, of tears."

[2] Cf. "of courtiership."     [3] "But that": cf. "than that which."

[4] "Respect": cf. "reserve."

hath given her selfe unheedfully for a pray to so wicked a spirite?

But to answere you beside[1] this wonderfull continencie of Alexander and Scipio which you have alleaged, I say, that I will not deny, but each of them did a deede worthie much praise. Notwithstanding least yee should say, that in rehearsing to you auncient matters, I tolde you fables, I will alleage a woman of our time of base degree, who notwithstanding shewed a far greater continencie than any of these two great estates.

I say unto you therefore, that I knew once a well favored and tender yong woman, whose name I tell you not, for giving matter to many lewd persons to reporte ill, which as soone as they understand a woman to be in love, make an ill descanting upon it.

She therefore beloved of a worthie and faire condicioned yong gentleman, was bent with heart and minde to love him. And of this not I alone, unto whom of her own accord she uttered trustfully the whole matter, no otherwise than if I had beene, I will not say a brother, but an inwarde sister of hers[2]: but all that beheld her in company of the beloved yong man, were well weeting of her passion.

She thus fervently loving, as a most loving mind could love, continued two yeares in such continencie, that she never made any token to this yong man of the love that she bore him, but such as she coulde not hide from him. At no time she would speake with him, nor receive any letters from him, or tokens, where there never passed day but she was tempted with both the one and the other.

And how she longed for it, that wot I well, for if otherwhile she coulde privily get any thing that had beene the yong mans, she was so tender over it, that a man would have thought that of it had sprong her life and all her joy. Yet would she never in so long a time content him with other, than to behold him, and be seene of him againe, and sometime happening to bee at open feastes, daunce with him as she did with others.

And because there was no great difference in their degree, she and the yong man coveted that so great a love might have a luckie ende, and be man and wife together.

All the men and women in the Citie desired the same, saving her cruel father, which of a weywarde and straunge opinion, minded to bestow her upon another more welthie. And this

[1] Cf. "further, touching that."      [2] Cf. "her dearest sister."

was not by the unluckie maiden otherwise gainestood, than with most bitter teares.

And after this unfortunate marriage was concluded with great compassion of the people there, and despairing of the poore lovers, yet did not this stroke of Fortune serve to root uppe so grounded a love in the heart of each other, but lasted afterwarde the terme of three yeares, albeit she full wisely dissembled it, and sought every way to cut in sunder those desires, which now were past hope. And in this while she followed on still in her set purpose of continencie, and perceiving she could not honestly have him, whom she worshipped in the world, she chose not to have him at all,[1] and continued in her wont not to accept messages, tokens nor yet his lookes.

And in this resolved determination the seely soule vanquished with most cruell affliction, and waxed through long passion very fainte, at the three yeares ende, died. Rather would she forgo her contentations and pleasures so much longed for, finally her life, than her honestie.

And yet wantede she no meanes nor waies to fulfill her desire most secretly, and without perill either of slander or any other losse. And for all that, refrained she from the thing of her selfe that she so much coveted, and for the which she was so côtinually attempted by the person whom alone in the worlde her desire was to please. And to this was she not driven for feare or any other respect, but onely for the zeale of true vertue.

What will you say of an other that for sixe monthes almost nightly laye with a most deare lover of his,[2] yet in a garden full of most savorie fruites, tempted with her owne most fervent longing and with the petitions and teares of him that was more deare to her than her owne selfe, refrained from tasting of them. And for all she was wrapped and tyed in the straight chaine of those beloved armes, yet never yeelded she her selfe as vanquished, but preserved undefiled the floure of her honestie.

Trow ye not (my Lorde Gasper) that these bee deedes of continencie alike to Alexanders? Which most fervently inamored, not with the women of Darius, but with this renowne and greatnesse, that pricked him forwarde with the spurres of glory to abide paines and daungers to make himselfe immortall, set at nought not onely other thinges, but his owne life, to get a name above all men? And doe we marvel with such thoughts in his hart that he refrained from a thing which he coveted not

---

[1] "To have him at all": cf. "to wish for him in any wise."
[2] "His": cf. "hers."

greatly? for since he never saw those women before, it is not possible that he should be in love with them at a blush, but rather perhaps abhorred them for Darius, his enimies sake.

And in this case everie wanton acte of his towarde them, had beene an injurie [1] and not love. And therefore no greater matter if Alexander which no lesse with noblenes of courage than martiall prowesse subdued the world, abstained from doing injurie to women.

The continencie in like case of Scipio is doubtlesse much to bee commended, yet if ye consider well, not to be compared to these two womens: for he in like manner also refrained from a thing that he coveted not, being in his enimies countrie, a fresh Captaine, in the beginning of a most waightie enterprise, leaving behinde him in his countrie, such expectation of himself, and having beside to give account to rigorous judges, that oftentimes chastised not onely the great but the least offences of all, and among them hee wist well hee had enimies, knowing also if he had otherwise done, because she was a noble damsell and espoused to a noble man, hee shoulde have purchased him so many enimies and in such sorte, that many woulde have driven off, and perchance have set him cleane besides his victorie.

Thus for so many respects and so waightie, hee abstained from a light and hurtfull appetite, in shewing continencie and freeharted well meaning, the which (as it is written) got him all the hartes of that people: and stood him in stead of another army with favor to vanquish mens harts, which perhaps by force of armes had beene invincible. So that this may rather be termed a warlike pollicie, than pure continencie: albeit beside, the report of this matter is not all of the purest: for some writers of authoritie affirme, that this Damsell was enjoyed of Scipio in the pleasures of love: and of this I tell you, yee may depose upon.

Phrisio saide: Perhaps ye have found it in the Gospell. I have seene it my selfe, answered the Lord Cesar, and therefore I have a much more certaintie of this, than you or any man els can have.

That Alcibiades arose no otherwise from Socrates bed than children doe from their fathers beds: for to say the truth, a straunge place and time was bed and night to view with fixed minde the pure beautie which is saide Socrates loved without any unhonest desire, especially loving better the beautie of the minde, than of the bodie: but in boyes, not in old men, for all they were wiser.

[1] Cf. "outrage."

And in good sooth a better example could not have beene picked out to praise the continencie of men, than this is of Xenocrates, which occupied in his studie, fastned and bounde by his profession, which is Philosophie, that consisteth in good manners and not in words, old, cleane spent of his naturall lustinesse, nothing able, no not in making proffer to bee able, refrained from a common haunted woman, which for the names sake might abhorre him.

I would sooner have believed he had beene continēt, if he had declared any token to have beene come to his right senses againe, and in that case have used continencie: or els abstained from the thing which olde men covete more than the battailes of Venus, namely from wine.

But to establish wel continencie in old age, it is written, that hee was full and laden with it. And what can be saide to bee more wider from the continencie of an olde man, than dronkennesse? And in case the shunning of Venus matters in that slow and cold age deserveth so much praise, how much shoulde it deserve in a tender maiden, as those two I have told you of? Of which the one most straightly bridling all her senses, not onely denyed her eyes their light, but also tooke from the hart those thoughts, which alone had beene a most sweete foode a long time to keepe her in life.

The other fervently in love, being so oftentimes alone in the armes of him whom she loved more a great deale than all the world beside, fighting against her own selfe and against hi.1 that was more deare to her than her owne selfe, overcame that fervent desire that many times hath and doth overcome so many wise men.

Trow ye not now (my Lorde Gasper) that writers may bee ashamed to make mentiō of Xenocrates in this case, and to reckon him for chaste? where if a man could come by the knowledge of it, I would lay a wager that he slept all that night untill the next day dinner time, like a dead bodie buried in wine: and for all the stirring that woman made, could not once open his eyes, as though he had beene cast into a deade sleepe.

Lord Gasper (quoth she [1]) if you will bethinke your selfe a litle better, I believe you shall finde out some other pretie example of continencie alike unto this.

The Lorde Cesar answered: Is not this other, think ye (Madam) a good example of continencie which he hath alleaged of Pericles? I muse much that hee hath not as well called to

[1] i.e. the Lady Emilia.

rehearsall the continencie and pretie saying that is written of him, that a woman asked too great a summe for one night, and he answered her, that he mineded not to buye repentance so deare.

They ceased not laughing and the Lord Cesar after he had stayed a while, my Lord Gaspar (quoth he) pardon me, if I tell truth. For in conclusion these be the wonderful continencies that men write of themselves, accusing women for incontinent, in whome are dayly seene infinite tokens of continencie.

And certes if ye ponder it aright, there is no fortresse so impregnable, nor so well fensed that being assaulted with the thousandeth part of the ingins and guiles that are practised to conquere the steadie minde of a woman, would not yeelde up at the first assault.

How many trained up by great estates and enriched through them and advanced to great promotion, having in their hands their fortresses, holdes, and castles, whereupon depended their whole state, their life, and all their goods, without shame or care to be named Traitors, have disloyally given them to whom they ought not?

And would God in our dayes there were such scarcitie of these kinde of persons, that we might not have much more adoe to finde out some one that in this case hath done that hee ought, than to name such as have failed therein.

See you not so many other that dayly wander about to kill men in thickets, and roving by sea, onely to robbe mens money? How many Prelates make marchandise with the goodes of the Church of God? How many Lawiers falsify testaments? What perjuries make they? how many false evidences, onely to get money? How many Phisitions poyson the diseased, onely for it? How many againe for feare of death doe most vile matters? And yet all these so stiffe and hard battailes doth a tender and delicate yong woman gainestand many times: for sundrie there have beene, that have chosen rather to dye than to lose their honestie.

Then saide the Lord Gasper: These (my Lord Cesar) be not I believe, in ye world nowadaies.

The Lord Cesar answered: And I will not alleage unto you them of olde time. But this I say, that many might be found out, and are dayly, that in this case passe not for death.[1] And now it commeth into my minde that when Capua was sacked by the Frenchmen (which is not yet so long since but you may full well beare it in mind) a well favored young gentle-

---

[1] "Passe not, etc.": cf. "do not fear to die."

woman of Capua, being lead out of her house where she had been taken by a company of Gascoignes, when she came to the river that runneth by Capua, she fained to plucke on her shoe, in so much that her leader let her goe a litle, and she straight way threw her selfe into the river.

What will you say of a poore countrie wench, that not many monthes agoe at Gazuolo beside Mantua, gone into the field a leazing [1] with a sister of hers, sore a thirst entred into a house to drink water, where the good man of the house, that was yong, seeing her meetely well favoured and alone, taking her in his armes, first with faire words, afterward with threatninges attempted to frame her to doe his pleasure, and where she strived stil more obstinatly, at length with many blowes and by force overcame her.

She thus tossed and sobbing, returned into the fielde to her sister: and for all the instance that she made upon her, would never disclose to her what outrage she received in that house, but still drawing homewarde, and shewing her selfe appeased by litle and litle, and to speak without disturbance, she gave her certaine instructions. Afterwarde when she came to the Olio, which is the river that runneth by Gazuolo, keeping her somewhat aloofe from her sister, that knew not, nor imagined that she minded to doe, sodainly cast her selfe into it.

Her sister sorrowfull and weeping, followed downe by the rivers side as fast as she coulde, which carried her a good pace away, and everie time the poore soule appeared above water, her sister threw into her a corde that she had brought with her to bind the corne withall. And for all the corde came to her handes more than once (for she was yet nigh inough the banke) the stedfast and resolved girle alwaies refused it, and pushed it from her. And thus shunning all succour that might save her life, in a short space died. She was neither stirred by noblenesse of bloude, nor by feare of death or slander, but only by the griefe of her lost maidenheade.

Now by this you may gather, how many other women doe deedes most worthie memorie, since (as a man may say) three dayes agoe this hath made such a triall of her vertue, and is not spoken of, ne yet her name knowne.

But had not the death folowed at that time of the bishop of Mantua uncle to our Dutchesse, the banke of the Olio in the place where she cast her selfe in, had now beene garnished with a verie faire sepulture, for a memorie of so glorious a soule,

[1] Cf. "to reap corn."

that deserved so much the more cleare renowne after death, as in life it dwelled in an unnoble body.

Here the Lord Cesar tooke respit a while, afterward hee set forwarde: In my dayes also in Rome there happened a like chaunce, and it was, that a well favoured and well borne yong gentlewoman of Rome, being long followed after of one that shewed to love her greatly, would never please him with any thing, no not so much as a look. So that this fellow by force of money corrupted a waiting woman of hers, who desirous to please him to finger more money, was in hande with her mistresse upon a day, no great holy day, to go visite Saint Sebastianes Church.

And giving the lover intelligence of the whole, and instructing him what he had to doe, lead the yong gentlewoman into one of the dark caves under grounde, that who so goe to Saint Sebastianes are wont to visite. And in it was the yong man first closely hid, which perceiving himselfe alone with her whom hee loved so much, beganne every way to exhort her with as faire language as he coulde, to have compassion upon him, and to chaunge her former rigor into love. But when he saw all his prayers could take none effect, he turned him to threatnings.

And when they prevailed not, he all to beat her.[1] In the ende hee was full and wholy bent to have his purpose, if not otherwise, by force, and therein used the helpe of the naughtie woman that had brought her thither. Yet could he never doe so much as make her graunt to him, but in words and deedes (although her force was but small) alwaies the seely yong woman defended her selfe in what she could possible. So that what for the spite hee conceived when he saw hee coulde not get his will, and what for feare least the matter shoulde come to her kinsfolkes eare, and make him punished for it, this mischievous person with the aide of the woman that doubted[2] ye same, strangled the unluckie yong woman, and there left her, and running his way provided for him selfe for being found out againe.

The waiting woman blinded with her owne offence, wist not to flee, and being taken upon certaine suspitions, confessed the whole matter, and was therefore punished according to her deserts.

The body of the constant and noble gentlewomā with great honour was taken out of the cave and carried to buriall within Rome with a garland of Laurell about her heade, accompanied with an infinite number of men and women: among which was

---

[1] Cf. "began to beat her cruelly."     [2] "Doubted": cf. "feared."

not one that brought his eyes to his home againe without teares. And thus generally of all the people was this rare soule no lesse bewailed than commended.

But to tell you of them that you your selfe know, remember you not that ye have heard tell, as the Ladie Fœlix della Rovere [1] was on her journey to Saona doubting lest certaine sailes that were descried a farre off, had beene Pope Alexanders vessels, that pursued her, was utterly resolved, if they had made toward her, and no remedie to escape, to cast her selfe into the Sea.

And this is not to bee thought that she did upon any lightnesse, for you as well as any man, doe know with what a wit and wisedom the singular beautie of that Ladie is accompanied.

I can no longer keepe in silence a word of our Dutchesse, who living fifteene yeares in company with her husband, like a widow, hath not onely beene stedfast in not uttering this to any person in the world, but also when she was perswaded by her owne friendes to forsake this widowhead,[2] she chose rather to suffer banishment, povertie, and all other kinde of miserie, than to agree to that, which all other men thought great favour and prosperitie of fortune. And as he still proceeded in talking of this, the Dutchesse saide.

Speake of somewhat els, and no more adoe in this matter, for yee have other thinges inough to talke of.

The Lord Cesar followed on. Full well I know that you will not deny mee this (my Lorde Gasper) nor you Phrisio.

No doubtlesse, answered Phrisio: but one maketh no number.[3]

Then saide the Lord Cesar: Truth it is that these so great effectes and rare vertues are seene in few women: Yet are they also that resist the battailes of love, all to be wondred at, and such as otherwhile bee overcome deserve much compassion. For surely the provocations of lovers, the crafts that they use, the snares that they lay in waite are such, and so applyed, that it is too great a wonder, that a tender girle should escape them.

What day, what houre passeth any time that the yong woman thus laide at is not tempted by her lover with money, tokens: and all thinges that he can imagine may please her?

At what time can she ever looke out at a window, but she seeth continually the earnest lover passe by? With silence [4] in

---

[1] Lady Felice della Rovere, natural daughter of Cardinal Giuliano della Rovere (at the time of these conversations Pope Julius II.) and cousin of "my Lord General."

[2] "Duke Guidobaldo's impotence is said to have given rise to the project of a divorce for his duchess"(Opdycke).

[3] Cf. "for one does not make a host."    [4] "With silence": cf. "Silent."

wordes, but with a paire of eyes that talke. With a vexed and faint countenance. With those kinled sighes. Oftentimes with most aboundant teares.

When doth she at any time issue out at her doores to Church or any other place, but he is alwaies in the face of her? And at every turning of a lane[1] meeteth her in the teeth, with such heavie passion painted in his eyes, that a man woulde weene that even at the instant hee were readie to dye?

I omit his precisenesse in sundrie thinges, inventions, merrie conceites, undertaking enterprises, sportes, daunces, games, maskeries, justes, tournaments, the which thinges she knoweth all to be taken in hande for her sake.

Againe, in the night time she can never awake, but she heareth musick, or at the least that unquiet spirite about the walles of her house, casting forth sighes and lamentable voices.

If by happe she talketh with one of her waiting women about her, she (being alreadie corrupted with money) hath straight way in a readinesse some pretie token, a letter, a rime, or some such matter, to present in her lovers behalfe and here entring to purpose, maketh her to understand how this seely soule burneth, how he setteth litle by his owne life, to doe her service, and how hee seeketh nothing of her but honestie, and that onely his desire is to speake with her.

Here then for all hard matters are found out remedies, counterfeite keyes, ladders of ropes, waies to cast into sleepe, a trifling matter is painted out,[2] examples are alleaged of others that doe much worse: so that every matter is made so easie, that she hath no more trouble but to say, I am content.[3] And in case the poore soule make resistance but a while, they ply her with such provocations, and finde such meanes, that with continuall beating at, they breake in sunder that is a let to her.

And many there be, that perceiving they can not prevaile with faire wordes, fall to threatnings, and say that they wil tell their husbands, they are that they be not.

Other bargaine boldly with their fathers, and many times with ye husbands, which for promotions sake give their owne daughters and wives for a pray against their will.

Other seeke by inchauntments, and witchcraftes, to take from them the libertie that God hath graunted to soules, wherein

---

[1] "Lane": cf. "street."
[2] "A trifling matter," etc.: cf. "the thing is painted as of little consequence."
[3] "Content": cf. "willing."

are seene wonderful conclusions.[1] But in a thousand yeare I could not repeat all the crafts that men use to frame women to their willes, which bee infinite.

And beside them which every man of him selfe findeth out, there hath not also wanted that have wittily made bookes,[2] and bestowed great studie to teach how in this behalfe women are to be deceived.

Now judge you how from so many nets these simple dooves can be safe, tempted with so sweete a baite. And what great matter is it then, in case a woman knowing her selfe so much beloved and worshipped many yeares together, of a noble and faire cōdicioned yong man, which a thousand times a day hazardeth his life to serve her, and never thinketh upon other but to please her. How with the continuall beating which the water maketh when it pearceth the most hard marble stone, at length is it brought to love it? And so she being vanquished by passions, yeeldeth to that whereof you spake, by reason of the imbecillitie of that sexe, she being by nature more desirous of that matter than the man that is in love.

Is this (thinke you) so hainous a trespasse, that the seely poore creature taken with so many entisements, deserveth not, if the worst should fall, the pardon that many times murtherers, theeves, fellons and traitors have?

Will you have this vice so uncomparable great, that because one woman is founde to runne into it, all women kinde should be cleane dispised for it, and generally counted void of continencie? Not regarding that many are found most invincible, that against the continuall flickering provocations of love are made of Diamonds,[3] and stiffe in their infinit stedinesse, more than the rocks, against the surges of the sea.

Then the Lorde Gasper when the L. Cesar stayed talking, began to make him answere, but the Lord Octavian smyling: Tush for love of God (quoth he) graunt him the victory, for I know ye shall doe small good, and me thinke I see you shall not onely make all the women your enimies, but also the more part of the men.

The Lord Gasper laughed and said: Nay, the women have rather great cause to thanke me. For had not I contraried the Lorde Julian and the Lorde Cesar, they should not have come to the knowledge of so many prayses as they have given them.

---

[1] "Wonderful conclusions": cf. "startling results."
[2] e.g. Ovid's *Ars Amandi*.
[3] Cf. "proof against love's continual enticements."

Then saide the Lord Cesar: The prayses which my Lorde Julian and I have given women, and many mo beside, were most knowne, therefore they have beene but superfluous.

Who woteth not that without women no contentation or delite can be felt in all this life of ours? which (set them aside) were rude, and without all sweetenesse, and rougher than the life of forrest wilde beastes?

Who knoweth not that women rid our harts of all vile and dastardly imaginations, vexations, miseries, and the troublesom heavines that so oftentimes accompanieth them?

And in case we will consider the truth, we shal know moreover, as touching the understanding of great matters, that they doe not stay our wits, but rather quicken them, and in warre make them [past] feare, and hardie passing measure.

And certes it is not possible, that in the hart of man, where once is entred the flame of love, there shoulde at any time raigne cowardlinesse.[1] For he that loveth, alwaies coveteth to make him selfe as lovely as he can, and evermore dreadeth that hee take no foile, that shoulde make him litle set by: and passeth not to goe a thousand times in a day to his death, to declare him selfe worthie of that love.

Therefore who so coulde gather an armie of lovers that should fight in the presence of the Ladies they loved, should subdue the whole world, unlesse against it on the contrarie part there were an other armie likewise in love. And to abide by,[2] the holding out of Troy tenne yeares against all Greece, proceeded of nothing els but of certaine lovers, which when they entended to issue out abroad to fight, armed them selves in the presence of their Ladies, and many times they[3] helped them, themselves, and at their setting forth rounded them some certaine word, y$^t$ set them on fire and made them more than men.

Afterwarde in fighting they wist well that they were beheld from the walles and towers by the Ladies, wherefore they deemed everie bold enterprise that they undertooke, was commended of them, which was the greatest rewarde to them that they coulde have in the world.

Many there be that holde opinion that the victorie of king Ferdinande and Isabell of Spaine, against the king of Granada was chiefely occasioned by women: for the most times when the armie of Spaine marched to encounter with the enimies, Queene

---

[1] Cf. "vileness."
[2] "And to abide by": cf. "And be well assured."
[3] "They": cf. "these women."

Isabel set forth also with all her Damsels: and there were many noble gentlemen that were in love, who till they came within sight of the enimies, alwaies went communing with their Ladies. Afterwarde echone taking his leave of his, in their presence marched on to encounter with the enimies, with that fiercenesse of courage, that love and desire to shew their Ladies that they were served with valiant men, gave them.

Whereupon it befell many times that a very few gentlemen of Spaine put to flight and slew an infinite number of Moores, thanked be the courteous and beloved women. Therefore I wot not (my Lorde Gasper) what waywarde judgement hath leade you to dispraise women.

Doe you not see that of all comely exercises and which delight the world, the cause is to be referred to no earthly thing, but to women? Who learneth to daunce featly for other, but to please women?

Who applyeth the sweetnesse of musicke for other cause, but for this? Who to write in meeter, at the least in the mother tongue, but to expresse the affections caused by women?

Judge you how many most noble Poemes we had beene without both in Greek and Latin had women beene smally regarded of Poets.

But in leaving all other apart, had it not beene a very great losse, in case maister Francis Petrarca, that writte so divinely his loves in this our tongue, had applyed his minde onely to Latin matters: as he would have done had not the love of ye Damsell Laura sometime staied him from it?

I name not unto you the fine wits that are now in the world, and here present, which dayly bring forth some noble fruite, and notwithstanding take their ground only of the vertue and beautie of women. See whether Salomon minding to write mystically verie high and heavenly matters, to cover them with a gracious vaile, did not faine a fervent Dialogue full of the affection of a lover with his woman, seeming to him that he coulde not finde here beneath among us any likenesse more meete and agreeing with heavenly matters, than the love towarde women: and in that wise, and manner, minded to give us a litle of the smacke [1] of that divinitie, which he both for his understanding and for the grace [2] above others, had knowledge of.

Therefore this needed no disputation (my Lorde Gasper) or at the least so many wordes in the matter. But you in gaine-saying the truth, have hindred the understanding of a thousand

---

[1] "Smacke": cf. "savour."  [2] Cf. "both by knowledge and by grace."

other pretie matters, and necessarie for the perfection of the gentlewoman of the Pallace.

The Lord Gasper answered: I believe there can no more be saide: Yet if you suppose that the Lorde Julian hath not garnished her throughly with good conditions, the fault is not in him, but in him that hath so wrought that there are no moe vertues in the worlde: for all that there be, he hath bestowed upon her.

The Dutchesse saide smiling: Well, you shall see that the Lord Julian wil yet finde out moe beside.

The Lord Julian answered: in good sooth (Madam) me seemeth I have sufficiently spoken. And for my part, I am well pleased with this my woman. And in case these Lordes will not have her as she is, let them leave her to me.

Here when all was whist, Sir Fredericke saide: My Lord Julian, to give you occasion to say somewhat els, I will but aske you a question, as touching that you have willed to bee the principall profession of the gentlewoman of the Pallace. And this it is, that I long to know how she should behave her selfe in a point that (to my seeming) is most necessarie.

For albeit the excellent qualities which you have given her, containe in them discretion, knowledge, jugement, sleight, sober mood,[1] and so many other vertues, whereby of reason she ought to have the understanding to entertaine every man, and in all kind of purpose, yet think I notwithstanding above any other thing, that it is requisite for her to know what belongeth to communication of love.[2]

For even as every honest gentleman for an instrument to obtaine the good will of women, practiseth those noble exercises, precise fashions[3] and good manners which we have named, even so to this purpose applyeth he also his wordes, and not onely when he is stirred thereto by some passion, but oftentimes also to doe honour to the woman he talketh withall, seeming to him that to declare to love her, is a witnesse that she is worthie of it, and that her beawtie and worthinesse is such, that it enforceth everie man to serve her.

Therefore would I know, how this woman in such a case shoulde behave her selfe uprightly, and how to answere him that loveth her in deed, and how him that maketh false semblant: and whether she ought to dissemble the understanding of it,

[1] "Discretion," etc.: cf. "genius, wisdom, good sense, ease of bearing modesty . . ."
[2] "Communication": cf. "discussions."
[3] "Precise fashions": cf. "elegancies."

or be answerable, or shun the matter,[1] and how to handle her selfe.

Then said the Lord Julian: It were first needfull to teach her to know them that make semblant to love, and them that love in deede. Afterwarde for being answerable in love or no, I believe she ought not to be guided by any other mans will, but by her owne selfe.

Sir Frederick said: Teach you her then what are the most certaine and surest tokens to discerne false love from true, and what tryall she shall thinke sufficient to content her selfe withall, to be out of doubt of the love shewed her.

The Lord Julian answered smiling: That wote not I, because men bee now a daies so craftie, that they make infinite false semblāts, and sometime weepe, when they have in deede a greater lust to laugh: therefore they should be sent to the constant Ile under the Arch of faithfull lovers. But lest this woman of mine (which is my charge and no mans els, because she is my creature) should runne into these errours which I have seene many other runne into, I woulde say that she shoulde not be light of credence that she is beloved: nor bee like unto some, that not onely make [not] wise[2] they understande him not that cōmuneth with them of love, be it never so farre of, but also at the first word accept all the prayses that be given them: or els deny them after such a sorte, that is rather an alluring for them to love them they commune withall, than a withdrawing of themselves.

Therefore the manner of entertainement in reasoning of love that I will have my woman of the Pallace to use, shal be alwaies to shunne believing that who so talketh of love, loveth her any whit the more. And in case the gentleman be (as many such there are abroad) malaperte, and hath small respect to her in his talke, she shall shape him such an answere, that he shall plainely understand she is not pleased withall. Againe, if he be demure and useth sober fashions and wordes of love covertly, in such honest manner, as I believe the Courtier whom these Lordes have fashioned will doe, the woman shall make wise not to understand him, and shall draw his wordes to another sense, seeking alwaies soberly with the discretion and wisedom that is alreadie saide becommeth her, to stray from that purpose.[3]

But in case the communication bee such that she can not faine not to understand it, she shall take the whole (as it were) for

---

[1] Cf. "whether to return his love or to refuse."
[2] "Make not wise": cf. "do not feign."
[3] "Stray," etc.: cf. "change the subject."

a merrie devise, and make wise that she knoweth it is spoken
to her rather to honour her withall, than that it is so in deede,
debasing her deserts, and acknowledging at the gentlemans
courtesie the prayses which he giveth her: and in this sort she
shall be counted discreete, and shall bee on the surer hande for [1]
being deceived.

Thus me seemeth the gentlewoman of the Pallace ought to
behave her selfe in communication of love.

Then Sir Fredericke. You debate this matter, my Lord
Julian (quoth he) as though it were requisite, that all such as
speake with women of love, should tell lyes, and seeke to deceive
them, the which in case it were so, I woulde say your lessons
were good. But if this gentleman that entertaineth, loveth in
very deede, and feeleth the passion that so tormenteth mens
hearts sometime, consider you not in what paine, in what
calamitie and death ye put him in, when at no time you will
that the woman shall believe him in any thing hee saith about
this purpose?

Shall othes, teares, and so many other tokens then, have no
force at all? Take heede (my Lord Julian) least a man may
thinke that beside y[e] naturall crueltie which many of these
women have in them, you teach them yet more.

The Lorde Julian answered: I have spoken, not of him that
loveth, but of him that entertaineth with communication of
love, wherein one of the necessariest points is, that wordes be
never to seeke: and true lovers as they have a burning heart so
have they a colde tongue, with broken talke and sodaine silence.

Therefore (may hap) it were no false principle to say, He that
loveth much, speaketh litle. Howbeit in this I believe there
can bee given no certaine rule, by reason of the diversitie of
mens manners. And I wot not what I should say, but that the
woman be good and heedfull, and alwaies beare in minde, that
men may with a great deale lesse daunger declare them selves
to love, than women.

The Lorde Gaspar saide laughing: Why (my Lorde Julian)
will not you that this your so excellent a woman shall love againe,
at the least when she knoweth certainely she is beloved, considering if the Courtier were not loved againe, it is not likely
he would continue in loving her: and so should she want many
favours, and chieflye the homage and reverence wherewithall
lovers obey, and (in a manner) worship the vertue of the
woman beloved.

---

[1] "on the surer hande for": cf. "safer against."

In this, answered the L. Julian, I will not counsell her. But I say perdee to love, as you now understãd, I judge it not meet, but for unmarried women. For when this love can not ende in matrimonie, the woman must needs have alwaies the remorse and pricking that is had of unlawfull matters, and she putteth in hazard to staine the renowne of honestie, that stãdeth her so much upon.

Then answered Sir Fredericke smyling: Me thinke (my Lord Julian) this opinion of yours is verie soure and crabbed, and I believe you have learned it of some Frier Preacher, of them that rebuke women in love with lay men, that their part may be the more. And me seemeth you set over hard lawes to married women, for many there be that their husbands beare very sore hatred unto without cause, and nippe them at the hart, some-time in loving other women, otherwhile in working them all the displeasures they can imagine.

Some are compelled by their fathers to take olde men full of diseases, uglesome and waywarde that make them leade their life in continuall miserie. And in case it were lawfull for such to bee devorced and severed from them they bee ill coupled withall, perhaps it were not to be allowed that they shoulde love any other than their husband. But when either through the starres, their enimies, or through ye diversitie of complexion, or any other casualtie, it befalleth that in bed, which ought to be the nest of agreement and love, the cursed furie of hell soweth the seede of his venome, which afterwarde bringeth forth disdaine, suspition, and the pricking thornes of hatred, that tormenteth those unluckie soules bound cruelly together in the fast lincked chaine that can not be broken but by death, why will not you have it lawfull for this woman to seeke some easement for so hard a scourge, and give unto another that which her husband not onely regardeth not, but rather cleane abhorreth?

I hold well, that such as have meete husbands and bee beloved of them, ought not to doe them injurie: but the other in not loving him that loveth them doe themselves injurie.

Nay, they doe themselves injurie in loving other beside their husband, answered the Lord Julian. Yet since not loving is not many times in our will, if this mishappe chaunce to the woman of the Pallace, that the hatred of her husband or the love of an other bendeth her to love I will have her to graunt her lover nothing els but the minde: nor at any time to make him any certaine token of love, neither in worde nor gesture, nor any other way that he may be fully assured of it.

Then saide maister Robert of Bari smiling, I appeale (my Lord Julian) from this judgement of yours, and I believe I shall have many fellowes. But since you will teach this currishnesse [1] (that I may terme it so) to married women, will ye also have the unmarried to bee so cruel and discourteous? and not please their lovers at the least in somewhat?

In case my woman of the Pallace, answered the Lorde Julian, be not married, minding to love, I will have her to love one she may marrie, neither will I thinke it an offence if she shew him some token of love. In which matter I will teach her one generall rule in few wordes, and that is, That she shew him whom she loveth all tokens of love, but such as may bring into the lovers minde a hope to obtaine of her any dishonest matter. And to this she must have a great respect, because it is an errour that infinite women runne into, which ordinarily covet nothing so much as to bee beautifull.

And because to have many lovers they suppose is a testimony of their beautie, they doe their best to winne them as many as they can. Therefore oftentimes they run at rovers in behaviours of small modesty, and leaving the temperate sober moode that is so sightly in them, use certaine wanton countenances, with baudie words and gestures full of unshamefastnesse, holding opinion that men marke them and give eare to them willingly for it, and with these fashions make themselves beloved, which is false.

Because the signes and tokens that bee made them, spring of an apetite moved by an opinion of easinesse,[2] not of love. Therefore will not I that my woman of the Pallace with dishonest behaviours shoulde appeare as though she woulde offer her selfe unto who so will have her, and allure what she can the eyes and affection of who so beholdeth her: but with her deserts and vertuous conditions, with amiablenesse and grace drive into the minde of who so seeth her, the very love that is due unto everie thing worthie to bee beloved, and the respect that alwaies taketh away hope from who so mindeth any dishonest matter.

He then that shall be beloved of such a woman, ought of reason to holde himselfe contented with every litle token, and more to esteeme a looke of hers with affection of love, than to be altogether maister of an other. And to such a woman I wot not what to adde more, but that she be beloved of so excellent

---

[1] "Currishnesse": cf. "rusticity."
[2] "By an opinion," etc.: cf. "belief in their willingness."

a Courtier, as these Lordes have fashioned, and she likewise to love him, that both the one and the other may have full and wholy his perfection.[1]

After the Lord Julian had thus spokē he held his peace, when the L. Gaspar laughing, now (quoth he) you can not complaine that the Lord Julian hath not fashioned this woman of the Pallace most excellent. And if perdee there bee any such to bee found, I say that she deserveth well to bee esteemed equall with the Courtier.

The Ladie Emilia answered: I will at all times be bound to find her, when you finde the Courtier.

Maister Robert said then: Doubtlesse it can not be said nay, but the Lorde Julians woman which he hath fashioned is most perfect. Yet in these her last properties as touching love, mee seemeth notwithstãding that he hath made her somewhat over crabbed, and especially where he will have her in wordes, gestures and countenance to take cleane away all hope from the lover, and settle him as nigh as she can in dispaire.

For (as all men know) the desires of man stretch not to such kinde of matters, whereof there is no hope to bee had. And although at times some women there have beene that perhaps bearing them selves loftie of their beautie and worthinesse: the first worde they have saide to them that communed with them of love hath beene, that they shoulde never looke to come by any thing of them that liked them[2]: yet in countenance, and dalliance together they have beene afterwarde more favourable to them, so that with their gentle deedes they have tempred in part their proude wordes.

But if this woman both in wordes, deedes, and behaviours take hope quite away, I believe our Courtier, if he be wise, will never love her, and so shall she have this imperfection, that she shall be without a lover.

Then the Lord Julian, I will not (quoth he) have my woman of the Pallace to take away the hope of every thing, but of dishonest matters, the which, in case the Courtier bee so courteous and discreete, as these Lordes have fashioned him, he will not onely not hope for, but not once motion.[3]

For if beautie, manners, wit, goodnesse, knowledge, sober moode, and so many other vertuous conditions which wee have given the woman, be the cause of the Courtiers love toward

---

[1] "May have," etc.: cf. "may attain their complete perfection."
[2] Cf. "never expect to have anything from them that he wished."
[3] "Motion": cf. "wish for."

her, the end also of this love must needes be vertuous, and if
noblenesse of birth, skilfulnesse in martiall feates, in letters,
in musicke, gentlenesse, being both in speech and behaviour
indowed with so many graces, be ye meanes wherewithall the
Courtier compasseth ye womans love, the ende of that love
must needes be of the same condition that the meanes are by
the which hee commeth to it. Beside that, as there bee in the
world sundrie kindes of beautie, so are there also sundrie desires
of men: and therfore it is seene that many, perceiving a woman
of so grave a beautie, that going, standing, jeasting, dallying,
and doing what she lusteth, so tempreth all her gestures, that
it driveth a certaine reverence into who so beholdeth her, are
agast and afeard to serve her.

And rather drawne with hope, love those garish and enticefull[1]
women, so delicate and tender, that in their wordes, gestures
and countenance, declare a certaine passion somewhat feeble,[2]
that promiseth to be easily brought and turned into love.

Some to be sure from deceites, love certaine other so lavish
both of their eyes, wordes and gestures, that they doe what ever
first commeth to minde, with a certaine plainenesse that hideth
not their thoughts.

There want not also many other noble courages,[3] that seeming
to them that vertue consisteth about hard matters (for it is
over sweet a victory to overcome that seemeth to another
impregnable) are soone bent to love the beauties of those women,
that in their eyes, wordes and gestures, declare a more churlish
gravitie[4] than the rest, for a tryall that their prowesse can enforce
an obstinate minde, and bend also stubborne willes and rebels
against love, to love.

Therefore such as have so great affiance in themselves because
they reckon themselves sure from deceite, love also willingly
certaine women, that with a sharpenesse of wit, and with arte
it seemeth in their beautie that they hide a thousand craftes.
Or els some other, that have accompanied with beautie a certaine
scornefull fashion,[5] in few wordes, litle laughing, after a sort as
though (in a manner) they smally regarded who so ever beholdeth
or serveth them.

Againe ther are found certaine other, that vouchsafe not to
love but women that in their countenance, in their speach and
in all their gestures have about them all hansomnesse, all faire

---

[1] "Garish and enticefull": cf. "attractive and enticing."
[2] Cf. "languorous passion."
[3] "Noble courages": cf. "generous souls."     [4] Cf. "austere severity."
[5] Cf. "coquettishly disdainful manner."

conditions, all knowledge, and all graces heaped together like one floure made of all the excellencies in the world.

Therefore in case my woman of the Pallace have scarcitie of their loves proceeding of an ill hope, she shal not for this be without a lover: because she shall not want them that shall be provoked through hir desertes and through the affiaunce of the prowesse in themselves, whereby they shall knowe themselves worthie to be loved of her.

Maister Robert still spake against him, but the Dutchesse tolde him that he was in the wrong, confirming the Lord Julians opinion: after that she added: We have no cause to complaine of the L. Julian, for doubtlesse I think that the woman of the Pallace whom hee hath fashioned, may be compared to the Courtier, and that with some advantage: for he hath taught her to love which these Lordes have not done their Courtier.

Then spake Unico Aretino: It is meete to teach women to love, because I never saw any that coulde doe it, for almost continually all of them accompanye their beautie with cruelty and unkindnesse towarde such as serve them most faithfully, and which for noblenesse of birth, honestie and vertue deserved a rewarde for their good wil: and yet many times give themselves for a pray to most blockish and cowardly men and very Asseheades,[1] and which not onely love them not, but abhorre them.

Therefore to shunne these so foule oversights, perhaps it had beene well done first to have taught them to make a choise of him that should deserve to be beloved, and afterwarde to love him. The which is not necessarie in men, for they know it too wel of themselves: and I my selfe can be a good witnesse of it, because love was never taught me, but by the divine beauty and most divine manners of a Ladie, so that it was not in my will not to worship her: and therefore needed I therein no arte nor teacher at all. And I believe that the like happeneth to as many as love truely.

Therefore the Courtier hath more neede to be taught to make him beloved than to love.

Then saide the Ladie Emilia: Doe you now reason of this then, maister Unico?

Unico answered: me think reason woulde that the good will of women shoulde be gotten in serving and pleasing of them. But it, wherein they reckon themselves served and pleased, I believe must bee learned of women themselves, which oftē times

---

[1] "Most blockish . . . men," etc.: cf. "men who are very silly, base, and of small account."

covet such straunge matters, that there is no man that would
imagin them, and otherwhile they themselves wot not what they
shoulde long for.

Therefore it were good you (madam) that are a woman, and
of right ought to know what pleaseth women, should take this
paine, to doe the world so great a profit.

Then saide the Ladie Emilia: For so much as you are generally
most acceptable to women, it is a good likelyhood that you
know all the waies how their good will is to be gotten. Therefore
is it perdee meete for you to teach it.

Madam, answered Unico, I can give a lover no profitable
advise than to procure that you beare no stroke [1] with y<sup>e</sup> woman
whose good will hee seeketh. For the small qualities which yet
seemed to the worlde sometime to be in me, with as faithfull
a love as ever was, were not of such force [2] to make me beloved,
as you to make mee be hated.

Then answered the Ladie Emilia: God save me (maister
Unico) for once thinking, and much more for working any thing
that should make you be hated. For beside that I shoulde doe
that I ought not, I shoulde bee thought of a slender judgement
to attempt a matter unpossible. But since ye provoke me in
this sort to speak of that pleaseth women, I will speake of it,
and if it displease you, lay the fault in your selfe.

I judge therefore, that who so entendeth to be beloved, ought
to love and to be lovely [3]: and these two pointes are inough to
obtaine the good will of women.

Now to answere to that which you lay to my charge, I say
that every man knoweth and seeth that you are most lovely:
Mary whether ye love so faithfully, as you say ye doe, I am verie
doubtful and perhaps others too. For, your being over lovely,
hath beene the cause that you have beene beloved of many
women: and great rivers divided into many armes become small
brookes: so love likewise scattred into mo than one body hath
small force.

But these your continuall complaintes and accusing of the
women whom you have served, of unkindnesse (which is not
likely, considering so many deserts of yours) is a certaine kinde
of discretion, to cloke the favours, contentations and pleasures
which you have received in love, and an assurance for the
women that love you and that have given themselves for a

_____
[1] "Beare no stroke": cf. "have no influence."
[2] "Were not . . . force": cf. "had not such power."
[3] "Lovely": cf. "lovable."

pray to you, that you will not disclose them. And therefore are they also well pleased, that you should thus openly shew false love to others, to cloke their true.

Wherefore if happly those women that you now make wise to love, are not so light of beliefe, as you would they were, it happeneth because this your arte in love beginneth to bee discovered, and not because I make you to be hated.

Then said maister Unico: I entend not to attempt to confute your words, because me seemeth it is as well my destinie not to be believed in truth, as it is yours to be believed in untruth.

Say hardly maister Unico, answered the Ladie Emilia, that you love not so, as you would have believed ye did. For if you did love, all your desires shoulde bee to please the woman beloved, and to will the selfe same thing that she willeth, for this is the law of love. But your complaining so much of her, betokeneth some deceite (as I have saide) or els it is a signe that you will that, that she willeth not.

Nay (quoth maister Unico) there is no doubt but I will that that she willeth, which is a signe I love her: but it greeveth mee because she willeth not that, that I will, which is a token she loveth not me, according to the very same law that you have alleaged.

The Ladie Emilia answered: he that taketh in hande to love, must also please and apply himselfe full and wholy to the appetites [1] of the wight beloved, and according to them frame his own: and make his owne desires, servants: and his veric soule, like an obedient handmaiden: nor at any time to think upon other, but to chaunge his, if it were possible, into the beloved wightes, and reckon this his chiefe joy and hapinesse, for so doe they that love truely.

My chiefe happinesse were jumpe, answered maister Unico, if one will alone ruled her soule and mine both.

It lyeth in you to doe it,[2] answered the Ladie Emilia. Then spake maister Bernarde interrupting them: Doubtlesse, who so loveth truely, directeth all his thoughtes, without other mens teaching, to serve and please the woman beloved. But because these services of love are not otherwhile well knowne, I believe that beside loving and serving, it is necessarie also to make some other shew of this love, so manifest, that the woman may not dissemble to knowe that she is beloved: yet with such modestie, that it may not appeare that hee beareth her litle reverence.

And therefore you (Madam) that have begun to declare how

[1] "Appetites": cf. "wishes."    [2] Cf. "to have it so."

the soule of the lover ought to be an obedient handmaiden to the beloved, teach us withall, I beseech you, this secrete matter, which mee thinke is most needefull.

The Lorde Cesar laughed and saide: If the lover be so bashfull, that he is ashamed to tell it her, let him write it her.

To this the Ladie Emilia saide: Nay, if he be descreete, as is meete, before he maketh the woman to understande it, hee ought to bee out of doubt, not to offend her.

Then saide the Lorde Gasper: All women have a delite to be sued to in love, although they were minded to deny that which they are sued unto for.

The Lorde Julian saide, you are much deceived. For I woulde not counsell the Courtier at any time to use this way, except he were sure not to have a repulse.

What should he then doe? quoth the Lord Gasper. The Lorde Julian answered: In case you will needs write or speake to her, doe it with such sober moode, and so warily, that the wordes may first attempt the minde, and so doubtfully touch her entent and will, that they may leave her a way and a certain issue to faine the understanding that those wordes containe love: to the entent if he finde any daunger, hee may draw backe and make wise to have spoken or written it to another ende, to enjoy these familiar cherishinges and daliances with assurance that oftentimes wome shew to such as should take them for friendship, afterwarde denye them as soone as they perceive they are taken for tokens of love.

Wherefore such as bee too rash, and venture so sawcily with certaine furies and plunges,[1] oftentimes lose them, and worthily: for it displeaseth alwaies everye honest gentlewoman, to bee litle regarded of who so without respect seeketh for love at her before he hath served her.

Therefore (in my minde) the way which the Courtier ought to take, to make his love knowne to the woman me think should be to declare them in signes and tokens more than in wordes. For assuredly there is otherwhile a greater affection of love perceived in a sigh, in a respect, in a feare,[2] than in a thousand wordes. Afterwarde, to make the eyes the trustie messengers, that may carrie the ambassades of the hart.

Because they oftentimes declare with a more force what passiō there is inwardly, than can the tongue, or letters, or

[1] "Venture . . . with certaine furies," etc.: cf. "venture thus presumptuously with a kind of fury and stubbornness."
[2] "In a respect," etc.: cf. "in reverence, in timidity."

messages, so that they not onely disclose the thoughtes, but also manie times kindle love in the hart of the person beloved. For those lively spirits that issue out at the eyes, because they are engendred nigh the hart, entring in like case into the eyes that they are levelled at, like a shaft to the pricke, naturally pearce to the hart, as to their resting place and there are at rest with those other spirits: and with the most subtill and fine nature of bloud which they carrie with them, infect the bloude about the hart, where they are come to, and warme it: and make it like unto themselves, and apt to receive the imprinting of the image, which they have carried away[1] with them. Wherefore by litle and litle comming and going the way through the eyes to the hart, and bringing backe with them the tunder and striking yron[2] of beautie and grace, these messengers kindle[3] with the puffing[4] of desire the fire that so burneth, and never ceaseth consuming, for alwaies they bring some matter of hope to nourish it.

Therefore it may full wel be saide, that the eyes are a guide in love, especially if they have a good grace and sweetnesse[5] in them, blacke, of a cleare and sightly blackenesse, or els gray, merrie and laughing, and so comely and pearcing in beholding, as some, in which a man thinketh verily that the waies that give an issue to the spirits are so deepe, that by them he may see as farre as the hart.

The eyes therefore lye lurking like souldiers in war, lying in waite in bushment, and if the forme of all the bodie be well favoured and of good proportion, it draweth unto it and allureth who so beholdeth it a farre off: untill he come nigh: and as soone as he is at hand, the eyes shoote, and like sorcerers bewitch, and especially when by a right line they send their glistering beames into the eyes of the wight beloved, at the time when they doe the like, because the spirites meete together, and in that sweete encounter the one taketh the others nature and qualitie: as it is seene in a sore eye, that beholding stedfastly a sound one, giveth him his disease. Therefore me thinke our Courtier may in this wise open a great parcell of the love to his woman.[6]

Truth it is, that in case the eyes bee not governed with arte,

---

[1] "Carried away": cf. "brought."
[2] "Tunder and striking yron": cf. "tinder and steel."
[3] "Kindle": the verb is far removed from its modifier, "by litle and litle."
[4] Cf. "breath."
[5] "Have a good grace," etc.: cf. "are kind and soft."
[6] "Woman": cf. "lady."

they discover many times the amorous desires more unto whom a man would least: for through them, (in a manner) visibly shine forth those burning passions, which the lover minding to disclose onely to the wight beloved, openeth them many times also unto whom he would most soonest hide them from.

Therefore hee that hath not lost the bridle of reason, handleth himselfe heedfully, and observeth the times and places: and when it needeth, refraineth from so stedfast beholding, for all it be a most savorie foode, because An open love is too hard a matter.

Count Lewis answered: Yet otherwhile to bee open it hurteth not: because in this case many times men suppose that those loves tend not to the end which every lover coveteth, when they see there is litle heede taken to hide them, and passe not whether they be knowne or no: and therefore with denyall a man chalengeth him a certaine libertie to talke openly, and to stand without suspition with the wight beloved. Which is not so in them that seeke to be secrete, because it appeareth that they stand in hope off, and are nigh some great rewarde, which they would not have other men to know.

I have also seene a most fervent love spring in the heart of a woman, towarde one that seemed at the first not to beare him the least affection in the worlde, onely for that she heard say, that the opinion of many was, that they loved together. And the cause of this (I believe) was that so generall a judgement seemed a sufficient witnesse, that he was worthie of her love. And it seemed (in a manner) that report brought the ambassade on the lovers behalfe much more truer and worthier to be believed, than he himselfe could have done with letters or wordes, or any other person for him: therefore sometime this common voice not onely hurteth not, but farthereth a mans purpose.

The Lord Julian answered: Loves that have reporte for their messenger, are verie perillous to make a man pointed to with a finger. And therefore who ever entendeth to walke this race [1] warily, needes must he make countenance to have a great deale lesse fire in his stomack, than in deede he hath, and content himselfe with that, that he thinketh a trifle, and dissemble his desires, jealosies, afflictions and pleasures, and many times laugh with mouth when the hart weepeth, and shew himselfe lavish of that he is most covetous of: and these thinges are so hard to be done, that (in a manner) they are unpossible.

[1] Cf. "travel this road."

Therefore if our Courtier would follow my counsell, I woulde exhort him to keepe his loves secrete.

Then saide maister Bernarde: You must then teach it him, and mee thinke it is much to purpose: for beside privie signes that some make otherwhile so closely, that (in a manner) without any gesture, the person whom they covet, in their countenance and eyes reade what they have in the hart.

I have sometime heard betweene two lovers a long and a large discourse of love, where of yet the standers by could not plainely understand any particular point, nor be out of doubt that it was of love. Such was the discretion and heedfulnesse of the talker: for without making any manner shew that they were not willing to bee heard, they rounded privily[1] the words onely that were most to purpose, and all the rest they spake aloud, which might bee applyed to divers meaninges.[2]

Then spake Sir Frederick: To reason thus in peecemeale of these rules of secretnesse, were a taking of an infinit matter in hand: therefore would I that we speake somewhat rather how the lover should keepe and maintaine his Ladies good will, which mee thinke is much more necessarie.

The Lord Julian answered: I believe, the meanes that serve him to compasse it, serve him also to keepe it: and all this consisteth in pleasing the woman beloved, without offending her at anye time. Therefore it were a hard matter to give any certaine rule, because who so is not discrete, infinite waies cōmitteth oversights, which otherwhile seeme matters of nothing, and yet offend they much the womans minde. And this happeneth more than to other, to such as be maistred with passion: as some that whensoever they have oportunitie to speake with the woman they love, lament and bewaile so bitterly, and covet many times thinges so unpossible, that through their unreasonablenesse they are lothed of them.

Other, if they bee pricked with any jealousie, stomack ye matter so grievously, that without stop they burst out in railing upon him they suspect, and otherwhile it is without trespasse[3] either of him, or yet of the woman.

And will not have her speake with him, nor once turne her eyes on that side where he is. And with these fashions many times, they doe not onely offend the woman, but also they are the cause that she bendeth her selfe to love him. Because the feare that a lover declareth to have otherwhile lest his Ladie

---

[1] Cf. "whispered."          [2] Cf. "construed," etc.
[3] "Otherwhile . . .": cf. "sometimes without fault."

forsake him for the other, betokeneth that he acknowledgeth himselfe inferiour in deserts and prowes to the other, and with opinion the woman is moved to love him. And perceiving that to put him out of favour he reporteth ill of him, although it be true, yet she believeth it not, and notwithstanding loveth him the more.

Then saide the Lorde Cesar: I confesse that I am not so wise that I coulde refraine speaking ill of my fellow lover, except you could teach me some other better way to dispatch him.

The Lord Julian answered smyling: it is saide in a proverbe, When a mans enimie is in the water up to the middle, let him reach him his hande, and helpe him from daunger: but when he is up to the chinne, set his foote on his head, and drowne him out of hande. Therefore certaine there bee that play so with their fellow lovers, and untill they have a sure meane to dispatch them, goe dissembling the matter, and rather shew themselves friendes than otherwise. Afterwarde when occasion serveth so fitlie, that they know they may overthrowe them with a sure riddance, reporting all evill of them, be it true or false, they doe it without sparing, with arte, deceite, and all waies that they can imagin.

But because I would not like that our courtier should at any time use any deceite, I would have him to withdraw the good will of his mistresse from his fellow lover with none other arte, but with loving, with serving and with being vertuous, of prowesse, discrete, sober, in conclusion with deserving more than he, and with being in every thing heedfull and wise, refraining from certaine lewd folies, into the which oftentimes many ignorant runne, and by sundrie wayes.

For in times past I have knowne some that in writing and speaking to womē, used evermore the wordes of Poliphilus, and ruffled so in their subtill pointes of Rethoricke, that the women were out of conceite with their owne selves, and reckoned themselves most ignorant, and an houre seemed a thousand yeare to them, to end that talke and to be rid of them. Other bragge and boast too beyond all measure.

Other speake things many times that redound to the blame and damage of themselves, as some that I am wont to laugh at, which make profession to be lovers and otherwhile say in the companie of women.

I never founde woman that ever loved me, and are not witting, that the hearers by and by judge that it can arise of none other cause, but that they deserve neither to be beloved, nor yet so much as the water they drinke, and count them Asseheades,[1] and would not love them for all the good [2] in the worlde: seeming to them [3] that in case they should love them, they were lesse worthie, than all the rest that have not loved them.

Other, to purchase hatred to some felow lover of theirs, are so fond that in like manner in the company of women they say: Such a one is the luckiest man in ye world, for once,[4] hee is neither well favoured, nor sober, nor of prowes, neither can hee doe or say more than other men, and yet all women love him, and rune after him, and thus uttering the spite they beare him for this good lucke, although neither in countenance nor deedes hee appeareth lovely, yet make they them believe that hee hath some hid matter in him, for the which hee deserveth the love of so many women.

Wherfore the women that heare them talke of him in this wise, they also upon this beliefe are moved to love him much more.

Then Count Lewis laughed and saide: I assure you our Courtier if he be discret, will never use this blockishnesse,[5] to get the good will of women.

The Lord Cæsar Gonzaga answered: nor yet another that a gentleman of reputation used in my dayes, who shall be namelesse for the honour of men.

The Dutchesse answered: tell us at the least what hee did. The Lord Cesar saide: this man being beloved of a great Ladie, at her request came privily to the towne where she lay. And after he had seene her and communed with her, as long as they thought meete and had time and leasure thereto, at his leave taking, with many biter teares and sighes in witnesse of the extreame griefe he felt for this departing, he required her to bee alwaies mindfull of him. And afterwarde hee added withall, That she would discharge his Inne, for since hee came thither at her request, he thoght meete that hee shoulde not stand to the charges of his being here, himselfe.

Then beganne all the Ladies to laugh, and saide that he was most unworthie of the name of a gentleman: and manie were ashamed with the selfe shame that he himselfe shoulde worthily have felt, if any time he had gotten so much understanding, that he might have perceived so shamefull an oversight.[6]

Then turned the Lord Gasper to the Lorde Cesar and saide: Better it had beene to have omitted the rehersall of this matter

---

[1] "Asseheades": cf. "men of slight account."
[2] "Good": cf. "gold"; [3] "Seeming to them": cf. "thinking."
[4] "For once": cf. "for although."
[5] Cf. "stupiditie." [6] "Oversight": cf. "fault."

for the honour of women, than the naming of him for the honour of men. For you may well imagine what a judgement that great Ladie had in loving so unreasonable a creature. And perhaps too, of many that served she chose him for the most discretest, leaving behind and shewing ill will unto them that hee was not worthie to waite upon.

Count Lewis laughed and saide: Who woteth whether hee was discrete in other thinges or no, and was out of y^e way only about Innes? But many times for overmuch love men commit great follies. And if you will tell the truth, perhaps it hath beene your chaunce to commit moe than one.

The L. Cesar answeared smiling: Of good fellowship let us not discover our owne oversightes. Yet we must discover them, aunsweared the Lord Gaspar, that wee may know how to amende them: then he proceeded. Now that the Courtier knoweth howe to winne and keepe the good will of his Lady, and take it from his fellow lover, you (my L. Julian) are dettour to teache her to keepe her loves secrete.

The L. Julian answeared: Me thinke I have sufficiently spoken, therefore get you now an other to talke of this secrete matter.

Then M. Bernard and all the rest began a fresh to be in hand with him instantly, and the Lorde Julian saide: you will tempt me. Ye are all the sort of you too great Clarkes in love. Yet if ye desire to know further, goe and reade Ovid.

And how, quoth maister Bernarde, shall I hope that his lessons are any thing worth in love, when he counselleth and saith that it is very good for a man in the company of his mistresse To faine the drunkarde? See what a goodly way it is to get good will withall. And he alleageth for a pretie devise to make a woman understande that he is in love with her, being at a banket, To dip his finger in wine and write it upon the table.

The Lorde Julian saide smiling: In those dayes it was no fault. And therefore (quoth maister Bernarde) seeing so sluttish a matter was not disalowed of men in those dayes, it is to bee thought that they had not so courtely behaviours to serve women in love, as we have. But let us not omit our first purpose, to teach to kepe love secrete.

Then saide the Lorde Julian: In mine advise to keepe love secrete, the causes are to be shunned that utter it, which are many: yet one principall, namely, To be over secrete and to put no person in trust. Because every lover coveteth to make his passions knowne to be beloved, and being alone, hee is driven to make many moe signes and more evident, than if hee were aided by some loving and faithfull friend. For the signes [1] that the lover himselfe maketh, give [2] a farre greater suspition, than those that he maketh by them that goe in message betweene.

And for so much as men naturally are greedie to understand, as soone as a stranger beginneth to suspect the matter, hee so applyeth it,[3] that he cōmeth to the knowledge of the truth, and when he once knoweth it, he passeth not for disclosing it, yea sometime he hath a delite to doe it. Which happeneth not to a friend, who beside that hee is a helpe to him with favour and counsel, doth many times remedie the oversights committed by the blinde lover, and alwaies procureth secretenesse, and preventeth manye matters which hee him selfe can not foresee: beside the great comfort that he feeleth, when he may utter his passions and griefes to a hartie friende, and the partening of them likewise encreaseth his contentations.

Then saide the Lord Gasper: there is an other cause that discovereth loves much more than this. What is that, answered the Lord Julian: The Lorde Gasper saide: Vaine greedinesse [4] joyned with the fondnesse and crueltie of women, which (as you your selfe have saide) procure as much as they can to get them a great number of lovers, and (if it were possible) they would have them all to burne and make ashes, and after death to returne to life, to dye againe. And though they love withall, yet rejoyce they at the torment of lovers, because they suppose the griefe, afflictions, and the calling every houre for death, is a true witnesse that they are beloved, and that with their beautie they can make men miserable and happie, and give them life and death, as pleaseth them. Wherefore they feede onely upon this foode, and are so greedy over it, that for wanting it they never throughly content lovers, nor yet put them out of hope.

But to keepe them still in afflictions and in desire, they use a certaine loftie sowernesse [5] of threatnings mingled with hope, and would have them to esteeme a worde, a countenance or a becke of theirs for a chiefe blisse.

And to make men count them chast and honest as wel others as their lovers, they find meanes that these sharp and discourteous manners of theirs, may bee in open sight, for every man to think that they will much worse handle the unworthie, since they handle them so, that deserve to be beloved. And under this beliefe, thinking themselves with this craft safe from

---

[1] "Signes": cf. "demonstrations."    [2] "Give": cf. "arouse."
[3] Cf. "employs such diligence."    [4] "Greedinesse": cf. "ambition."
[5] Cf. "dominating severity."

slander, oftentimes they lye nightly with most vile men and whom they scarce know. So that to rejoyce at the calamitie and continuall complaintes of some worthie Gentleman, and beloved of them, they barre themselves from those pleasures, which perhaps with some excuse they might come by, and are the cause that the poore lover by very debating of the matter is driven to use waies by the which the thing commeth to light, that with all diligence should have beene kept most secrete.

Certaine other there are, which if with deceite they can bring many in beliefe that they are beloved of them, nourish among them jealousies, with cherishing and making [1] of the one in the others presence. And when they see that he also whom they love best, is now assured and out of doubt that hee is beloved through the signes and tokens that bee made him, many times with doubtfull words and fained disdaines they put him in uncertaintie.

And nip him at the very hart, making wise not to passe for him, and to give them selves full and wholy to the other.

Whereupon arise malice, enimities, and infinite occasions of strife and utter confusion. For needes must a man shew in that case the extreame passion which he feeleth, although it redound to the blame and slander of the woman.

Other, not satisfied with this only torment of jealosie, after the lover hath declared all his tokens of love and faithfull service, and they received the same with some signe to bee answerable in good will, without purpose and when it is least looked for, [2] they beginne to bethinke themselves, [3] and make wise to believe that he is slacked, and faining new suspitions that they are not beloved, they make a countenāce that they will in any wise put him out of their favour.

Wherefore through these incōveniences the poore soule is constrained of verie force to beginne a fresh, and to make her signes, as though he beganne his service but then, and all the day long passe up and downe through the streete, and when the woman goeth forth of her doores to accompany her to Church and to every place where she goeth, and never to turne his eyes to other place.

And here he returneth to weeping, to sighes, to heavie countenances, and when he can talke with her, to swearing, to blapheming, to desperation, and to all rages which unhappie

---

[1] Cf. "bestowing caresses and favour . . ."
[2] "Without purpose": cf. "without cause"; "looked for": cf. "expected."
[3] "Bethinke themselves": cf. "draw back."

lovers are led to by these wilde beastes, that have greater thirst of bloud than the verie Tygres.

Such sorrowfull tokens as these bee, are too often seene and known, and manie times more of others than of the causer of them: and thus are they in few daies so published, that a step can not be made, nor the least signe that is, but it is noted with a thousand eyes.

It happeneth then, that long before there be any pleasures of love betwixt them, they are gessed and judged of all the worlde. For when they see yet their lover now nigh deathes doore, cleane vanquished with the crueltie and torments they put him to, determineth advisedly and in good earnest to draw back, then begin they to make signe that they love him hartily, and do him all pleasures and give themselves to him, least if that fervent desire should faile in him, the fruite of love should withall be the lesse acceptable to him, and he ken them the lesse thanke for doing all thinges contrarily.

And in case this love bee alreadie knowne abroad, at this same time are all the effects knowne in like manner abroad that come of it, and so lose they their reputation, and the lover findeth that he hath lost time and labour and shortned his life in afflictions without any fruit or pleasure.

Because he came by his desires, not whē they should have beene so acceptable to him that they woulde have made him a most happie creature, but when hee set litle or nothing by them. For his hart was now so mortified with those bitter passions, that he had no more sense to tast the delite or contentation offred him.

Then saide the Lord Octavian smyling: you held your peace a while and refrained from speaking ill of women, but now you have so well hit them home, that it appeared ye waited a time to plucke up your strength, like them that retire backwarde to give a greater push at the enconter. And to say the truth, it is ill done of you, for now mee thinke ye may have done and bee pacified.

The Ladie Emilia laughed, and turninge her to the Dutches she said: See Madam, our enemies beginne to breake and to square one with an other.

Geve me not thys name aunswered the L. Octavian, for I am not your adversary, but this contention hath displeased me, not because I am sory to see the victory upon womens side, but because it hath lead the L. Gaspar to revile them more than hee ought, and the L. Julian and the L. Cesar to praise them perhaps somwhat more than due: beside that through the length of the talke wee have lost the understandinge of many other pretie matters that are yet behind to be said of the Courtier.

See quoth the Ladie Emilia, whether you bee not [1] our adversarie, for the talke that is past greeveth you, and you would not that this so excellent a gentlewoman of the Pallace had beene fashioned: not for that you have any more to say of the Courtier (for these Lordes have spoken alreadie what they know, and I believe neither you, ne any man els can adde ought thereto) but for the malice you beare to the honour of women.

It is out of doubt, answered the Lorde Octavian, beside that is alreadie spoken of the Courtier, I coulde wish much more in him. But since every man is pleased that he shall be as he is, I am well pleased too, and would not have him altered in any point, saving in making him somewhat more friendly to women, than the Lorde Gaspar is, yet not perhaps, so much as some of these other Lords are.

Then spake the Dutchesse: In any case we must see whether your witte bee such that it can give the Courtier a greater perfection, than these Lordes have alreadie done.

Therefore dispose your selfe to utter that you have in your minde, els will wee thinke that you also can not adde unto him more than hath alreadie beene saide, but that you minded to diminish the prayses and worthinesse of the gentlewoman of the Pallace, seeing ye judge she is equall with the Courtier, whom by this meane you woulde have believed might be much more perfect than these Lordes have fashioned him.

The Lord Octavian laughed and saide: The prayses and dispraises given women more than due, have so filled the eares and minde of the hearers, that they have left no voide roome for any thing els to stand in: beside that (in mine opinion) it is verie late.

Then said the Dutchesse: If we tarrie till to morrow, we shall have the more time, and the prayses and disprayses, which (you say) are given women on both sides passing measure, in the mean season will we be cleane out of these Lordes mindes, and so shall they bee apt to conceive the truth that you will tell us.

When the Dutchesse had thus spoken, she arose upon her feet, and courteously dismissing them all, withdrew her to her bedchamber, and every man gotte him to his rest.

[1] Cf. "You see . . . that you are . . ."

# FOURTH BOOK

## THE FOURTH BOOKE OF THE COURTIER, OF COUNT BALDESSER CASTILION, UNTO MAISTER ALFONSUS ARIOSTO

THINKING to write out the communicatiō[1] that was had the fourth night after the other mentioned in the former bookes, I feele among sundry discourses a bitter thought that gripeth me in my mind, and maketh me to call to remembrance worldly miseries and our deceitful hopes, and how fortune many times in the verie middest of our race, otherwhile nigh the ende disapointeth our fraile and vaine purposes, sometime drowneth them before they can once come to have a sight of the Haven a farre off.

It causeth me therefore to remember that not long after these reasoninges were had, cruell death bereaved our house of three most rare gentlemen, when in their prosperous age and forwardnesse of honour[2] they most flourished.

And of them the first was the Lord Gaspar Pallavicine, who assaulted with a sharpe disease, and more than once brought to the last cast, although his minde was of such courage that for a time in spite of death hee kept the soule and bodie together, yet did he end his natural course long before he came to his ripe age.

A very great losse, not in our house onely, and to his friendes and kinsfolke, but to his Countrie and to all Lumbardie.

Not long after dyed the Lord Cesar Gonzaga, which to all that were acquainted with him, left a bitter and sorrowfull remembrance of his death. For since nature so seldom times bringeth forth such kinde of men, as she doth, meete it seemed that she should not so soone have bereaved us of him. For undoubtedly a man may say that the Lord Cesar was taken from us even at the very time when hee began to shew more than a hope[3] of himselfe, and to bee esteemed as his excellent

---

[1] "Communicatiō": cf. "discussions."
[2] "Prosperous age," etc.: cf. "flower of robust age and hope of honour."
[3] "Shew more than a hope": cf. "give more than a promise."

qualities deserved. For with many vertuous acts he alreadie
gave a good testimonie of his worthinesse, and beside his noblenesse of birth, he excelled also in the ornamēt of letters, of
marciall prowesse, and of every worthie qualitie. So that for
his goodnesse, wit, nature, and knowledge,[1] there was nothing
so high, that might not have beene hoped for at his hands.

Within a short while after the death of maister Robert of
Bary was also a great heavinesse to yᵉ whole house: for reason
seemed to perswade every man to take heavily the death of a
yong man of good behaviour, pleasant and most rare in the
beautie of physnomie, and in the making of his person, with a
luckie and lively towardnes,[2] as a man coulde have wished.

These men therefore, had they lived, I believe woulde have
come to passe, that unto who so had knowne them, they woulde
have shewed a manifest proofe, how much the Court of Urbin
was worthie to bee commended, and how furnished it was with
noble knights, which (in a manner) all yᵉ rest have done that
were brought up in it.

For truely there never issued out of the horse of Troy so many
great men and Captains, as there have come men out of this
house for vertue verie singular and in great estimation with
all men.

For as you know Sir Frederick Fregoso was made Archbishoppe
of Salerno, Count Lewis, bishop of Baious. The Lorde Octavian
Fregoso, Duke of Genua: maister Bernarde Bibiena, Cardinall
of Sancta Maria in Portico: maister Peter Bembo, Secretarie
to Pope Leo. The Lord Julian was exalted to the Dukedome of
Nemours, and to the great estate he is presently in. The Lord
Francesco Maria della Rovere generall of Rome, he was also
made Duke of Urbin: although a much more prayse may be
given to the house where hee was brought up, that in it he
hath proved so rare and excellent a Lord in all vertuous qualities,
(as a man may behold) than that hee attained unto the Dukedom
of Urbin.

And no small cause thereof (I thinke) was the noble companie
where in dayly conversatiõ he alwaies heard and saw commendable nourture.

Therefore (mee thinke) whether it bee by happe, or through
the favour of the starres, the same cause that so long a time
hath graunted unto Urbin very good governours, doth still
continue and bringeth forth the like effects. And therefore it is

---

[1] "Goodnesse," etc.: cf. "goodness, capacity, courage, and wisdom."
[2] "Luckie and lively," etc.: cf. "of very rare personal grace."

to be hoped, that prosperous fortune will still encrease these so vertuous doinges, that the happinesse of the house, and of the state shall not onely not diminish, but rather dayly encrease: And thereof we see alreadie many evidēt tokens, among which I reckon the chiefest to bee, that the heaven hath graunted such a Ladie as is the Ladie Eleonor Gonzaga the new Dutchesse.

For if ever there were coupled in one bodie alone, knowledge, wit, grace, beautie, sober conversatiō, gentlenesse, and every other honest qualitie, in her they are so linked together, that there is made thereof a chaine, which frameth and setteth forth everie gesture of hers, with all these conditions together.

Let us therefore proceede in our reasoninges upon the Courtier, with hope that after us there shall not wante such as shal take notable and worthy examples of vertue at the present Court of Urbin, as wee now doe at the former.

It was thought therfore (as the L. Gaspar Pallavicin was wont to rehearse) that the next day after the reasoninges conteyned in the last booke, the L. Octavian was not muche seene: for manye deemed that hee had gotten himselfe out of company to thinke well upon that he had to say without trouble.[1]

Therefore when the company was assembled at the accustomed houre where the Dutchesse was, they made the L. Octavian to bee diligently sought for, which in a good while appeared not, so that many of the Gentlemen and Damosels of the Court fell to dauncing and to mind other pastimes, supposing for that night they shoulde have no more talke of the Courtier. And now were they all setled about one thing or an other, when the Lorde Octavian came in (almost) no more looked for.

And beholding the Lorde Cesar Gonzaga and the L. Gasper dauncing, after hee had made his reverence to the Dutchesse, he saide smyling: I had well hoped wee should have heard the Lorde Gaspar speak some ill of women this night too, but since I see him daunce with one, I imagine he is agreed withall. And I am glad that the controversie, or (to terme it better) the reasoning of the Courtier is thus ended.

Not ended, I warrant you, answered the Dutchesse, for I am not such an enimie to men, as you be to women, and therefore I will not have the Courtier bereaved from his due honour and the ornaments which you your selfe promised him yesternight.

And when that she had thus spoken, she commanded them all after that dance was ended, to place themselves after the

[1] Cf. "that he might without hindrance think carefully . . ."

wonted manner, the which was done. And as they stood all with heedfull expectation, the Lord Octavian saide.

Madam, since for that I wished many other good qualities in the Courtier, it followeth by promise that I must entreat upon them, I am well willing to utter my minde: not with opinion that I can speake all that may be saide in the matter, but onely so much as shall suffice to roote that out of your minde, which yesternight was objected to mee: namely that I speake it more to withdraw the prayses from the gentlewoman of the Pallace, in doing you falsely to believe,[1] that other excellent qualities might be added to the Courtier, and with that pollicie preferre him before her, than for that it is so in deede.

Therefore to frame my selfe also to the houre, which is later than it was wont to be, when wee beganne our reasonings at other times, I will be briefe.

Thus continuing in the talke that these Lordes have ministred, which I full and wholy allow and confirme, I say, that of thinges which we call good, some there bee that simply and of themselves are alwaies good, as temperance, valiant courage, health, and all vertues that bring quietnesse to mens mindes. Other be good for divers respects and for the end they be applied unto, as the lawes, liberallitie, riches, and other like.

I thinke therefore that the Courtier (if he be of the perfection that Count Lewis and Sir Frederick have described him) may indeede bee a good thing and worthy praise, but for all that not simply, nor of himself but for respect of that whereto he may be applied.

For doubtlesse if the Courtier with his noblenes of birth, comely behaviour, pleasantnesse and practise in so manye exercises, shoulde bring foorth no other fruite, but to be such a one for himselfe, I would not thinke to come by this perfect trade of Courtiershippe, that a man should of reason bestow so much studie and paines about it, as who so will compasse it must do. But I would say rather that many of the qualities appointed him, as dauncing, singing, and sporting, were lightnes and vanitie, and in a man of estimation rather to be dispraised than commended.

Because those precise fashions, the setting forth of ones selfe, merry talke[2] and such other matters belōging to entertainement of women and love (although perhaps many other be of a contrarie opinion) doe many times nothing els but womanish

---

[1] "In doing," etc.: cf. "by raising a false belief."
[2] "Fashions," etc.: cf. "elegancies, devices, mottoes."

the mindes, corrupt youth, and bring them to a most wanton trade of living: whereupon afterwarde ensue these effects, that the name of Italy is brought into slaunder: and few there bee that have the courage, I will not say to jeopard their life, but to enter once into a daunger.

And without peradventure there bee infinite other thinges, that if a man bestow his labour and studie about them, woulde bring forth much more profit both in peace and warre, than this trade of Courtiership of it selfe alone.

But in case the Courtiers doings be directed to the good ende they ought to be, and which I meane: mee thinke then they should not only not be hurtful or vaine, but most profitable, and deserve infinite prayse.

The ende therefore of a perfect Courtier (whereof hetherto nothing hath beene spoken) I believe is to purchase him, by the meane of the qualities which these Lordes have given him, in such wise the good will and favour of the Prince he is in service withall, that he may breake his minde to him, and alwaies enforme him franckly of the truth of every matter meete for him to understand, without fear or perill to displease him. And when hee knoweth his [1] minde is bent to commit any thing unseemely for him, to be bold to stand with [2] him in it, and to take courage after an honest sorte at the favor which he hath gotten him through his good qualities, to disswade him from every ill purpose, and to set him in the way of vertue. And so shall the Courtier, if he have the goodnesse in him that these Lordes have given him accompanied with readinesse of wit, pleasantnesse, wisedom, knowledge in letters, and so many other thinges, understand how to behave himselfe readily in all occurrents to drive into his Princes heade [3] what honour and profit shall ensue to him and to his by justice, liberallitie, valiantnesse of courage, meekenesse, and by the other vertues that belong to a good prince, and contrariwise what slander, and damage commeth of the vices contrarie to them.

And therefore in mine opinion, as musicke, sportes, pastimes, and other pleasant fashions, are (as a man woulde say) the floure of Courtlinesse, even so is the training and helping forwarde of the Prince to goodnesse, and the fearing him from evil, the fruite of it.

And because the prayses of well doing cōsisteth chiefly in two pointes, whereof the one is, in choosing out an end that

---

[1] "His": cf. "his prince's."　　　　　[2] Cf. "oppose."
[3] "Drive into his," etc.: cf. "be able deftly to show."

our purpose is directed unto, that is good in deede, the other, the knowledge to finde out apt and meete meanes to bring it to the appointed good ende: sure it is that the minde of him which thinketh to worke so, that his Prince shall not bee deceived, nor lead with flatterers, railers, and lyers, but shall know both the good and the bad, and beare love to the one, and hatred to the other, is directed to a verie good end.

Me thinke againe, that the qualities which these Lords have given the Courtier, may bee a good meanes to compasse it: and that, because among many vices that we see now a dayes in many of our Princes, the greatest are ignorance and selfe liking.

And the roote of these two mischiefes is nothing els but lying, which vice is worthely abhorred of God and man, and more hurtfull to Princes than any other, because they have more scarcitie than of any thing els, of that which they neede to have more plentie of, than of any other thing: namely, of such as should tell them the truth, and put them in mind of goodnesse: for enimies bee not driven of love to doe these offices, but they delight rather to have them live wickedly and never to amend: on the other side, they dare not rebuke them openly for feare they be punished.

As for friendes, few of them have free passage to them, and those few have a respect to reprehend their vices so freely as they doe private mens. And many times to currie favour and to purchase good will, they give themselves to nothing els but to feede them with matters that may delight and content their minde, though they be foule and dishonest. So that of friendes they become flatterers.

And to make a hand [1] by that straight familiaritie, they speake and worke alwaies to please, and for the most part open the way with lyes, which in the Princes minde engender ignorance, not of outwarde matters onely, but also of his owne selfe. And this may be saide to be the greatest and foulest lye of all other, because the ignorant minde deceiveth himselfe, and inwardly maketh lies of himselfe.

Of this it commeth, that great men, beside that they never understand the truth of any thing, drunken with the licentious libertie that rule bringeth with it, and with aboundance of delicats drowned in pleasures, are so farre out of the way, and their minde is so corrupted in seeing themselves alwaies obeied, and (as it were) worshipped with so much reverence and praise, without not onely any reproofe at all, but also gainsaying, that

[1] Cf. "profit."

through this ignorance they wade to an extreame selfe liking,[1] so that afterwarde they admit no counsell nor advise of others.

And because they believe that the understanding how to rule is a most easie matter, and to compasse it, there needeth neither arte nor learning, but onely stoutnesse, they bend their mind and all their thoughts to the maintenance of that porte they keepe, thinking it the true happinesse to do what a man lusteth.

Therefore doe some abhorre reason and justice, because they weene it a bridle and a certain meane to bring them in bondage, and to minish in them the contentation and hearts ease that they have to beare rule, if they should observe it: and their rule were not perfect nor whole, if they should be compelled to obey unto duetie and honestie, because they have opinion, that Who so obeyeth, is no right Lorde in deede.

Therefore taking these principles for a president, and suffering themselves to bee leade with selfe liking, they waxe lofty, and with a stately countenance, with sharpe and cruell conditions,[2] with pompous garments, golde and jewels, and with comming (in a manner) never abroad to be seene, they thinke to get estimation and authoritie among men, and to bee counted (almost) Gods.

But they are (in my judgement) like the Colosses that were made in Rome the last year upon the feast daye of the place of Agone, which outwardly declared a likenesse of great men and horses of triumph, and inwardly were full of towe and ragges.

But the Princes of this sorte are so much worse, as the Colosses by their owne waighty peise stand upright of themselves, and they because they be ill counterpeised, and without line and levell placed upon unequall ground, through their owne waightines overthrow them selves, and from one errour runne into infinite. Because their ignorance being annexed with this false opinion, that they can not erre, and that the port they keepe commeth of their knowledge, leadeth them every way by right or by wrong to lay hand upon possessions boldly, so they may come by them. But in case they would take advisement to know and to worke that that they ought, they would as well strive not to raigne, as they doe to raigne.

Because they should perceive what a naughtie and dangerous matter it were for subjects that ought to be governed, to be wiser than the Princes that should governe.

[1] Cf. "boundless self-esteem."    [2] Cf. "haughty looks and stern behaviour."

You may see that ignorance in musicke, in dancing, in riding, hurteth no man, yet he that is no musition is ashamed and afraide to sing in the presence of others, or to daunce, he that can not, or he that sitteth not well a horse to ride.

But of the unskilfulnesse to governe people arise so many evils, deathes, destructions, mischiefes, and confusions, that it may bee called the deadlyest plague upon the earth. And yet some Princes most ignorant in governement, are not bashfull nor ashamed to take upon them to governe, I wil not say in the presence of foure, or halfe a dosen persons, but in the face of the world: for their degree is set so on loft, that all eyes beholde them, and therefore not their great vices onely, but their least faults of all are continually noted.

As it is written, that Cimon was ill spoken of because he loved wine, Scipio, sleepe, Lucullus, banquets. But would God the Princes of these our times would couple their vices with so many vertues, as did they of olde time: which if they were out of the way in any point, yet refused they not the exhortations and lessons of such as they deemed meete to correct those faultes: Yea they sought with great instance to frame their life by the rule of notable personages: As Epaminondas by Lysias of Pythagoras sect: Agesilaus by Xenophon: Scipio by Panetius, and infinite others.

But in case a grave Philosopher shoulde come before any of our Princes, or who ever beside, that would shew them plainly and without anie circumstance the horrible[1] face of true vertue, and teach them good manners, and what the life of a good Prince ought to be, I am assured they woulde abhorre him at the first sight, as a most venemous serpent, or els they woulde make him a laughing stocke, as a most vile matter.[2]

I say therefore, that since now a days Princes are so corrupt through ill usages, ignorance and false selfe liking, and that it is so harde a matter to give them the knowledge of the truth, and to bend them to vertue, and men with lyes and flatterie, and such naughtie meanes seeke to currie favour with them, the Courtier by the meane of those honest[3] qualities that Count Lewis and Sir Fredericke have given him, may soone,[4] and ought to goe about so to purchase him the good will, and allure unto him ye mind of his Prince, that he may make him a free and safe passage to commune with him in every matter without troubling him.[5] And if he be such a one as is saide, hee shall

---

[1] "Horrible": cf. "frightful."  [2] Cf. "thing."  [3] Cf. "gentle."
[4] "May soone": cf. "can with ease."  [5] Cf. "being irksome."

compasse it with small paine, and so may he alwaies open unto him the trueth of every matter at ease.

Beside this, by litle and litle distil into his mind goodnesse, and teach him continencie, stoutnesse of courage, justice, temperance, making him to tast what sweetnesse is hid under that litle bitternesse, which at the first sight appeareth unto him that withstandeth vices, which are alwaies hurtfull, displeasant and accompanied with ill report and shame, even as vertues are profitable, pleasant and prayseable, and enflame him to them with examples of manye famous captaines, and of other notable personages, unto whome they of olde time used to make images of mettall and marble, and sometime of golde, and to set them up in common haunted places, as well for the honour of them, as for an encouraging of others, that with an honest envie they might also endevor themselves to reach unto that glorie.

In this wise may hee leade him through the rough way of vertue (as it were) decking it aboute with boughes to shadow it, and strowing it over with sightlye flowers, to ease the griefe of the painefull jorney in him that is but of a weake force. And sometime with musicke, sometime with armes, and horses, sometime with rymes, and meeter, otherwhile with communication of love, and with all those waies that these Lords have spoken of, continually keepe that minde of his occupied in honest pleasure [1]: imprinting notwithstanding therein alwaies beside (as I have saide) in company with these flickering provocations [2] some vertuous condition, and beguiling him with a holesom craft, as the warie Phisitions doe, who many times when they minister to yong and tender children in their sicknesse, a medicine of a bitter taste, annoint the cup about the brimme with some sweete licour.

The Courtier therefore applying to such a purpose this veile of pleasure, in every time, in every place, and in everie exercise he shall attain to his end, and deserve much more praise and recompence, than for any other good worke that he can doe in the world.

Because there is no treasure that doth so universally profit, as doth a good prince, nor any mischiefe so universally hurt, as an ill Prince. Therefore is there also no paine so bitter and cruel that were a sufficient punishment for those naughtie and wicked Courtiers, that make their honest and pleasant manners, and their good qualities a cloake for an ill end, and by meane

---

[1] "Honest pleasure": cf. "worthy pleasures."
[2] "Flickering provocations": cf. "allurements."

of them seeke to come in favour with their Princes for to corupt them, and to cause them to stray from the way of vertue, and to lead them to vice.

For a man may say, that such as these be, doe infect with deadly poyson, not one vessel whereof one man alone drinketh, but the common fountaine that all the people resorteth to.

The Lord Octavian helde his peace, as though hee woulde have saide no more, but the Lord Gaspar, I can not see my Lorde Octavian (saide he) that this goodnesse of mind and continencie, and the other vertues which you will have the Courtier to shew his Lord, may bee learned: but I suppose that they are given the men that have them, by nature and of God.

And that it is so, you may see that there is no man so wicked and of so ill conditions in the world, nor so untemperate and unjust, which if he be asked the question, will confesse himselfe such a one. But every man be he never so wicked, is glad to be counted just, continent and good: which should not be so, in case these vertues might be learned.

Because it is no shame not to know the thing that a man hath not studied, but a rebuke,[1] it is not to have that which wee ought to be endowed withall of nature.

Therefore doth each man seeke to cover the defaultes of nature, as well in the mind, as also in y⁰ bodie: the which is to bee seene in the blinde, lame, crooked and other maimed and deformed creatures. For although these imperfections may be laide to nature, yet doth it greeve each man to have them in himself: because it seemeth by the testimonie of the selfe same nature that a man hath that default or blemish (as it were) for a patent and token of his ill inclination.

The fable that is reported of Epimetheus doth also confirme mine opinion, which was so unskilfull in dividing the giftes of nature unto men, that hee left them much more needy of every thing, than all other living creatures.

Whereupon Prometheus stole the politike wisedome[2] from Minerva and Vulcan that men have to get their living withall. Yet had they not for all that, civil wisedom to gather themselves together into Cities, and the knowledge to live with civilitie, because it was kept in the Castle of Jupiter by most circumspect overseers, which put Prometheus in such feare that hee durst not approch nigh them. Whereupon Jupiter taking pitie upon the miserie of men, that coulde not fellowship together for lacke of civill vertue, but were torne in peeces by wilde beastes, he

---

[1] "Rebuke": cf. "reproach."　　　　　[2] Cf. "artful cunning."

sent Mercurie to the earth to carrie justice and shame, that these two things might furnish cities, and gather citizens together.

And willed that they should be given them, not as other artes were, wherein one cunning man sufficeth for many ignorant, as Phisicke, but that they shoulde be imprinted in every man. And ordeined a law, that all such as were without justice and shame, shoulde be banished and put to death as contagious to the Citie.

Behold then (my Lorde Octavian) God hath graunted these vertues to men, and they are not to be learned, but be naturall.

Then the Lord Octavian somewhat smiling: will you then my Lord Gaspar (quoth he) have men to be so unfortunate and of so peevish a judgement, that with policie they have founde out an arte to tame the natures of wilde beastes and beares, wolves, Lions, and may with the same teach a pretie bird to flie as a man list, and returne backe from the wood and from his naturall libertie of his owne accorde to snares and bondage, and with the same policie can not or wil not find out artes wherby they may profit themselves, and with studie and diligence make their minde more perfect?

This (in mine opinion) were like as if Phisitions should studie with all diligence to have the arte onely to heale fellons in fingers, and the red gumme in yong children, and laye aside the cure of fevers, pleurisie and other sore diseases, the which how out of reason it were every man may consider.

I believe therefore that the morall vertues are not in us altogether by nature, because nothing can at any time be accustomed unto it, that is naturally his contrarie: as it is seene in a stone, the which though it bee cast upward ten thousand times, yet will he never accustome to goe up of it selfe.

Therefore in case vertues were as naturall to us, as heavinesse to the stone, wee should never accustome our selves to vice.

Nor yet are vices natural in this sorte, for then should we never be vertuous: and a great wickednesse and folly it were, to punish men for their faults, that came of nature without our offence.

And this errour shoulde the lawes commit, which appoint not punishment to the offenders for the trespasse that is past, because it can not be brought to passe, that the thing that is done, may not be done, but they have a respect to the time to come, that who so hath offended may offend no more, or els with ill president give not a cause for others to offend. And thus yet they are in opinion, that vertues may be learned, which is most true, because we are borne apt to receive them, and in like manner vices.

And therefore there groweth a custome in us of both the one and yᵉ other through long use, so that first we practise vertue or vice, after that, we are vertuous or vitious.

The contrarie is known in the thinges that bee given us of nature, for first wee have the power to practise them, after that wee doe practise: as it is in the senses, for first we can see, heare, feele, after that, we do see, heare and feele: although notwithstanding many of these doinges bee also set out more sightly with teaching.

Whereupon good schoolemaisters doe not onely instruct their children in letters, but also in good nurture, in eating, drinking, talking, and going, with certaine gestures meete for the purpose.

Therefore even as in the other artes, so also in the vertues it is behofefull to have a teacher, that with lessons and good exhortations may stirre up and quicken in us those moral vertues, whereof wee have the seede inclosed and buried in the soule, and like the good husbandman till them and open the way for them, weeding from about them the briers and darnell of appetites, which many times so shadow and choke our mindes, that they suffer them not to budde nor to bring forth the happie fruites, which alone ought to be wished to growe in the harts of men.

In this sorte then is naturally in every one of us justice and shame, which you say Jupiter sent to the earth for all men. But even as a bodie without eyes, how sturdie soever he be, if he remove to any certaine place, ofttimes faileth: so the roote of these vertues that be potentially engendred in our mindes, if it bee not aided with teaching, doth often come to nought.[1] Because if it shoulde bee brought into doing, and to his perfect custome, it is not satisfied (as is saide) with nature alone: but hath neede of a politike usage and of reason, which may clense and scoure that soule, taking away the dim vaile of ignorance, whereof arise (in a manner) all the errours of men.

For in case good and ill were well knowne and perceived, every man woulde alwaies choose the good, and shunne the ill. Therefore may vertue be saide to be (as it were) a wisedom and an understanding to choose the good: and vice, a lacke of foresight and an ignorance that leadeth to judge falsely. Because

---

[1] Cf. "for if it is to ripen into action and perfect character, nature alone is not enough."

men never choose the ill with opinion that it is ill, but they are deceived through a certaine likenesse of good.

Then answered the Lorde Gaspar: yet are there many that know plainely they doe ill, and doe it notwithstanding, and that because they more esteeme the present pleasure which they feele, than the punishment that they doubt shall fall upon them, as theeves, murtherers and such other.

The Lord Octavian saide: true pleasure is alwaies good, and true sorrow, evil: therefore these be deceived in taking false pleasure for true, and true sorrow for false: whereupon manye times through false pleasures, they run into true displeasures.

The arte therefore that teacheth to discerne this truth from falshood, may in like case be learned: and the vertue by the which wee choose this good in deede, and not that which falsely appeareth to be, may bee called true knowledge, and more available for mans life, than any other, because it expelleth ignorance, of the which (as I have saide) spring all evil.

Then maister Peter Bembo, I wot not my Lord Octavian (quoth hee) how the Lorde Gaspar should graunt you, that of ignorance should spring all evils, and that there be not many which in offending know for certaintie that they doe offend, neither are they any deale deceived in the true pleasure, nor yet in the true sorrow, because it is sure that such as be incontinent, judge with reason and uprightly, and knowe it, whereunto they are provoked by lust contrarie to due, to be ill, and therefore they make resistance and set reason to match greedie desire, whereupon ariseth the battaile of pleasure and sorrow against judgement.

Finally reason overcome by greedy desire, farre the mightier, is cleane without succour, like a ship, that for a time defendeth her selfe from the tempestuous sea-stormes, at the end beaten with the too raging violence of windes, her gables and tacklinges broken, yeeldeth up to be driven at the will of fortune, without occupying helme or any manner helpe of Pilot for her safegarde.

Forthwith therefore commit they the offences with a certaine doubtfull remorse of conscience, and (in a manner) whether they will or no, the which they woulde not doe, unlesse they knewe the thing that they doe to be ill, but without striving of reason would runne wholy headlong after greedie desire, and then should they not be incontinent, but untemperate, which is much worse.

Therefore is incontinencie saide to bee a diminished vice, because it hath in it a part of reason, and likewise continencie an unperfect vertue, because it hath in it part of affection:[1] therefore mee thinke that it can not be said that the offences of the incontinent come of ignorance, or that they bee deceived and offend not, when they know for a truth that they doe offend.

The Lord Octavian answered: Certesse (maister Peter) your argumēt is good, yet (in my minde) it is more apparant than true.[2] For although the incontinent offend with that doubtfulnesse, and reason in their minde striveth against greedie desire, and that that is ill seemeth unto them to be ill in deed, yet have they no perfect knowledge of it, nor understand it so throughly as need requireth.

Therefore of this, it is rather a feeble opinion in them, than certaine knowledge, whereby they agree[3] to have reason overcome by affection: but if they had in them true knowledge, there is no doubt, but they woulde not offend: because evermore the thing whereby greedy desire overcommeth reason, is ignorance, neither can true knowledge bee ever overcome by affection, that proceedeth from the bodie and not from the minde, and in case that it be well ruled and governed by reason, it becommeth a vertue: if not, it becommeth a vice.

But such force reason hath, that she maketh the sense alwaies to obey, and by wondrous meanes and waies perceth, lest ignorance should possesse[4] that which she ought to have: so that although the spirits and the sinewes and the bones have no reason in them, yet when there springeth in us the motion of minde, that the imagination (as it were) pricketh forwarde, and shaketh the bridle to the spirits, all the members are in a readinesse, the feete to runne, the handes to take or to doe that which the mind thinketh upon.

And this is also manifestly knowne in many, which unwittingly otherwhile eate some lothsom and abhorring meate, but so wel dressed that to their taste it appeareth most delicate: afterward understanding what manner thing it was, it doth not onely greeve them and loath them in their mind, but the bodie also agreeth with the judgement of the minde, that of force they cast that meat up againe.

The Lord Octavian followed on still in his talke, but the Lorde Julian interrupting him. My Lord Octavian (quoth he) if I have well understood, you have saide that Continencie is

---

[1] "Affection": cf. "passion."
[2] "Apparant than true": cf. "specious than sound."
[3] "Agree": cf. "allow."
[4] "Perceth," etc.: cf. "enters in . . ., provided ignorance does not possess . . ."

an unperfect vertue, because it hath in it part of affection: and me seemeth that the vertue (where there is in our mind a variance betwen reason and greedie desire) which fighteth and giveth the victory to reason, ought to be reckoned more perfect, than that which overcommeth, having neither greedie desire nor any affectiō to withstand it.

Because (it seemeth) that that minde abstaineth not from ill for vertues sake, but refraineth the doing it, because he hath no will to it.

Then the Lord Octavian, which (quoth he) woulde you esteeme the valianter Captaine, either he that hazardeth himselfe in open fight, and notwithstanding vanquisheth his enimies, or hee that by his vertue and knowledge weakeneth them in bringing them in case not able to fight, and so without battaile or any jeopardie discomfit them?

He (quoth the Lorde Julian) that overcommeth with most suretie, is out of doubt most to bee praised, so that this assured victorie of his proceede not through the slacknesse of the enimies.

The Lorde Octavian answered: you have judged aright. And therefore I say unto you, that continencie may be compared to a Captaine that fighteth manly, and though his enimies bee strong and well appointed, yet giveth he them the overthrow, but for all that not without much ado and danger. But temperance free from all disquieting, is like the Captaine that without resistance overcommeth and raigneth. And having in the mind where she is, not onely aswaged, but cleane quenched the fire of greedy desire, even as a good prince in civil warre dispatcheth the seditious inward enimies, and giveth the scepter and whole rule to reason.

So in like case this vertue not enforcing the mind, but pouring thereinto through most quiet waies a vehement perswasion that may incline him to honestie, maketh him quiet and full of rest, in every part equall and of good proportion: and on every side framed of a certaine agreement with himself, that filleth him with such a cleare calmenesse, that hee is never out of patience: and becommeth wholy and most obedient to reason, and readie to turne unto her all his motions, and follow her where she lust to leade him, without any resistance, like a tender lambe that runneth, standeth and goeth alwaies by the Ewes side, and moveth onely as he seeth her doe.

This vertue therefore is most perfect, and is chiefely requisite in Princes, because of it arise many other.

Then the Lorde Cesar Gonzaga, I wot not (quoth he) what

vertues requisit for princes may arise of this temperance, if it be she that riddeth the minde of affections (as you say) which perhaps were meete for some Monke, or Heremite, but I can not see how it shoulde be requisite for a Prince that is couragious, freeharted, and of prowesse in martiall feats, for whatsoever is done to him, never to have anger, hatred, good will, disdaine, lust, nor any affection in him: nor how without this he can get him authoritie among the people and souldiers.

The Lorde Octavian answered: I have not said that temperance should throughly rid and root out of mens mindes affections: neither should it bee well so to doe, because there bee yet in affections some parts good: but that which in affections is corrupt and striving against honestie, she bringeth to obey unto reason.

Therefore it is not meete, to ridde the troublesom disquietnesse of the minde, to roote up affections cleane, for this were as if to avoide dronkennesse, there shoulde be an acte established, that no man should drinke wine: or because otherwhile in running a man taketh a fall, every man shoulde bee forbid running.

Marke them that breake horses, they breake them not from their running and comming on loft,[1] but they will have them to doe it at the time and obedience of the rider.

The affections therefore that be cleansed and tried by temperance are assistant to vertue, as anger, that helpeth manlinesse: hatred against the wicked helpeth justice, and likewise the other vertues are aided by affections, which in case they were clean taken away, they woulde leave reason very feeble and faint, so that it shoulde litle prevaile, like a shipmaister that is without winde in a great calme.

Marvell ye not then (my Lorde Cesar) if I have saide, that of temperance arise many other vertues: for when a minde is in tune with this harmony, by the meane of reason he easily received afterwarde true manlinesse, which maketh him bold and safe from all daunger, and (in a manner) above worldlye passions. Likewise justice an undefiled virgin, friende to sober mood and goodnesse, Queene of all other vertues, because she teacheth to doe that which a man ought to doe, and to shun that a man ought to shunne, and therefore is the most perfect, because through her the works of the other vertues are brought to passe, and she is a helpe to him that hath her both for himselfe and for others: without the which (as it is commonly saide) Jupiter himselfe could not well governe his kingdom.

---

[1] "Comming on loft": cf. "leaping."

Stoutnesse of courage [1] doth also follow after these, and maketh them all the greater, but she can not stand alone, because who so hath not other vertues, can not be of a stout courage.

Of these then wisedom is guide, which consisteth in a certaine judgement to choose well. And in this happie chaine are also lincked liberallitie, sumpteousnesse,[2] the desire to save a mans estimation, meekenesse, pleasantnesse, courtesie in talke, and many other which is now no time to speake of.

But in case our Courtier will doe as we have saide, he shall finde them all in his Princes minde: and dayly he shall see spring such beautifull floures and fruites, as all the delicious gardens in the world have not the like: and he shall feele very great contentation within himself, when he remembreth that he hath given him, not yᵉ things which foolish persons give, which is, golde, or silver, plate, garments, and such matters, whereof he that giveth them hath himselfe very great scarcitie, and he that receiveth them exceeding great store: but that vertue, which perhaps among all the matters that belong unto man is the chiefest and rarest, that is to say, the manner and way to rule and to raigne in the right kinde. Which alone were sufficient to make men happie, and to bring once againe into the world the golden age, which is written to have beene whē Saturnus raigned in the olde time.

Here, when the Lord Octavian had paused a litle as though he woulde have taken respite, the Lorde Gaspar saide: which reckon you (my Lord Octavian) the happiest government and that were most to purpose to bring into the world againe that golden age which you have made mention of, either the raigne of so good a Prince, or the governmēt of so good a common weale?

The Lorde Octavian answered, I woulde alwaies preferre the raigne of a good Prince, because it is a good governement more agreeable to nature, and if it bee lawfull to compare small matters with infinite, more like unto Gods, which one and alone governeth the universall.

But leaving this, ye see that in whatsoever is broght to passe with the pollicie of man, as armies, great sayling vessels, buildinges and other like matters, the whole is committed to one alone, to dispose thereof at his will.

Likewise in our bodie all the members travaile and are occupied

---

[1] "Stoutnesse of courage": cf. "magnanimity" —in the Aristotelian sense of the entire greatness of life.
[2] Cf. "magnificence."

as the hart thinketh good. Beside this, it seemeth meete that people should as well bee governed by one Prince, as many other living creatures bee, whom nature teacheth this obedience, as a most soveraigne matter.[1]

Marke ye whether Deere, Cranes, and many other foules, when they take their flight doe not alwaies set a Prince before, whom they follow and obey. And Bees (as it were) with discourse of reason, and with such reverence honour their King, as the most obedientest people in the world can do.

And therefore all this is a verie great argument that the soveraigntie of a Prince is more according to nature, than a common weales.

Then maister Peter Bembo: and me thinke (quoth he) that since God hath given libertie for a soveraigne gift, it is not reason that it should be taken from us: nor that one man should be partner of it more than another, which happeneth under the rule of Princes, who for the most part keepe their people in most straight bondage. But in common weales wel in order this libertie is well kept.

Beside that, both in judgements and in advisements it happeneth oftener that the opinion of one alone is false, than the opinion of many, because troublous affection either through anger, or through spite, or through lust, sooner entreth into the minde of one alone than into the multitudes, which (in a manner) like a great quantitie of water, is less subject to corruption, than a small deale.

I say againe, that the example of the beastes and foules doth not make to purpose, for both Deere and Cranes and the rest doe not alwaies set one and the selfe formost for them to follow and obey, but they stil change and varie, giving this preferment sometime to one, otherwhile to another, and in this manner it becommeth rather the forme of a common weale, than of a kingdom, and this may be called a true and equall libertie, when they that sometime command, obey againe an otherwhile.

The example likewise of the Bees (me thinke) is not alike, because that king of theirs is not of their owne kinde: And therefore he that will give unto men a worthy head in deede, must bee faine to finde him of another kind, and of a more noble nature than mans, if men (of reason) shoulde obey him, as flockes and heardes of cattell that obey, not a beast their like, but a shepeheard and a heardman, which is a man and of a more worthie kinde, than theirs.

[1] Cf. "salutary."

For these respects, I think (my Lord Octavian) the government of a cōmon weale is more to be coveted, than of a king.

Then the Lord Octavian, against your opinion, maister Peter (quoth he) I will alleage but one reason: which is, that of waies to rule people well, there be onely three kindes. The one a kingdome. The other, the rule of good men, which they of olde time called Optimates. The third, the government of the people.

And the transgressing[1] (to terme it so) and contrarie vice that every one of these is changed into being appaired and corrupted, is when the kingdome becommeth a Tyranny: and when the governance of good men is chaunged into the handes of a few great men and not good: and when the rule of the people is at the disposition of the communalty,[2] which making a meddlie[3] of the orders, suffereth the governance of the whole at the will[4] of the multitude.

Of these three ill governments (it is sure) the tyranny is the worst of all, as it may be proved by many reasons. It followeth then, that of the three good, the kingdom is the best, because it is contrarie to the worst, for (as you know) the effects of contrarie causes, they be also contrarie among themselves.

Now as touching it, that you have spoken of libertie, I answere, that true libertie ought not to be saide, to live as a man will, but to live according to good lawes. And to obey is no lesse naturall, profitable and necessary, than to command. And some thinges are borne and so appointed and ordained by nature to command, as some other to obeysance.

Truth it is, that there bee two kinds of bearing rule, the one Lordly and forcible, as maisters over slaves, and in this[5] doth the soule command the bodie. The other more milde and tractable, as good Princes by way of the lawes over their subjectes, and in this reason commandeth greedy desire. And eche of these two waies is profitable: because the bodie is created of nature apt to obey the soule, and so is desire, reason.

There be also many men whose doinges bee applyed[6] onely about the use of the bodie: and such as these bee are so farre wide from the vertues, as the soule from the bodie, and yet because[7] they be reasonable creatures, they be so much partners of reason, as they doe no more but know it, for they possesse it not, ne yet have they the use of it.

---

[1] "Transgressing": cf. "excess."  [2] Cf. "rabble."
[3] "Making a meddlie": cf. "breaks down distinctions."
[4] Cf. "caprice."  [5] "In this": cf. "in this way.'
[6] "Bee applyed": cf. "have to do."  [7] "Because": cf. "although."

These therefore be naturally bondmen, and better it is for them, and more profitable to obey, than to beare sway.

Then saide the Lord Gaspar: In what manner wise be they then to bee commanded that be discret and vertuous, and not by nature bound?

The Lorde Octavian answeared: With that tractable commaundement[1] kingly and civill. And to such it is well done otherwhile to committe the bearing of such offices as be meete for them, that they may likewise beare sway and rule over others of lesse wit than they bee, yet so that the principall governement may full and wholy depend upon the chiefe Prince.

And because you have said, that it is an easier matter to corrupt the mind of one, then of a great sort, I say, that it is also an easier matter to find one good and wise, than a great sort.[2] Both good and wise ought a man to suppose a king may be of a noble progeny, inclined to vertue of hys owne naturall motion, and through the famous memorie of his auncestors, and brought up in right good conditions. And though he be not of an other kinde than man, as you have saide is among the Bees, yet if he be helped forwarde with the instructions, bringing up, and arte of the Courtier, whom these Lordes have fashioned so wise and good, he shall bee most wise, most continent, most temperate, most manly, and most just, full of liberallitie, majestie, holinesse, and mercy: finally, hee shall be most glorious and most dearely beloved to God and man: through whose grace hee shall attaine unto that heroicall and noble vertue, that shall make him passe the boundes of the nature of man, and shall rather be called a demy God, than a man mortall. For God deliteth in and is the defender not of those Princes that will follow and counterfeit him in shewing great power, and make themselves to be worshipped of men, but of such as beside power, whereby they are mightie, endevour themselves to resemble him also in goodnesse and wisedom, wherby they may have a will and a knowledge to doe well and to bee his ministers, distributing for the behoufe of man the benefits and gifts that they receive of him.

Therefore even as in the firmament the sunne and the moone and the other starres shew to the worlde (as it were) in a glasse, a certaine likenesse of God: So upon the earth a much more liker image of God are those good Princes that love and worship him, and shew unto the people the cleare light of his justice,

---

[1] "Tractable commaundement": cf. "gentle rule."
[2] "A great sort": cf. "many."

accompanied with a shadow [1] of the heavenly reason and understanding.

And such as these be doth God make partners of his true
dealing, righteousnesse, justice and goodnesse, and of those
other happie benefits which I can not name, that disclose unto
the worlde a much more evident proofe of the Godhead, than
doth the light of the sunne, or the continuall turning of the
firmament with the sundrie course of the starres.

It is God therefore that hath appointed the people under
the custody of princes, which ought to have a diligent care
over them, that they may make him account of it, as good
stewardes doe their Lorde, and love them, and thinke their
owne, all the profit and losse that happeneth to them, and
principally above all things provide for their good estate and
welfare.

Therfore ought the prince not onely to be good, but also to
make others good, like the Carpenters square, that is not onely
straight and just it selfe, but also maketh straight and just
whatsoever it is occupied about.

And the greatest proofe that the Prince is good, is when the
people are good: because the life of the prince is a law and
ringleader of Citizens, and upon the conditions of him [2] must
needes all others depend: neither is it meete for one that is
ignorant, to teach: nor for him that is out of order, to give
order: nor for him that falleth, to helpe up an other.

Therefore if the Prince will execute these offices aright, it
is requisite that hee apply all his studie and diligence to get
knowledge, afterwarde to fashion within himselfe and observe
unchangeably in every thing the law of reason, not writtē in
papers or in mettall, but graven in his owne minde, that it
may be to him alwaies not onely familiar, but inwarde, and
live with him as a parcell of him: to the intent it may night and
day, in every time and place, admonish him, and speake to him
within his hart, ridding him of those troublous affections that
untemperate mindes feele, which because on the one side they
be (as it were) cast into a most deepe sleepe of ignorance, on
the other overwhelmed with the unquietnesse which they feele
through their wayward and blinde desires, they are stirred
with an unquiet rage, [3] as he that sleepeth otherwhile with
straunge and horrible visions.

Heaping then a great power upon their naughtie desire, there

[1] Cf. "reflection."     [2] Cf. "his behaviour."
[3] Cf. "tossed by a relentless fury."

*K 807

is heaped also a great trouble withall. And when the Prince can doe what he will, then is it great jeopardie lest hee will the thing that he ought not.

Therefore said Bias well, that promotiōs declare[1] what men be: for even as vessels while they are empty, though they have some chincke in them it can ill bee perceived, but if they be filled with licour, they shew by and by on what side the fault is, so corrupted and ill disposed mindes seldom discover their vices, but when they be filled with authoritie. For then they are not able to carrie the heavie burden of power, but forsake themselves, and scatter on every side greedy desire, pride, wrath, solemnesse,[2] and such tyrannicall fashions as they have within them.

Whereupon without regard they persecute the good and wise, and promote the wicked. And they can not abide to have friendship, assemblies and conferences among Citizens in Cities. But maintaine spies, promoters, murtherers and cutthroates to put men in feare and make them to become faint harted. And they sow debate and strife to keepe them in division and weake.

And of these manners insue infinite damages and the utter undoing of the poore people, and oftentimes cruel slaughter, or at the least continuall feare to the Tyrants themselves. For good Princes feare not for themselves, but for their sakes whome they rule over: and Tyrants feare very them whom they rule over.

Therefor the more number of people they rule over, and the mightier they are, the more is their feare, and the more enimies they have.

How fearefull (thinke ye) and of what unquiet minde was Clearcus Tiranne of Pontus every time he went into the market place, or into the theater, or to any banket, or other haunted place? For (as it is written) hee slept shut into a chest. Or Aristodemus of Argos, which of his bed had made to himselfe a prison (or litle better) for in his pallace hee had a litle roome hanging in the aire, and so high that hee should climbe to it with a ladder, and there slept hee with a woman of his, whose mother overnight tooke away the ladder, and in the morning set it to againe.

Cleane contrarie to this therefore ought the life of a good Prince to bee free and safe and as deare to his subjects as their owne: and so framed, that he may have a part of both

---

[1] "Promotiōs declare": cf. "office shows."
[2] "Solemnesse": cf. "insolence."

the doing and beholding[1] life, as much as shall be behoveful for the benefit of the people.

Then the Lorde Gaspar: And which of the two lives, my Lorde Octavian (quoth he) doe you thinke most meete for a Prince?

The Lorde Octavian answered smyling: ye thinke perhaps that I stand in mine owne conceite to be the excellent courtier that ought to know so many matters, and to apply them to the good end I have spoken of. But remember your selfe, that these Lordes have fashioned him with many qualities that be not in me: therefore let us first doe our best to finde him out, for I remit me to him[2] both in this and in all other thinges that belong to a good Prince.

Then the Lorde Gaspar: I thinke (quoth he) that if any of the qualities given the Courtier want in you, it is rather musicke and daunsing and the rest of small account, than such as belong to the instructing of a prince, and to this end of Courtlinesse.

The Lord Octavian answered: They are not of small account all of them that helpe to purchase a man the favour of a prince, which is necessarie (as wee have saide) before the Courtier aventure to teach him vertue, the which (I trow) I have shewed you may bee learned, and profiteth as much as ignorance hurteth, whereof spring all vices, and especially that false liking a man hath of himselfe. Therefore (in mine opinion) I have sufficiently saide, and perhaps more than my promise was.

Then the Dutchesse, wee shall bee so much the more bound (quoth she) to your gentlenesse, as ye shall satisfie us more than promise. Therfore sticke not to speak your fansie concerning the Lord Gaspars request. And of good felowship shew us beside whatsoever you would teach your Prince, if he had neede of instructions.

And set the case that you have throughly gotten his favour, so as it may be lawful for you to tell him frankly what ever commeth in your minde.

The L. Octavian laughed and saide: If I had the favour of some Prince[3] that I know, and should tell him franckly mine opinion (I doubt me) I shoulde soone loose it: Beside that, to teach him, I shoulde neede first to learne my selfe. Notwithstanding, since it is your pleasure that I shall answere the Lorde Gaspar in this point also, I say, that (in my minde) princes ought to give themselves both to the one and the other

---

[1] Cf. "active and contemplative."    [2] Cf. "leave to him."
[3] "Some Prince": cf. "a certain prince."

of the two lives, but yet somewhat more to the beholding: Because this in them is devided into two partes, whereof the one consisteth in knowing well and judging: the other in commanding aright, and in such wise as it shoulde be done, and reasonable matters,[1] and such as they have authoritie in, commanding them to him, that of reason ought to obey, and in time and place accordingly.

And of this spake Duke Fredericke, when he saide, He that can command, is alwaies obeyed. And to commande is evermore the principall office of princes, which notwithstanding ought many times also to see with their eyes, and to be present at the deede doing, and according to the time and the businesse otherwhile also be doing themselves,[2] and yet hath all this a part with action or practise.

But the end of the active or doing life ought to be the beholding,[3] as of war, peace, and of paines, rest. Therefore is it also the office of a good Prince so to trade[4] his people and with such lawes and statutes, that they may live in rest and in peace, without daunger and with increase of wealth, and injoy peaceably this ende of their practises and actions, which ought to be quietnesse. Because there have beene oftentimes many common weales and Princes, that in warre were alwaies most florishing and mightie, and immediatly after they have had peace, fell in decay and lost their puissance and brightnesse, like iron unoccupied. And this came of nothing els, but because they had no good trade of living in peace, nor the knowledge to injoy the benefit of ease.

And it is not a matter lawful to be alwaies in war, without seeking at the ende to come to a peace: although some Princes suppose that their drift ought principally to be, to bring in subjection their borders, and therefore to traine up their people in a warlike wildenesse of[5] spoile and murther, and such matters: they wage them to exercise it, and call it vertue.

Whereupon in the olde time it was an usage among the Scythes, that who so had not slaine one enimie of his, coulde not drinke in solemne bankets of the goblet that was carried about to his companions.

In other places the manner was to reare about ones sepulture so many Obeliskes, as he that lay there buried had slaine of

---

[1] "Reasonable matters": cf. "things reasonable."
[2] "According," etc.: cf. "ought also sometimes to take part themselves."
[3] Cf. "contemplative."
[4] "To trade": cf. "to establish."     [5] Cf. "ferocity for."

his enimies. And all these thinges and many moe, were invented to make men warlike, onely to bring others in subjection, which was a matter (almost) unpossible, because it is an infinite peece of worke, untill all the worlde be brought under obeysance: and not very reasonable, according to the law of nature which will not have, that in others thing shoulde please us, which in our selves is a griefe to us.

Therefore ought Princes to make their people warlike, not for a greedie desire to rule, but to defend themselves the better and their owne people from who so would attempt to bring them in bondage, or to doe them wrong in any point: or els to drive out Tyrants, and to governe the people well that were ill handled. Or els to bring into bondage them that of nature were such, that they deserved to bee made bondmen, with intent to governe them well, and to give them ease, rest, and peace.

And to this ende also ought to be applied y^e lawes, and all statutes of justice, in punishing the ill, not for malice, but because there should be no ill, and lest they should bee a hindrance to the quiet living of the good.

Because in very deede it is an uncomely matter and worthie of blame, that in warre (which of it selfe is nought [1]) men shoulde shew themselves stout and wise, and in peace and rest (which is good) ignorant, and so blockish that they wist not how to enjoy a benefit.

Even as therefore in war they ought to bend their people to the profitable and necessarie vertues to come by the end (which is, peace) so in peace, to come by the end thereof also (which is, quietnesse) they ought to bend them to honest vertues, which be the end of the profitable. And in this wise shall the subjects be good, and the Prince shall have many moe to commend and to rewarde, than to chastise. And the rule both for the subjects and for the prince shalbe most happie, not Lordly, as the maister over his bondman, but soft and meeke, as a good father over his good childe.

Then the Lorde Gaspar: gladly (quoth he) woulde I understand what manner vertues these are, that bee profitable and necessarie in warre, and what honest in peace.

The Lorde Octavian answered: All be good and helpe the turne, because they tend to a good end. Yet chiefly in warre is much set by that true manlinesse, which maketh the mind voide from all passions, so that he not onely feareth not perils,

___
[1] "Nought": cf. "bad."

but passeth not upon them. Likewise stedfastnesse, and patience, abiding with a quiet and untroubled mind all the strokes of fortune.

It is behovefull likewise in war and at all other times to have all the vertues that belong to honestie,[1] as justice, stayednesse, sober mood: but much more in peace and rest, because oftentimes men in prosperitie and rest, when favourable Fortune fauneth upon them, waxe unrighteous, untemperate, and suffer themselves to bee corrupted with pleasures.

Therefore such as bee in this state have verie great neede of these vertues, because rest bringeth ill conditions too soone into mens mindes.

Whereupon arose a Proverbe in olde time, that Rest is not to bee given to bondmen: And it is thought that the Pyramides of Egipt were made to keepe the people occupied, because Unto every man, use to abide paines is most profitable.

There be moreover many other vertues, all helpfull, but it sufficeth for this time to have spoken thus much: for if I could teach my prince and traine him in this manner and so vertuous a bringing up (as wee have set forth) in doing it without any more (I would believe) that I had sufficiently well compassed the ende of a good Courtier.

Then the Lorde Gaspar, My Lord Octavian (quoth he) because you have much praysed good bringing up, and seemed (in a manner) to believe that it is the chiefe cause to make a man vertuous and good, I would know whether the Courtiers instructing of his prince, ought to beginne first of use and (as it were) dayly fashions,[2] that unawares to him may make him to accustome himselfe to well doing: or els whether he ought to begin it himselfe in opening unto him with reason the propertie of good and ill, and in making him to perceive before hee take the matter in hand, which is the good way, and to be followed: and which is the ill, and to be shunned: finally,[3] whether into the mind of his, the vertues ought to bee driven and grounded with reason and understanding first, or with custome.

The Lord Octavian said: you bring me into overlong a discourse: yet because you shall not thinke that I will slacke, for that I am not willing to make answere to your requestes, I say, that like as the soule and the bodie in us are two thinges, so is the soule devided into two parts: whereof the one hath in it reason, and the other appetite.

---

[1] Cf. "make for right."
[2] "Of use," etc.: cf. "with practice and with daily behaviour."
[3] Cf "in short."

Even as therefore in generation the body goeth before the soule, so doth the unreasonable part of the soule goe before the reasonable: the which is plainely to bee discerned in yong babes, who (in a manner) immediatly after their birth utter anger and fervent appetite, but afterwarde in processe of time reason appeareth.

Therefore first must the bodie bee cherished before the soule: after that, the appetite before reason: but the cherishing of the bodie for a respect to the soule, and of the appetite for a respect to reason. For as the vertue of the minde is made perfect with learning, so is the civill with custome.

Therefore ought there to be a ground made first with custome,[1] which may governe the appetites not yet apt to conceive reason: and with that good use leade them to goodnesse: afterwarde settle them with understanding, the which although she be last to shew her light, yet doth she the more perfectly make the vertues to be injoyed of who so hath his minde well instructed with manners,[2] wherein (in mine opinion) consisteth y^e whole.

The Lorde Gaspar saide: Before ye proceede any further, I woulde know how the bodie should be cherished: because you have saide that we must cherish it before the soule.

The Lorde Octavian answered smyling: know of these men that make much of it and are faire and round, as for mine (as you see) it is not halfe well cherished. Yet may there also be much saide in this behalfe: As, the time meete for marriage, that children be neither too nigh nor too farre off from the fathers age: Exercises, and bringing up soone after their birth, and in the rest of their life, to make them handsome, towardly, and lively.

The Lord Gaspar answered: The thing that woulde best please women to make their children handsome and wellfavoured (in my minde) were the fellowship that[3] Plato will have of them in his common weale, and in that wise.

Then the Ladie Emilia smyling: It is not in the covenant (quoth she) that ye should a fresh fall to speake ill of women. I suppose answered the Lord Gaspar, that I give them a great prayse, in saying that they shoulde desire to have a custome brought up, which is alowed of so worthie a man.

The Lorde Cesar Gonzaga saide laughing: Let us see whether

[1] "Therefore ought there," etc.: cf. "We ought, therefore, first to teach through habit."

[2] Cf. "trained by practice."

[3] "Fellowship that," etc.: cf. "community wherein."

among the Lorde Octavians lessons (yet I wot not whether hee have spoken all or no) this may take place: and whether it were well done the Prince should establish it for a law or no.

The few that I have spoken, answered the Lord Octavian, may perhaps bee inough to make a good prince as princes goe now a dayes. Although if a man woulde go more narrowly to worke in the matter, there were much more for him yet to say.

Then said the Dutchesse: Since it costeth us nothing but wordes, shew us of good fellowship that, that woulde come in your minde to teach your Prince.

The Lorde Octavian answered: Many other matters I woulde teach him (madam) if I knew them my selfe: and among the rest, that hee shoulde picke out a certaine number of gentlemen among his subjects, of the noblest and wisest, with whom he shoulde debate all matters, and give them authoritie and free leave to utter their minde franckly unto him without respect: and to take such order with them that they may well perceive, that in every thing he would know the truth and abhorre lying.

And beside this Counsell of the nobilitie, I woulde perswade him to choose out others among the people of a baser degree, of whom hee should make an honest substantial Councel, that should debate with the Councel of the nobilitie the affaires of the Citie, belonging to the common and private estate. And in this wise should bee made, of the Prince, as of the heade, of the nobilitie and commons, as of the members, one bodie alone knitte together, the governance whereof should chiefly depend upon the Prince, yet should the rest beare a stroke also in it: and so should this state have the forme and manner of the three good governments, which is, a kingdom, men of the best sorte, and the people.

Afterwarde I woulde shew him, that of cares belonging to a Prince, the chiefest is of justice: for maintenance whereof wise and well tryed men shoulde bee chosen out for officers, whose wisedom were very wisedome in deed, accompanied with goodnesse, for els is it no wisedom, but craft. And where there is a want of this goodnesse, alwaies the arte and subtiltie of Lawiers is nothing els but the utter decay and destruction of the lawes and judgements: and the fault of every offence of theirs is to bee laide in him that put them in office.

I woulde tell him how that of justice also dependeth the zeale toward God, which belongeth unto all men, and especially to Princes, who ought to love him above all things, and to direct all their doings unto him, as unto the true end: And (as Xenophon saith) to honour and love him alwaies, but much more in prosperitie, because they may afterwarde lawfully with a more confidence call to him for assistance when they be in any adversitie: for it is not possible to governe either himselfe or others well, without the help of God, who unto the good sendeth otherwhile good fortune for his minister, to helpe them out of great dangers, sometime adversitie, lest they shoulde slumber so much in prosperitie, that they might happen to forget him, or the wisedome of man, which many times redresseth ill fortune, as a good player the ill chaunces of the dice, with cunning play at tables.

I would not forget also to put the Prince in minde to be devoute in deede, not superstitious, nor given to the vanitie of ignorance and prophecies: for in case hee have accompanied with the wisedome of man, a godly zeale of true religion, he shall also have good lucke,[1] and God his defendor, who will alwaies increase his prosperitie both in peace and war.

Beside, I would declare unto him how he should love his Countrie and his people, keeping them not in too much bondage, for being[2] hated of them, whereof arise seditions, conspiracies, and a thousand mischiefes beside: nor yet in too much libertie, least he bee set at nought, whereof proceedeth the licentious and riotous living of the people, theft, roberie and murther without anie feare of lawes, oftentimes the decay and utter destruction of Cities and kingdomes.

Moreover how he should love them that bee nighest to him, from one degree to another, observing among them all in certaine matters a like equalitie, as in justice, and liberallitie, and in some matters a reasonable partialitie,[3] as in being liberall, in recompensing, in bestowing promotions and honours according to the unequalnesse of deserts, which ought not alwaies[4] to exceede, but to bee exceeded with recompences. And that in thus doing hee should not onely not be beloved, but (in a manner) worshipped of his subjects, neither shoulde he neede to commit the guarde of his person to straungers, for his owne (for the better safegard and profitte of themselves) would guarde him in their owne person: and each man woulde willingly obey the lawes, when they should see him to obey them him-

[1] "Lucke": cf. "fortune."       [2] "For being": cf. "lest he be."
[3] Cf. "judicious inequality."
[4] "Ought not alwaies": cf. "always ought not."

selfe, and be (as it were) an uncorrupted keeper and minister of them.

And so shall he make all men to conceive such an assured confidence of him, that if he should happen otherwhile to goe beyond them in anie point, every one woulde know it were done for a good intent: the selfe same respect and reverence they woulde have to his will, as they have to the lawes. And thus should the Citizens mindes bee tempered in such sorte, that the good would not seeke for more than is requisite, and the bad shoulde not bee able.[1]

Because many times aboundance of wealth is cause of great destruction, as in poore Italy, which hath been and still is, a pray and bootie in the teeth of straunge nations, as well for the ill government, as for the aboundance of riches that is in it.

Therefore the best way were, to have the greater part of the Citizens, neither verie wealthie, nor verye poore: because the overwealthie many time waxe stiffe necked and recklesse,[2] the poore, desperate and picking.[3] But the meane sorte lye not in waite for others, and live with a quiet mind that none lye in waite for them. And where this meane sorte are the greater number, they are withall the mightier. And therfore neither the poore nor rich can worke any conspiracie against the Prince, or against others, nor move sedition.

Wherefore to avoide this evill, the most surest way is universally to maintaine a meane.

I woulde counsell him therefore to use these and many other remedies for the purpose, that in the minde of the subjects there spring not a longing after new matters and alteration of state, which most commonly they doe, either for gaine, or els for promotion that they hope upon, or for losse, or els for some toile that they be afearde of. And these sturres in their mindes be engendred sometime of hatred and despite that maketh them desperate for the wronges and unshamefull dealing that they receive through the covetousnesse, pride and crueltie, or un-lawfull lust of the higher powers: otherwhile of a contempt and litle regarde that ariseth in them through negligence and ill handling and lacke of foresight in Princes.

And these two faults must be prevēted with purchasing him the love of the people, and authority, which is done in rewarding and prompting the good, and in finding wisely a remedie, and sometime with rigour, that the evill and seditions waxe not

---

[1] Cf. "could not" (seek for more than they needed).
[2] Cf. "insolent and rash."          [3] Cf. "base and dishonest."

great: the which thing is easier to be stopped before they come to it, than to plucke them down againe after they are once on loft.

And I would say, to restraine the people from running into those inconveniences, there is no better way than to keepe them from ill customes, and especially such as be put in use, and creepe in unawares by litle and litle, because they be secrete infections that corrupt cities before a man can not onely remedie them, but spye them out.

With such meanes I would counsel the Prince to doe his best to preserve his subjects in quiet estate, and to give them the goods of the mind, and of the bodie, and of fortune: but them of the bodie and of fortune, that they exercise them of the minde: which the greater and plentier they be, so much the more profitable be they: that happeneth not in them of the bodie, nor of fortune.

In case therefore the subjects be good and of worthinesse, and well bent to the end of happinesse, that prince shall be a verie great Lorde: for that is a true and a great governmēt, under the which the subjects be good, well ruled, and well commanded.

Then the Lord Gaspar, I suppose[1] (quoth hee) that he should be but a small Lorde, under whom the subjectes were all good. For in every place there be few good.

The Lorde Octavian answered: In case some certain Circe should turn into wilde beastes all the French kings subjects, woulde not you thinke him a small Lord for all he raigned over so many thousand beastes? And contrariwise, if onely the Cattel that scatter abroad feeding about our mountaines here, might become wise men, and valiant gentlemen, woulde not you thinke that yᵉ heardmen that shoulde governe them and have them obedient to them, of heardmen were become great Lords.

You may see then, that not the multitude of subjectes, but the worthinesse of them maketh princes great.

The Dutchesse, the Ladie Emilia, and all the rest gave very diligent care to the L. Octavians talke for a good while together, but after hee had here made a litle stoppe, as though hee had made an end of his talke, the Lorde Cesar Gonzaga said.

Certesse (my Lord Octavian) it can not be saide, but your lessons be good and profitable: yet should I believe, that if yee instructed your Prince with them, yee deserve rather the name

[1] "Suppose": cf. "think."

of a good scholemaister than of a good Courtier: and hee of a good governour rather than of a good Prince.

Yet my meaning is not, but that the care of Princes should be to have their people well ruled with justice and good usages, notwithstanding it may be sufficient for them (in my minde) to choose out good ministers to execute these kinde of matters, but the verie office of them is farre higher.

Therfore if I thought my selfe to be the excellent courtier that these Lordes have fashioned, and in my Princes favour, without peradventure I would never encline him to any vitious matter: but to attaine unto the good end you speake of, and the which I confirme ought to be the fruite of the Courtiers travailes and doinges, I would endevour to put into his heade a certaine greatnesse, with that princely sumptuousnesse and readinesse of courage, and unconquered prowesse in armes, that should make him beloved and reverenced of all men, in such wise,[1] that for this in especiall he should be famous and notable to the world.

I would shew him also, that hee ought to accompany with his greatnesse, a familiar gentle behavior, with a soft and lovely kindnesse, and good cast to make much of his subjects and straungers discreetly more and lesse according to their deserts, observing alwaies notwithstanding the majestie meete for his degree, that shoulde not in any point suffer him to diminish his authoritie through overmuch abasing, nor yet purchase him hatred through overmuch rigorousnesse.

That he ought to be full of liberality and sumptuous, and give unto every man without stint, for God (as they say) is the treasurer of freeharted Princes: make gorgeous banquets, feastes, games, people pleasing shewes, keepe a great number of faire horses for profit in warre, and for pleasure in peace: Haukes, houndes, and all other matters that belong to the contentation of great Princes and the people. As in our dayes we have seene the Lorde Francis Gonzaga marquesse of Mantua[2] do, which in these things seemeth rather king of all Italy, than Lord over one Citie.

I would assay also to bring him to make great buildings both

---

[1] Cf. "to such a degree."
[2] Francesco Gonzaga (born 1466, died 1519), Marquess of Mantua, and a brother of "my Lady Duchess." Castiglione left his court in 1504 for that of Urbino, and remained in his displeasure (which at one time threatened imprisonment) until 1516, when their old relationship was restored. This part of *The Courtier* was written after the peace, or when it was in prospect.

for his honour in life, and to give a memorie of him to his posteritie, as did duke Fredericke in this noble pallace, and now doeth Pope July in the temple of Saint Peter, and the way that goeth from the pallace to his house of pleasure Belvedere, and many other buildings, as also the old auncient Romanes did, whereof so many remnants are to be seene about Rome, Naples, Pozzolo, Baie, Civita vecchia, Porto, and also of Italy, and so many other places, which be a great witnesse of the prowesse of those divine courages.

So did Alexander the great in like manner, which not satisfied with the fame that he got him worthily for subduing the worlde with martiall prowesse, built Alexandria in Egypt, Bucephalia in India, and other Cities in other Countries: and entended to bring the mountaine Athos into the shape of a man, and in the left hand of him to builde a very large Citie, and in the right a great bolle, into the which should gather all the rivers that ranne from it, and thence should fall downe towarde the sea, a purpose in very deed princely and meete for the great Alexander.

These thinges (thinke I) my Lord Octavian, become a noble and a right Prince, and shall make him both in peace and warre most triumphant, and not put him in the head of such particular and small matters, and have a respect to take weapon in hand onely to conquere and vanquish such as deserve to be conquered, or to profit his subjects withall, or to dispossesse them that governe not as they ought.

For in case that the Romanes, Alexander, Hannibal and the rest had had these respects, they shoulde never have reached to the toppe of the glory they did.

The Lorde Octavian answered them smiling: such as had not these respects should have done the better in case they had had them: although if ye consider well, ye shall finde that many had them: especially those auncientest of olde time, as Theseus and Hercules.

And thinke not that Procustes, Scyron, Caccus, Diomides, Antheus, and Gerion were any other than cruell and wicked tyrants, against whom these noble couraged Demigods kept continuall and mortall warre.

And therefore for ridding the world of such intollerable monsters (for tyrants ought not to bee called by other name) unto Hercules were made temples, and sacrifices, and goodly honours given him, because the benefit to roote up tyrants is so profitable to the worlde, that who so doth it, deserveth a farre greater rewarde, than whatsoever is meete for a mortall man.

And of them you have named. Doe you not thinke that Alexander did profitte with his victories the vanquished? since he so traded those barbarous Nations which hee overcame with such good manners, that of wilde beastes he made them men? He built many beautifull Cities in Countries ill inhabited, planting therein civil kinde of living, and (as it were) coupled Asia and Europe together with the bond of amitie and holy lawes, so that the vanquished by him were more happie than the rest.

Because among some hee brought in matrimonie: among other, husbandrie: among other, Religion: among other, not to slay, but to make much of their parents in their old age: among other, the refraining from bedding with their mothers, and a thousand other matters, that might be saide for a witnesse of the profit which his victories brought unto the world.

But leaving aside them of olde time, what enterprise were more noble, more glorious, and also more profitable, than if Christians would bende their force to conquere the infidels: would you not thinke that this war prosperously atchieved, and being the cause of so many a thousand to be brought from the false sect of Mahumet to the light of the Christian truth, it should be a profit as well to the vanquished, as to the subduers?

And undoubtedly, as Themistocles in times past being banished out of his countrie, and embraced of the king of Persia, and much made of, and honoured with infinite and most rich gifts, said unto his traine: Oh sirs, we had beene undone, had wee not beene undone,[1] even so might then the Turkes and the Moores speak the verie same with good cause, for that in their losse should consist their welfare.

This happinesse therefore (I hope) we shall come to the sight of, if God graunt so long life to Monseigneur d'Angoulesme, that he may come to y^e croune of Fraunce, who sheweth such a hope of himselfe, as foure nights agoe the Lorde Julian spake of. And to the crowne of England the Lorde Henry prince of Wales, who presently groweth under his most noble father, in all kind of vertue, like a tender Impe under the shadow of an excellent tree, and laden with fruite to renue him much more beautifull and plenteous when the time shall come.

[1] Cf. "we should have been undone but for our undoing": i.e. they were in a bad way until defeat brought them to this comfort.

For as our Castilio writeth from thence,[1] and promiseth at his returne to tell us more at the full, a man can judge no lesse, but that nature was willing in this prince to shew her cunning, in one bodie alone so many excellent vertues, as were sufficient to decke out infinit.

Then saide maister Bernard Bibiena: A very great hope of himselfe promiseth also the Lord Charles prince of Spaine, who not yet fully ten yeares of age, declareth now such a wit, and so certaine tokens of goodnesse, wisedom, modestie, noble courage and of every vertue, that if the Empire of Christendom (as it is thought) come to his handes, it is to be reckened upon, that hee will darken the name of many Emperors of olde time, and in renowne be compared to the most famous that ever were in the world.

The Lorde Octavian proceeded, I believe therefore that God hath sent such and so heavenly Princes upon the earth, and made them one like another in youth, in mightinesse of armes, in state, in handsomnesse and disposition of person, that they may also bee minded alike in this good purpose [2]: and in case any manner envie or strife of matching others arise at anye time among them, it shall be, who shall be the first, and most enclined and most couragious in so glorious an enterprise.

But let us leave this kind of talke, and returne unto our owne. Unto you therefore (my Lord Cesar) I say, that such thinges as you would have the Prince to doe, be very great and worthie much praise. But you must understand that if hee be not skilfull in that I have saide hee ought to have a knowledg in, and have not framed his minde in this wise, and bent it to the way of vertue, it shall be hard for him to have the knowledge to be noble couraged, liberall, just, quicke spirited, wise, or to have any other of those qualities that belong unto him: neither woulde I have him to be such a one for any other thing, but to have the understanding to put in use these conditions.

For as they that builde bee not all good workemen: so they that give, be not all liberall: for vertue never hurteth any man: and many there be, that lay hand on other mens goods to give,

---

[1] "Castilio"—Castiglione. He had returned, but pretends that he was yet away.

[2] A vain, if pious hope. Sir Walter Raleigh, born almost in their time, later commented upon what the world must needs expect when its rule was shared out among such sparks. "M. d'Angoulesme" became Francis I. of France in 1515; "Lord Charles," the Emperor Charles V., in 1519. "The Lord Henry" had succeeded his father in 1509. Cf. pp. 312, 313.

and so are lavish of an other mans substance. Some give to them they ought not, and leave in wretchednesse and misery such as they be bound to. Other give with a certaine ill will, and (as it were) with a despite, so that it is knowne they doe it, because they can doe none other. Other doe not onely not keepe it secrete, but they call witnesse of it, and (in a manner) cause their liberalities to bee cryed. Other foolishly at a sodaine empty the fountaine of liberalitie, so that afterwarde they can use it no more.

Therefore in this point (as in all other matters) hee must have a knowledge, and governe himselfe with the wisedom that is a companion unto all the other vertues, which for that they are in the middle, be nigh unto the two extremities, that be vices.

Wherefore hee that hath not knowledge rūneth soone into them. For as it is a hard matter in a circle to find out the pricke in the centre, which is the middle, so is it hard to find out the pricke of vertue placed in the middle between two extreeme vices, the one for the overmuch, and the other for the over litle.

And unto these we are enclined, sometime to the one, sometime to the other: and this is knowne by the pleasure and griefe that is felt within us, for through the one wee doe the thing that we ought not, and through the other wee leave undone that which we ought to doe: although pleasure bee much more dangerous, because our judgement is soone led by it to be corrupted. But because the perseverance [1] how farre a man is wide from the centre of vertue, is a hard matter, we ought by litle and litle to draw backe of our selves to the contrary parte of this extremitie, which wee know we be enclined unto, as they doe, that make straight crooked staves, for by that means we shall draw nigh unto vertue, which is placed (as I have saide) in that pricke of the meane.

Whereby it commeth that by many waies we be wide, and by one alone we doe our office and duetie: like as Archers by one way alone hitte the marke, and by many misse the pricke. Therefore oftentimes a Prince to be gentle and lowly, doth many thinges contrarie to comelinesse, and so humbleth himselfe that he is nought set by.

Some other to shew a grave majestie with authoritie according, becommeth cruel and untollerable.

Some one, to be counted eloquēt, entreth into a thousand straunge matters and long processes, with curious wordes giving

---

[1] "Perseverance": cf. "to perceive."

eare to him selfe, so that other men can not for lothsomnesse heare him.

Therefore my (Lord Cesar) doe you not call a small matter any thing that may better a Prince, how small so ever it be. Nor thinke that I judge it to bee in the reproofe of my lessons, where you say, that a good governour might better thus bee formed, than a good Prince.

For perhaps there can not be a greater praise nor more comely for a Prince, than to call him a good governour.

Therefore if it should fall to my lotte to instruct him, he shoulde have a care not onely to governe the matters alreadie spoken of, but also farre lesser, and understand in peecemeale whatsoever belongeth to his people, as much as were possible: and never credit nor trust any officer so much, as to give him the bridle wholy into his hands, and the disposing of the whole government.

For no man is most apt to all things. And much more hurt commeth of the light beliefe of Princes, than of mistrusting, which otherwhile doth not onely not hurt, but oftentimes profiteth exceedingly. Yet in this point a good judgement is very necessarie in a Prince, to discerne who deserveth to bee put in trust, and who not.

I would he shoulde have a care to understand the doings, and to bee an overseer of his officers and ministers. To breake and to ende controversies among his subjects. To take up matters betweene them, and to knitte them together in allyance by marriage. To provide so, that the citie may be all joyned together and agreeing in amitie, like a privat house, well peopled, not poore, quiet, and full of good artificers. To shew favour to marchant men, and to helpe them also with stockes.[1] To be liberall and honourable in house keeping[2] toward straungers and religious persons. To temper all superfluous matters, because through the offences committed in these thinges, albeit they appeare but small, Cities many times fall in decay.

Therefore it is reason that the Prince set a stint to the over sumptuous buildinges of private men, banquetings, unmeasurable dowries of women, their riotous excesse,[3] their pompe in jewels and apparell, which is nothing els but a token of their follie.

For (beside that through ambition and malice that one of them beareth another, they many times lavish out their live-

<hr>

[1] Cf. "money."  [2] Cf. "hospitality."
[3] "Riotous excesse": cf. "luxury."

lode and husbandes substance, otherwhile for some pretie jewell or other matter of fancie) sometime they sell their honestie to him that will buye it.

Then saide maister Bernard Bibiena smiling: You beginne (my Lord Octavian) to take the Lord Gaspars and Phrisios parte.

Then the Lord Octavian answered in like manner, smiling. The controversie is ended, and I entend not now to renue it. Therefore will I speake no more of women, but returne to my Prince.

Phrisio answered: You may now leave him hardly, and bee contented to have him such a one as you have instructed him. For doubtlesse it were an easier matter to find out a woman of the qualities the Lorde Julian hath spoken of, than a prince of the qualities you woulde have in him.

Therefore (I feare me) he is like the common weale of Plato, and wee shall never see such a one, unlesse it bee perhaps in heaven.

The Lorde Octavian answered: thinges possible, though they be hard, yet is it to bee hoped that they may be: therefore may we yet perhaps see him upon the earth in our time.

For although the heavens be so scant in bringing forth excellent princes, that in so many hundred yeares wee doe scantly see one, yet may this good lucke happen to us.

Then saide Count Lewis: I have a good hope of it. For beside the three great ones that wee have named, of whom may be hoped it that belongeth to the high degree of a perfect Prince, there be also now a daies in Italy certaine Princes children, which although they be not like to have such power, may hap will supply it with vertue: and he that among them all declareth a more towardnesse, and promiseth of him selfe a greater hope than any of the rest (me thinke) is the L. Fredericke Gonzaga sonne and heire to the Marquesse of Mantua, and Nephew to our Dutchesse here.

For beside the honest inclination to good nourture, and the discretion that he declareth in these tender yeares, they that have the bringing up of him, reporte such wonderous thinges, as touching his being wittie, desirous of glorie, stoutharted, courteous, freeharted, friendly to justice, so that of so good a beginning, there can not be looked for but a very good ende.

Then Phrisio, well, no more of this (quoth he) we will pray unto God that we may see this your hope fulfilled.

Here the Lorde Octavian turning him towarde the Dutchesse, after a sort as though hee had ended as much as he had to say.

You have now heard Madam (quoth he) what I am able to say of the end of y^e Courtier, wherein though I have not satisfied in all pointes, it shall suffice me yet, that I have shewed, that some other perfection may be given him beside the matters which these Lordes have spoken of, who (I believe) have left out both this and whatsoever I am able to say, not because they knew it not better than I, but because they were loth to take the paines.

Therefore will I give them leave to goe forwarde, if they have anye thing els left behinde to bee saide.

Then said the Dutchesse: Beside that it is late (for within a while it will bee time for us to make an ende for this night) me thinke, we ought not to mingle any other talke with this, wherein you have gathered together such sundrie and goodly matters, that concerning the end of Courtlinesse, it may be saide, that you are not onely the perfect Courtier whom we seeke for, and able to instruct your Prince well, but also (if fortune be so favourable on your side) ye may be the good prince your selfe, which should not be without great profit to your Countrie.[1]

Then laughed the Lorde Octavian, and said: perhaps (madam) were I in that estate, it would be with me as it is with many others that can better say well, than doe well.

Here after a little debating of the matter to and fro among the company, with certaine contentions tending to the commendation of that that had beene spoken, and agreeing on all hands not yet to be bed time, the Lord Julian saide smyling.

Madam, I am so very an enimie to craft and guile, that needes must I speake against the Lord Octavian: who for that hee is (as I much doubt him) a secret conspiratour with the Lord Gaspar against women, hath overshot him selfe in committing two errors (in mine opinion) very great: whereof the one is, that meaning to prefer the Courtier before the gentlewoman of the pallace, and to make him to passe those bounds, that she is not able to reach to, he hath also preferred him before the Prince, which is most unseemely. The other, that he hath given him such an ende, that it is evermore hard and otherwhile unpossible for him to come by it: and yet when he doth come by it, he ought not to have the name of a Courtier.

[1] These lines were written after Ottaviano Fregoso—"the L. Octavian" —had been elected Doge of Genoa, dispossessing the French (Opdycke, 414). Francis I. regained the city in 1515, but continued him as governor. In 1522 "L. Charles" (see pp. 291-3), now Charles V., captured and sacked the place, and Fregoso was sent as prisoner to Ischia, where he died of ill-treatment, for which the Marquess of Pescara (Vittoria Colonna's husband) must be held responsible.

I can not see, quoth the Ladie Emilia, how it is hard or unpossible for the Courtier to come by this his end, nor yet how the Lord Octavian hath preferred him before the Prince.

Graunt it him not, answered the Lord Octavian: for I have not preferred y^e Courtier before the Prince. And as touching the end of courtlinesse, I dare undertake that I am not over-seene in any point.[1]

Then answered the Lorde Julian: You can not say (my L. Octavian) that alwaies the cause, by the which the effect is such as it is, is no more such as the effect is.[2] Therefore needes must the Courtier, by whose instruction the Prince must bee of such an excellencie, bee more excellent than the Prince: and in this wise shall hee be also of a more worthinesse than the Prince himselfe, which is most unfitting.

Then concerning the ende of Courtlinesse, that which you have spoken may follow when there is litle betweene the age of the Prince and the Courtiers: yet very hardly, for where there is small difference of age, it is likely there is also small difference of knowledge. But in case the Prince be olde and the Courtier yong: it is meete that the olde Prince know more than the yong Courtier, and where this followeth not alwaies, it fol-loweth sometime, and then is the end which you have appointed to the Courtier unpossible.

In case againe the Prince be yong, and the Courtier aged, much adoe shall the Courtier have to win him the good will of the Prince with those qualities that you have given him. For (to say the truth) feates of armes and the other exercises belong unto yong men, and be not comely in age: and musicke, dauncing, feastings, sportings, and love, be matters to be laughed at in olde men, and (me thinke) to an instructer of the life and manners of a Prince, who ought to bee a grave person and of authoritie, ripe in years and experience, and if it were possible, a good Philosopher, a good Captaine, and to have the know-ledge almost of every thing, it is most seemely.

Wherfore he that instructeth a Prince (I believe) ought not to bee called a Courtier, but deserveth a farre greater and a more honourable name.

Therefore (my Lord Octavian) pardon me, in case I have opened this your craftie conveyance, which I thinke my selfe bound to do, for the honour of my woman, whom you would

---

[1] "Overseene," etc.: cf. "in any error."
[2] Cf. "does not always have more of that quality than its result has."

have to bee of lesse worthinesse than this courtier of yours, and I will none of that.

The L. Octavian laughed and saide: I more prayse it were for the gentlewoman of the pallace (my Lorde Julian) to exalt her so much that she may bee equall with the Courtier, than so much to debase the Courtier that hee shoulde bee equall with the gentlewoman of the pallace: for it were not unfit for the woman also to instruct her Ladie, and with her to draw to the same end of Courtlinesse, which I have said is meete for the Courtier with his Prince. But you seeke more to dispraise the Courtier, than to praise the gentlewoman of the pallace.

Therefore shall it become me also to take parte with the Courtier. Nowe to make you aunswere to your objections, you shall understand that I have not sayde, that the instruction of the Courtier ought to be the only cause why the Prince should bee such a one, for in case he be not inclined of nature and apt to be such a one, all diligence and exhortation of ye Courtier were in vaine. As in like maner every good husbandman should labor in vaine, that woulde take in hande to till and sowe wyth good graine the barraine sand of the Sea, because this barrennesse in that place is naturall. But when to the good seede in a fruitfull soyle with the temperatenes of ayre and raine meete for the season of the yere, there is also applied the diligēce of mans husbandinge the grounde, alwayes great aboundaunce of corne is seene to spring plenteously: yet for all this, is it to be said that the husbandman alone is the cause of it, although without hym all the other thinges doe little or nothing helpe the purpose.

There bee therefore many Princes, that would be good in case their mindes were wel tilled, and of them speake I, not of such as be like the barraine Countrey, and of nature so farre wide from good conditions, that no teaching wer able to frame their mind to a right trade.

And forsomuch as (as we have already sayde) such customes and properties be ingendred in us, as our doings are,[1] and vertue consisteth in doing and practise, it is not unpossible nor any marvel, that the Courtier shoulde traine his Prince in many vertues, as justice, liberalitie, noble courage, the practising whereof hee through his greatnesse may lightly put in use, and make it custome, which the Courtier can not doe, because he hath no meanes to practise them.

[1] Cf. "our actions are what our habits are"

And thus the Prince inclined to vertue by y^e Courtier, may become more vertuous than the Courtier: beside that, you must conceive that the whetstone which cutteth not a whit, doth yet make a toole sharpe: therefore although the Courtier instructeth his Prince, yet (me thinke) it is not to be saide that he is of a more worthinesse than his Prince.

That the ende of this Courtier is hard, and sometime unpossible, and that when the Courtier doth come, he ought not to be named a Courtier, but deserveth a greater name, I tell you plainely, that I deny not this hardnesse, because it is no lesse hard to find out so excellent a Courtier, than to come by such an end.

Yet by reason (me thinke) the unpossiblenesse of the matter lyeth not in the point that you have alleaged. For in case the Courtier bee so yong that he hath not understanding in the thing, which he ought to have a knowledge in, it is not to the purpose to speake of him, because he is not the Courtier that we entreat upon, neither is it possible for him that must have a sight in so manye things to be very yong. And if it happen moreover the Prince to bee so wise and good of himselfe, that he needeth no exhortatiōs or councell of others (although it be so hard a matter as every man knoweth) it sufficeth that the Courtier be such a one, as if his prince had need, he coulde make him vertuous: and then may he in effect fulfill the other part, not to suffer him to be deceived, and to worke that evermore he may understand the truth of every thing, and bolster him against flatterers, and railers, and al such as should endevour to corrupt his minde with honest delights. And in this wise shall he yet come by a part of his ende though hee can not practise the whole.

Which can not bee justly laide to him for a fault, since he refraineth the doing of it upon so good a ground. For were an excellent Phisition in place where al were found and in health, a man ought not therefore to say, that the Phisition (although he cured no diseased) wanted of his end.

Wherefore as the Phisitions respect ought to bee the health of men, even so the Courtiers, the vertue of his Prince: and it sufficeth them both to have this ende inwardly graft in them,[1] when the want of uttering it outwardly in practise is occasioned by the subject, to the which this end is directed.

But in case the Courtier were so olde, that it became him not to bee doing in musicke, feastings, sportinges, martiall feates,

---

[1] Cf. "latent within their power."

and the other sleights of the bodie, yet can it not be saide notwithstanding, that it were unpossible for him to enter that way in favour with his Prince: for where his age taketh away the practising of those thinges, it taketh not away the understanding of them, and if he have practised them in his youth, it maketh him to have so much the more perfect judgement in them, and giveth a knowledg to teach them his Prince so much the more perfectly, as yeares and experience bring knowledge of all thinges with them.

And thus shall the aged Courtier, although hee exercise not the qualities that he is endowed withall, come by his end at length, to instruct well his prince. And in case you will not call him a Courtier, it shall nothing offend me: for nature hath not appointed such narrow boundes to the dignities of men, that one may not come up from one to another.

Therefore many times meane souldiers arise to bee Captaines: private men, Kinges: priests, Popes: and scholers, maisters: and so with their degree or dignitie, they take their name accordingly. Wherefore perhaps a man may say, that to become the instructer of a Prince, were the ende of a Courtier, although I perceive not who should refuse this name of a perfect Courtier, which (in my minde) is worthie very great praise.

And I can not see but Homer, as hee fashioned two most excellent personages for example of mans life, the one in practises, which was Achilles, the other in passions and sufferances, which was Ulisses: even so in like manner minded to fashion a perfect courtier (which was Phœnix) who after rehersall of his loves and many other matters of youth, declareth that he was sent to Achilles by his father Peleus, to be in his company, and to teach him to speake, and to doe: which is nothing els but the end that we have appointed for our Courtier.

Neither can I thinke that Aristotle and Plato tooke scorne of the name of a perfect Courtier, because it is plainely to be seene that they practised the deeds of Courtiership, and gave themselves to this end, the one with the great Alexander, the other with the kinges of Sicilia.

And because it is the office of a good Courtier to know the nature and inclination of his Prince, and so according to the businesse, and as occasion serveth with slightnesse[1] to enter in favour with him (as we have saide) by those waies that make him a sure entrie, and afterwarde bend him to vertue. Aristotle so well knew the nature of Alexander, and with slightnesse

---

[1] "With slightnesse": cf. "tactfully."

framed him selfe so well thereafter that he was beloved and honoured of him more than a father.

Wherefore among many other tokens that Alexander shewed him for a witnesse of his good will, he caused Stagira the citie where hee was borne, once destroyed, to bee builded new againe. And Aristotle, beside the directing him to that glorious ende, that was to make the world onely a general[1] countrie, and all men as one people, that should live in amitie and agreement together, under one government and one law, that like the sunne, should generally give light to all, hee instructed him in the natural sciences, and in the vertues of the mind full and wholy, that he made him most wise, most manly, most continent, and a true morall Philosopher, not in wordes onely, but in deedes.

For there can not be imagined a more noble Philosophie, than to bring to a civill trade of living such wilde people as were the inhabitants of Bactria and Caucasus, India, and Scythia, and to teach them matrimony, husbandrie, to honour their fathers, to abstaine from robbing and killing, and from other naughtie conditions, and to builde so many noble cities in strange countries, so that infinite through those lawes were brought from a wilde life to live like men.

And of these thinges in Alexander, the author was Aristotle, in practising the waies of a good Courtier: the which Calisthenes coulde not do, for all Aristotle shewed him the way of it, who because he was a right philosopher, and so sharpe a minister of the bare truth without mingling it with courtlinesse, hee lost his life and profited not, but rather gave a slaunder to Alexander.

With the very same way of Courtlinesse Plato framed Dion the Syracusan. But when he met afterward with Dionysius the tyrant, like a booke all full of faultes and errors, and rather needfull to be cleane blotted out, than altered or corrected, because it was not possible to scrape out of him that blot of tyranny wherewithall he was stained so long together, he would not practise therein the waies of Courtiership, for he thought they shoulde be all in vaine.

The which our Courtier ought to doe also, if his chaunce be to serve a prince of so ill a nature, that by long custome is growne in use with vices, as they that have the consumption of the lunges with their disease. For in this case he ought to forsake his service, lest hee beare the blame of his Lords ill

[1] Cf. "one single universal . . ."

practises, or feele the hartgriefe that all good men have which serve the wicked.

Here when the Lord Octavian had made a stay, the Lorde Gaspar saide: I had not thought our Courtier had beene so worthie a personage. But since Aristotle and Plato be his mates, I judge no man ought to disdaine this name any more.

Yet wote I not whether I may believe that Aristotle and Plato ever daunced, or were Musitions in all their life time, or practised other feates of chivalrie.

The Lorde Octavian answered: almost it is not lawful to thinke that these two divine wits were not skilful in every thing, and therefore it is to be presupposed, that they practised what ever belonged to Courtlinesse.

For where it commeth to purpose, they so penne the matter, that the verie crafts masters themselves know by their writings, that they understood the whole, even the pith and innermost roots.

Wherefore to a Courtier or instructer of a prince (how ever ye lust to terme him) that tendeth to the good ende which we have spoken of, it is not to be saide, but that all the good qualities which these Lordes have given him doe belong, though he were never so grave a Philosopher or holy in his manners [1]: because they strive not against goodnesse, discretion, knowledge and will, in all age, and in all time and place.

Then the Lorde Gaspar, I remember (quoth he) that these Lordes, yesternight reasoning of the Courtiers qualities, did allow him to be a lover, and in making a rehersall of as much as hetherto hath beene spoken, a man may picke out a conclusion, That the Courtier (which with his worthinesse and credit must encline his prince to vertue) must in manner of necessitie bee aged, for knowledge commeth verye seldom times before yeares, and especially in matters that be learned with experience: I can not see, when he is well drawne in yeares, how it will stand well with him to be a lover, considering (as it hath beene saide the other night) Love frameth not with olde men, and the trickes that in yong men be galantnesse, courtesie and precisenesse [2] so acceptable to women, in them are mere follies, and fondnesse to bee laughed at, and purchase him that useth them hatred of women, and mockes of others.

Therefore in case this your Aristotle and olde Courtier were a lover, and practised the feates that yong lovers doe (as some that we have seene in our dayes) I feare me, he would forget to

---

[1] Cf. "saintly in his behaviour."      [2] "Precisenesse": cf. "elegancies."

teach his Prince: and peradventure boyes would mocke him behinde his backe, and women would have none other delight in him, but to make him a jesting stocke.

Then saide the Lord Octavian: Since all the other qualities appointed to the Courtier are meete for him, although hee be olde, mee thinke we shoulde not then barre him from his happinesse to love.

Nay rather, quoth the Lorde Gaspar, to take his love from him, is a perfection over and above,[1] and making him to live happily out of miserie and wretchednesse.

Maister Peter Bembo said: remember you not (my Lord Gaspar) that the Lord Octavian declared the other night in his devise of pastimes, although he be not skilfull in love, to know yet that there be some Lovers, which reckon the disdaines, the angers, the debates and torments which they receive of their Ladies, sweete? Whereupon hee required to bee taught y<sup>e</sup> cause of this sweetnesse.

Therefore in case our Courtier (though he bee olde) were kindled with those loves that bee sweete without any bitter smacke, he should feele no miserie nor wretchednesse at all. And being wise, as we set case he is, he should not be deceived in thinking to be meete for him whatsoever were meete for yong men.

But in loving should perhaps love after a sorte, that might not onely bring him in slaunder, but to much praise and happinesse, without any lothsomnesse at all, the which very seldom or (in a manner) never happeneth to yong men: and so should he neither lay aside the teaching of his Prince, nor yet commit any thing that should deserve the mocking of boyes.

Then spake the Dutchesse: I am glad (maister Peter) that you have not beene much troubled in our reasonings this night, for now we may be the bolder to give you in charge to speake, and to teach the Courtier this so happie a love, which bringeth with it neither slaunder, nor any inconveniencie: for perhaps it shall be one of the necessariest and profitablest qualities that hetherto hath beene given him, therefore speake of good felowship as much as you know therein.

Maister Peter laughed and saide: I would be loath (madam) where I say that it is lawfull for old men to love, it should be an occasion for these Ladies to thinke mee olde: therefore hardly give ye this enterprise to an other.

The Dutchesse answered: you ought not to refuse to be counted

[1] "Is a perfection," etc.: cf. "is to give him an added perfection."

old in knowledge, though ye be yong in yeares. Therefore say on, and excuse your selfe no more.

Maister Peter saide: surely (madam) if I must entreate upon this matter, I must first goe aske counsell of my Hermit Lavinello.[1]

The Ladie Emilia saide then halfe in anger: There is never a one in all the company so disobedient as you be (maister Peter) therefore shoulde the Dutchesse doe well to chastice you somewhat for it.

Maister Peter saide smiling: for love of God (madam) be not angry with me, for I will say what ever you will have me. Goe to, say on then, answered the Ladie Emilia.

Then maister Peter after a whiles silence, somewhat setling himselfe as though he should entreat upō a waightie matter, saide thus: My Lordes, to shew that olde men may love not onely without slaunder, but otherwhile more happily than yong men, I must be enforced to make a litle discourse to declare what love is, and wherein consisteth the happinesse that lovers may have. Therfore I beseech you give the hearing with heedefulnesse, for I hope to make you understand, that it were not unfitting for anie man here to bee a lover, in case he were fifteene or twentie yeares elder than M. Morello.

And here after they had laughed a while, M. Peter proceeded. I say therefore that according as it is defined of the wise men of olde time, Love is nothing else but a certaine coveting to enjoy beautie: and for somuch as coveting longeth for nothing, but for things known,[2] it is requisite that knowledge goe evermore before coveting,[3] which of his owne nature willeth the good,[4] but of himselfe is blind, and knoweth it not. Therefore hath nature so ordained that to every vertue of knowledge[5] there is annexed a vertue of longing. And because in our soule there be three manner waies to know, namely, by sense, reason, and understanding: of sense there ariseth appetite or longing, which is common to us with brute beastes: of reason ariseth election or choice, which is proper to man: of understanding, by the which man may be partner with Angels, ariseth will.

[1] "Lavinello": Opdycke notes, "a hermit discourses to Lavinello on the beauty of mystical Christian love" in Bembo's *Gli Asolani* (Book III.): "much of the following disquisition seems to be drawn" from that work, and from Plato. "As Bembo is known to have revised *The Courtier* before publication, we may assume that he was content with the form and substance of the discourse here attributed to him."

[2] Cf. "perceived."

[3] "It is requisite," etc.: cf. "perception must needs always precede desire."

[4] "Willeth the good": cf. "wishes good things."

[5] Cf. "faculty of perception."

Even as therefore the sense knoweth not but sensible matters, and that which may be felt, so the appetite or coveting onely deserveth the same: and even as the understanding is bent but to behold things that may bee understood, so is that will onely fedde with sprituall goods.

Man of nature indowed with reason, placed (as it were) in the middle betweene these two extremities, may through his choice inclining to sense, or reaching to understanding, come nigh to the coveting sometime of the one, sometime of the other part.

In these sortes therefore may beautie be coveted, the generall name wherfore may be applyed to all thinges, either naturall or artificiall, that are framed in good proportion, and due temper, as their nature beareth.

But speaking of the beautie that we meane, which is onely it, that appeareth in bodies, and especially in the face of man, and moveth this fervent coveting which wee call Love, we will terme it an influence of the heavenly bountifulnesse, the which for all it stretcheth over all thinges that be created (like the light of the sunne) yet when it findeth out a face well proportioned, and framed with a certaine lively agreement of several colours, and set forth with lights and shadowes, and with an orderly distance and limits of lines,[1] thereinto it distilleth it selfe and appeareth most welfavored, and decketh out and lightneth the subject where it shineth with a marvellous grace and glistering (like the sunne beames that strike against beautifull plate of fine golde wrought and set with precious jewels).

So that it draweth unto it mens eyes with pleasure, and pearcing through them, imprinteth himselfe in the soule, and with an unwonted sweetnesse all to stirreth her and deliteth, and setting her on fire maketh her to covet him.

When the soule then is taken with coveting to enjoy this beautie as a good thing, in case she suffer her selfe to be guided with the judgement of sense, she falleth into most deepe errours, and judgeth the bodie in which beauty is discerned to be the principall cause thereof: whereupon to enjoy it she reckoneth it necessarie to joine as inwardly as she can, with that bodie, which is false.

And therfore who so thinketh in possessing the bodie to enjoy Beautie, he is farre deceived, and is moved to it, not with true knowledge by the choice of reason, but with false

[1] "Lines": cf. "outlines."

opinion by the longing of sense. Whereupon the pleasure that followeth it, is also false and of necesitie full of errors.

And therefore into one of the two vices runne all those lovers that satisfie their unhonest lusts [1] with ye women whom they love: For either as soone as they be come to the coveted ende, they not only feele a fulnesse and lothsomnesse, but also conceive a hatred against the wight beloved, as though longing repented him of his offence, and knowledged the deceite wrought him by the false judgement of sense, that made him believe the ill to be good: or els they continue in the very same coveting and greedinesse, as though they were not in deed come to the end which they sought for. And albeit through the blind opinion that hath made them dronken (to their seeming) in that instant they feele a contentation, as the diseased otherwhile, that dreame they drinke of some cleare spring, yet be they not satisfied, nor leave of so.

And because of possessing coveted goodnesse, there ariseth alwaies quietnesse and satisfaction in the possessors minde, in case this were the true and right ende of their coveting, when they possesse it they would be at quietnes and throughly satisfied which they be not: but rather deceived through that likenesse, they forthwith returne again to unbridled coveting, and with the very same trouble which they felt at the first, they fall againe into the raging and most burning thirst of the thing, that they hope in vaine to possesse perfectly.

These kinde of lovers therefore love most unluckily,[2] for either they never come by their covetings, which is a great unluckinesse: or els if they doe come by them, they come by their hurt, and ende their miseries with other greater miseries: for both in the beginning and middle of this love, there is never other thing felt, but afflictions, torments, griefes, pining, travaile, so that to be wan, vexed with continuall teares and sighes, to live with a discontented minde, to be alwaies dumbe, or to lament, to covet death, in conclusion most unluckie are the properties which (they say) belong to lovers.

The cause therefore of this wretchednesse in mens mindes, is principally Sense, which in youthfull age beareth most sway, because the lustinesse of the flesh and of the bloud, in that season addeth unto him even so much force, as it withdraweth frō reason.

Therefore doth it easily traine the soule to follow appetite or longing, for when she seeth her selfe drowned in the earthly

---

[1] Among them Bembo could write himself.    [2] Cf. "unhappily."

prison, because she is set in the office to governe the bodie, she can not of her selfe understand plainly at the first the truth of spirituall beholding. Wherefore to compasse the understanding of thinges, she must goe begge the beginning [1] at the senses, and therefore she believeth them, and giveth eare to them, and is contented to be lead by them, especially when they have so much courage, that (in a manner) they enforce her.

And because they bee deceitfull, they fill her with errours and false opinions. Whereupon most commonly it happeneth, that yong men be wrapped in this sensuall love, which is a very rebel against reason, and therefore they make themselves unworthie to enjoy the favors and benefits which love bestoweth upon his true subjects, neither in love feele they any other pleasures, than what beastes without reason doe, but much more grievous afflictions.

Setting case therefore this to be so, which is most true, I say, that the contrarie chaunceth to them of a more ripe age. For in case they, when the soule is not now so much wayed downe with the bodily burden, and when the naturall burning aswageth and draweth to a warmth, if they be inflamed with beautie, and to it bend their coveting, guided by reasonable choice, they bee not deceived, and possesse beautie perfectly, and therefore through the possessing of it, alwaies goodnesse ensueth to them: because beautie is good, and consequently the true love of it is most good and holy, and evermore bringeth forth good fruites in the soules of them, that with the bridle of reason restraine the ill disposition of sense, the which olde men can much sooner do than yong.

It is not therefore out of reason to say, that olde men may also love without slander, and more happily, than yong men: taking notwithstanding this name Old, not for the age at the pits brinke, nor when the cannelles of the bodie be so feeble, that the soule can not through them worke her feates, but when knowledge in us is in his right strength.

And I will not also hide this from you: namely, that I suppose, where sensuall love in every age is naught, yet in yong men it deserveth excuse, and perhaps in some case lawfull: for although it putteth them in afflictions, dangers, travels, and the unfortunatnesse that is said, yet are there many that to winne them the good will of their Ladies practise vertuous thinges, which for all they be not bent to a good end, yet are they good of them selves.

[1] "The beginning": cf. "first notions."

And so of that much bitternesse they picke out a litle sweetnesse, and through the adversities which they sustaine, in the ende they acknowledge their errour.

As I judge therefore, those yong men that bridle their appetites, and love with reason, to be godly: so doe I hold excused such as yeelde to sensuall love, whereunto they be so enclined through the weakenesse and frailtie of man: so they show therein meekenes, courtesie, and prowesse, and the other worthie conditions that these Lords have spoken of, and when these youthfull yeares bee gone and past, leave it off cleane, keeping aloofe from this sensuall coveting as frō the lowest step of the stayres, by the which a man may ascend to true love.

But in case after they draw in yeares once, they reserve still in their colde hart the fire of appetites, and bring stoute reason in subjection to feeble sense, it can not be said how much they are to be blamed: for like men without sense they deserve with an everlasting shame to be put in the number of unreasonable living creatures, because the thoughts and waies of sensuall love bee farre unfitting for ripe age.

Here Bembo paused a while as though he woulde breath him, and when all thinges were whist, maister Morello of Ortona saide: And in case there were some olde man more fresh and lustie and of a better complexion than many yong men, why would you not have it lawfull for him to love with the love that yong men love?

The Dutchesse laughed and said: If the love of yong men bee so unluckie, why would you (maister Morello) that olde men should also love with this unluckinesse? But in case you were olde (as these men say you bee) you would not thus procure the hurt of olde men.

Maister Morello answered: the hurt of olde men (me seemeth) maister Peter Bembo procureth, who will have them to love after a sorte, that I for my part understand not: and (me think) the possessing of this beautie which he prayseth so much, without the bodie, is a dreame.

Doe you believe maister Morello, quoth then Count Lewis, that beautie is alwaies so good a thing as maister Peter Bembo speaketh of?

Not I in good sooth, answered maister Morello: But I remember rather that I have seene many beautifull women of a most ill inclination, cruell, and spitefull, and it seemeth that (in a manner) it happeneth alwaies so, for beautie maketh them proud: and pride, cruel.

Count Lewis saide smiling: To you perhaps they seeme cruell, because they content you not with it, that you would have. But cause maister Peter Bembo to teach you in what sorte olde men ought to covet beautie, and what to seeke at their Ladies handes, and what to content themselves withall: and in not passing out of these boundes, ye shall see that they shall bee neither proude nor cruel: and will satisfie you with what you shall require.

Maister Morello seemed then somewhat out of patience, and saide: I will not know the thing that toucheth me not. But cause you to be taught how the yong men ought to covet this beautie, that are not so fresh and lustie as old men be.

Here Sir Fredericke to pacify maister Morello, and to breake their talke, would not suffer Count Lewis to make answere, but interrupting him, saide.

Perhaps maister Morello is not altogether out of the way in saying that beautie is not alwaies good, for the beautie of women is many times cause of infinit evils in the world, hatred, warre, mortalitie, and destruction, whereof the rasing of Troye can be a good witnesse. And beautifull women for the most part bee either proude and cruell (as is saide) or unchast, but maister Morello would finde no fault with that.

There be also many wicked men that have the comlinesse of a beautifull countenance, and it seemeth nature hath so shaped them, because they may bee the readier to deceive, and that this amiable looke were like a baite that covereth the hooke.

Then maister Peter Bembo, believe not (quoth hee) but beautie is alwaies good. Here Count Lewis because he would returne againe to his former purpose, interrupted him and saide.

Since maister Morello passeth not to understand that, which is so necessarie for him, teach it me, and shew me how olde men may come by this happinesse of love, for I will not care to be counted olde, so it may profit me.

Maister Peter Bembo laughed and saide: first will I take the error out of these gentlemens minde: and afterwarde will I satisfie you also. So beginning a fresh: My Lordes (quoth hee) I would not that with speaking ill of beautie, which is a holy thing, any of us as prophane and wicked should purchase him the wrath of God. Therefore to give maister Morello and Sir Frederick warning, that they lose not their sight, as Stesichorus did, a paine most meete for who so dispraiseth beautie. I say that beautie commeth of God, and is like a circle, the goodnesse whereof is the Centre. And therefore, as there can be no circle without a centre, no more can beautie be without goodnesse.

Whereupon doth very seldom an ill soule dwell in a beautifull bodie. And therefore is the outwarde beautie a true signe of the inwarde goodnesse, and in bodies this comelines is imprinted more and lesse (as it were) for a marke of the soule, whereby she is outwardly knowne: as in trees, in which the beautie of the buddes giveth a testimonie of the goodnesse of the fruite. And the very same happeneth in bodies, as it is seene, that Palmestrers[1] by the visage knowe manie times the conditions, and otherwhile the thoughts of men. And which is more, in beastes also a man may discerne by the face the qualitie of the courage, which in the body declareth it selfe as much as it can.

Judge you how plainely in the face of a Lyon, a horse, and an Eagle, a man shall discerne anger, fiercenesse, and stoutnesse: in lambes and doves simplenesse and verie innocencie: the craftie suttletie in foxes and wolves, and the like (in a manner) in all other living creatures.

The soule therefore for the most part bee also evil, and ye beautifull good. Therefore it may be said that beautie is a face pleasant, merrie, comely, and to be desired for goodnesse: and foulenesse a face darke, uglesome, unpleasant, and to bee shunned for ill. And in case you will consider all thinges, ye shall find, that whatsoever is good and profitable, hath also evermore the comelinesse of beautie.

Behold the state of this great Ingin[2] of the worlde, which God created for the health and preservation of every thing that was made. The heaven rounde besette with so many heavēly lights: and in the middle, the earth environed with the Elements, and upheld with the waight of it selfe: the sunne, that compassing about giveth light to the whole, and in winter season draweth to the lowermost signe, afterwarde by litle and litle climbeth againe to the other part: The moone, that of him taketh her light, according as she draweth nigh, or goeth farther from him: And the other five starres, that diverslye keepe the very same course.

These thinges among themselves have such force by the knitting together of an order so necessarily framed, that with altering them any one jotte, they should be all lowsed, and the world would decay. They have also such beautie and comelinesse, that all the wits men have, can not imagin a more beautifull matter Thinke now of the shape of man, which may be called a litle

---

[1] Cf. "physiognomists."       [2] Cf. "fabric."

world: in whom every parcell of his bodie is seene to be necessarily framed by arte and not by happe, and then the forme altogether most beautifull, so that it were a hard matter to judge, whether the members, as the eyes, the nose, the mouth, the eares, the armes, y^e breast, and in like manner the other partes, give either more profit to the countenance and the rest of the bodie, or comelinesse. The like may bee saide of all other living creatures.

Beholde the feathers of foules, the leaves and boughes of trees, which be given them of nature to keepe them in their being, and yet have they withall a very great slightnesse.

Leave nature, and come to arte. What thing is so necessarie in sayling vessels, as the fore part, the sides, the mainyardes, the maste, the sailes, the sterne, oares, ankers, and tacklinges? All these thinges notwithstanding are so well favoured in the eye, that unto who so beholdeth them, they seeme to have beene found out as wel for pleasure, as for profit.

Pillers, and great beames upholde high buildings and pallaces, and yet are they no lesse pleasurefull unto the eyes of the beholders, than profitable to the buildings.

When men began first to builde, in the middle of the temples and houses, they reared the ridge of the roofe, not to make the workes to have a better shew, but because the water might the more commodiously avoide on both sides: yet unto profit there was forthwith adjoyned a faire sightlinesse, so that if under y^e skye where there falleth neither haile nor raine a man should builde a Temple without a reared ridge, it is to bee thought, that it coulde have neither a sightly shew nor any beautie.

Beside other things therfore it giveth a great praise to the world, in saying that it is beautifull. It is praysed, in saying, the beautifull heaven, beautifull earth, beautifull sea, beautifull rivers, beautiful woodes, trees, gardens, beautifull cities, beautifull churches, houses, armies. In conclusion this comely and holy beautie is a wondrous setting out of everie thing.[1] And it may bee saide, that Good and beautifull be after a sorte one selfe thing, especially in the bodies of men: of the beautie whereof the nighest cause (I suppose) is the beautie of the soule: the which as a partner of the right and heavenly beauty, maketh sightly and beautiful what ever she toucheth, and most of all, if the bodie, where she dwelleth, be not of so vile a matter, that she can not imprint in it her propertie.

[1] "In conclusion," etc.: cf. "In short, this gracious and sacred beauty gives highest ornament to everything."

Therefore Beautie is the true monument and spoile of the victory of the soule, when she with heavenly influence beareth rule over martiall and grosse nature, and with her light overcommeth the darkenesse of the bodie.

It is not then to bee spoken that beauty maketh women proude or cruel, although it seeme so to maister Morello. Neither yet ought beautifull women to beare the blame of that hatred, mortalitie, and destruction, which the unbridled appetites of men are the cause of.

I will not now deny, but it is possible also to finde in the world beautifull women unchaste, yet not because beautie inclineth them to unchaste living, for it rather plucketh them from it, and leadeth them into the way of vertuous conditions, through the affinitie that beautie hath with goodnesse.

But otherwhile ill bringing up, the cōtinuall provocations of lovers, tokens, povertie, hope, deceites, feare, and a thousand other matters overcome the stedfastnesse, yea of beautifull and good women: and for these and like causes may also beautifull men become wicked.

Then saide the Lord Cesar: In case the Lord Gaspars saying be true of yesternight, there is no doubt, but the faire women be more chaste than the foule.

And what was my saying quoth the Lorde Gaspar? The Lorde Cesar answered: If I do well beare in mind, your saying was, that the women that are sued to, alwaies refuse to satisfie him that sueth to them, but those that are not sued to, sue to others.

There is no doubt but the beautifull women have alwaies more suters, and be more instantly laide at in love, than the foule. Therefore the beautifull alwaies deny, and consequently bee more chaste than the foule, which not being sued to, sue to others.

Maister Peter Bembo laughed and saide: This argument can not be answered to. Afterwarde he proceeded. It chanceth also oftentimes, that as to other senses, so the sight is deceived, and judgeth a face beautifull, which in deed is not beautifull. And because in the eyes, and in the whole countenance of some women, a man beholdeth otherwhile a certaine lavish wantonnesse painted with dishonest flickeringes,[1] many whom that manner delighteth, because it promiseth them an easinesse to come by the thing that they covet, call it beautie: but in deede

---

[1] "Dishonest flickeringes": cf. "unseemly blandishments."

it is a cloked unshamefastnesse [1] unworthie of so honourable and holy a name.

Maister Peter Bembo held his peace, and those Lordes still were earnest upon him to speake somewhat more of this love, and of the way to enjoy beautie aright, and at the last.

Me thinke (quoth he) I have shewed plainly inough, that old men may love more happily than yong, which was my drift, therefore it becometh not me to enter any farther.

Count Lewis answered: You have better declared the unluckinesse of yong men, than the happinesse of olde men, whom you have not as yet taught what they must follow in this love of theirs: onely you have saide, that they must suffer themselves to bee guided by reason, and the opinion of many is, that it is unpossible for love to stand with reason.

Bembo notwithstanding sought to make an ende of reasoning, but the Dutchesse desired him to say on, and he beganne thus a fresh.

Too unluckie were the nature of man, if our soule (in the which this so fervent coveting may lightly arise) should bee driven to nourish it with that onely, which is common to her with beasts, and could not turne it to the other noble parte, which is proper to her.

Therefore since it is so your pleasure: I will not refuse to reason upon this noble matter. And because I know my selfe unworthie to talke of the most holy mysteries of love, I beseech him to leade my thought and my tongue so, that I may shew this excellent Courtier how to love contrary to the wonted manner of the common ignorant sorte.

And even as from my childhood I have dedicated all my whole life unto him, so also now that my wordes may bee answerable to the same intent, and to the praise of him.

I say therefore, that since the nature of man in youthfull age is so much enclined to sense, it may be graunted the Courtier, while hee is yong, to love sensually. But in case afterwarde also in his ripe yeares, he chaunce to be set on fire with this coveting of love, hee ought to bee good and circumspect and heedfull, that he beguile not himselfe, to bee lead willfully into the wretchednesse, that in yong men deserveth more to bee pittied than blamed: and contrariwise in old men, more to be blamed than pittied.

Therefore when an amiable countenance of a beautifull woman commeth in his sight, that is accompanied with noble

---

[1] Cf. "immodesty."

conditions and honest behaviours, so that as one practised in love, hee woteth well that his hew hath an agreement with hers, as soone as hee is aware that his eyes snatch that image and carrie it to the hart, and that the soule beginneth to beholde it with pleasure, and feeleth within her selfe the influence that stirreth her, and by litle and litle setteth her in heate, and that those lively spirits, that twinckle out through the eyes, put continuall fresh nourishment to the fire: hee ought in this beginning to seeke a speedy remedie and to raise up reason, and with her to sense the fortresse of his hart, and to shut in such wise the passages against sense and appetites, that they may enter neither with force nor subtil practise.

Thus if the flame bee quenched, the jeopardie is also quenched. But in case it continue or encrease, then must the Courtier determine (when he perceiveth hee is taken) to shunne throughly al filthinesse of common love, and so enter into the holy way of love, with the guide of reason.

And first consider that the body, where that beautie shineth, is not the fountaine from whence beautie springeth, but rather because beautie is bodilesse, and (as wee have saide) an heavenly shining beame, she loseth much of her honour when she is coupled with that vile subject and full of corruption, because the lesse she is partner thereof, the more perfect she is, and clean sundred from it, is most perfect.

And as a man heareth not with his mouth, nor smelleth with his eares: no more can he also in any manner wise enjoy beautie, nor satisfie the desire that she stirreth up in our mindes, with feeling, but with the sense, unto whom beautie is the very butte to level at: namely, the vertue of seeing.

Let him lay aside therefore the blinde judgement of the sense, and enjoy with his eyes ye brightnesse, the comelinesse, the loving sparkels, laughters, gestures, and all the other pleasant furnitures of beautie: especially with hearing the sweetnesse of her voice, the tunablenesse of her wordes, the melody of her singing and playing on instruments (in case the woman be-loved bee a musitian) and so shall he with most daintie foode feede the soule through the meanes of these two senses, which have litle bodily substance in them, and be the ministers of reason, without entring farther towarde the bodie, with coveting unto any longing otherwise than honest.

Afterwarde let him obey, please, and honour with all reverence his woman, and recken her more deare to him than his owne life, and preferre all her commodities and pleasures before his

owne, and love no lesse in her the beautie of minde, than of
the bodie.

Therefore let him have a care not to suffer her to run into
an errour, but with lessons and good exhortations seeke alwaies
to frame her to modestie, to temperance, to true honestie, and
so to worke that there may never take place in her other than
pure thoughts, and farre wide from all filthinesse of vices. And
thus in sowing of vertue in the garden of that minde, he shall
also gather the fruites of most beautiful conditions, and savour
them with a marvellous good relise.

And this shal be the right engendring and imprinting of
beautie in beautie, the which some holde opinion to be the end
of love. In this manner shall our Courtier bee most acceptable
to his Ladie, and she will alwaies shew her selfe towarde him
tractable, lowly and sweete in language, and as willing to please
him, as to be beloved of him: and the willes of them both shall
bee most honest and agreeable, and they consequently shall
bee most happie.

Here maister Morello. The engendring (quoth he) of beautie
in beautie aright, were the engendring of a beautifull childe in a
beautifull woman, and I woulde thinke it a more manifest token
a great deale that shee loved her lover, if she pleased him with
this, than with the sweetnesse of language that you speake of.

Maister Peter Bembo laughed, and saide: You must not
(maister Morello) passe your boundes. I may tell you, it is not
a small token that a woman loveth, when she giveth unto her
lover her beautie, which is so precious a matter: and by the
wayes that be a passage to the soule, that is to say, the sight
and the hearing, sendeth the lookes of her eyes, the image of
her countenance, and the voice of her wordes, that pearce into
the lovers hart, and give a witnesse of her love.

Maister Morello saide: Lookes and wordes may be, and oftentimes are false witnesses. Therefore who so hath not a better
pledge of love (in my judgement) he is in an ill assurance. And
surely I looked still that you would have made this woman of
yours somewhat more courteous and free towarde the Courtier,
than my Lorde Julian hath made his: but (me seemeth) ye be
both of the propertie of those judges, that (to appeare wise)
give sentence against their owne.

Bembo saide: I am well pleased to have this woman much
more courteous towarde my Courtier not yong, than the Lorde
Julians is to the yong: and that with good reason, because mine
coveteth but honest matters, and therefore may y^e woman graunt

him them all without blame. But my Lorde Julians woman that is not so assured of the modestie of the yong man, ought to graunt him the honest matters onely, and deny him the dishonest.

Therefore more happie is mine, that hath graunted him whatsoever hee requireth, than the other, that hath part graunted, and part denyed.

And because you may moreover the better understand, that reasonable love is more happy than sensuall, I say unto you that selfe same thinges in sensuall ought to be denyed otherwhile, and in reasonable, graunted: because in the one, they bee honest, and in the other dishonest.

Therefore the woman to please her good lover, beside the graunting him mery countenances, familiar and secret talke, jeasting, dalying, hand in hand, may also lawfully and without blame come to kissing: which in sensual love according to the Lord Julians rules, is not lawfull. For since a kisse is a knitting together both of bodie and soule, it is to bee feared, lest the sensuall lover will be more enclined to the part of the bodie, than of the soule: but the reasonable lover woteth well, that although the mouth be a parcell of the bodie, yet is it an issue for the wordes, that be the interpreters of the soule, and for the inwarde breath, which is also called the soule.

And therefore hath a delite to joyne his mouth with the womans beloved with a kisse: not to stirre him to any dishonest desire, but because hee feeleth that that bonde is the opening of an entrie to the soules, which drawne with a coveting the one of the other, poure them selves by turne the one into the others bodie, and bee so mingled together, that each of them hath two soules.

And one alone so framed of them both ruleth (in a manner) two bodies. Whereupon, a kisse may be saide to be rather a coupling together of the soule, than of the body, because it hath such force in her, that it draweth her unto it, and (as it were) separateth her from the bodie.

For this doe all chaste lovers covet a kisse, as a coupling of soules together. And therefore Plato the devine lover saith, that in kissing, his soule came as farre as his lippes to depart out of the bodie.

And because the separating of the soule from the matters of the sense, and the through coupling her with matters of understanding may be betokened by a kisse, Salomon saith in his heavenly booke of Balates,[1] O that he would kisse me with

[1] Cf. "divine book of the Song."

a kisse of his mouth, to expresse the desire he had, that his soule might be ravished through heavenly love to the beholding of heavenly beautie, in such manner, that coupling her selfe inwardly with it, she might forsake the bodie.

They stood all harkening heedfully to Bembo, reasoning, and after he had staied a while, and saw that none spake, he saide: Since you have made me to beginne to shew our not yong Courtier this happie love, I will leade him yet somewhat farther forwards, because to stand still at this stay were somewhat perillous for him, considering (as we have oftentimes saide) the soule is most inclined to the senses.

And for all reason with discourse chooseth well, and knoweth that beautie not to spring of the bodie, and therfore setteth a bridle to the unhonest desires, yet to behold it alwaies in that bodie, doth oftentimes corrupt the right judgement. And where no other inconvenience insueth upon it, once absence from the wight beloved carrieth a great passion with it.

Because the influence of that beautie when it is present, giveth a wonderous delite to the lover, and setting his hart on fire, quickeneth and melteth certaine vertues in a traunce and congeled in the soule, the which nourished with the heate of love, flow about and goe bubbling nigh the hart, and thrust out through the eyes those spirits which bee most fine vapours made of the purest and clearest part of the bloud, which receive the image of beautie, and decke it with a thousande sundrie furnitures.

Whereupon the soule taketh a delite, and with a certaine wonder is agast,[1] and yet enjoyeth she it, and (as it were) astonied together with the pleasure, feeleth the feare and reverence that men accustomably have towarde holy matters and thinketh her selfe to be in Paradise.

The lover therefore that considereth onely the beautie in the bodie, loseth this treasure and happinesse, as soone as the woman beloved with her departure leaveth the eies without their brightnesse, and consequently the soule as a widdow without her joy. For since beautie is farre off, that influence of love setteth not the hart on fire, as it did in presence.

Whereupon the poares be dryed up and withered, and yet doth the remembrance of beautie somewhat stirre those vertues of the soule in such wise, that they seeke to scatter abroade the spirits, and they finding the wayes closed up, have no issue, and still they seeke to get out, and so with those shootings

[1] "Is agast": cf. "trembles with awe."

inclosed, pricke the soule, and torment her bitterly, as yong children, when in their tender gummes they beginne to breed teeth.

And hence come the teares, sighes, vexations and torments of lovers: because the soule is alwaies in affliction and travell and (in a manner) waxeth woode, until the beloved beautie commeth before her once againe, and then is she immediatly pacified and taketh breath, and throughly bent to it, is nourished with most daintie food, and by her will, would never depart from so sweet a sight.

To avoide therefore the torment of his absence, and to enjoy beautie without passion, the Courtier by the helpe of reason must full and wholy call backe againe the coveting of the bodie to beautie alone, and (in what he can) beholde it in it selfe simple and pure, and frame it within in his imagination sundred from all matter, and so make it friendly and loving to his soule, and there enjoy it, and have it with him day and night, in every time and place, without mistrust ever to lose it: keeping alwaies fast in minde, that the bodie is a most diverse thing from beautie, and not onely not encreaseth, but diminisheth the perfection of it.

In this wise shall our not yong Courtier bee out of all bitternesse and wretchednesse that yong men feele (in a manner) continually, as jelousies, suspitions, disdaines, angers, desperations and certaine rages full of madnesse, whereby many times they be ledde into so great errour, that some doe not onely beate y^e woman whom they love, but ridde themselves out of their life.

He shall doe no wrong to the husband, father, brethren or kinsfolke of y^e woman beloved. He shall not bring her in slander. He shall not be in case, with much a doe otherwhile to refraine his eyes and tongue from discovering his desires to others. He shal not take thought at departure or in absence, because he shall evermore carrie his precious treasure about with him shutte fast within his hart.

And beside, through the vertue of imagination, hee shall fashion with himselfe that beautie much more faire than it is in deede. But among these commodities, the lover shall find another yet farre greater, in case hee will take this love for a stayre (as it were) to climbe up to another farre higher than it. The which he shall bring to passe, if he will goe and consider with himselfe, what a straight bond it is to bee alwaies in the trouble to behold the beautie of one bodie alone. And therefore to come out of this so narrowe a roome, hee shall gather in his thought by litle and litle so many ornaments, that meddling all beautie together, he shal make an universall conceite, and bring the multitude of them to the unitie of one alone, that is generally spred over all the nature of man. And thus shall he beholde no more the particular beautie of one woman, but an universall, that decketh out all bodies.

Whereupon being made dimme with this greater light, he shall not passe upon the lesser, and burning in a more excellent flame, he shall litle esteeme it, that hee set great store by at the first.

This stayre [1] of love, though it be very noble and such as few arive at it, yet is it not in this sorte to be called perfect, forsomuch as where the imagination is of force to make conveyance, and hath no knowledge, but through those beginninges that ye senses helpe her withall, she is not cleane purged from grosse darknesse: and therefore though she do consider that universall beautie in sunder and in it selfe alone, yet doth she not well and clearely discerne it, nor without some doubtfulnesse, by reason of the agreement that the fancies have with the bodie.

Wherefore such as come to this love, are like to yong birdes almost flush, which for all they flitter a litle their tender winges, yet dare they not stray farre from the nest, nor commit themselves to the winde and open weather.

When our Courtier therfore shall bee come to this point, although hee may bee called a good and happie lover, in respect of them that be drowned in the miserie of sensuall love, yet will I not have him to set his hart at rest, but boldly proceede farther, following the high way after his guide, that leadeth him to the point of true happinesse. And thus in steade of going out of his wit with thought, as he must doe that will consider the bodily beautie, hee may come into his wit, to beholde the beautie that is seene with the eyes of the minde, which then begin to be sharpe and throughly seeing, when the eyes of the bodie lose the floure of their sightlinesse.

Therefore the soule ridde of vices, purged with the studies of true Philosophie, occupied in spirituall, and exercised in matters of understanding, turning her to the beholding of her owne substance, as it were raised out of a most deepe sleepe, openeth the eyes that all men have, and few occupie, and seeth in her selfe a shining beame of that light, which is the true image of

[1] Cf. "stage."

the Angelike beautie partened with [1] her, whereof she also partneth with the bodie a feeble [2] shadow.

Therefore waxed blinde about earthly matters, is made most quicke of sight about heavenly. And otherwhile when the stirring vertues [3] of the bodie are withdrawne [4] alone through earnest beholding, either fast bound through sleepe, when she is not hindred by them, she feeleth a certaine privie smell [5] of the right Angelike beautie, and ravished with the shining of that light, beginneth to be inflamed, and so greedely [6] followeth after, that (in a manner) she waxeth dronken and beside her selfe, for coveting to couple her self with it, [7] having found (to her weening) the footesteps of God, in the beholding of whom (as in her happie [8] ende) she seeketh to settle her selfe.

And therefore burning in this most happie flame, she ariseth to the noblest part of her which is the understanding, and there no more shadowed with the darke night of earthly matters, seeth the heavenly beautie: but yet doth she not for all that enjoy it altogether perfectly, because she beholdeth it onely in her particular understanding, which can not conceive the passing great universall beautie.

Whereupon not throughly satisfied with this benefit, love giveth unto the soule a greater happinesse. For like as through the particular beautie of one bodie hee guideth her to the universall beautie of all bodies: Even so in the least degree of perfection through particular understanding hee guideth her to the universall understanding.

Thus the soule kindled in the most holy fire of true heavenly love, fleeth to couple her selfe with the nature of Angels, and not onely cleane forsaketh sense, but hath no more neede of the discourse of reason, for being chaunged into an Angell, she understandeth all thinges that may be understood: and without any veil or cloud, she seeth the maine sea of the pure heavenly beautie and receiveth it into her, and enjoyeth the soveraigne happinesse, that can not be comprehended of the senses.

Since therefore the beauties, which we dayly see with these our dimme eyes in bodies subject to corruption, that neverthe-

---

[1] "Partened with": cf. "communicated to."
[2] "Feeble": cf. "faint."   [3] Cf. "motive forces."   [4] Cf. "absorbed."
[5] Cf. "she is conscious of a certain far-off perfume."
[6] Cf. "eagerly."
[7] Cf. "she almost becomes frenzied with desire to unite herself to that beauty."
[8] "Happie": cf. "beatific."

lesse be nothing els but dreames and most thinne shadowes of beautie, seeme unto us so well favored and comely, that oftentimes they kindle in us a most burning fire, and with such delight, that we reckon no happinesse may bee compared to it, that wee feele otherwhile throughe the onely love which the beloved countenance of a woman casteth at us.

What happie wonder, what blessed abashment [1] may we reckon that to bee, that taketh the soules, which come to have a sight of the heavenly beauty? what sweet flame? What sweete incense may a man believe that to be, which ariseth of the fountaine of the soveraigne and right beautie? Which is the originall of all other beautie which never encreaseth nor diminisheth, alwaies beautifull, and of it selfe, as well on the one part as on the other, most simply, onely like it selfe, and partner of non other, but in such wise beautifull, that all other beautifull thinges be beautifull, because they be partners of the beautie of it.

This is the beautie unseperable from ye high bountie, which with her voice calleth and draweth to her al thinges: and not onely to the indowed with understanding giveth understanding, to the reasonable reason, to the sensuall sense and appetite to live, but also partaketh with plantes and stones (as a print of her self) stirring, and the natural provocation [2] of their properties.

So much therefore is this love greater and happier than others, as the cause that stirreth it, is more excellent. And therefore, as common fire tryeth gold and maketh it fine, so this most holy fire in soules destroyeth and consumeth whatsoever there is mortall in them, and relieveth and maketh beautifull the heavenly part, which at the first by reason of the sense was deade and buried in them.

This is the great fire in the which (the Poets write) that Hercules was buried on the toppe of the mountaine Oeta: and through that consuming with fire, after his death was holy and immortall.

This is the fiery bush of Moses: The devided tongues of fire: the inflamed Chariot of Helias: which doubleth grace and happinesse in their soules that be worthie to see it, when they forsake this earthly basenesse, and flee up unto heaven.

Let us therefore bend all our force and thoughtes of soule to this most holy light, that sheweth us the way which leadeth to heaven: and after it, putting off the affections we were clad at our coming downe, let us climbe up the staires, which at the lowermost steppe have the shadow of sensuall beautie, to the

---

[1] Cf. "awe."          [2] "Provocation": cf. "instinct."

high mansion place where the heavenly, amiable and right beautie dwelleth, which lyeth hidden in the innermost secretes of God, lest unhalowed eyes shoulde come to the sight of it: and there shall wee finde a most happie end for our desires, true rest for our travels, certaine remedie for miseries, a most healthfull medicine for sicknesse, a most sure haven in y° troublesome stormes of the tempestuous sea of this life.'

What tongue mortall is there then (O most holy love) that can sufficiently prayse thy worthines? Thou most beautifull, most good, most wise, art derived of the unitie of the heavenly beautie, goodnesse and wisedom, and therein dost thou abide, and unto it through it, (as in a circle) turnest about.

Thou the most sweete bond of the world, a meane betwixt heavenly and earthly thinges, with a bountifull temper [1] bendest the high vertues to the government of the lower,[2] and turning backe the mindes of mortall men to their beginning, couplest them with it.

Thou with agreement bringest the Elements in one, stirrest nature to bring forth, and that which ariseth and is borne for the succession of the life.[3] Thou bringest severed matters into one, to the unperfect givest perfection, to the unlike likenesse, to enimitie amitie, to the earth fruites, to the Sea calmnesse, to the heaven, lively light.

Thou art the father of true pleasures, of grace, peace, lowlinesse, and good will, enimy to rude wildnesse, and sluggishnesse: to be short, the beginning, and end of all goodnesse.

And forsomuch as thou delightest to dwell in the floure of beautifull bodies and beautifull soules, I suppose that thy abiding place is now here among us, and from above otherwhile shewest thy selfe a litle to the eyes and mindes of them that bee not worthie to see thee.

Therefore vouchsafe (Lorde) to hearken to our prayers, pour thy selfe into our harts, and with the brightnesse of thy most holy fire lighten our darkenesse, and like a trustie guide in this blinde mase shew us the right way: correct the falshood of the senses, and after long wandring in vanitie, give us the right and sound joy. Make us to smell those spirituall savours that relieve [4] the vertues of the understanding, and to heare the heavenly harmony so tunable, that no discorde of passion take

---

[1] "Bountifull temper": cf. "benignant sway."

[2] "High vertues," etc.: cf. "the supernal powers to rule the lower powers."

[3] Cf. "and that which is born, to the perpetuation of life."

[4] "Relieve": cf. "quicken."

place any more in us. Make us dronken with the bottomlesse fountaine of contentation,[1] that alwaies doth delight, and never giveth fill, and that giveth a smacke of the right blisse[2] unto who so drinketh of the renuing and cleare water therof. Purge with the shining beames of thy light our eyes from mistie ignorance, that they may no more set by mortall beautie, and well perceive that the thinges which at the first they thought them selves to see, be not in deede, and those that they saw not, to be in effect. Accept our soules, that bee offered unto thee for a sacrifice. Burne them in the lively flame that wasteth all grosse filthinesse, that after they be cleane sundred from the bodie, they may bee coupled with an everlasting and most sweete bond to the heavenly beautie. And wee severed from ourselves, may bee changed like right lovers into the beloved, and after we be drawn from the earth, admitted to the feast of the angels, where fed with immortall ambrosia and nectar, in the end we may dye a most happie and lively[3] death, as in times past died the fathers of olde time, whose soules with most fervent zeale of beholding, thou didst hale from the bodie, and coupledst them with God.

When Bembo had hetherto spoken with such vehemencie, that a man woulde have thought him (as it were) ravished and beside himselfe, hee stood still without once moving, holding his eyes towarde heaven as astonied: when the Ladie Emilia, which together with the rest gave most diligent eare to this talke, tooke him by the plaite of his garment, and plucking him a little said.

Take heede (maister Peter) that these thoughts make not your soule also to forsake the bodie.

Madam, answered maister Peter, it should not be the first miracle that love hath wrought in me. Then the Dutchesse and all the rest began a fresh to bee instant upon maister Bembo that he would proceede once more in his talke, and every one thought he felt in his minde (as it were) a certaine sparkell of that godly love that pricked him, and they all coveted to heare farther: but maister Bembo,

My Lords (quoth hee) I have spoken what the holy furie of love hath (unsought for) indited to me: now that (it seemeth) he inspireth mee no more, I wot not what to say. And I thinke verily that love will not have his secretes discovered any farther, nor that the Courtier should passe the degree that his pleasure

[1] "Make us dronken," etc.: cf. "Fill us with that inexhaustible fountain of content . . ."
[2] "A smacke," etc.: cf. "a taste of true beatitude."     [3] Cf. "living."

is I should shew him,[1] and therefore it is not perhaps lawfull to speake any more of this matter.

Surely, quoth the Dutchesse, if the not yong Courtier be such a one, that he can follow this way which you have shewed him, of right he ought to be satisfied with so great a happinesse, and not to envie the yonger.

Then the Lord Cesar Gonzaga, the way (quoth he) that leadeth to this happinesse is so steepe (in my mind) that (I believe) it will be much adoe to get to it.

The Lord Gaspar saide: I believe it be hard to get up for men, but unpossible for women.

The Ladie Emilia laughed and saide: If ye fall so often to offend us, I promise you, ye shall be no more forgiven.

The Lorde Gaspar answered: It is no offence to you, in saying, that womens soules be not so purged from passions as mens be, nor so accustomed in beholding,[2] as maister Peter hath saide, it is necessary for them to be, that will taste of the heavenly love.

Therefore it is not read that ever woman hath had this grace: but many men have had it, as Plato, Socrates, Plotinus and many other: and a number of our holy fathers, as Saint Francis, in whom a fervent spirite of love imprinted the most holy seale of five woundes.

And nothing but the vertue of love coulde hale up Saint Paule the Apostle to the sight of those secretes, which is not lawfull for man to speake of, nor shewe S. Stephen the heavens open.

Here answered the Lord Julian. In this point men shall nothing passe women, for Socrates himselfe doth confesse that all mysteries of love which he knew, were opened unto him by a woman, which was Diotima. And the Angell that with the fire of love imprinted the five woundes in Saint Francis, hath also made some women worthie of the same print in our age.

You must remember moreover that Saint Marie Magdalen had many faultes forgiven her, because she loved much: and perhaps with no lesse grace than Saint Paule, was she many times through Angelike love haled up to the third heaven. And many other (as I shewed you yesterday more at large) that for love of the name of Christ have not passed upon life, nor feared torments, nor any other kind of death how terrible and cruel so ever it were. And they were not (as maister Peter will have his Courtier to be) aged, but soft and tender maidens,

---

[1] i.e. should have shown.
[2] "Accustomed," etc.: cf. "given to contemplation."

and in the age, when he saith that sensuall love ought to be borne withall in men.

The Lord Gaspar began to prepare himselfe to speake to the Duchesse. Of this (quoth shee) let maister Peter be judge, and the matter shall stand to his verdite, Whether women be not as meete for heavenlie love as men. But because the plea betweene you may happen be too long, it shall not be amis to defer it until to morrow.

Nay, to night, quoth the Lord Cesar Gonzaga. And how can it be to night, quoth the Dutchesse?

The Lord Cesar answered: Because it is day alredy, and shewed her the light that began to enter in at the clifts of the windowes.

Then every man arose upon his feete with much wonder, because they had not thought that the reasonings had lasted longer than the accustomed wont, saving only that they were begon much later, and with their pleasantnesse had deceived so the Lordes mindes, that they wist not of the going away of the houres. And not one of them felt any hevinesse of sleepe in his eies, the which often happeneth when a man is up after his accustomed houre to goe to bed.

When the windowes then were opened on the side of the Pallaice that hath his prospect towarde the high top of Mount Catri, they sawe already in the East a faire morning like unto the colour of roses, and all starres voyded, saving only the sweete Governesse of heaven, Venus which keepeth the boundes of the night and day, from which appeared to blowe a sweete blast, that filling the aire with a biting colde,[1] began to quicken the tunable notes of the prettie birdes,[2] among the hushing[3] woodes of the hils at hand.

Whereupon they all taking their leave with reverence of the Dutchesse, departed toward their lodgings without torche, the light of the day suffising. And as they were nowe passing out of the great Chamber doore, the Lord Generall turned him to the Dutchesse, and said: Madam, to take up the variance betweene the Lord Gasper and the Lord Julian, wee will asemble this night with the judge sooner than we did yesterday. The Lady Emilia answered, upon condition, that in case my Lorde Gasper will accuse women, and give them (as his wont is) some false report, he will also put us in suretie to stand to triall, for I recken him a wavering starter.[4]

---

[1] Cf. "crisp coolness."
[2] "Tunable notes," etc., "sweet choruses of joyous birds . . ."
[3] "Hushing": cf. "murmuring."
[4] Cf. "shifty disputant."

# EVERYMAN'S LIBRARY

## A LIST OF THE 979 VOLUMES
## ARRANGED UNDER AUTHORS

*Anonymous works are given under titles.*

*Anthologies, Dictionaries, etc. are arranged at the end of the list.*

# LONDON: J. M. DENT & SONS LTD.
# NEW YORK: E. P. DUTTON & CO. INC.

*The Publishers regret that, owing to wartime difficulties and shortages, some of the volumes may be found to be temporarily out of print.*